ANTISEMITISM

A Reference Handbook

Other Titles in ABC-CLIO's
CONTEMPORARY
WORLD ISSUES
Series

Books in the Contemporary World Issues series address vital issues in today's society such as genetic engineering, pollution, and biodiversity. Written by professional writers, scholars, and nonacademic experts, these books are authoritative, clearly written, up-to-date, and objective. They provide a good starting point for research by high school and college students, scholars, and general readers as well as by legislators, businesspeople, activists, and others.

Each book, carefully organized and easy to use, contains an overview of the subject, a detailed chronology, biographical sketches, facts and data and/or documents and other primary-source material, a directory of organizations and agencies, annotated lists of print and nonprint resources, and an index.

Readers of books in the Contemporary World Issues series will find the information they need in order to have a better understanding of the social, political, environmental, and economic issues facing the world today.

ANTISEMITISM

A Reference Handbook

Jerome A. Chanes

**CONTEMPORARY
WORLD ISSUES**

A B C ✽ C L I O

Santa Barbara, California
Denver, Colorado
Oxford, England

Library of Congress Cataloging-in-Publication Data

Chanes, Jerome A.
    Antisemitism / Jerome A. Chanes.
        p. cm. — (Contemporary world issues)
    Includes bibliographical references and index.
    ISBN 1-57607-209-6 (hardback : alk. paper); ISBN 1-85109-497-0 (eBook)
1. Antisemitism. 2. Antisemitism—History. I. Title. II. Series.

    DS145.C464 2004
    305.892'4—dc22

                                        2004020608

08   07   06   05   04   10   9   8   7   6   5   4   3   2   1

This book is also available on the World Wide Web as an eBook. Visit abc-clio.com for details.

ABC-CLIO, Inc.
130 Cremona Drive, P.O. Box 1911
Santa Barbara, California 93116-1911

This book is printed on acid-free paper ∞ .
Manufactured in the United States of America

Contents

Preface

Is antisemitism another form of group prejudice? Or is it *sui generis*, a most ancient hatred, appearing, like a Hindu god, in many different forms throughout history? *Antisemitism: A Reference Handbook* takes the reader through the many manifestations of antisemitism throughout history and in the current time and acts as a "road-map" to this most ancient prejudice and hatred. As such, this book will provide scholars, public affairs and government officials, journalists, students, researchers, and lawyers a detailed overview of the past and present of this most complex social problem. Especially valuable will be the annotated bibliography of resource materials that is central to work in this arena.

My interest in antisemitism derives, paradoxically enough, from my belief in—indeed obsession with—American pluralism, which has manifested itself in researching, writing, lecturing, and teaching. My work in the history and sociology of antisemitism derives from twin interests: intergroup relations and the sociology of American Jews, which I have taught for many years at the university level, and from my work over many years in the public policy arena.

Antisemitism: A Reference Handbook begins with an introductory essay that sets a context for the study of antisemitism and enables the researcher to have an overview of the area as of 2004. Chapter 2, a history of antisemitism (with a chronological time line), develops a historical context for looking at antisemitism and explores those dynamics in history that informed the three historical "types" of antisemitism: cultural or ethnic antisemitism in the ancient world, religious antisemitism during the period of the development and maturing of Christianity, and racialist antisemitism of the modern period.

Chapter 3 consists of brief biographical sketches of individuals who are notable either for their antisemitic expression or for their work in the counteraction of antisemitism. Chapters 4 and 5—the core of the book—include primary sources on antisemitism and its counteraction and a country-by-country survey of the status of antisemitism. Chapter 5 consists of primary sources on antisemitism and its counteraction—the researcher's "meat and potatoes"—and summaries of international legal documents on discrimination and group prejudice.

Chapter 6 is a directory of national and international organizations involved in the monitoring, study, and counteraction of antisemitism. The book concludes (Chapter 7) with a detailed guide to resources—print and nonprint—on every conceivable aspect of antisemitism. The annotated bibliography will be of considerable value to scholars, researchers, and journalists as well as to the casual reader.

Acknowledgments

I am indebted to a number of individuals who assisted me in the preparation of this book. Michael Skakun's skill in tracking down countless facts, and his keen journalist's eye, were invaluable in this project.

Libraries and librarians, and academic colleagues, make a project such as this work. Warmest thanks to Cyma Horowitz and Michele Anish of the American Jewish Committee library for their assistance in this project. Cyma and Michele have been friends and dependable colleagues on many projects over many years. A debt of gratitude as well goes to the staff of the Barnard College Library—especially to Jenna Freedman—for their gracious assistance. Jenna enabled me to use research tools that melted hours of work into minutes. I thank Frank Unlandherm, Middle East and Judaica bibliographer at Columbia, and Zalman Alpert, "erudite" *nonpareil*, of Yeshiva University's Mendel Gottesman Library, for their assistance. Thanks as well to Anne Bayefsky of the Columbia Law School for helping me unravel the arcana of international agreements; to my friend and colleague Lawrence Grossman, for alerting me to materials new and old; to my mentor, friend, and colleague, Columbia's polymath, David Sidorsky, for his insights; to my teacher and colleague, Louis H. Feldman, for guiding me through the Classical world; to good friends and film-scholars Annette Insdorf of Columbia University and Stuart Klawans for their steel-trap minds when it comes to factual data on films; to Barnard's Joel Kaye, medievalist *extraordinaire;* and to Ken Jacobson for his challenging observations and his encouragement. I am saddened that my friend, colleague, guru, and basketball nemesis Gary Rubin *zt"l* did not live to see this work. He contributed to it.

The professional staffs of human relations agencies were helpful in sharing materials and expertise. I thank Jeffrey P. Sinensky, Felice Gaer, and Sybil Kessler of the American Jewish Committee; Marc D. Stern of the American Jewish Congress; and Eugene Korn, Alan M. Schwartz, and Steve Freeman of the Anti-Defamation League.

Donald Altschiller, whose book *Hate Crimes* graces the Contemporary World Issues series, was most generous in sharing his professional expertise. I thank also Mike Edison and Daniel Feldman for their research assistance when this project was a'borning.

Gratitude is owed to my ABC-CLIO editors, Alicia Merritt and Carla Roberts, for guiding this work toward its conclusion and to my friend and *chavrutha* of many decades, Rabbi Jay Miller—Jay gives the characterization "best teacher I ever had" new meaning—and to my mentor of many years, Rabbi Dr. Moses D. Tendler, for his encouragement. Thanks as well to my teacher and friend, Edwin Hymovitz, a man of vast erudition (hardly limited to modal shifts in Chopin).

Finally—*acharona chaviva*—to my wife, Dr. Eva (Chaviva) Fogelman, to whom this book is lovingly dedicated, for her unflagging encouragement and support and for her numerous helpful and practical suggestions at every stage; and to my son, Adam Chanes, who—even at age six—asked challenging questions ("But Rashi doesn't say that!"), deeper gratitude than words can express.

A Note on the Spelling and Usage of *Antisemitism*

Historian Yehuda Bauer wrote as follows:

The term "antisemitism" was coined in 1879 by a professed antisemite, the German radical writer and politician Wilhelm Marr. The old term, "Jew-hatred," had become obsolete, for it described traditional Christian antipathy toward Jews, and did not suit the modern, pseudoscientific, nationalist, anti-Christian ideology which arose during the second half of the nineteenth century. The standard bearers of the new—or revised—ideology sought a neutral, sanitized term that did not contain the word "Jew," and that would sound as though it had come from the world of the new social sciences. Marr's neologism came from the field of comparative philology, which had labeled certain languages, particularly Hebrew, Arabic, and Aramaic, as "Semitic."

Sometimes in English the word is written as a hyphen. "Anti-Semitism," however, is altogether an absurd construction, since there is no such thing as "Semitism" to which it might be opposed. In German—and Hebrew—there is no hyphen and the word has no precise meaning, although its connotations are well understood. Despite this rather elliptical reference, Marr's readers, his colleagues, and his disciples did not have to struggle with the meaning of "anti-Semitism." They knew what he meant (Bauer 1994).

The use of the hyphen and upper case, as in "anti-Semitism," as Bauer pointed out, emphasizes a fictitious and imaginary

"Semitism," characterizing a racially defined (rather than linguistic) "Semitic" group. Such a usage gives the antisemites a victory
right off the mark.

    Antisemitism will be the spelling in this book.

Reference

Yehuda Bauer, "In Search of a Definition of Antisemitism," in
Approaches to Antisemitism: Context and Curriculum, ed. Michael
Brown, 22–34 (New York: American Jewish Committee, 1994).

1

Introduction and Overview

The Nature of Antisemitism

A sampling of recent headlines from Europe includes the following:

"There Is More Antisemitism Today than in the 1930s."
—Simon Wiesenthal, April 2003

"Antisemitism Is the Burden of Europe."
—Rudolph Giuliani, former New York City mayor and head of the U.S. delegation to the OSCE (Organization on Security and Cooperation in Europe) Conference on Antisemitism, June 2003

United Kingdom: Five hundred gravestones were damaged in East London in the worst recorded desecration . . .

Germany: An Orthodox Jewish student was attacked, a man wearing a Jewish Star of David was kicked and spat on, and a religious Jew was assaulted . . .

Italy: Photos of "veiled Palestinian women" were displayed above pictures of Holocaust victims . . .

France: A British Allied cemetery was desecrated in northern France . . .

Austria: A rabbi in Vienna was attacked by two youths . . .

Croatia: Plans for a monument honoring thousands of Croat Nazi troops . . .

Belarus: A Jewish graveyard was defaced with Nazi swastikas . . .

Russia: The Russian Interior Ministry says there are currently up to 15,000 skinheads in Russia . . .

Belgium: Nazi sympathizer, Michel Delacroix, has been appointed . . .

Greece: A Greek professor from the London School of Economics wrote an article in the largest Greek newspaper blaming the Jews . . .

What Is Antisemitism?

These headlines, culled from European newspapers, suggest to some that there is an atmosphere developing in which antisemitism is once again a major issue of concern around the world. Do these news stories reflect a new reality of antisemitism? Are societal conditions once again ripe for an outburst of antisemitic expression, the way they were in central Europe in the 1930s? Or does the worldwide decline in antisemitism, evident over the past half century and more, continue?

Antisemitism means different things to different people. The irrational antipathy—indeed hatred—expressed toward any group appears to be a universal phenomenon. But is antisemitism another form of group prejudice, or is it *sui generis?*

First there is the question of definition: What is antisemitism? The old saw states: "An antisemite is someone who dislikes Jews more than is absolutely necessary." Even this tired one-liner tells us something about the nature, irrationality, and unpredictability of hatred toward Jews. For the purpose of this book, however, we use the following definition: Antisemitism is all forms of hostility manifested toward the Jews throughout history that results from no legitimate cause.

The term *antisemitism* was coined in 1879 by Wilhelm Marr, a German polemicist who denounced Jews on what he claimed to be scientific racial, rather than religious, grounds. The adoption of this term marked an awareness that it was no longer fashionable in some circles of late-nineteenth-century Europe to be anti-Jewish on *religious* grounds. By the late nineteenth century, religious hostility was regarded by many European intellectuals as medieval and backward. The new paradigm for anti-Jewishness—antisemitism—was more neutral, objective, and "scientific." The term *antisemitism* has never referred to hatred of Semites, which designates speakers of a group of languages (Hebrew, Arabic, Aramaic, and so on). Rather, the term *antisemitism* is directed at Jews; it is the modern locution of Jew-hatred.

However one defines antisemitism, there is a commonality among antisemitism and many other forms of group conflict and group prejudice. Antisemitism presupposes that *the Jews are radically "Other,"* fundamentally different from the mainstream population—different, therefore deviant. Or, as in historian Salo Baron's trenchant formulation during a conference on antisemitism at Columbia University in 1983: "Antisemitism is the dislike of the unlike." This simple, central point is a universal characteristic of antisemitism throughout the ages. As author Leon Wieseltier has observed, Jewish "apartness"—the "otherness" of Jews—was their great offense. Jews were viewed as being fundamentally unassimilable: in ancient times, Jews were viewed as misanthropes; in the supersessionist theology of the medieval Church, the Jews were attacked for their spiritual incorrigibility, for which they were impugned and oppressed; in the modern period, Jews were resented for their "corporateness"— Jews were attacked as "a state within a state" (Wieseltier 2003). In *Histories*, the Roman historian Tacitus observed that the Jews have separated themselves to such a degree as to incur the hatred of all. Even when Jews did assimilate—unwillingly, under coercion in fifteenth- and sixteenth-century Iberia; willingly in the nineteenth and twentieth centuries—they were subjected to an antisemitism of a racialist or biological nature.

To Jews themselves, however, the intolerance of the majority was never to be confused with the exclusiveness of the minority, which Jews zealously guarded. They were, in effect, saying, "I am not the 'other'; I am merely *myself.*" So a three-step process ensued: (1) Non-Jews never accepted the exclusiveness of Jews, which they interpreted as "otherness" and therefore deviant; (2) There was nothing Jews could—or would—do to mitigate this cause of anti-Jewish animus—except to disappear; (3) The refusal to disappear was maliciously interpreted by non-Jews as an attitude of defiance and contempt.

Another view, on the extreme end of the continuum, is a traditional Jewish rabbinic formulation: "An established principle: Esau hates Jacob" is the classic representation of antisemitism: Babylonia, Rome, Christendom as Edom—the antisemitic descendants of Esau: antisemitism incarnate, antisemitism universal, antisemitism unending, antisemitism eternal, antisemitism immutable.

There have been many other efforts aimed at defining antisemitism, from the elaborate formulations reflected in attitudinal surveys, which suggest a definition not along the lines of anti-Jewish expression but of anti-Jewish attitudes that are uncomfortable for Jews; to the basic question of whether antisemites can be converted?—*Is* antisemitism immutable?—an elaboration of the "Esau-hates-Jacob" locution.

For Jews themselves, antisemitism is a puzzler. Antisemitism has been a constant blight on the otherwise rich and complicated history of the Jews. As historian Allan Nadler remarked, "Despite a string of theological explanations and strategies—ranging from repentance to self-immolation and even apostasy—the Jews have never quite comprehended, let alone been able to free themselves of, this hatred" (Nadler 2003, **10**).

The patterns of antisemitism are irrational: A pariah people for most of their history, Jews have been persecuted for believing in Judaism and excoriated for being nonbelievers; despised when poor and loathed when rich; shamed for their ignorance of the host culture and rebuffed for mastering it; denounced as capitalists and assailed as communists; derided for their separatism and reviled for their assimilationism.

During its long history, antisemitism has assumed a number of disguises and has cloaked itself in religious or pseudoreligious garb: Christian theological "teachings of contempt" for the Jews; theories of alleged Jewish economic and media control and manipulation; the idea that Jews dominate the political system or pollute national cultures; and most recently, the idea that "Zionism Equals Racism" and other forms of Israelophobia, a denial of the very peoplehood of the Jews—all these are either subterfuges for what, at bottom, is antisemitism, or blatant antisemitism itself.

Antisemitism had been transnational and transcultural in its themes, images, and ideas. Racist theories articulated in Europe in the nineteenth century played a role in the passage of restrictive immigration laws in the 1920s in the United States. The antisemitic forgery *The Protocols of the Elders of Zion*, consigned yesterday to the ash-heap of history, has today been resurrected for use by propagandists in some Arab states.

One important point that is important to emphasize at the beginning of any exploration of antisemitism is that although antisemitism has been an important factor in Jewish history, it does not *define* Jewish history. Antisemitism is not the central dynamic of the Jewish experience. Indeed, the experience of the Jews vis-à-vis the non-Jewish world is a complicated experience, with an interplay of many factors, one of which is antipathy toward Jews. The historians Cecil Roth and Salo Baron decried the "lachrymose" views of Jewish history—historiographies that placed antisemitism front and center of the history of the Jews.

The Stages of Antisemitism

The *categorization* of anti-Jewish behavior is an important part of defining antisemitism. Historically, there are no specific social or political periods or conditions that especially favor the rise or dissemination of antisemitism; antisemitism has been a factor in many different societies, under different political, religious, social, and economic conditions. Although unrest or distress of any kind, arising from any source, favors antisemitism, there is no social dynamic that is peculiar to any period that obliges antisemitism. No specific accusations characterize antisemitism, even though certain myths tend to recur: the "blood libel" (an accusation that Jews murder non-Jewish children and use their blood in the preparation of matza for the Passover holiday), Jews and money, and Jewish domination are examples. Each succeeding era of antisemites took the anti-Jewish mythology of the preceding and carried the ball themselves. As psychologist Mortimer Ostow has observed: "Even after the subsidence of Church influence [with attendant Christian anti-Jewish activity], that is, even among the deists of the seventeenth and eighteenth centuries, and certainly among the Nazis, Christian demonization of the Jews was accepted, exploited, and elaborated" (Ostow 1996, 176).

We can identify at least six stages in antisemitism.[1] Antisemitism is easily classified historically as pointing to at least half-a-dozen varieties. (1) The pre-Christian anti-Jewish activity in the ancient Greco-Roman world, most of which was not what we would call "antisemitism," was primarily ethnic in nature. (2) There is the classic Christian antisemitism of antiquity and the Middle Ages, which was religious in nature and which extended into modern times. (3) Traditional Muslim antisemitism is—at least in its classical form—highly nuanced in that Jews are *Dhimmi*, members of a protected class. (4) There is the political, social, and economic antisemitism of Enlightenment and post-Enlightenment Europe, which laid the groundwork for racialist antisemitism. (5) There is the racial antisemitism that arose in the nineteenth century out of Enlightenment thinking and that culminated in Nazism. (6) Finally, the contemporary antisemitism of Israelophobia and "Zionism Equals Racism," a relatively new phenomenon, is what many characterize as the New Antisemitism.

(We may note an important case study in antisemitism, that of Nazi Germany. The antisemitism that arose in Nazi Germany developed out of three sources: [1] a political party whose platform was that of destruction and extermination of Jews as individuals and as a people; [2] a powerful war machine, that enabled the Nazi regime to impose its will—and prosecute its policy of destruction of the Jews—throughout Europe; and [3] the lack of significant opposition to—and in many cases complicity with—the Nazi agenda.)

We may telescope these six categories to three: ancient antisemitism, which was primarily *ethnic* in nature; Christian antisemitism, which was *religious;* and the *racial* antisemitism of the nineteenth and twentieth centuries.[2] If there is indeed any such thing as a New Antisemitism (a fourth category), it is "new" in the sense that it does not fit the pattern of these three categories.

The Psychology of Antisemitism

How antisemitism is *defined* is related to how antisemitism is *described* from a psychological perspective. Psychologically speaking, antisemitism, like any racial prejudice, is not of one piece. But generalizations about the psychology of antisemitism are useful. For comprehensive analyses, the reader is referred to works cited in Chapter 7, especially Mortimer Ostow, Martin Bergmann (in Chanes), and Dennis Wrong (in Stember).

The most comprehensive generalization about the forces that promote group prejudice is the psychodynamic approach. Prejudice—including antisemitism—functions independently of the target group's real attributes and of the actual social relationships between prejudiced persons (antisemites, in this case) and members of the group they despise (Jews). From the simple theory of "scapegoating," which has significant currency, to the elaborate technical conceptions of projections of id and superego, the psychodynamic approach to antisemitism has dominated research and theory over the past sixty years.

Among most antisemites, their irrational hatred is the expression of what psychologists call "primary process thinking," that is, thought that is driven by *feeling* and not subjected to the discipline of reason, logic, or reality-testing. Psychologically speaking, in individual cases of antisemites (and this is true for bigots, generally), the individual is looking for a "principle of evil," an explanation for evil in the world that is less far-fetched than invisible demons. Beginning with early Christian teachings, that principle was the Jew, and this principle has been passed on through the ages and is active among "post-Christian" antisemites. Identifying mythologies such as this is central to understanding the psychology of antisemitism.

A critique of the psychodynamic approach, in brief, is threefold: first, psychodynamics (especially the method known as psychoanalysis) do not explain the ebbs and flows, rises and declines, of antisemitism; they do not explore the interaction between the individual and the group. Second, psychodynamics do not explain why a *particular* ethnic group—Jews, for example—becomes the object of prejudice. Finally, as a practical matter, psychodynamics do not take into account the realities and actualities of intergroup relations. Jews are not a figment of the majority group's diseased imagination but are real people with real relations to members of the majority. A corollary of this is that psychoanalysis does not constitute an efficacious counteraction of antisemitism; law and social action, which turn on changing the conditions of society, not of the individual, do.

In terms of individual psychology, at bottom, two psychological characteristics are present in the individual antisemite: excessive hostility and the need (and a capacity) to project one's aggression on other groups. Persons who have these traits generally suffer from feelings of inadequacy and from the feeling that their own personal borders, psychologically speaking, are easily invaded by others. In psychological language, the ego boundary of such an individual is weak and requires the protection of prejudice in order for the person to maintain his or her equilibrium. What are projected by such an individual are those parts of the self that are unacceptable and repudiated. And when the expression of the bigoted aggression of an individual is sanctioned by a group, it becomes much easier for the individual to express that aggression. When the institutions of power—for example, the government in Nazi Germany—sanction prejudice, all of the conditions are in place for antisemitism to flourish.

Antisemitism, Prejudice, and Jewish Security: A Crucial Nexus

Psychologist Gordon Allport, who wrote at length about the topic, offered a number of definitions of prejudice: "Prejudice is thinking ill of others without sufficient warrant"; prejudice is "a feeling, favorable or unfavorable, toward a person or thing, prior to, or not based on, actual experience" (Allport 1954, 6).[3]

These two definitions identify three important characteristics of prejudice: (1) prejudice is irrational, (2) prejudice is based on prejudgments, and (3) the prejudgment/prejudice is generally not reversible when exposed to new knowledge. In other words, the data of social science tell us that attitudes do not change.

Allport offered as well a fuller approach to prejudice that includes the ingredient of functional significance: "Prejudice is a pattern of hostility in interpersonal relationships which is directed against an entire group, or against its individual members; it fulfills a specific irrational function for its bearers" (Allport 1954, 12). The final phrase of this definition suggests that a negative attitude is not a prejudice unless there is a functional element in the attitude, so that the attitude serves a self-gratifying purpose for the person who holds that attitude.

Among the most strongly held and widespread of society's prejudices is racism; racism—a biologically-based prejudice, in which the biology is deeply flawed—indeed satisfies all of the criteria we have noted. The questions at hand: Is antisemitism a form of racism? What is the relationship of antisemitism and racism?

Although antisemitism is related to racism, distinctions between antisemitism and racism ought be noted. Racialism or racism, as awful and repugnant are its manifestations, is premised on observable physical differences between groups of people. The world of antisemitism represents deeper, more profound, more irrational antipathy that moves its adherents and practitioners in attitude and behavior. Antisemitism in its modern manifestations clearly has racialist elements, but a distinction between antisemitism and classic racist expression ought be borne.

A second distinction needs to be suggested. In any analysis of antisemitism, a crucial distinction must be made between *antisemitism*, which does exist and must be monitored, repudiated, and counteracted, and *Jewish security*, which in 2004—with some notable exceptions—is strong. *Jewish security, at bottom, is the ability of Jews, individually and collectively, to participate in the workings of their society without fear of anti-Jewish animus.* Although antisemitism and Jewish security are concentric circles and therefore obviously related, the distinction between them is important when discussing the issue of antisemitism anywhere in the world.

Trends in Antisemitism

The Measurement of Antisemitism

Assessment of antisemitism is rooted in the criteria by which antisemitism is measured. There are two kinds of antisemitism—following sociologist Robert Merton's model—*behavioral* and *attitudinal:* what people *do* and what people *think.* There is a crucial relationship between what people *think* and what people *do,* between attitudinal and behavioral antisemitism. Antisemitism of both kinds is assessed along a broad range of evaluative criteria.[4] The data on antisemitism, along these criteria, indicate that both behavioral and attitudinal antisemitism have declined everywhere over the past fifty years, even as there are recurring danger signals. This finding is amply confirmed by evidence both anecdotal and research generated. Nonetheless, the finding calls for some analysis in terms of both behavioral and attitudinal manifestations.

Behavioral antisemitism is manifest, of course, in many different ways, from acts of antisemitic vandalism to jokes and comments to political rhetoric. The reality is that behavioral antisemitism of any kind, in most parts of the world—especially in Western societies—is no longer a significant factor. Such behavioral antisemitism includes large-scale discrimination against Jews; the cynical use of antisemitism in political rhetoric in order to achieve political gains, arguably the most virulent form of antisemitism; and most important, the inability or reluctance of the Jewish community to express itself on issues of concern in the society because of anti-Jewish animus. Obviously, this is a very general proposition; there are vast differences from country to country, and there are countries in which this proposition is simply not true. This kind of antisemitism has declined steadily and dramatically over the past four decades and more.

It is virtually impossible for social scientists to measure the security of any ethnic, religious, or racial group, using mathematical criteria. Such evaluations are done qualitatively and anecdotally. Measurements are useful and appropriate in assessing the *negatives* in a society; attitudinal antisemitism—what people think about Jews—has been the subject of surveys and polls, particularly in the United States, less so in other countries.[5]

The question with respect to attitudinal antisemitism is a basic one: What do people think about Jews? On this fairly narrow question there are fairly conclusive findings. The cumulative data of attitudinal surveys conducted by a range of researchers over the years have consistently substantiated the view that the level of conventional antisemitic beliefs has continued in its forty-year decline. Simply put, there are fewer people in most countries who profess unfavorable images of Jews.

It is important to identify some degree of specificity in this generalization. The statement obviously does not refer to Muslim and Arab countries, where levels of antisemitic attitudes remain high. The generalization is also nuanced when it comes to Europe; *conventional* attitudinal antisemitism has declined in most European countries, but levels of anti-Zionist sentiment—an Israelophobia that can fairly be characterized as antisemitism—have risen in the early part of the present decade.[6]

The usual explanation for this transformation in terms of attitudinal antisemitism is generational and is most dramatically evident in the United States. It is not that the antisemites are being converted, but that each succeeding age-group tends to display fewer antisemitic attitudes than the preceding generation of that age group. Committed antisemites are swayed to virtue neither by events nor by prejudice-reduction programs. Research findings clearly, strongly, and consistently suggest that a younger, better educated, more affluent population is less antisemitic. This pattern, a negative correlation of education level and antisemitism, obtains across the board.

A number of recent attitudinal surveys are identified in the annotated bibliography in Chapter 7 and are discussed in Chapter 4. These include periodic surveys of American and European attitudes of Jews, commissioned by the Anti-Defamation League; and surveys on a range of intergroup attitudes, commissioned by the American Jewish Committee. Attitudinal surveys generate data that are highly significant, even as there are some questions with respect to how the surveys are designed and interpreted. For the purpose of this discussion, four questions ought be noted.

The first question has less to do with the study and everything to do with the way in which data on antisemitism are presented and interpreted by surveys. Numerical data reported by surveys always need to be contextualized—"Compared to *when?*" and "Compared to *what?*" It is only with appropriate contextualization that the data can tell researchers anything about the nature and extent of antisemitism.

Second, some of the questions in the indices of antisemitic attitudes often used by researchers may not have been perceived by respondents as reflecting negatively on Jews; they indeed may not measure antisemitism. Questions about Jews sticking together, to take but one example, may have reflected antisemitism in the 1950s and 1960s; they hardly do so today. The lesson: a number of questions in an index may be measuring not antisemitism but some other beliefs or feelings that may indeed represent some anti-Jewish animus or may in fact be reflective of positive attitudes toward Jews.

Third, and a more serious issue: attitudes are much more nuanced than the three groupings "most antisemitic," "middle," "not antisemitic" that are used in some of the standard Anti-Defamation League surveys, which use an eleven-question "index" to measure attitudes toward Jews. There is a basic ambiguity in most responses that needs to be noted. A respondent who answered "yes" to six or seven questions (some of which may in fact *not* measure antisemitism, as we just noted) has been just fine on four or five. (And even some of these questions may *not* measure antisemitism, as we have noted.) Even among the "most antisemitic," therefore, there exist identifiable pro-Jewish attitudes. (Among the "not antisemitic," the reverse is true: they may very well hold anti-Jewish attitudes.) A more sophisticated conceptual scheme is clearly needed, one that takes into account these ambiguities.

Fourth, and most troubling: Attitudinal surveys may be leading researchers toward a new definition of antisemitism: attitudes toward Jews that are distasteful, rather than the classic definition of antisemitism as expressed hostility toward Jews.[7]

The General State of Antisemitism

The condition of Jews around the world with respect to their security is discussed in detail in the first sections of Chapter 4. As a general proposition, and notwithstanding antisemitic expressions in the early years of this century related to the Arab-Israeli conflict, antisemitism has declined in the overwhelming majority of countries over the past fifty years, and the security of Jews around the world has improved. For most Jews around the world, antisemitism is not a matter that compromises their ability to participate in the working of their societies and polities.

Much is made, however, of the New Antisemitism. What is the New Antisemitism, if it is indeed "new"? In order to answer this question, we need to probe antisemitism in Europe, a phenomenon related to anti-Zionist and anti-Israel rhetoric. Antisemitism in Europe is historically linked to the political contours of each era and of each country during a given era.[8] The physiognomy of European antisemitism in any given era is a function of the primary political challenge facing Europeans in that time and place. An example: nationalism in the nineteenth century and its relationship to racialist antisemitism.

The primary political challenge for Europe today is that of moving beyond the nation-state, a problem that is framed in the clash between nationalism and postnationalism. It comes as no surprise that Israel (and the United States) are reviled for acting like the nation-states they are. Israel, as the product of nineteenth-century European nationalism (so the analysis goes), acts as the ideology of nationalism suggests that sovereign states should and do act: it is ready to employ the force of arms to defend the nation's interests. This behavior is what disturbs many Europeans; it strikes their postnationalist sensibilities as retrograde and racist. Israel squares off against the Arabs in the same benighted manner as the French used to against the Germans. Hence, European antisemitism. Zionism, the darling of the Left seventy years ago, became successful—that is, it created a nation-state—precisely at a time when the nation-state fell out of fashion.

It is important to note that most Europeans who articulate this view—and surveys show that substantial pluralities in many European counties do (Anti-Defamation League 2002)—distinguish themselves as not holding classical antisemitic prejudices.

What about recent manifestations of anti-Israel rhetoric and accompanying expressions of antisemitism in Europe? The question is: At which point does criticism of the policies of the State of Israel become antisemitism? This question—as are many others in the antisemitism arena—is a threshold question and therefore is subjective. One evaluative standard that is offered: criticism—indeed, harsh criticism—of the policies of Israel is legitimate. The point at which it becomes antisemitism is the point at which the *legitimacy* of the State of Israel, and by extension the Zionist enterprise, is questioned, because it is at that point that the legitimacy of Jewish peoplehood is called into question. This, tautologically, is antisemitism.

But this may be too high a threshold. It might be legitimately argued that criticism of Israel is in itself a form of antisemitism; it creates an atmosphere that is conducive to antisemitism, and much of it may be motivated by antisemitic sentiments. In this regard the geopolitical analysis offered above on postnationalism is instructive. If there is such a thing as the New Antisemitism, it is precisely the "double standard" applied to Israel as a nation-state defending itself.

If there indeed be any such thing as a New Antisemitism, then, it is "new" in the sense that it does not fit the pattern of ethnic (ancient), religious (Christian), or racial (nineteenth- and twentieth-century) antisemitism. Many analysts argue that there is a double standard—the assertion that Jews may not defend themselves as may any other people or person and by extension the illegitimacy of a Jewish historical particularism—that is close to antisemitism. Related to and indeed deriving from this, of course, are the isolation of the State of Israel and the relegation of Israel to the status of "pariah state."

Having said this, the reality is that in the twenty-first century, whatever antisemitic manifestations there may be, there is no regime or government in Europe that has an agenda of the murder of Jews. Indeed, the only regimes today that *do* believe in an ideology and pursue a program of Jewish destruction are those in the Arab world.

The Counteraction of Antisemitism

As a general proposition, the conditions for successful counteraction of antisemitism have never been better. The historical context in this regard is crucial: The destiny of the Jews has, after many centuries, left Europe. Throughout the history of Europe, Jews were traditionally at the mercy of "rights" granted by rulers, parliaments, and clerics. Jewish destiny is for the most part now in Israel, where Jews have sovereignty; and in the United States, where Jews enjoy with others the benefits of a pluralist democracy. The example of the United States, home of the world's largest Jewish community, is instructive. The United States is not just another "address" for Jews on the run from persecution but is a place that is, because of its pluralist structure, fundamentally hospitable to Jews. It is a principle of pluralism that Jews can comfortably be "a state within a state" without fear of hostility. Although antisemitism and other forms of bigotry can and do exist in a pluralist society, the conditions of pluralism are necessary for successful counteraction of antisemitism.

It is useful to place contemporary counteraction of antisemitism in the context of responses to antisemitism in history. There have been three historical models of Jewish responses to antisemitism.[9]

First, in the "pre-modern" period, there was no concept of antisemitism as humanly fashioned ideology or as political problem; anti-Judaism was a reflection of God's will and of divine "natural law," and it was "natural" that Jews (in the classic rabbinic formulation discussed earlier under "What is Antisemitism?") were hated by non-Jews. Not only was there no point in trying to fight antisemitism, argued the rabbinic leadership, but there was something somewhat impious about any such effort. The overwhelming Jewish belief was that inordinate Jewish suffering—all of the many calamities of Jewish history going back to the destruction of the Temples and even further back in history, and going forward: the Crusades, the Inquisition and expulsions, and so on—was the consequence of sinfulness.

This response—and response it was, not to be confused with the "quietism" that was the norm in the modern period—was primarily theological and rooted in *orthopraxis:* prayer and repentance and awaiting divine salvation.

Second, during the period of the European Enlightenment, non-Jewish hatred of Jews was identified by Jews as a social and political problem to be addressed strategically by the Jewish community. Unfortunately, however, even though the diagnosis of the causes and nature of antisemitism was radically different from that of the classical rabbis—divine providence was no longer part of the equation—there was yet the tendency to "blame the victim." Many in the Jewish leadership in western Europe—particularly those who were influenced by Enlightenment thinking—were convinced that non-Jewish hatred of Jews was the consequence of the behavior, dress, etiquette, and language of Jews. The prevalent view was that once Jews ceased to stand out among non-Jews, the problem of antisemitism would wither and ultimately disappear. This "quietist" approach expressed itself as well as Jewish dependence on "rights" being granted to Jews by sovereigns and parliaments in Europe.

The third historical response to antisemitism, that of the late nineteenth and the twentieth centuries, emerged when it became clear that the first two responses were failures. In the late nineteenth century it was evident that neither a purely religious response to antisemitism, nor a quietistic program of Jewish "improvement," would alleviate Jew-hatred. On the contrary, antisemitism in Europe was growing in intensity, with new racialist ideologies and manifestations. A small group of Jewish political visionaries realized that the only solution to the deepening problem of European antisemitism was the removal of Jews from the lands in which antisemitism was rife and the creation of a Jewish state. This approach was proposed indeed by individuals who were mostly the products of an assimilationist approach to the problem. It was clear to these thinkers that antisemitism was an incurable spiritual disease of Europe and that only the removal of the Jews themselves from the unhealthy and unnatural environment of Europe to their natural homeland could "cure" the hatred of them. The early Zionists were indeed convinced not so much that Israel would serve to protect Jews against the violent designs of their enemies but that the very existence of a Jewish national homeland would dissolve antisemitism once and for all.

It is worth going into this level of detail on the history of the counteraction of antisemitism because all contemporary Jewish approaches to counteraction (and for that matter, approaches to the counteraction of any prejudiced or racist activity) are informed by the premise that "blaming the victim" is not a legitimate approach to the problem; and, further, contemporary counteraction is influenced by the Zionist insistence that antisemitism must be dealt with aggressively and decisively, using *political* means. In short, in the contemporary era—especially since the Holocaust—there is a consensus among Jews that the victims of this most vile and ancient hatred need neither apologize for their existence nor emasculate themselves in response to antisemitism but must take action—be that action political, legislative, or judicial—against it.

The means of counteraction of antisemitism are many. We identify the most visible and efficacious.

Popular among Jewish "defense" agencies has been the use of a variety of prejudice-reduction programs (such as the World of Difference program of the Anti-Defamation League), although there are limited data that such programs result in the diminution of attitudinal antisemitism among members of the broad population. The weight of the data suggests that the lessening of prejudice is a result of generational changes in social, economic, and educational status rather than in the "conversion" of individual bigots. Nonetheless, prejudice-reduction programs are useful in that they demonstrate that populations that participate in the programs are committed to the diminution of prejudice.

Legislative and judicial remedies—hate-crimes laws, for example—likewise are questionable in terms of their efficacy at reducing antisemitism; it is not clear that they prevent expressions of antisemitic bias. Such legislation is nevertheless extremely important (assuming that the laws are crafted in a way that does not inhibit legitimate freedom of expression, and they thereby pass constitutional muster) in that the laws send the message that the central institutions of power in the society—in this case, government—will not tolerate bigoted behavior.[10]

The most efficacious counteraction of antisemitism, in the view of this author, is the improving of social and economic conditions. The data, without fail, assert that in any population, in any geographic area, at any time, in which the conditions of society are improved—primarily economic and educational conditions—bigotry and racism decrease.[11]

Transcending all of these types of counteraction—and this goes not to the question of *antisemitism,* but to *Jewish security*—is the enhancement of the kinds of constitutional protections taken for granted in the United States and gaining currency in some other countries. In the United States, these protections are chiefly those embodied in the First Amendment to the U.S. Constitution, and most centrally the separation of church and state. For American Jews there is no surer guarantor of security than the strength of constitutional institutions. Any institutions in society that strengthen and thereby enhance pluralism will act as a preventative to antisemitism.

What Do We *Not* Know about Antisemitism?

Finally, what is the research agenda for the many questions that remain about antisemitism?

A research agenda on antisemitism needs to be aggressively pursued; public officials and social scientists need to understand better the various forms of antisemitism and their distinguishing features, the perceptions of antisemitism, and the efficacy of the different methods of counteraction. Primarily non-Jews are those who ought be interested in the understanding of antisemitism and not only as a matter of understanding a form of group prejudice. Historian Yehuda Bauer said: "The last time Jew-hatred became official policy in a major nation, it contributed significantly to the outbreak of a war in which 35 million lives were lost. Most of the casualties were not Jews. This would seem to be reason enough for non-Jews to oppose antisemitism with all their energy" (Bauer 1994, 21).

First, there is the question of the "perception gap" found in many countries—chief of which is the United States—in which the data show that antisemitism is declining both behaviorally and attitudinally, but in which majorities of Jews at the grassroots level assert that it is a serious problem and indeed rising. What explains this perception gap?

In the first instance, it is necessary to understand what Jews *are* saying when they say that antisemitism is a serious problem. On this question there are some data. A 1991 study, conducted by Brandeis University's Perlmutter Institute for Jewish Advocacy, revealed that Jews in the United States, when asked about specific areas of "seriousness" of the antisemitism they were reporting, did not for the most part pinpoint economic, power, or political areas—the more serious manifestations of antisemitism—but rather incidents of vandalism. Or they are saying "I heard from my neighbor that he heard on the radio. . . ."

Second, in terms of explaining the perception gap, it is clear that much of the anxiety felt by many is obviously related to the historical experience of the Jews, particularly that of the Holocaust. History has made Jews unusually sensitive, and it is a sensitivity worth maintaining. This gut reaction is a response not to antisemitism but to a foreboding of latent antisemitism possibly turning into actual. We recall the classic one-liner: What's the definition of a Jewish telegram? "Start worrying. Letter follows." The 80 to 90 percent in the United States who are responding "Yes" to the question "Is antisemitism a serious problem?" are responding not to antisemitism but to the Jewish telegram.

Earl Raab, who has articulated much of the vocabulary of the Jewish community relations field in the United States, has written about this foreboding at length.[12] Raab suggested that the foreboding felt by most Jews in the United States and elsewhere is that of an antisemitism that is latent among many in the society, requiring some radical social dislocation to cause its actual expression. This foreboding is useful. But Raab suggested that it will not help Jews much if they only see anti-Israel activity as the latest version of atavistic Jew-hatred. At best, the foreboding does lead to an understanding that the best fight against latent anti-semitism is the fight to strengthen positive American self-interest attitudes toward Jews (Raab 1992).

But there is more to the gap between the perception of anti-semitism and the reality of Jewish security than just the foreboding of latent antisemitism. Sociologist Steven M. Cohen has found that more than half of all American Jews (to take one important example) continue to hold traditional negative stereotypes of non-Jews (Cohen and Liebman 1990). Whatever the data on the actual decline of antisemitism, these negative images resonate in the perception of an antisemitism re-emergent. And this dynamic reinforces itself: the perception that non-Jews are hostile may very well lead Jews to avoid non-Jewish intimacies and associa-tions. In turn, the absence of such contact sustains the negative image of the non-Jew and reinforces Jews' fear of non-Jews—in a word, of antisemitism.

Further, the perception of antisemitism found among many Jews, particularly American Jews, may be a vestige of a time when antisemitism *was* very real—periods in which large-scale social and economic discrimination against Jews was norma-tive—and when every Jew was insecure vis-à-vis non-Jews. If these outmoded social and cultural perceptions of the non-Jew persist, it may be too soon to measure the reactions of American Jews to questions about Jewish security against the *true* state of Jewish security.

Further, there is, in the United States, the inevitable intrusion of issues from the public affairs agenda into the consciousness of many Jews. The Christian "religious right" and the notion of the United States as a "Christian nation"[13] and related attacks on the separation of church and state—threats all, in my view, to Jewish security—suggest to some Jews a renewed wafting of antisemitic odors. Questions with respect to the "religious right" evangelical political movement in the United States occasionally go beyond, and are deeper than, debates over public-policy issues. The con-troversy over the sometimes questionable assertions about Jews found in the writings and public utterances of the Reverend Pat Robertson, leader of the Christian Coalition, which portray a worldwide conspiracy of international bankers, communists, and freemasons (code-words all for classic *antisemitica*), further sug-gests that there remains a reservoir of antisemitism that may in-form much of the activity of the "religious right." At the very least, the apocalyptic vision that underlies much of the support of the "religious right" and evangelical political movement for the State of Israel is in essence conversionary and not especially friendly to Jews.

There are additional obvious influences on the perception of Jews of antisemitism. Anti-Israel and anti-Zionist rhetoric has a profound influence on Jewish perceptions, and antisemitic activity in Europe has had an important effect as well. The effects of Israelophobia, particularly in its virulent expressions in the United Nation's World Conference against Racism held in Durban, South Africa, in 2001, are profound and far transcend in the minds of many Jews the realities of Jewish security that they enjoy in their home countries. Jews also cannot discount the effects of societal traumas they have experienced, such as the impact on American Jews of the 1991 riots in the Crown Heights neighborhood of Brooklyn. Important as well is the effect of intergroup tensions in general. The sense of this author is that the source of anxiety for many Jews around the world (again, especially in the United States) is not be antisemitism per se; it is the rise of intergroup conflict across the map. The relationship of intergroup tension to antisemitism is an area that requires significant study.

A second important area for research is that social scientists and historians need to know more about the taboos and controls surrounding expression of antisemitism, controls that cause non-antisemites to become anti-antisemites. The question is not one of who are the antisemites? But one of who are those who are *not* antisemites? There are three types of people in any society in terms of how they relate to Jews: philosemites, non-antisemites, and anti-antisemites.[14] The security of Jews does not depend on people being non-antisemites; for most people in most countries, Jews are simply not an issue.

There are many people who do not care about the Jews one way or another but who may be unconstrained enough to support an antisemite for political office if such support appears to serve their needs. These are the non-antisemites. The dynamic at work in non-antisemitism lies at the interface of the social control and trigger mechanisms.

The real security of Jews lies in people being *anti*-antisemites, for whom antisemitism is totally illegitimate and must be repudiated. A relatively small number of people fall in the anti-antisemite category, and not much is known about the taboo that informs anti-antisemitism.

Third is the question of triggers of antisemitism. With respect to triggers of antisemitism, it is not enough to mouth the simple formula of "bad times equals increased antisemitism." Bad economic times can be the background; they do not constitute the trigger. What is required is a combination and interaction of *background* and context; antisemitic *attitudes* of the population that are measured; and *trigger*.[15]

Fourth, there are forms of antisemitism that are difficult to observe and measure, namely hidden and latent antisemitism. Additionally, traditional, cruder forms of antisemitism may not have been eliminated but may have been revamped and repackaged for a new generation. Israelophobia is an example of this area. These new forms, articulated in a different, perhaps less blatant manner, more subtle and nuanced, call for study. The difficulty is that even though new forms of antisemitism may be open and observable (as compared with hidden and latent antisemitism), they are often encrypted.[16]

Fifth is the question of threshold. The different points at which individuals *perceive* antisemitism need to be probed. What yardstick are people using when they measure situations that they themselves perceive or experience as antisemitism? Should survivors of the Holocaust, on the one hand, and college students who never experienced behavioral antisemitism until they reached the campus, on the other, be categorized in the same manner? Both groups, from opposite ends of the spectrum, have very low thresholds for perceiving antisemitism.[17] This is a difficult and sensitive area.

Sixth, we need a new look at the attitudinal surveys. The surveys, which may be either antiquated or irrelevant, need to be retooled, and new questionnaires, which respond to the realities of the twenty-first century, need to be crafted.

Seventh, a hierarchy of antisemitism needs to be developed. This is extremely important. Not all forms of antisemitism carry equal weight. It is absurd to equate political antisemitism—a most virulent form of antisemitism—with an incident of antisemitic vandalism. No one would want to minimize any form of antisemitic expression—any person who is at the receiving end of such expression is an abused person—but a serious weighting system needs to be developed by social scientists.

Eighth, the relationship of bigotry in general and antisemitism needs to be explored.

Ninth, and most crucial: what is the relationship between attitude and behavior? This question has been around for decades and has bedeviled the research psychologists as much as the sociologists.

Conclusion

The historian Lucy Dawidowicz, writing in *Commentary* magazine in 1970, asked a simple question: "Can anti-Semitism be measured?" (Dawidowicz 1970). Dawidowicz suggested that survey analysis, which presents a picture frozen in a moment in time and which provides much of the data upon which we rely, is by its nature unequipped to investigate the historic images and themes that yet flourish; it is certainly unequipped to trace the passage of these themes from one culture to another. How much more difficult to locate a specific variety of antisemitism within a meaningful historical continuum and translate this form of antisemitism in a responsible way for researchers? It is this last question that, ultimately, is our charge in evaluating and interpreting antisemitism.

In sum, there is no answer to the questions, "Why antisemitism?" and "How much antisemitism?" or even to the question, "How can antisemitism be eradicated?" The continued monitoring, measurement, evaluation, and assessment of antisemitism must continue as a centerpiece of research on the part of social scientists and public affairs officials. There are few who maintain that legislative remedies will eradicate anti-Jewish behavior; there are certainly no remedies for antisemitic attitudes and beliefs. But the variety of approaches to antisemitism—to bigotry in general—will send a powerful message that to the central institutions of society antisemitism is wrong and must be rejected.

Notes

1. See Chapter 2 for a full historical narrative and analysis of antisemitism.

2. On the New Antisemitism, see below, "The General State of Antisemitism."

3. For a full discussion, see Allport, *The Nature of Prejudice* (1954), chap. 1 and *passim*.

4. Among the criteria for assessing antisemitism, developed by the National Jewish Community Relations Advisory Council (NJCRAC, now the Jewish Council for Public Affairs—JCPA), are prevailing attitudes toward Jews; acts of aggression, covert or overt, toward Jews; discrimination against Jews; expressions of antisemitism by public figures; expressions of antisemitism by religious figures; response to conflict situations; official reactions to antisemitism; antisemitic "mass" movements; personal experience with antisemitism; anti-Zionist manifestations in which the legitimacy of the State of Israel—and therefore the legitimacy of the peoplehood of the Jews—is questioned. (This does not include criticism of the policies of the Israeli government.) NJCRAC, *NJCRAC 1985–86 Joint Program Plan* (New York: NJCRAC, 1986).

5. See Chapter 7 for bibliographical references to surveys—specifically those conducted on American and European attitude by the Anti-Defamation League and on intergroup relations by the American Jewish Committee—conducted in a number of countries of antisemitic attitudes.

6. See Chapter 4 for data.

7. For a review and analysis of attitudinal surveys, see Jerome A. Chanes, "Antisemitism and Jewish Security in America: Why Can't Jews Take 'Yes' for an Answer?" in *Jews in America: A Contemporary Reader,* ed. Roberta Rosenberg Farber and Chaim I. Waxman, 129–134 (Hanover, NH: Brandeis University Press, 1999). The analysis holds true for surveys conducted since 1999.

8. A fine analysis is offered by Mark Lilla, "The End of Politics: Europe, the Nation-State, and the Jews," *The New Republic,* 23 June 2003, 29–34.

9. The author acknowledges the work of historian Allan Nadler, who suggested this construct.

10. For a comprehensive review of the hate-crimes arena, see Donald Altschiller, *Hate Crimes: A Reference Handbook* (Santa Barbara, CA: ABC-CLIO, 1999).

11. See, for example, data from studies conducted over the past two decades by Marttila and Kiley/the Marttila Communications Group for the Anti-Defamation League (*1998 Survey on Anti-Semitism and Prejudice in America; 2002 Survey on Anti-Semitism in America*). This inverse correlation—social conditions up, antisemitism down—holds true, contrary to conventional wisdom, across racial lines as well.

12. See Earl Raab, "Can Antisemitism Disappear?" in *Antisemitism in America Today,* ed. Jerome A. Chanes, 84–99 (New York: Carol Publishing/Birch Lane Press, 1995).

13. Revealing was the observation of Senator Howell Heflin (D-Alabama), who, in his opening remarks in Senate subcommittee hearings in Washington, D.C., on 10 October 1994 on language on religious harass-

ment in the workplace for Equal Employment Opportunity Commission guidelines, averred, "We have [in this country] Americans, Jews, and others." Heflin thought he was being a nice guy.

14. The philosemitism phenomenon is a social-psychological phenomenon that calls for a discrete treatment.

15. Earl Raab, "Taking the Measure of Anti-Semitism" (1992), explored this area.

16. For a comprehensive discussion of hidden and latent antisemitism, see Tom W. Smith, *Anti-Semitism in Contemporary America New York: American Jewish Committee, 1994*, 19–22, (New York: American Jewish Committee, 1994).

17. I thank Dr. David Singer of the American Jewish Committee for suggesting this example.

References

Allport, Gordon W. 1954. *The Nature of Prejudice*. Menlo Park, CA: Addison-Wesley.

Anti-Defamation League. 2002. *European Attitudes toward Jews: A Five Country Survey*. New York: Anti-Defamation League.

Bauer, Yehuda. 1994. "In Search of a Definition of Antisemitism." In *Approaches to Antisemitism: Context and Curriculum,* ed. Michael Brown, 10–21. New York: American Jewish Committee.

Cohen, Steven M., and Charles S. Liebman. 1990. *Two Worlds of Judaism: The Israeli and American Experiences*. New Haven: Yale University Press.

Dawidowicz, Lucy. 1970. "Can Anti-Semitism Be Measured?" *Commentary* 50, no. 1 (July): 36–43.

Nadler, Allan. 2003. "The Barbed Embrace." *Forward* 56, no. 31 (June 20): 450.

Ostow, Mortimer. 1996. *Myth and Madness: The Psychodynamics of Antisemitism*. New Brunswick, NJ: Transaction.

Raab, Earl. 1992. "Taking the Measure of Anti-Semitism in the 21st Century." Address to the Plenary Session of the National Jewish Community Relations Advisory Council, 16 February 1992 (unpublished address).

Survey of Jewish Attitudes. 1991. Perlmutter Institute for Jewish Advocacy, Brandeis University.

Wieseltier, Leon. 2003. "Old Demons, New Debates." YIVO Conference on Antisemitism, New York, 12 May 2003 (unpublished address).

2

Historical Narrative and Chronology

The Ancient World

A ntisemitism is not, contrary to conventional wisdom, as old as the Jews themselves. While living in a homeland of their own and developing their own civilization, the Jews of ancient Israel encountered the rivalries and even hostilities that were and are normal among peoples and powers in a given region. These normal geopolitical tensions, whatever else they might signify, ought not be characterized facially as antisemitism.

It is indeed possible that the first stirrings of antisemitism occurred during the period of the First Commonwealth monarchy in Palestine, that is, up to the sixth century BCE. There were significant numbers of non-Jews living in the land of Israel during that period, and the seeds of future friction were present even in the early years.

But the first clear manifestations of antisemitism do not come about until the creation of an involuntary *Diaspora*, after the destruction of the first temple in Jerusalem and the dispersion of the Jews—the Babylonian captivity—in 586 BCE. We find that in the first centuries of the Jewish dispersion, the Jews had settled far beyond the geographical limits of the Mediterranean world.

Thus, the negative picture of the Jew as homeless wanderer—society's castoff—did not begin with the development of Christian theology. Such descriptions are found in writings dating from pre-Hasmonean times.[1] In the third century BCE there was a sizable Jewish community in Egypt, centered in Alexandria. Egypt indeed had become the heart of the Diaspora; it was also the center of Hellenization. Alexandria was a second Athens. Jewish refusal to accept common religious and social standards was resented by the strongly Hellenized indigenous Egyptian population. Alexandria became the chief center of recognizable antisemitism in the ancient world.

The main popularizer of antisemitic themes was the third-century Egyptian priest and historian Manetho. Manetho taught that Jews were originally a group of Egyptian lepers who, when expelled from Egypt, became a tribe of misanthropic wanderers. Manetho, as an official historian, had credibility in Alexandria. From the third century on, the themes of leprous origins and misanthropy were rarely absent from the litanies of pagan antisemitism. These themes have continued to resonate down to the present day.

But a more serious manifestation was the concentrated attack on the Jewish religion in the days of Antiochus IV (Epiphanes) in the second century BCE (Jews know this history well as central to the Chanukah story). Under Antiochus, Jews were compelled to reject many of the laws of their fathers. But were the Antiochan decrees manifestations of antisemitism? Hardly; the "villains" of the narrative were the Jewish Hellenizers in Jerusalem, who sought to introduce and indeed impose secular culture. Antiochus's actions were informed by geopolitical realties, rather than anti-Jewish animus. The distinction is an important one and ought be borne in mind by students of antisemitism and other forms of group prejudice.[2]

But it was the experience during the Hellenistic period that enables us to draw a picture and develop an understanding of the alleged antipathy of Jews to other nations as well as the antipathy toward Jews that derived from Jewish social and religious practices, which is represented by the dynamic of difference: Jews *were* different from their neighbors and for the most part did not identify with other peoples. For example: no other nation or people denied the gods of its neighbors; on the contrary, panreligiosity—identifying others' gods with one's own—was the norm. Important was the fact that none of the peoples was unequivocally hostile toward intermarriage, except the Jews. The Jews were characterized by their Hellenistic neighbors and masters as misanthropes and worse, a people who flagrantly denied the Hellenic principle of the unity of mankind.

How Should Ancient Antisemitism Be Evaluated?

Despite the clash of religious views, and sometimes of political imperatives, between the followers of the God of Israel and those of Zeus or Jupiter, pagan antisemitism was not primarily theological. We do not observe in pagan times the anti-Jewish reactions on the part of large segments of the Greek or Roman body-politic that would render precarious the lot of Jews. Foreign theologies were generally tolerated—indeed were considered legitimate—so long as their adherents refrained from acts that were hostile to the imperial religion and gave some sort of nod to Jupiter. In point of fact, Jews were even exempt from this last requirement; Judaism was permitted as a discrete religion in the Roman empire.

So it is not clear that the first antisemitism was ethnic, or racialist. Neither was it economic, as has been a familiar pattern down the ages. Economic factors may have been present but not sufficient to enable the characterization of antisemitism. There was no disproportion of Jews in commerce, or of wealthy Jews, during Greek or Roman times.

Anti-Jewish feeling took the shape of a national xenophobia—fear or dislike of outsiders, of people who were different—played out in political settings. As we have seen, antisemitism was in large measure manifested as a literary phenomenon, flowing as it did from the pens of a nativistic intelligentsia.

One ought not underestimate the early manifestations of anti-Jewish animus. There are two points that ought be borne in mind. First, antisemitism, of whatever period, rests in an important way on a *prescriptive*—and in the eyes of Jews, positive—manifestation of Judaism: the Biblical injunction to be separate from—to be "other" from—other nations and other peoples, as being witness and faithful to one God and his Torah. Pagan (and later) antisemitism turned this commandment on its head in a display of resentment, hatred, and destruction. The originally *positive* ingredient at the heart of antisemitism has often been overlooked when historians and social scientists analyze the subject. The second point is that antisemitism during Greek and Roman times was not a function of theological imperatives or racialist ideologies, as it became during Christian or modern periods.

The Christian World

Anti-Jewish themes manifested themselves early in Christianity's first centuries and were constant and uniform. As the church in the first century of its existence expanded into the Gentile world and became less recognizably "Jewish" with respect to beliefs and practices, attitudes vis-à-vis Judaism became embedded in theology. The church, according to the Christian theology as articulated by the third-century church father Origen, antedated ancient Israel—it was thereby a church of *all* people; the Laws of Moses were only for the Jews, and they were a yoke imposed upon the Jews because of their unworthiness and their sins; the Jews were an apostate nation; and so on. The church, embodying the fulfillment of God's will, replaced the synagogue; Christians became the "new Israel"; the church became *Verus Israel*, "the true Israel." The second-century church father Justin set the tone for the ominous theme that would resonate until the mid-twentieth century: Jewish misfortune—destruction of Jerusalem, desolation of their land and exile from it—was the consequence of divine punishment for the death of Christ.

The Christian view is essentially as follows: In the view of the Apostle Paul (as adopted by some of the church fathers), the political bondage of the Jews, the *Galut*—the "Exile"—was the visible manifestation of a more fundamental bondage, foretold by the prophets of ancient Israel. The Christian interpretation of the *Galut* as the embodiment of the "wandering Jew" is a watershed in the history of antisemitism. The doctrine held that Jews are to be preserved, in a meager and mean state, until the end of days. The Jews are scattered throughout the world in order that they may serve, by means of their miserable condition, as a testimony to the truth of Christianity. The persistence of Israel, seemingly a contradiction of the Christian conception of the church as *Verus Israel*, "the True Israel," led the church fathers, notably Augustine (fourth–fifth centuries CE), to elaborate the doctrine of the Jews as "witness" to the truth of Christianity; their existence was justified in attesting through their humiliation the triumph of church over synagogue.

The rivalry for proselytes also set Jews and Christians against each other. Contemporary sources suggest that during the first two centuries Jewish proselytization remained active, and Jewish attractiveness to proselytes likewise remained. Proselytization was in all likelihood directed in equal measure toward early Christians and to pagans, and among the pagans it is possible that many a potential follower of nascent Christianity was attracted instead to Judaism.

No century was more fateful for Jewish-Christian relations than the fourth. For the emerging church it was an hour of triumph: it was powerful in number and influence; more important, Christianity was now exalted as church of the Roman state.

The fourth century was a century in ferment: the Councils of Nicea and Constantinople canonized the essentials of Catholic belief; the age of the church fathers was at its height; internal christological controversies raged; and the Roman Empire split east and west. And the Jews, uncowed, continued by their very existence—indeed they were thriving—to challenge the foundations of Christianity.

From the year 315 on, anti-Jewish measures were promulgated by the Emperor Constantine and others. Mild at first, in due course they included edicts prohibiting Jewish pilgrimages to Jerusalem and forbidding conversion to Judaism. Rabbis were prohibited from meeting in conclave. And the decrees became increasingly harsh not only in content but in language as well: Jews were a "pernicious" and "despicable sect" that met in "sacrilegious assemblies." Such terminology became all too well known as permanent features of later Christian rulers.

Whatever the reasons, the fact is that after Christianity became the official religion of the Roman state—this happened, during the reign of Constantine, in 321—the rulers of the realm began translating the theology into practice: they took the concepts and claims of the church fathers and early theologians and began using these ideas against the Jews. Successive Roman emperors withdrew privileges granted to the Jews as being part of the Roman Empire. Rabbinical jurisdiction was curtailed and eventually abolished. Proselytization was made punishable by death. Jews were excluded from holding high office.

It is important to make an effort to gauge the effect of these transformations on the Jewish leadership. Emperor Constantine's conversion to Christianity early in the fourth century must have stunned Jewish leaders. They doubtless realized that the legislation initiated by him and those who followed him differed from the anti-Jewish measures of earlier emperors, to which they had become inured. For the first time, the inner life, religious observance, community organizations, and nonpolitical public utterances of the Jews became an important concern of the central government. In addition to the heavy hand of the government, there appeared on the scene a new factor, one with which the Jews would from now on have to contend: the Christian clergy. An important distinction from pagan anti-Jewish activity became apparent: temple priests as a rule merely followed the lead of state authorities, whereas bishops and other clerics considered it a duty to set the pace for the state, particularly in all matters having any bearing on religion. The Jewish question was of religious concern to the Christian state. With its universality and hierarchic discipline, the Christian clergy became a decisive force on both the local and imperial levels.

The Crusades and Their Aftermath

The First Crusade is, to many, a turning point in the history of antisemitism and brought home to Jews the salient point: that of the utter instability of the Jewish position in the Western world. Previous outbreaks of intolerance, even murderous riots, were local and sporadic in nature. They lacked premeditation and widespread concerted action. The First Crusade set a new pattern: from this time on, anti-Jewish persecutions exercised a dangerously contagious appeal, nurtured by emotional stress, informed by religion that degenerated into mass psychosis. This phenomenon was one that transcended national boundaries. It established also the pattern of the commingling of religious excitation with the greed for gain and riches.

The massacres of the spring and summer of 1096, and the Jerusalem killings of 1099, therefore, leave a permanent imprint on any evaluation of Jewish-Christian relations. It was the First Crusade that left Jews forever after with the overpowering feelings and concerns of alienation and insecurity vis-à-vis the Christian world.

The First Crusade was preached by Pope Urban II on 27 November 1095. Urban's proclamation was a signal for noblemen and common people to engage in a campaign against infidels. Almost immediately, the French nobleman Godfrey of Bouillon vowed that he would not set out for the Holy Land until the crucifixion was avenged by the blood of the Jews. The call for vengeance for the blood of Jesus became a common one in crusader poetry and in popular sermons, and these easily turned the masses of crusaders against the Jews.

The first group of crusaders, gathering in France on their way to Germany, attacked the Jewish community in Rouen and possibly other cities. Jews in Rhine Valley communities, however, felt secure, relying on the protection of local bishops and rulers. Nevertheless, as bands of crusaders, under the leadership of the crusader Emicho, poured into Germany in April through June of 1096, riots broke out in the Rhine basin. Crusader bands attacked and murdered Jews in Speier, Worms—where they massacred Jews in their houses and later those who sought an illusory refuge in the bishop's castle—and Mainz, with no Jews of this great Jewish center surviving. A comparable disaster occurred in Cologne, where again the bishop made an effort to protect the city's Jews. The details of these or many other massacres of Jews during the First Crusade need not be rehearsed; they are well documented in both Christian and Jewish sources. In the end, there were more than 5,000 Jewish victims in Europe and the destruction of whole communities.

Upon arriving in Jerusalem in June 1099, and on capturing the city on 15 July, Godfrey and his army entered the Jewish Quarter. Jews took refuge in their synagogues, which were set on fire by the crusaders. A terrible massacre ensued; the Jewish community of Jerusalem was utterly destroyed. Contemporary Christian commentators, either ironically or with candor, described how, after massacring Jews and other "infidels," crusaders went with tears to worship at the Holy Sepulchre.

It is important to understand the role of the church in the effects of the Crusades against the Jews. Although religious fanaticism, informed by classic church teachings and by the church councils, was the main propelling force, the church leadership—pope and bishops—was in the main not responsible for most of the bloodshed. It is true that Pope Urban II remained remarkably silent when the news of the massacres reached him.[3]

The records clearly indicate that the bishops in many instances made efforts to protect Jews. Most often these efforts were ineffectual. Many bishops, themselves engrossed in local power struggles, did not pay much attention to what was happening to the relatively small Jewish communities under their jurisdiction.

What were the legacies of the Crusades (including those subsequent to the First Crusade) in terms of antisemitism? Most important, there was the ever-deepening enmity toward Jews on the part of the Christian masses. There was the willingness of Christian folk to accept, as part of popular culture, unfounded and even bizarre accusations about Jews and for entire communities to be blamed for the misdeeds—whether attested by evidence or not. In sum, for the Jews the Crusades became the symbol of the intractable antagonism between Judaism and Christianity. The unprecedented persecutions and massacres of Jews by Christians increased manyfold the level of tension between the two communities. The Crusades revealed the physical danger in which the Jewish communities then existed and, more important, the impotence of their ecclesiastical masters in protecting them. There began now a period of intermittently recurring massacre and persecution that marked European Jewish experience for many centuries. The Crusades became firmly imprinted in the historic consciousness of the Jews as the symbol of all subsequent tragedy that would befall them.

Antisemitism in Late Medieval Europe

The Crusades marked a turning point in Jewish history and particularly in the history of antisemitism. For the first time the church itself was forced to define its position vis-à-vis large-scale popular persecution of the Jews. The aftermath of the Crusades in terms of Jewish-Christian relations was significant. Papal decrees stipulated that Jews should not be deprived of what rights they had, that their lives should not be endangered, that they ought not be baptized by force, that their cemeteries should not be desecrated.

Nonetheless, there was the strong objection on the part of Christians, at every level, to the participation of Jews in any profession that would secure Jews a respected status among the Christians or authority over Christians. Incitement of the mob was increasingly employed as a method of applying pressure.

The age of the Crusades brought a vast increase in church influence as well as a change for the worse in the status of Jews. This influence was especially apparent in church councils that were convened during this period and in the authority of the regulations passed by these councils. The Fourth Lateran Council in 1215, for example, extended anti-Jewish enactments of previous councils in a number of directions: special taxes on Jewish-owned lands; the prohibition against Jews having more than one synagogue in a town; some calls to proscribe Talmudic and other rabbinic literature (although this matter was generally left to the popes). But the most baleful influence of the Fourth Lateran Council—again the beginnings of a woeful pattern—was the enactment of a rule that Jews must dress so as to be easily distinguishable from Christians. Before too long this was institutionalized into the Jewish "badge," the subject of resolutions and canons enacted by more than forty councils in every part of Europe during the thirteenth and fourteenth centuries.

The most implacable and intractable enemies of the Jews increasingly came from the rising middle class, and also from among certain orders of Christian monks, particularly the mendicant Franciscans and Dominicans. But the pattern of anti-Jewish activity varied from country to country. In Spain, for example, the slow pace of Christian reconquest from the Muslims—a process lasting from the eleventh to the fifteenth centuries—enabled the Jews to continue benefiting from a relatively privileged situation. Antisemitic currents found in Europe, and prevalent in some areas, took time to penetrate the Iberian Peninsula.

In tracing the situation of Jewish communities during the centuries following the Crusades, there is, as was noted at the outset, a conflicting pattern. On the one hand, rulers were often protective of Jews in their realms, granting them charters and taking other benevolent measures; on the other hand, the ecclesiastical view was represented by anti-Jewish enactments of the church councils. But even the royal charters increasingly reflected an old/new concept, one that was rooted in Christian theology and that was eagerly accepted by the masses: the concept of *Jewish servitude.* The progressive humiliation of Jews in medieval Europe derived from the consistent and thorough application of this idea by rulers and by the church.

The most significant anti-Jewish manifestations in Europe—other than the antisemitic libels, which will be discussed later in this chapter—came about as a result of the changes in the legal status of the Jews. At bottom, in Spain, France, and Germany, Jews became serfs of the king. Although a measure of protection was afforded the Jews by virtue of this status, the status included grave disabilities for Jews. The status ensured the social, legal, and personal humiliation of the Jews. From the viewpoint of the general Christian populace, Jewish serfdom substantiated the religious and popular view of the degradation and wickedness of the Jews.

Among the most serious of these manifestations, which reverberate to the present day, were those of the libels: the leveling of false charges against Jews, particularly the *blood libel* and the *libel of desecrating the host*. Libels against Jews came to overshadow all other antisemitic horrors experienced by Jews. Libeling by its nature is a vicious circle: each false charge added to the negative and indeed terrifying image of the Jew; and the worsening of that image as a result of the libel lent greater credence to constantly renewed and inflated accusations. False charges grew out of popular Christian superstition and were sustained and disseminated by monks and priests.

In 1144 the Jews of Norwich in England were accused of the murder of a Christian child. From that time on charges of this kind were leveled against Jews all over Europe. The explanation for the libel, and logic of those who believed it, was that once the Jews had crucified Jesus, they thirsted for pure and innocent blood. Since the formerly incarnate God, Jesus, was now in heaven, the Jews aspired to the blood of the most innocent of Christian believers, namely Christian children. It follows that the season in which most ritual-murder charges were brought was that of Passover, close in time to the Crucifixion.

There is evidence from contemporary sources that most Christians believed these libels to be the literal truth; public proclamations, whether from popes or princes, were of no avail in destroying the belief.

The seriousness of the effects of the blood libel cannot be minimized. Throughout the centuries many Jews, including in some instances entire communities, were cruelly slain as a result of the libel. But it was the social and psychological damage that was the most enduring legacy of this most awful and fantastic libel in human history: within the western European cultural milieu of the Middle Ages the image of the Jew as menacing demon was grossly reinforced.

The libel of desecrating the host was, predictably, leveled against the Jews as soon as it became part of Christian dogma that the bread and wine of the Christian sacrament are literally transubstantiated into the body and blood of Jesus. Christians began believing in the miraculous power of the host. Since the Jews had once slain the incarnated God, Jesus—now transubstantiated into the host—what else could one expect but that these wicked people would continue to "slay" God—Jesus—by defiling the host?

According to some scholars, the first recorded charge of this bizarre and crude accusation dated from 1243 Berlin and provided the pattern for the libel, which usually ran as follows: a Jew was supposed to have bribed a Christian to provide him with a piece of the host. This was then taken to the Jew's home, or to a synagogue, where the host—that is, Jesus—was tortured. It was stabbed, beaten, or trampled upon, fulfilling the Jews' desire, in the words of the Christians, "to torture Jesus again." Jews suspected of such action were usually burnt; families and communities were punished. Entire areas of Jewish communities, mostly in Germany, were devastated as a result of this libel.

The libels were of profound importance in the history of antisemitism, both in and of themselves and what they signified. The charge of desecrating the host, even more than the blood or ritual-murder libel, clearly showed how Christians viewed the Jews in the Middle Ages. In the view of the average Christian, Jews were fully aware that a priest brought about the mystery of transubstantiation of Jesus in the bread. Yet not only did Jews deny this mystery—the most sacred in the Christian religion— but they did everything possible to profane Christian sanctities and indeed to strike at, torture, and kill God. Once again, the grotesque and crude image of Jew as demon was reinforced in this awful manner.

Contemporary Christian chronicles from France, Germany, and England make it clear that, although the populace lusted for the blood of the Jews, they lusted more for Jewish treasures. What was taking place was arguably as much social revolution as it was out-and-out antisemitism. The Jews, by their loans to the nobility, enabled nobles to resist the efforts of opposing forces in the cities to gain ascendancy. And in the cities proper, the Jews tended to side with the patrician class in its struggle against the guilds. Thus the guilds became the bitter enemies of the Jews, and where guild leaders succeeded in getting control of the government (as in Strasbourg), they destroyed the Jewish community. Of course, the desired effect, from the point of view of the guilds, was just the opposite: once the nobility and city patricians were rid of their debts to the Jews, they became only the stronger. The net result: everyone was enriched at the expense of the hapless victims, the Jews.

The beginnings of the ghetto are to be found in the history of the Jews of Germany of that period. Antisemitic activities in Germany, sparked by the Crusades, reached their culmination in the persecutions of 1348–1349. From that time on, the Jews were enclosed in special quarters—ghettos—the gates to which were locked each night so that none might leave or enter.

Spanish Inquisition and Expulsion

For the purpose of context, recall what was happening elsewhere in Europe. From 1298 to 1348, in central Europe, blood libels, denunciations of the Talmud, and charges of desecrations of the host led to massacres and riots that cut a path through Germany. The animosity toward Jews and persecution of them reached their peak during the Black Death, in the massacres of 1348–1349. Social unrest, coupled with scapegoating of the Jews for a natural catastrophe that could not be explained, resulted in fifty years of horror for the Jews of Europe.

The events of 1348 cast a heavy shadow over the lives of Spanish Jews, even as their own condition was relatively stable. During the second half of the fourteenth century, however, with the increasing social tension that marked all of Christian Spain, with competing royal houses (and the decline in power of some of these houses), there was a notable decline in the situation of the Jews, culminating in violent outbursts against Jews in 1391, beginning in Seville and spreading throughout the entire country. The genesis of these riots was in inflammatory sermons preached, beginning in 1378, by Ferrand Martinez of Seville. Martinez soon became the virtual ruler of Seville, and he intensified his anti-Jewish campaign. Unfortunately, the royal authorities did not check Martinez, and as a cumulative result of his virulent preachings, riots broke out in June 1391 and ultimately spread throughout the country. Many Jewish communities were utterly destroyed. From that year—1391—until the expulsion from Spain almost exactly one century later, the Jews of Christian Spain lived under the relentless pressure of recurring antisemitic outbreaks against them. It ought be noted that by 1450, much of this activity was conducted against the Marranos or *Conversos* (see below); nonetheless the pressure against Jews was very real.

The antisemitic rabble-rousing that characterized late-fourteenth-century Spain was nourished not only by the classic hatreds but also by envy of Jews occupying official posts and enjoying a good economic position. A highly important additional factor was the fresh envy of the forced converts to Christianity, the New Christians—we know them by the derogatory name given them by the Christian community at the time: the Marranos. The question of the Marranos or *Conversos*—those Jews who were forced to convert—is a complicated one. It is important to note, however, that the Marranos enjoyed equal rights in all re-

spects with the rest of the Christian population and steadily infil-
trated the sources of livelihood, and social positions as well, of
Spain, thus enraging the "old" Christians.

Additionally, these *converso* New Christians were suspected
by church authorities (often with justification) of "relapsing" into
Judaism. Much of the antisemitic activity of the fifteenth century,
particularly the activities of the Inquisition, was generated by
popular and institutional antipathy toward these *Conversos*.

For the Jewish communities of Spain, the antisemitic experience of the fifteenth century was significant not only in terms
of the losses of life and property suffered. More serious was the
widening chasm between Jews and their Christian neighbors,
fostered by the fanatical churchmen of Spain, eventually playing itself out in institutional antisemitism on the part of the
Spanish Catholic Church. The pattern of restrictive legislation
reemerged in fifteenth-century Spain, side by side with by-now
classic libels. In 1410, the charge of desecrating the host was preferred against the Jews of Segovia; torture and death of Jews followed. In 1412 legislation was passed that in every way was designed to reduce the Jews to poverty and to humiliate them.
Jews were to keep strictly to their quarters; they were shut out
from the professions; they were not to engage in handicrafts or
deal in wine, meat, and bread or act as brokers; they were not
permitted to hire Christians—indeed, all social intercourse with
Christians was forbidden. Jews were not permitted to levy their
own communal taxes, and their own rabbinical courts were
abolished. Jews could not bear arms. Further, they were required to wear special clothes.

Although these regulations—among the harshest that we
have seen—were subsequently somewhat mitigated, the 1412 law
was illustrative of the tone and tenor of the times. Indeed, in 1415,
following the celebrated disputation in the city of Tortosa, Pope
Benedict issued his infamous bull, decreeing, among other things,
the prohibition against study of the Talmud. (There was, however, no significant enforcement of the ban.) Any written attack
on the church was prohibited. Jewish judges lost their authority.
Finally, the Jews in Aragon were confined to a special quarter—
one of the first instances of the ghetto.

The Inquisition was originally established by Pope Gregory
IX in the thirteenth century as a church mechanism by whose
means heretics could be judged. The inquisitorial mission was en-
trusted mainly to the Dominican order. Originally, the Inquisition

was not authorized to interfere in the internal affairs of the Jews, but this rule was abridged on the grounds that the presence of Jews in a Christian milieu caused heresy to develop. Handbooks used by inquisitors in the middle of the fourteenth century made the point that Jews attempted, when and wherever they could, secretly to pervert Christians and to attract them to the "Jewish perfidy," acting particularly in the case of those who had been Jews, but who were now "New Christians." This idea informed the thrust of the Spanish Inquisition.

The Inquisition from its earliest days took on a decidedly anti-Jewish cast. In 1242 the Inquisition in Paris condemned the Talmud. And in 1288, also in France, the first mass burning at the stake of Jews took place under Inquisition directives.

The principle objective of the Inquisition in Spain, however, was the persecution of those who were inclined toward Judaism and not the Jews themselves. It was therefore chiefly directed at *Conversos*, the New Christians, whom the fanatical Dominicans who conducted the Inquisition suspected as being less than Christian. Before too long the Inquisition spread to include the destruction of all heretics, and although the Inquisition as such did not destroy the Jewish community, the community was clearly implicated.

It is important to bear in mind that the Inquisition was both an *ecclesiastical* and *political* institution. The anti-Jewish persecutions of 1391 and 1412–1414 resulted in the creation of a class of New Christians (the *Conversos*), many of whom achieved political, economic, and social status. The Inquisition's function, aside from rooting out religious relapses on the part of these New Christians, was to protect the status of the older Christian society. This function was pursued especially vigorously after the ascent of Ferdinand and Isabella to their thrones.

The chief figure of the late-fifteenth-century Spanish Inquisition is Tomas de Torquemada. Torquemada was appointed to direct the machinery of the Inquisition in 1483; it was from this date on that the Jewish community was more directly implicated in the workings of the dreaded office. After 1483, for example, Jews were obliged by the Inquisition to bring themselves to betray their brethren. The Inquisition compelled Jewish communal leaders to proclaim that any Jew knowing of Marranos who adhered to Judaism, and who did not bring this information to the Inquisition, would be laid under *herem*, the Jewish communal ban.

Although the Inquisition was mostly directed against the Marranos, it brought terror to Jews everywhere in the realm, because the Jews were inevitably linked to the Marranos. At every trial suspicions were voiced against the community of Jews, and efforts were made to obtain from the authorities new decrees against them. With regard to antisemitism, by this time the mass animosity that prepared Christians to believe any evil of the Jews and New Christians alike had assumed a distinctly racist tone.

Moreover, in terms of blatant antisemitism, the Inquisition was used as an instrument that served the purposes of spreading anti-Jewish libels. At Avila it was charged that five Jews, together with some Marranos, had killed a Christian child for ritual purposes. The denounced persons, brought before the Inquisition, were burned alive. The whole fabricated story served as a pretext for removing Jews, first by killing, later by expulsion. It is clear that the Inquisition was prepared to go to great lengths in order to attain its ends.

The significance of the Inquisition is that with the Inquisition, the transformation of Christian antisemitism into institutional patterns, embedded in the formal institutions of power, was complete.

But the worst—expulsion—was yet to come. After the anti-Jewish riots of 1391, and the edicts of 1412 and 1415, the situation of the Jews in Spain deteriorated. In 1415 the Spanish king, responding to the papal bull prohibiting study of the Talmud, extended the whole series of anti-Jewish laws previously enacted. Although many of these regulations were rescinded before too many years passed, they served as precedent for the future.

There were three significant factors that led to the expulsion. First was the "Christian-Christian" conflict discussed earlier, engendered and deepened by the Marranos and inevitably spilling over against the Jews. Second, the marriage of Isabella and Ferdinand in 1469, uniting the kingdom in 1479, had disastrous consequences for Spanish Jewry. At first the monarchs took little notice of the Jews as such, but they did consider the Marranos to be a danger to Christian, and therefore to national, unity. But after the monarchs introduced the Inquisition, launching a frontal attack on the Marranos, the Jews were in serious trouble. Certainly the Avila libel, in which the Inquisition exploited a charge that had no factual foundation, helped prepare the ground for the expulsion two years later of professed Jews. A harbinger of things to come were the events in Andalusia in 1483. In that year the Jews were expelled from Andalusia because the inquisitors were convinced that it was impossible to root out Jewish heresies from among the Marranos while practicing Jews still lived in their midst.

The third factor leading to expulsion was the final victory, in January 1492, of the Spanish Catholics over the Muslims in the Iberian Peninsula. With the end of Muslim power, the almost fanatical urge toward complete religious unity of the kingdom was reinforced. The scandal (to Catholics) of New Christians who had remained true to Judaism had clearly demonstrated that limitations of the rights of Jews, and other harsh measures, did not suffice to suppress their influence. The conclusion: Jews must be totally and irrevocably removed, en masse, from Spain. On 31 March 1492, the edict of expulsion was signed. By 30 July, not a single Jew was to remain in the realm.

The sad aftermath of the expulsion is all too well known. Spanish Jews were allowed three months to emigrate—popular history has recorded the date of their departure as the Ninth of Av, the day of mourning for the fall of Jerusalem and the destruction of the Temple. They went to Italy, to Muslim countries of North Africa, and 100,000 of them to Portugal, where they met with a bitter fate: a terrifying forced conversion upon their arrival—the masses of expelled Jews were admitted by the Portuguese and then in 1496, as children were separated from parents, were compelled, with inhuman cruelty, to accept Christianity. The Spanish, or Sephardi, diaspora spread throughout northern Africa and Italy and even to Palestine, and west, to the Netherlands.

Anticipating a pattern that became horribly familiar, many Spanish religious and governmental institutions introduced *Limpieza de Sangre*—blood purity—statutes. On the basis of Jewish blood flowing through their veins, New Christians and their descendants were denied entrance to the institutions of the society: religious orders, universities, public office. The motivation for these discriminatory regulations was the obligation of Christian society to defend itself against the "dangerous schemings" of the community whose Christianity merely masked a Jewish interior. The regulations often referred to the "polluted blood" of the New Christians. It is clear, therefore, that the expulsion of Jews from Spain did not put an end to the "Jewish question" of the Spanish world; Christian antisemitism, transmuted, continued in its new form.

Islam and the Jews

At the beginning of the Muslim expansion during the seventh century, the Arab conquerors placed no great value on converting their newly subjugated peoples. This fact, together with the romance of the "Golden Age" of the Jews in Muslim Spain, has given rise to the picture of a Jewish life that was unfettered and without restraints during the Islamic period. This picture is a largely flawed one. There were, in fact, periods during which Jewish communities under Islam experienced antisemitism. It is an irenic misreading of history to confuse great religious, intellectual, and cultural achievements with situations and conditions in society arising out of religious, political, and social dynamics that lead to anti-Jewish attitudes and behavior.

The legal status of Jews under Islam was determined by the principles applied by Muslims to all non-Muslims who qualified as being "people of the Book." Muslims called such people *dhimmis*, or protected minorities. According to Islamic legal theory, *dhimmi* status was granted equally to Jews, Christians, Zoroastrians, and members of a few other religions. *Dhimmis* may have been protected; they were nonetheless clearly second-class citizens. They paid a poll tax; they endured economic and social discrimination. The inferior status of Jews, Christians, Zoroastrians, and others basically derived from the *dhimma*—the construct of the "protected minority."

Nevertheless, *dhimmis,* including Jews, were granted religious tolerance, and, it is important to note, they were guaranteed security of life and property. Islamic legal sources, unlike Christian sources, which talk pejoratively about the status of Jews specifically, have relatively little to say *specifically* about Jews. Islamic legal sources refer to *dhimmis* in general. Jews generally were not, at least in theory, singled out.

For most of the fourteen hundred some years of the Arab-Jewish encounter, Arabs were not in fact antisemitic in the sense in which the word is used in this book. The crucial difference is not that the Arabs have some sort of special kinship to the Jews, but that the Arabs for the most part *are not Christians.* In Islam, the Christian testament has no place in education; Muslim children are not raised on stories of Jewish deicide; there is no *theological* tradition of antisemitism. And as we have seen, the Muslim encounters with Jews during the early days of Islam were very different both in circumstance and outcome from early Christian encounters. Additionally, and very important, the Muslims did not conceive or present themselves as the new Israel or as *Verus Israel*—the "true Israel." They did not therefore feel threatened—as did the Christians—by the obstinate survival of the old Israel. The difference from Christianity is that the Koran was offered not as a *fulfillment* of Judaism, as in Christianity, but as a *new revelation*, superseding both the Jewish and Christian scriptures. The difference is not as subtle as it might seem; it is an important one. It is noteworthy that Islam, unlike Christianity, did not retain in its sacred canon the Hebrew Bible—the Old Testament—and no clash of interpretations between Judaism and Islam could therefore arise.

The treatment of Jews in the Koran itself is mixed; there are many passages in the Koran, and in other early Islamic writings, in which harsh words are used about the Jews. These are concerned, for the most part, with Muhammad's own armed conflict—in which he was victorious—with the Jews of his region. These harsh passages are to some extent balanced by other passages that speak more respectfully of the Jews as the bearers of an older tradition and that prescribe a degree of tolerance to be accorded to Jews. The key point here is that in Islam there is no tradition of Jewish *guilt* that, as we have seen and will continue to demonstrate, has informed and colored Christian attitudes toward the Jewish religion and to its practitioners.

Having said this, one ought add that within this framework there were certain clear stipulations regarding non-Muslim behavior: non-Muslims were enjoined from mocking Muslim worship; proselytization was prohibited; and, reminiscent of other patterns, a distinctive dress was prescribed for "unbelievers." (This prescription may have influenced the Christian requirement of distinctive garb for Jews.) We should understand that among the early Muslims there was a "pecking order," a sort of infidel aristocracy of non-Muslims, with Christians ranking immediately below the True Believers—the Muslims—and above Jews. Christians were considered to be more sincere than Jews and less treacherous.

But generally speaking, during much of the history of the contact between Jew and Muslim, the two peoples habituated themselves to one another, and much of the harshness that we have come to expect as resulting from these kinds of vexing regulations either simply did not emerge.

It is useful to point out that there are areas of resemblance of Islam to Judaism, in order to understand why this harshness was not present. The details of comparative religion are beyond the scope of this discussion; suffice it to say that the law and religion in the two faiths have much in common.

In exploring the question of Muslim treatment of Jews, it is helpful to look at the different periods of Islamic history and use these as a framework. The first period, that of so-called Classical Islam, consisted of the first seven or eight centuries of Muslim history that ended during the time of the retreat of Islam before the advance of Christian Europe. The Muslim conquest of Constantinople took place in 1453. By the late twelfth and the thirteenth centuries the decline was already setting in; it was, in many ways, downhill after Constantinople. That period was one of strength and confidence, during which the Islamic world was advancing in power and expanding in territory. The position of Jews, as of other minorities, varied enormously during these centuries, but an important point must be noted: even at their worst, anti-Jewish persecutions did not have the distinctive characteristics of Christian antisemitism. Although there were some fears of domination by *dhimmis* that did crop up from time to time, there were no fears specifically of Jewish domination. Likewise, there were no fears of Jewish conspiracy; no charges of diabolic evil. Jews were not accused of poisoning wells, of spreading the plague. Even the obscene blood libel did not appear among the Muslims until it was introduced—interestingly enough, by their own newly conquered Christian subjects—in the fifteenth century (and consistently rejected, we might add, by the Ottoman rulers).

Antisemitic activity of a severe nature—violent persecution, forced conversion, banishment—was rare during this first period, although it was not unknown. These manifestations occurred, as would be expected, during times of stress and danger, when the Islamic world perceived a danger either from within or without. The war against the Crusaders, for example (which we have discussed from the Christian side), led to a harsh and repressive attitude toward non-Muslims. During the Crusader conflict Jews and other non-Muslims were subjected, for the first time since the rise of Islam, to social segregation. Christians, to be sure, were the main target, but Jews were also affected.

Each successive wave of enemy invasion of Islam—the Crusaders, the Mongols, the modern European empires—led to tensions between Muslim and non-Muslim. (One notable exception was the Almohades of the twelfth and thirteenth centuries, who were the major persecutors of medieval Jews and who were not affected by enemy invasion.) But it was the third wave, the era of

European invasion, that caused profound changes in Muslim society, changes that had important implications for non-Muslims,
especially Jews. The succession of Muslim defeats at the hands of
their European enemies took its toll on Muslim self-confidence
and, with it, Muslim willingness to tolerate others.

Non-Muslim subjects came to be viewed as disaffected and
disloyal subjects whose sympathies lay with the Europeans. Such
suspicions were reinforced by the wealth and prominence Christians and Jews were able to acquire during times of European influence. During the course of the nineteenth and twentieth centuries, these suspicions deepened in a manner that had profound
implications for Jews. Muslim hostility toward Jews, always tempered by some measure of tolerance, sometimes descending even
into severe repression, became something quite different with the
changed circumstances of European domination. The non-Muslim ceased being merely contemptible in Muslim eyes and became perceived as *dangerous*. In the case of Jews, this new attitude
was reinforced by the importation of certain ideas characteristic
of European antisemitism, such as Jewish conspiracy and domination—ideas that had been previously unknown even to the
most prejudiced among the Muslims.

The process, argue a number of historians, began in the nineteenth century, not with Muslims but with the *Christian* Arab minorities, which of all the communities in the Middle East had the
closest contacts with the West and which were constantly receiving priests and missionary emissaries. The Christian minorities in
Muslim lands did not like the Jews for practical reasons, as well
as religious: Jews were their main commercial competitors. But it
was during the nineteenth century that Christian Arab antisemitism went beyond anti-Jewish agitation and called for boy-
cotts. Antisemitism took on an ugly form: accusations of ritual
murder began turning up all over the Ottoman Empire, in the
Arab as well as the Greek and Turkish provinces.

In the second half of the nineteenth century, Arabic versions
of European antisemitic writings began appearing. These writings included the ever-popular forgeries. For example, some
tracts purported to be the confessions of a converted rabbi and revealed the "horrors" of the Jewish religion; others were compila-
tions of antisemitic myths, accusing Jews of ritual human sacrifice
and other obscenities.

As we have witnessed in other times and places, these attempts to spread virulent antisemitism were not totally unre-

sisted. In Ottoman Turkey, the authorities stopped publication of particularly vicious tracts and from time to time closed down newspapers that published anti-Jewish incitements, seen as a threat to the public order.

But the rising tide of hostility to Jews in Arab lands was unremitting. The status of non-Muslim minorities—*Dhimmi*—was changing, as was the way in which the *Dhimmi* were viewed by Muslims. The old relationship prescribed by Muslim law and usage, which combined tolerance with inequality, had worked well enough for a thousand years. But it was no longer acceptable to the Muslims of the nineteenth and twentieth centuries.

Curiously enough, but entirely understandable, it was the improvement in the lot of non-Muslims, including Jews, that resulted in the worsening of their condition. With the gradual abandonment of the old order, Jews were better off than before. Instead of subject communities in a state defined by Islam, they were now citizens of a country. But, as is often the case, the advance of Jews in education, wealth, and even power aroused resentment among Muslims, who saw no good reason to accept as equals those whom they had always regarded as inferiors.

From a religious and social point of view, many conservative Muslims, deeply offended by turn-of-the-century revolutions—such as the Young Turk Revolution of 1908—alleged that such revolutions were due to Jewish machinations. These accusations were given a new sophistication, based on the antisemitic doctrines about conspiracies and the like imported from Europe, and achieved a certain amount of credence among Muslims.

The importation from Europe of new-style antisemitism included the ritual-murder and blood libel. When the libel had in the past appeared in the Middle East, it had derived exclusively from Christian sources. The most famous, in 1840, was the Damascus affair, begun by Catholic monks and energetically fostered by French government officials in that city. By the end of the nineteenth century, however, the blood libel and other forms of classic antisemitica were coming from Muslim sources; in the twentieth century this became commonplace. A new call, heard early in the century, was for a Christian-Muslim alliance to confront the common Jewish enemy. With the resurgence of Muslim fundamentalism in recent decades, this theme is rarely heard anymore. And, of course, Zionism and the establishment and flourishing of the State of Israel have served as triggers for Muslim antisemitism in our day.

Socioreligious Struggles in Western Europe: The Beginnings of the Ghetto

The events surrounding the Reformation—events that were no less than revolutionary within Christianity—had profound implications for the Jews of Europe as well. These implications were particularly significant in terms of the divergences of antisemitic attitude and expression among the emerging Protestant groups.

The central voice of the Reformation was, of course, Martin Luther. Luther, as Muhammad before him, courted the Jews as he founded his new faith. Luther was confident that the Jews would be won over to a Christianity stripped of popish trappings. When he realized that Jews did not meet his expectations, Luther's attitude toward the Jews became one that before too long was blatantly antisemitic. In 1542 Luther published a tract, "Concerning the Jews and Their Lies," soon followed by another essay, which excoriated the Jews in language that equaled in virulence anything uttered against them before or since. Luther, in language both sarcastic and scatological, renewed all the old charges of the past, perpetuating patterns with which we have become familiar during the course of this book: Jews are poisoners; Jews are usurers; Jews are parasites on Christian society; Jews consort with Satan himself; Jews are doomed to Hell. In Luther's writings a new locution of an old image of the Jew emerged: the Jew as Antichrist.

Luther did not leave to his readers' imagination what he conceived as the appropriate agenda to deal with the Jews. He was quite explicit: their synagogues should be burned, their books seized; they should be forced into back-breaking manual labor; better still, they should be expelled by the kings and princes from their territories. Not for the Luther the well-established— although often fruitless—practice of bishops and princes making an effort to protect Jews within their domains! During his last years (he died in 1546), Luther engaged in efforts to have the German princes expel the Jews or at least oppress them. Indeed, his very last sermon, delivered a few days before his death, was fully expressive of what had become an obsession with Jews. He urgently called for their expulsion from Germany.

What were the effects of Luther's teachings about Jews? Most observers argue that Martin Luther's emphasis on the Jewish Bible—the Old Testament—tended to mitigate some of the harshness of traditional Christian teachings and eventually to alleviate the lot of Jews who were under Protestant hegemony. His immediate impact, however, was probably negative. Protestant Germany, paying attention more to his denunciations, maintained the vexations of the past. Violence against Jews was not frequent in Germany during the seventeenth century, but it did take place. The savage attack in 1614 on the ghetto of Frankfort-am-Main is but one example. In 1670, in a pattern becoming more familiar, Jews were expelled from Vienna. In 1747, Maria Theresa's order of expulsion of all Jews from Bohemia was not carried out, thanks chiefly to the intercession of *Hofjuden*—court Jews—before a number of European sovereigns, who themselves interceded with Maria Theresa.

The overall impact of the Reformation on the evolution of antisemitism is more complex than that of early Catholicism. The repercussions of the reformation were indeed sometimes contradictory. Protestantism developed in different directions. One branch, Calvinism and the sects and movements influenced by the teachings of John Calvin, proved over the centuries to be less Judeophobic than was Catholicism. The other main branch, Lutheranism, became antisemitic. The divergence in terms of antisemitism between the two branches of Protestantism is rooted in the differences between these two movements in social thought more than in theology. From their beginnings, the Calvinist movements (which included, by the way, the Puritans in England and America) emphasized in their social thinking individual responsibility. Calvinists embraced social values and energetic moral action. To many Calvinists, leadership and flock alike, the ideals of social action left somewhat less room for active anti-Judaism. Additionally, the significant role played by the Hebrew Bible—the Old Testament—in Calvinism had an important influence on Calvinist groups in terms of their thinking about Jews. Indeed, Calvinist and Puritan groups identified themselves with the Jews of the Bible and reflected favorably on their attitude toward Jews of their own time. The French Calvinists (as one example), who were themselves persecuted up until the French Revolution, developed sympathies that were markedly pro-Jewish. This outlook informed the salutary behavior of some Huguenot communities during World War II and is retained to the present day.

For Lutherans, however, theology gave a radically different twist to social action. The Calvinist idea of "salvation through works"—that good works might be an indication of a state of grace—was not part of classical Lutheran thinking. To Lutheranism, justification of the religion by faith willy-nilly implied a renunciation of civic responsibility. Indeed, Luther himself referred sneeringly to the active faith of good works as *Juedischer Glaube*, "Jewish faith."

The immediate consequence of the Reformation was to aggravate the position of Jews in those areas of Europe that remained Catholic. We know the history of the Catholic counterreformation: the popes of the counterreformation were determined to restore ecclesiastical usages, strict application of Church religious law, and harmony within the Church. With the advent of the counterreformation, the theses of the early Church fathers—the Jew as a miserable witness to the truth of Christianity, and so on—began being applied to the letter.

One result, from the second half of the sixteenth century on, was the introduction of the ghetto, first in Italy, afterward in the Austrian Empire. Why the ghetto, particularly during the period of counterreformation? Contemporary Catholic theologians were of the view that the Jewish ghetto was better proof of the truth of Christianity than theological argument. The ghetto became the convenient additional demonstration of the "error" of Judaism.

The origins of the word *ghetto* are not clear; the word probably describes a quarter of Venice that was enclosed in the year 1516 and declared to be the only part of the city in which Jews could live. Whatever the origins of the term, it came to Christian leadership that the most effective way of segregating Jews from Christians was to shut the Jews up in quarters of their own, particularly if these quarters were surrounded by walls with a gate opened up only during the day. *Enforced segregation* was the operative principle of the ghetto.

The pattern that developed in the formation of the ghetto was one in which the Church, in principle, took up the cudgels for that infamous institution and left the details to state and local authorities. We ought to recall the fact that Jewish quarters had a long, often voluntary, tradition, antedating the Christian Roman Empire. Jewish quarters often satisfied deep-rooted segregationist desires of the Jewish community itself. The question at hand, however, is the enforced segregation of Jews in the medieval ghetto.

Although the idea of enforced Jewish segregation appears in Christian writings from the twelfth century on—it was discussed at the Third Lateran Council—it was from the fifteenth century on that the ghetto idea was included in the formal anti-Jewish program of the Christian religious orders. Included in these Judeophobic programs were the imposition of wearing of the Jewish badge and regulations severely restricting Jewish economic activity. Additionally, Jews were compelled to listen to conversionary sermons.

The Jews of sixteenth-century Europe who managed lives outside the ghetto were few. The rank and file languished in the ghetto, where their lives were strictly regulated. In addition to the restrictions and regulations that have been mentioned, there were others, often of the most petty nature. Jews were not permitted to walk in twos; they could not appear in public when a prince was in town; they could not make a purchase ahead of a Christian at the market; they could not frequent certain streets. Jews had to have a pass for intercity travel, and they had to pay a body tax in transit. The number of guests they could invite to a wedding was limited. Even their manner of dress was prescribed.

Most drastic for Jews, never a sizable population, was the regulation of their marriages, regulations designed to prevent a rapid multiplication of Jews. In some areas Jewish marriages were limited to the number of deaths in the community. In others, only the eldest son was permitted to marry; or only one son, sometimes two, could inherit. We see the beginnings of patterns of social antisemitism that resonate for us in the twentieth century: Jews were often made the butt of coarse jokes. On the streets even the most educated Jews could be and were accosted in the most crude manner. Jews had to doff their hats to passersby.

Anti-Jewish literature took its cue—and its legitimacy—from Luther's attacks, which reflected existing Jew-hatred. Old charges and libels, now refurbished to fit new circumstances, were trotted out; new libels were added: Jews consume Christian blood to be rid of their bad odor; Jews engage in a range of secret crimes, many of a sexual nature. We begin to sense a new direction in the libels of the sixteenth century. The crude mythological and moralistic libels of the medieval writers were gradually being given a *racial* cast: Jews are not only evil and perverted people; they are *constitutionally* and *racially* evil.

One other development in the history of antisemitism that ought be explored at this point is the so-called Jewish badge. During the course of this discussion we have noted on a number of occasions the promulgation of regulations obliging the Jews to don some sort of distinctive garb. This regulation varied with time and place throughout the Middle Ages and thereafter. The original source of the requirement for Jews to distinguish themselves was the Lateran Council of 1215, which resolved that intimacies between Jews and Christians be prevented and to that end states and municipalities should enact measures enabling Jews to be distinguished from Christians. By the fifteenth century the badge had spread throughout Europe. It took different forms. Here a yellow wheel to be affixed to the garment; there a red wheel. In Heidelberg a blue hat; in other parts of Germany a conical hat. Whatever form the badge took, whatever the shape or color, it served as reminder to all of the Jew as outsider, the Jew as object of scorn.

One significant development during this period merits some comment, and that is the invention of printing. This new device, together with the growing secularization of letters, aggravated the situation in terms of popular conceptions of Jews. It became all the more easy to present stereotyped images of unsavory Jewish characters, simultaneously reflecting and intensifying popular aversions. The stage especially became an instrument of anti-Jewish warfare. By the time that Christopher Marlowe's fifteenth-century play, *The Jew of Malta,* for example, became a part of the repertoire, many a play with anti-Jewish characters had been presented, in translation or adaptation, in theaters throughout Europe.

As the eighteenth century dawned, the Talmud—the vast compendium of Jewish normative tradition—once again came under attack. Assiduous efforts were made by European antisemites to turn up blasphemies and evidence of ritual murder or poisoning in the Talmud. One of the most influential of these hate mongers was Johann Eisenmenger, who happened to be a first-rate scholar of Semitic languages and who also happened to be a virulent antisemite who accepted as truth all the old slanders against Jews. Eisenmenger took it as his mission to comb through the Talmud to ferret out references to these libels. In 1700 Eisenmenger published a book, *Entdecktes Judentum (Judaism Unmasked)*, which is nothing less than an antisemitic encyclopedia. It is noteworthy that official permission, and thereby official sanction, for publication of Eisenmenger's book was granted in 1711 by Emperor Frederick of Prussia. Eisenmenger's book was influential for two centuries and more.

Some observers suggest that the period beginning with the sixteenth century was the nadir of postbiblical Jewish history, at least in terms of the level of anti-Jewish activity. Once again, however, we must use caution against identifying the history of antisemitism with Jewish history, of which antisemitism was but one element, albeit an important element. But by the sixteenth and seventeenth centuries Christian antisemitism had come to full fruition, and the fruits of Christian anti-Jewish thought and belief wrought devastating effects on Jewish life throughout Europe. We must recall that Jews had been almost totally eliminated from most of western Europe by expulsions from England, Spain and Portugal, and France. Although it is true that the various pogroms, regulations, and expulsions did not consist of an uninterrupted chain of catastrophe in Jewish history, it is equally valid to suggest that the cumulative psychological effect on the Jewish community was enormous. Few Jewish communities ever really felt secure. By the end of the Middle Ages, and into the next centuries, the European Jew personified both in the mind of the non-Jew—and perhaps even in his own—the "Wandering Jew" of Christian thought.

New factors began developing during that period. Alongside the flowering of humanistic thought was the emergence of the ominous insinuations of physical and mental inferiorities in the Jew. These assumed a place in the ever-waxing antisemitic stereotype, gradually increasing in importance. Christian theological antisemitism was no longer alone. Racialism gradually became a dominant factor, ultimately informing, among other pernicious movements, Nazism.

Enlightenment and Emancipation

Some real anti-Jewish expression did emerge in the writings of the *philosophes*—the class of intellectuals in France who denounced organized religion, particularly Christianity, and touted "natural religion" or deism and who ushered in the secularism of the modern era. As result of the efforts of the *philosophes,* for the first time in centuries the status of the Jews became a matter for debate. Judaism, whatever its *relative* virtues might have been, was considered to be a particularly antisocial religion, one that nurtured a stubborn sense of particularism and created divisions within the society. The most common argument for emancipation of the Jews—the removal of legal disabilities and thereby incorporating Jews into the mainstream society—was that it would convert the Jews to the majority culture, thus relieving society of their most obnoxious traits.

Voltaire, the most famous of the French Enlightenment *philosophes*, was the most blatant of this group in antisemitic expression. During Hitler's domination of Europe, a history teacher in France had no difficulty in compiling a 250-page book of Voltaire's anti-Jewish writings. Highly revealing is Voltaire's masterwork, the *Dictionnaire Philosophique*. Noteworthy is that of its 118 articles, treating everything under the sun, no fewer than thirty attack the Jews in one way or another. "The most abominable people in the world . . . whose laws do not say a word about spirituality and the immortality of the soul." "Our masters and our enemies, whom we believe and whom we detest." The article on "Jew" is the longest in Voltaire's *Dictionnaire*—thirty pages—and includes the following: "You will find them an ignorant and barbarous people, who for a long time have combined the most sordid greed with the most detestable superstition and the most invincible hatred for all the peoples who tolerate them and enrich them."[4] To Voltaire, Jews were ignorant by nature and could never be integrated into modern society.

With the *philosophes*, we have observed that a central point of rationalist thinking was antireligion, expressed largely as anti-Christian rhetoric. With Voltaire, anti-Christianity was something more and something different. Contemporaries suggested that Voltaire opposed Christianity so much because Christianity was born into a nation he abhorred.

One might legitimately refer to Voltaire as the main founder of modern secular, "rational" antisemitism. His agenda was the destruction of the traditional beliefs fundamental to the eighteenth-century society, particularly that of the infallibility of the Church. From both the psychological and tactical points of view, Voltaire's antisemitism was primarily the result of his hatred for the Church. The better to ridicule the established Church, Voltaire preferred to concentrate his attacks on the traditional Jewish Hebrew Bible (the so-called Old Testament), the root source of organized religion, and on the followers of the Hebrew Bible, the Jews. Voltaire and others did not hesitate to pour scorn on Christianity by reviling its Jewish origins. Voltaire expressed his anti-Jewish rhetoric in such a manner that in the antisemitic campaigns of the next two centuries he was used as an authority and was frequently quoted.

Eisenmenger's *Entdecktes Judentum,* discussed earlier, bridged the gap between medieval anti-Judaism and modern antisemitism. It was the last flare-up of denunciation based on the traditional Jewish-Christian schism. But the rationalism emerging from the Enlightenment did not vitiate the classic denunciations. Eisenmenger's book did not drop out of sight; the book in fact served to nourish the burgeoning antisemitic movement directly and indirectly for the next two centuries.

During this period racialist antisemitism emerged. In general, the tendency during the century of the Enlightenment—the eighteenth century—was to view the individual as the protagonist of science and the creator of progress, indeed to take the place of God in creation. One of the results of this view of the individual was that science began to elaborate a widening gap between human beings and other creatures and indeed between educated humans and "savages." The emancipation of science from ecclesiastical teachings, the abandonment of the biblical approaches to creation, left the way clear for racialist theories. It did not require a major leap to go from the rationalist teaching of a human/savage dichotomy to that of German nineteenth-century philosophers, who were to discover the existence of two human races: the "pale, beautiful" race and the "dark, ugly" race. The distinction between the white man and the black, brown, and yellow easily led to distinctions between various European peoples. Beginning in the eighteenth century, continuing into the nineteenth, some writers began characterizing the Jews as a "race," and the myth of the "Aryan race" developed. Modern German antisemitism was forged by German Romantic nationalism from the idea—which had arisen in the forests of Germany—of an organic identity in which the Jew could not participate: the *Volk,* an organic folk people.

But there is a more general question than that of racialism in terms of the significance of the Enlightenment and the emancipation. It is indeed true that Christianity had lost some of its former hold on people's minds and its determining influence on state and society. But Christianity was not eclipsed; it was far from defunct. Christianity still provided the universal discourse for some in society, for whom the traditional conception of the role of the Jew in history remained valid. The negative image attached to the word *Jew* retained its ideological moorings.

Moreover, even among those for whom the dogmatic truth of Christianity was not an issue, the Christian religion was sustained as a component of nationalism. Christianity was presented as the guarantor of nationalism and retained the doctrine of Christian superiority over Judaism. This was easily transformed, during the nineteenth century, into overt antisemitism.

The seminal work that developed the racialist theories that were pressed into service in support of the idea that Jews were a non-Aryan, alien element whose very nature was different from that of the northern Europeans was that of Joseph Gobineau, a French diplomat and author whose book, *Essai sur L'inegalite des Races Humaines,* articulated views on the "racial factor" in history that had currency. According to Gobineau, there was a hierarchy of race: white, yellow, black. The white—the so-called Aryan—race was the creator of civilization. Only the white race embodied and personified the supreme human virtues of honor and love of freedom. Gobineau asserted—and this assertion was central—that these qualities could be perpetuated only if the race remained pure. Gobineau, who held no particular brief against the Jews specifically, believed that both the Latin and Semitic peoples had degenerated throughout history and that this degeneration had come about as a result of racial intermixtures. According to Gobineau, only the Germans had preserved their "Aryan" purity, but there was for Germans a danger as well, and that was that the evolution of the modern world condemned them also to crossbreeding and, therefore, to degeneracy. Western civilization, averred Gobineau in a gloomy peroration to his readers, must be resigned to its fate. Gobineau's influence on the antisemitic ideology of racism was due less to his own personal views about Jews and more to the construction given to his themes by other European Jew-haters.

Racist themes of antisemitism found easy acceptance among central Europeans of all stripes, especially as Jews were identified with the capitalist oppressors of the working class. All the themes—economic, racialist, traditional stereotypes—coalesced into the image of the successful, nonnational, non-Aryan, unproductive, parasitic foreigner, whose power resided in money and in his ability to manipulate and indeed control others. By the end of the nineteenth century, as the other areas of the emancipation were bearing fruit, antisemitism had become an acceptable element in German political life and could be manipulated by political leaders seeking popular lower- and middle-class support.

In terms of popular culture in central Europe, mention ought be made of a particularly gross and crude stereotype that, having first emerged in the thirteenth century, achieved renewed currency in the eighteenth and nineteenth centuries. This was the libel of the *Judensau*, the Jewish sow, in which Jews in a bizarre manner were associated with the unclean pig that was forbidden them by the laws of *kashruth*. Many variations of this crude association appeared through the century in art and verse, usually portraying Jews suckling from a sow, straddling the animal, sucking its tail, or eating its excrement. Other caricatures show Jews, having suckled from the *Judensau*, sitting down in the synagogue to partake of a meal of forbidden pig.

Entering the Twentieth Century: Eastern Europe

The differences in the nineteenth century, in terms of the situation of the Jews, between western Europe and eastern Europe, primarily in the Russian Empire, were vast. States in western Europe were not anti-Jewish in any formal sense; rights and privileges had been granted the Jews throughout Europe. There was, to be sure, significant expression of antisemitism, and there were new trends of racist and nationalist antisemitism, trends that were to be of profound and lasting significance, but the atmosphere in western Europe was by and large one of increasing liberalization. Not so in the east. What informed Russian policy toward Jews over centuries was that the czarist regime regarded it as a duty to protect the population against the Jews. Curiously enough, in the eighteenth century Russia became the first country in Europe in which the Jews were permitted to elect and be elected to guild councils and municipal bodies; but this development aggravated the tension that existed between urban dwellers and the Jews. In 1782 the central authorities ruled that burghers and merchants (included in the guilds) must reside in towns and not in villages. This laid the foundation—indeed, was the first step—for the demand, later emphatic, that the Jews be banished from the villages. This was one of the central trends of Russian policy toward the Jews in the nineteenth century.

Further: the attempts made by Jewish merchants to trade in central Russia engendered friction with local merchants. One of the consequences of this friction was a law passed in 1791 prohibiting the Jews from permanently leaving certain provinces. This development created a situation that later was codified into what became known as the notorious Pale of Settlement—an expansion of the idea of ghetto on a countrywide basis.

But before we continue further into the history of Russian antisemitism in the nineteenth century, we take a look back at a series of events in the seventeenth century that colored eastern European Jewish history for centuries, namely the Chmielnicki massacres.

One of the significant clusters of events in modern Jewish history up to the Holocaust was that of the massacres in 1648–1649 of the Jews of the Ukraine at the hands of Bogdan Chmielnicki. Chmielnicki was the nationalist leader of the Cossack and peasant uprising against Polish rule in the Ukraine in 1648. His aim was to establish an autonomous Ukraine; his secondary goal was the eradication of the Jews from the Ukraine. Chmielnicki's anti-Polish propaganda, nurtured in the soil of social and religious unrest, bore fruit among many in the Ukrainian peasantry and among the Cossacks. For Chmielnicki, hatred of Jews was a convenient rallying point for his people. The Jews of the Ukraine were, once again, caught between conflicting forces. In this case, they were caught between nobility and peasantry, between Pole and Ukrainian, between Ukrainian and Cossack, between Catholic and Orthodox. They were accused by each side of loyalty to the other and victimized, accordingly, by each. A familiar pattern.

In the annals of Jewish history, and especially in the history of antisemitism, Chmielnicki is reviled as one of the most sinister oppressors of Jews in any generation. In the course of their campaigns, Chmielnicki's followers acted with savage and unremitting cruelty against the Jews. These campaigns are well known to all Jews as the terrible massacres of 1648–1649—*G'zeroth Tah v'Tat*—'The Evil Decrees of '48 and '49."[5] Jews do not use the word *holocaust* lightly, but the term may be an approximation of the destruction of large segments of Polish and Ukrainian Jewry during the seventeenth century, a destruction for which Chmielnicki bears the principle burden of responsibility.

Most of the massacres took place from May to November 1648, beginning with Jewish communities east of the Dnieper River, then spreading westward. By the end of the year there were no more Jews to be found in the villages; whatever Jews remained crowded into fortified cities. These cities were unable to sustain the siege of the peasant hordes, and after they were taken by Chmielnicki's men, most of the Jews were butchered.

It is impossible to determine with accuracy the number of victims who perished at Chmielnicki's hand; contemporary Jewish chronicles say 100,000 were killed. Historians today put the number killed at the tens of thousands. Whatever the number, the collective trauma was so severe as to recall the massacres during the Crusades; indeed, the trauma was even more severe: at least during the Crusades many bishops and temporal rulers made efforts to protect Jews in their realm. Such was not the case during *Tah v'Tat*. No wonder that the massacres of 1648–1649 have been referred to by some Jewish authors as "the Third Destruction" and that the horror of the massacres has been expressed in the Jewish liturgy and in Hebrew literature.

One final point on the Chmielnicki massacres. It has been the fashion among some Polish and Ukrainian historians to make an effort to fasten the responsibility for the bloodshed on the Jews, particularly Jewish administrators of estates of nobles in the area, asserting that these lessees engaged in persecution of the peasants in their midst. But contemporary sources yield no evidence of such persecution of peasants by Jews. This analysis is another example of blaming the Jews—blaming the very presence of the victims themselves—for misfortunes and evils visited upon them by others.

The critically important event in Russian antisemitism took place in 1881, with the assassination of Czar Alexander II by revolutionary terrorists, one of whom was a Jew. Reactionary newspapers immediately began whipping up anti-Jewish sentiment, and the result was a wave of pogroms in some 160 cities throughout Russia. Although the government did not directly organize these riots, it stood aside as Jews were murdered and brutalized, setting a pattern for the pogrom. The assassination was also used as a pretext for the passage of the infamous May Laws of 1882, severe anti-Jewish economic legislation. It was in this set of decrees that the government chose, in a most extreme way, to formulate and implement its antisemitic policy, the "protection of the basic population against Jewish exploitation." Local bureaucracies, together with the police, took these decrees as open indications of the central authorities' intentions and began openly harassing the Jews, and worse.

The next czar, Nicholas II, made no secret of his personal membership in the antisemitic Black Hundreds. This body was associated with the government in directly fomenting and indeed organizing pogroms during 1903 and, again, the most severe pogroms in 1905. Also in 1905 the notorious antisemitic forgery, *The Protocols of the Elders of Zion*, was published under the auspices of the secret police of the czar by the press of the czar.

But the worst was yet to come, and it came in the classic form: the blood libel. The very fact of a blood-libel accusation being taken seriously—and coming before a court of law as legitimate—attests to the hysterical antisemitic atmosphere of disintegrating czarism. The background of the libel case was a conference of associations of nobles in 1911 in which the participants, first demanding that Russia be rid of Jews, proceeded then to bring forth "experts" who claimed that Jews needed Christian blood for the observance of their religion—the classic libel. In fact, not unexpectedly, shortly afterwards a Jew named Mendel Beilis was accused of the murder of a Christian boy for the purpose of using his blood for ritual purposes. The police, cooperating with the antisemitic organs of government, knew and kept quiet about the identity of the true murderers. The case became a vehicle for the struggle between the regime and opposition forces. Beilis was eventually acquitted for lack of evidence. The jury, not able to agree on convicting Beilis, nonetheless affirmed the blood libel.

Despite occasional victories of liberalism in Russia, such as those that flamed briefly during the first two revolutionary decades of the twentieth century, the antisemitic current in Russia was much too strong to give Jews much hope of swimming against it.

Arguably the single most famous—or infamous—antisemitic document in history was *The Protocols of the Elders of Zion*. The *Protocols* purports to reveal the minutes of a secret meeting held by world Jewish leaders, the "Elders of Zion," who are conspiring to take over the world. The document consists of twenty-four "protocols" and professes to be the confidential minutes of a Jewish conclave convened in secret in the last years of the nineteenth century. This forgery places in the mouths of the "Jewish conspirators" a host of incredible statements and plans, a number of which derive from libels that we have discussed. For example, the *Protocols* charges, in a crude manner, the Jews with secretly subverting the morals of the non-Jewish world; it describes Jewish control of the world's economies and of the wealth of nations by Jewish bankers; it tells of Jewish control of the press; it describes Jewish plans for the destruction of civilization by means of Jewish control.

A creation of the Russian secret police, the *Protocols* was first circulated during the late nineteenth century. It is most likely that the source of the document was based on a volume written by a French lawyer, Maurice Joly, in 1865, entitled *Dialogue in Hell between Machiavelli and Montesquieu: or the Politics of Machiavelli in the Nineteenth Century.* Joly's book, which cast Machiavelli as the conspirator bent on world conquest, had a political purpose and was not antisemitic. The author of the *Protocols,* however, made use of large portions of Joly's book, simply attributing to Jewish "Elders of Zion" the aims of world conquest that Joly had attributed to Machiavelli.

The *Protocols* itself is most likely the work of the Paris branch of the Russian secret police, which undertook during the last decade of the nineteenth century the preparation of a series of antisemitic forgeries. Most scholars agree that the original intent of the *Protocols* was not to incite the masses against the Jews but to frighten the czar into complying with the demands of the reactionary right wing in Russia by throwing suspicion on the relatively moderate prime minister, Count Witte, as being an agent of international Jewry. But almost immediately the forgery became an instrument of antisemitism of the most virulent sort, even to the present day.

It was apparent soon after the book appeared that the *Protocols* was a crude forgery and a hoax. But most significant about the *Protocols* is that it is the single document that has had the greatest influence on antisemitic activity in the twentieth century; antisemites of every conceivable stripe, in every country, of every political persuasion, have utilized the *Protocols* or have kept it close at hand. Beginning with the aftermath of the Bolshevik Revolution, émigré czarists portrayed the revolution as part of a Jewish plot to enslave the world and pointed to the *Protocols* as the blueprint for this plan. The uniting, by the *Protocols,* of the Jews with the Bolsheviks and with revolution had profound repercussions for decades after.

The use of the *Protocols* as a fundamental tool of antisemitism soon spread: in Great Britain in the 1920s; in interwar Poland, where the Catholic bishops invoked the *Protocols;* in the Middle East, where Arabs took up the document to arouse passions against Jewish settlers in Palestine; even in the United States in the 1920s; and, of course, in Nazi Germany, where the myth of the *Protocols* fit in well with the strains of German nationalism and Central European racism.

In summing up the influence of *The Protocols of the Elders of Zion*—and relevant to the other libels that have been discussed in this book—a central principle can be identified: People continue reading and using the *Protocols* because the masses often find vast untruths more credible than small ones. The *Protocols* is one of the biggest lies ever devised, and for that reason there will always be evildoers to exploit it and fools to believe it.

Entering the Twentieth Century: Western Europe

The nineteenth century unification of Germany introduced new facets to European antisemitism. Liberalism became the target of Volkist hostility and antisemitism. The expansive role of capital in the new German state intensified charges that the Jews were using their newly acquired rights to exploit Germans. The economic crisis of 1873 was adduced by antisemites as further evidence that the Jews were undermining the country in order to advance their own interests. During the six years of depression following the 1873 crash, German politics took an authoritarian right turn. The attack on both Jews and liberals, from both right-wing conservatives and from populist agitators, gathered momentum.

The first assault came from Wilhelm Marr, who was an unsuccessful journalist. Marr's pamphlet *Der Sieg des Judentums Uber das Germanentum* (*The Victory of Jewry over Germandom*), was published in the critical year, 1873, and was circulated widely. Drawing on the parallel ideas of race and Volkist nationalism, Marr argued that the Jews' "racial qualities" had enabled them not only to survive through the ages but also to become "the first major power in the West." Marr's pessimistic conclusion was that the Germanic state had degenerated too far for the *Volk* to withstand Jewish superiority.

The beginnings of *political* antisemitism were in the activities of Adolf Stoecker. In 1878 Stoecker founded the Christian Social Workers' Party. (It is important to note that the word *Christian* in a European organization's name during that period was a code word for antisemitism.) Although this party was not overtly antisemitic, the later activities of this influential Berlin preacher convinced him that antisemitism struck a responsive chord in his listeners and provided him with a unifying platform. In 1879 Stoecker delivered a blatantly antisemitic speech in which he characterized Jews as being a "force against religion" and "a great danger to German national life" because they represented an indigestible foreign element. Stoecker's recommendation: protection against the Jews by means of enacting "wise" (by which he meant antisemitic) legislation. Stoecker's proposals included provisions that would have removed Jewish teachers from the schools and limited the number of appointments of Jewish judges.

Stoecker's thinking was both leftist and rightist in its populist origins. His leftist proposals were those directed toward control of the stock exchange and other economic behemoths and were at least implicitly antisemitic, since in the popular mind big capital was Jewish. The rightist proposals were explicitly antisemitic and caught a popular fancy.

Building upon the experience of previous decades, a torrent of antisemitism that did not abate until the turn of the century began in 1879 (the same year as Stoecker's speech) with the activities of Heinrich von Treitschke, a historian who combined fervent Lutheranism with Germanism. Treitschke, a prominent professor of history at the University of Berlin, contributed an antisemitic series of articles to the *Preussiche Jahrbucher*. Treitschke maintained that, in characterizing the Jews as a misfortune that befell German Christians, he was expressing the resentful reaction of popular opinion against a foreign element.

This thought is significant, because antisemitism achieved a respectability in German-speaking lands; antisemitic movements and parties proliferated. Numerous student fraternities excluded Jews. More academics authored antisemitic treatises, and the fact that these works came out of a respectable academic world gave the hate literature all the more credibility. In politics, antisemitism, particularly in Austria, made its mark.

The arrest, trial, convicting, and sentencing of Captain Alfred Dreyfus, which took place in 1894, was the coming together of French xenophobic antisemitism with the obsessive need to protect the honor of the greatest of French institutions, the army.

The history of nineteenth-century French antisemitism, an oscillation between virulence and enlightened public opinion, deserves a more discursive presentation than is possible in this book. During the 1880s, no fewer than three antisemitic weeklies were launched in France, with one, *L'Antisemitique*, founded in 1883, maintaining publication for more than a year. The clique responsible for *L'Antisemitique* made an effort to establish an international antisemitic league and made overtures to German and Hungarian counterparts. Their plans came to naught, in all likelihood because they could not cooperate with other European antisemitic groups.

The failure of *L'Antisemitique* was in glaring contrast to the immense success of Edouard Drumont's *La France Juive*, published in 1886. Drumont, who became the master of French antisemitic agitation, was a little-known journalist whose book went through some hundred printings within one year. The central thesis of this haphazardly organized collection of gossip and spurious arguments was that the Jews, members of an inferior race, had made themselves the masters of modern France. Indeed, the book is an echo of Wilhelm Marr's slogan of the Jewish conquest of Germany. But although Drumont received some inspiration from foreign sources, he relied in the main upon the French anti-Jewish tradition. He found in this tradition a more than adequate foundation upon which to build one of the most extensive and most vitriolic of antisemitic treatises.

There has been much discussion of late-nineteenth-century French antisemitism, particularly the discrepancy between the collapse of *L'Antisemitique* and the success of *La France Juive*. Historian Jacob Katz suggested that the attitudes assumed by the two publications were a microcosm of those of society with regard to the Christian tradition and the Jews. *L'Antisemitique* used all the popular invectives against the Jews, especially their alleged devastating role in the economic life of France, but its underpinnings were a kind of "Voltairian" antisemitism: the noxiousness of the Jews was ascribed to qualities already evident in the laws and personalities of the Old Testament. This kind of rhetoric did not necessarily play with otherwise sympathetic readers, who would be ready to accept antisemitic accusations but not at the price of disparaging what Christian tradition also held in awe.

It is important to keep in mind a central difference between Drumont and antisemitic rhetoric that had appeal in German-speaking lands: *La France Juive* was a polemic compounded of ritual murder and conspiratorial financial control, whereas across the Rhine racist and antisemitic activity was engaged in constructing a theory of a master race.

With Drumont and other agitators the stage was set for *L'af-faire Dreyfus*.[6] The Dreyfus matter, from October to December 1894, was not a deliberate plot to frame an innocent man. It was the outcome of a reasonable suspicion reinforced by some circumstantial evidence, personal dislike, and highly significant, instinctive prejudice. Captain Alfred Dreyfus, a Jew—the eternal alien—was a natural suspect to absorb the stain of treason.

In the Dreyfus affair two dynamics worked hand in hand: French xenophobic prejudice and antisemitism (that we have outlined in this chapter) and the esteem of the army of France. The army was more than a body of the Republic; it *was* the Republic. Historian Barbara Tuchman said it best: "In the eyes of the people the Army was above politics; it was the nation, it was France, it was the greatness of France."[7] Anatole France: "It is all that is left of our glorious past."[8]

The details of the case—the arrest and conviction of Dreyfus on espionage charges; his incarceration on Devil's Island; the crystallization of French antisemitism around the case; Dreyfus's retrial and pardon in 1896 and full acquittal in 1906—are beyond the scope of this book, and we need not rehearse them here.[9] The salient point is that French antisemitism, as has been the case in other places and other times, required the coming together of *instigator* with *circumstance*. The instigator in late-nineteenth-century France was Drumont, whose *La France Juive* played on fear of the evil power of Jewish finance. The founding by Drumont in 1892 of his newspaper *La Libre Parole*—a logical next step after the success of his book—came at a time when the anger of losers in financial scandals fell upon leading financiers, some of whom were Jews. When Dreyfus was condemned, *La Libre Parole* explained his motive to the French public: revenge for slights received as a Jew and the desire of his race for France's ruin. Throughout the course of the affair, *La Libre Parole* reinforced the choice of "Dreyfus or the army's honor" by invoking the Jewish connection.

A classic and important manifestation of the antisemitism that sparked and was in turn sparked by the affair was the "Syndicate." A creation of the antisemitic press, it was purported to be a subterranean fellowship of Jews, a sinister conspiracy whose forces were mobilized to reverse Dreyfus's conviction and to substitute a Christian in his place. The theory held that purpose of the Syndicate was to break down the faith in the army and to open the nation's gates to the enemy (Germany). As the animus

of the affair grew, so did the Syndicate in antisemitic eyes, growing into a monstrous league of Jews, freemasons, Socialists, foreigners, and other evil types. Any French problem or defeat was
the result of Syndicate activity. The Syndicate was everywhere; it
embodied the hates and fears of the French Right. The Jew, as
master of the Syndicate, was the enemy incarnate.

The cries of "Death to the Jew!" outside the parade ground
where the ceremony of Dreyfus's degradation took place were
heard by Theodor Herzl, a secular Hungarian/Austrian Jew who
was the Paris correspondent of the Vienna *Neue Freie Presse.*
"Where [is this taking place]?" Herzl wrote. "In France. In republican modern, civilized France, a hundred years after the Declaration of the Rights of Man."[10] The shock of *L'affaire Dreyfus,* together with his own personal history, clarified for Herzl the
problems of antisemitism. Herzl's *Der Judenstaat,* whose opening
statement calling for the "restoration of the Jewish state" articulated its aim, was a result, as was the convening of the First Zionist Congress in August 1897 out of the most disorganized and
fractional community in the world. The Dreyfus affair gave the
impulse to a new factor in world affairs—the emergence of Jewish nationalist and political identity—that had lain dormant for
close to two millennia.

World War II: The Destruction of European Jewry

The Weimar Republic emerged from the despair of World War I
with a new constitution that at long last provided the Jews of
Germany with complete equality. But at the very moment that
Jews had just begun to enjoy those political and civil rights for
which they had been long striving, antisemitism burst forth in its
classic worst forms. In the minds of large numbers of Germans,
the Jews were to blame for Germany's defeat, for the revolution
in Germany, for the loss of the monarchy—indeed for the loss of
the past.

On 24 February 1920, barely six months after the Weimar
constitution was enacted, the Nazi Party issued its twenty-five-
point program that asserted that no Jew could be a member of the
German people, the *Volk,* and that only persons of German blood

could be members of the German state. But it was not only the Nazis who were spouting anti-Jewish venom; the heretofore nonantisemitic right-wing German Nationalist People's Party, nationalist and Christian, was likewise seized by the antisemitic madness. In 1920 its party program took a formal stand "against the predominance of Jewry in government and public life."

The 1920s, the one decade of Jewish participation in German parliamentary life, witnessed the proliferation of antisemitic associations and societies (as many as 430 of these organizations) and of antisemitic periodicals (as many as 700). Antisemitic legislation was introduced regularly in legislatures. And before the end of 1920, the notorious antisemitic forgery, *The Protocols of the Elders of Zion*, just translated into German, had sold an astounding 120,000 copies.

In 1923 the Nazis had won 800,000 votes; by 1930 they had 6.5 million; and in 1932, in the last free election of the Weimar Republic, 14 million—one-third of the population—voted for the National Socialists. On 30 January 1933, the oath of office of chancellor of the German Republic was administered to Adolf Hitler. Hitler came to power legally, exploiting the letter of the law to subvert the law.

During the earliest years of Nazi rule, a series of anti-Jewish activities was initiated and laws passed. One activity, the organization by the government of an anti-Jewish boycott, was significant in that it demonstrated Hitler's talent for rationalizing and politicizing antisemitism, channeling the passion for pogrom on the part of rank-and-file antisemites into political action. Originated in 1933 as spontaneous violence of Nazi hooligans against Jewish businesses, the boycott soon involved a number of organs of government and semiofficial ones as well, such as the vicious antisemitic newspaper *Der Stürmer*.

A range of anti-Jewish laws and decrees was passed, the net effect of which was to undermine, by legal means, the rights and the position of German Jews. From the first law in April 1933 authorizing the elimination from the civil service of Jews, some 400 laws and decrees were passed over the next decade. In rapid succession came laws denying admission to the bar of "non-Aryan" lawyers; excluding Jews from the judiciary and from dentistry; limiting the attendance of non-Aryan Germans in German schools to a tiny proportion of the population; and on and on. Early on came the decree defining the "non-Aryan" as anyone "descended from non-Aryan, especially Jewish, parents or grand-parents." And the Reich Citizenship Law, passed in 1935, codified that citizenship was not a matter of an individual right but derived from membership in the German *Volk*. Citizenship was now related to race, and race was the determining factor in the drafting of the Nuremberg Laws, also in 1935.

The year 1935 was an infamous one in the history of antisemitism; it was in that year that, once again, the violence of antisemitism was channeled into law, in this case, the Nuremberg Laws, that defined legally and socially the National Socialist antisemitic agenda. The law and its thirteen supplemental decrees legitimated racialist antisemitism and transmuted the "purity of German blood" into a legal category. The laws forbade marriage and sexual relations between Germans and Jews and disenfranchised those subjects of Germany who were not of German blood. This last aspect—the disenfranchisement of Jews—embodied the most fundamental demand of every antisemitic movement from the beginning of the emancipation.

After the passage of the Nuremberg Laws there was yet more anti-Jewish legislation passed. An important factor in Nazi antisemitism, however, became the Schutzstaffel (SS), the dreaded enforcer of the National Socialist movement, which began asserting its control and supremacy over other party and state institutions with regard to the Jews.

With the passage of the Nuremberg Laws and their companion legislation and decrees, the centrality of "blood and race" that obsessed National Socialism was transformed with bureaucratic fastidiousness into legal racial categories. The Jews, henceforth, were outside the protection of the state. The Nuremberg Laws completed the total disenfranchisement of the Jews of Germany; but Hitler himself, in introducing the laws to the Reichstag assembled at Nuremberg, ominously hinted at the next stage of the Nazi agenda, when he used the term "final solution" in discussing the "problem" of Jews in Germany.

One other key event needs to be mentioned at this juncture in our review of antisemitism in prewar Germany: Kristallnacht—the "night of broken glass"—9–11 November 1938. The event followed a classic pattern of antisemitism, namely the cynical exploitation of mob feelings to further both antisemitic and political goals.

What happened at Kristallnacht, and why? Hitler's plans for the end of 1938 had included war over Czechoslovakia and with it the expropriation of Jews and violence against them. But with the Munich conference in September of that year, the plan misfired. Nonetheless, an unexpected opportunity for dealing with the Jews opened up with the assassination on 7 November of Ernst vom Rath, a third secretary in the German embassy in Paris, by Hershl Grynszpan, a seventeen-year-old Polish Jewish student. The incitement of the Jews of Germany in response to vom Rath's assassination began on 8 November with an incendiary editorial in the Nazi newspaper, the *Volkischer Beobachter*. Meetings all over Germany, incited by Minister of Propaganda Joseph Goebbels, were called on 8 and 9 November; at these meetings the local party leaders agitated the assembled mob, which then went into action, setting fire to synagogues, destroying Jewish businesses and homes, and beating Jews. It was precisely at that point in Nazi German history, with war fever running high, and the Jews already clearly identified as the enemies, that the rank-and-file Nazis, eager for a little action, were unleashed in mob violence.

When it was learned on 9 November that vom Rath had died of his wounds, Goebbels called for "spontaneous" demonstrations across the country: Jewish blood was to flow for the death of vom Rath. That night fires were ignited all over Germany, and the shattered plate glass that was to give the pogrom (although Kristallnacht was worse than any pogrom) its name littered the streets of German cities and towns. Synagogues and other Jewish institutions were burned to the ground. More than 7,000 Jewish businesses were destroyed. Some 100 Jews were killed, and thousands were subjected to violence and torments. Some 30,000 Jewish men were arrested and sent to concentration camps.

Kristallnacht served to complete the first Nazi agenda vis-à-vis the Jews: their total expropriation and the complete removal of their freedom. The result of Kristallnacht was the elimination of the Jews from the economy, educational system, and places of public accommodation of Germany. The Jewish community was assessed a fine of 1 billion marks.

By the beginning of 1939 it appeared that all aspects of the Nazi antisemitic agenda had been disposed of, except for the Jews themselves. This last issue was the subject in early 1942 of the Wannsee Conference of Nazi leadership, at which the coordination with respect to the "final solution"—the physical liquidation of the remaining Jews—was effected.

A final observation on the Hitlerian plan for the destruction of the Jews: Hitler's ideas about what became known as the final solution were shaped in his book *Mein Kampf*, written in 1924–1925, in which, as we know, he developed his anti-Jewish ideas into an all-embracing schema. Hitler meant quite literally what he advocated: the elimination, through destruction, of the Jews. He advocated a systematic, two-stage approach, which he put into practice: first, a preliminary stage in which Jews were deprived of their rights; and second, the accomplishment of the ultimate objective—"removal of the Jews."

It is probably true that without Hitler, the charismatic *Fuhrer*, the destruction of European Jewry would not have occurred. But it is equally true that without that assertive and enduring tradition of antisemitism by which the Germans sought self-definition, Hitler would not have had the soil in which to grow his organization and spread its propaganda. And with the third element—the humiliation of Versailles, economic distress, political upheavals—added to German antisemitism plus Hitler, Hitler was able to transform the German brand of antisemitism into a radical doctrine of mass murder.

Antisemitism in the United States

Overall, the historical record shows that there has been *relatively* little manifestation of antisemitism in the United States, certainly as compared with the European experience. There are four structural differences between the United States and Europe that collectively account for American exceptionalism and uniqueness.

1. The separation of church and state tautologically meant that Jews were not living in a "Christian" society—or in *any* kind of religious society. It was church-state separation that lifted pluralism from being a conceptual or philosophical ideal and made it a *legal* obligation.[11] In the United States, from the very beginning of the American polity, the public sphere was viewed, by legal fiat, as being a neutral place. Church-state separation therefore asserted that Jews (and other minorities and individuals) would not be merely tolerated but *accepted*. Maintaining a firm line of separation between church and state, therefore, is central to religious voluntarism and to religious freedom; by extension, it fosters the distinctive survival and creativity of religious groups, including Jews.

2. American society was a postemancipation society from its very beginnings. This reality was, in my view, most crucial in ensuring that political antisemitism of the kind that arose in nineteenth-century Europe did not come to be in the United States. Before the late eighteenth century, Jews everywhere in Europe were legally defined as outsiders in society and therefore alien to the polity. The opening for Jews to become citizens came as a result of the Enlightenment—with the French Revolution acting as the engine for Enlightenment ideas—with the result that Jews began entering the mainstream of European societies.

America did not carry the European pre-Enlightenment baggage—the bulk of U.S. Jewish history begins after the Declaration of Independence and the Constitution were drafted—with the result that Jews no less than any others were entitled to equal status in the body politic.

3. The United States was a new nation—a frontier society—made up people of diverse backgrounds without "insiders" and "outsiders." In contrast, in Europe, Jews had to cope with the fact that the nation-states in which they were citizens as a result of the emancipation had historical memories, deriving from a Christian context, going back centuries, and that they, the Jews, were not part of these memories except as aliens and enemies.

4. The United states, as a nation of immigrants, was inherently pluralist. Indeed, even when the ideology of choice was the "melting pot," the reality was always cultural and democratic pluralism, and pluralism became a uniquely U.S. way of positioning oneself as a member of American society, even as that person (or group) retained religious and ethnic identity. An important byproduct of a pluralist society was that it removed the onus under which Jews had been compelled to live in many other societies.

The sum result of these four dynamics is that antisemitism did not invade in the formal institutions of power, as it did in Europe.

The key point to bear in mind is that in this country antisemitism has not been embedded in the institutions of power—often the formal institutions of power—as it was in Europe over the course of many centuries. This factor is absolutely central and needs to be recalled especially by those who would identify the conditions of the United States in the 1990s with those of Germany in the 1920s.

Antisemitism first became an issue in the Civil War. In 1862, General Ulysses S. Grant, at the time Union commander in the Tennessee district, issued an order in which he unfairly named Jews as being the worst offenders in a smuggling operation and expelled all Jews "as a class" from all the territory under his jurisdiction, which included Kentucky, Tennessee, and Mississippi. This order, the infamous General Orders Number 11, is unique in the history of the United States: it is the one official overtly anti-Jewish decree in the American experience. The immediate questions of who was doing what kind of smuggling in Tennessee, and the role of Jews in competition with non-Jews in that smuggling, were not and are not the issue in General Orders Number 11. Jews were singled out in Grant's order because antisemitism, heretofore almost nonexistent in the United States, had been aroused by the turmoil of the war. The pattern of Jewish scapegoating was again experienced, with Jewish financiers attacked as "Jew-bankers" who were supporters of the Confederacy. The northern press repeated the charge that Jews dominated the speculation of gold and were engaged in destroying the national economy. Together with General Orders Number 11, these charges were a restatement of a classic theme of antisemitism: the Jews are doing too well; their agenda is one of financial control; Jewish bankers are controlling the economy. Economic antisemitism tinged with classic libel had once again become a factor, this time in the United States.

It ought be noted that Grant's General Orders Number 11 was revoked by order of President Abraham Lincoln, primarily because of constitutional strictures against any agency of the federal government singling out any group for special treatment.

Whatever antisemitism existed during and after the Civil War, it was not sufficient to inflict substantial damage upon the Jewish community. What was a problem, however, was the growing perception of the Jew as different, as somehow "other"—a pattern that has been noted since antiquity—owing this time to the concentration of Jews in very few pursuits: they were clothing manufacturers, shopkeepers, department store owners. The "German" Jews of the nineteenth century—the group actually comprised German, Austrian, Polish, Bohemian, and other Jews—as they pursued these trades and cohered as a group, found their separateness reinforced by an increasing social antisemitism. This practice—which played itself out in so-called restricted resorts and clubs—was widespread and became more so further into the twentieth century and set a pattern that continued through most of the century, with vestiges of this social discrimination remaining today.

Antisemitism of an ideological and racialist bent emerged in the United States during the highly nationalistic 1890s, a period during which the large-scale immigration of Jews from eastern Europe that characterized the next three decades began. The anti-Jewish stereotype of old, containing the elements of Christian antisemitism and the picture of the Jew as the wielder of undue power, was adopted by nativist thinkers and authors, including some of prominence, such as Henry Adams, who represented an eastern patrician intellectual class.

The incorporation of frank racism into American antisemitism, following the European pattern that has been discussed in previous sections, took place during the early part of the twentieth century and informed the movement for restriction of immigration. Although restrictionism was not on its face antisemitic, there is no question that the intellectual and legislative fathers of the movement considered Jewish immigration as deleterious to the welfare of the nation. The point was most sharply expressed in the writings of a leading nativist, the racist Madison Grant, whose writings paralleled the pseudoscientific racist themes popularized in European antisemitica. Grant's book, *The Passing of the Great Race*, published in 1916, condemned the Jews for mongrelizing the nation. The result of restrictionism was the passage of the Immigration Act of 1924, which established a national origins quota system that discriminated heavily against eastern European—largely Jewish—immigration.

We ought not to enter the twentieth century without a mention of the one actual instance of a pogrom inflicted upon Jews in this country. In 1902 the funeral of Rabbi Jacob Joseph, who had served unhappily as chief rabbi of New York, turned into a riot when the cortege was set upon by Jew-hating hecklers and debris throwers. The police, inadequately deployed, either stood by or, as confirmed by subsequent investigation, actively joined the mob, spurred on by the cry of "Kill those sheenies!" by the police inspector in charge. The funeral riot resulted from two factors: first, a total insensitivity of police to minority rights (a dynamic that resonates even in today's newspaper headlines); second, the intense interethnic animosity—primarily between Jews and the older and established Irish—that had developed in New York with the huge influx of Jews in the last two decades of the nineteenth century and the early years of the twentieth. The issues of ethnic composition and competition likewise continue to be significant factors in the intergroup-relations challenges of the present-day United States.

During the first decades of the twentieth century two other events took place that galvanized Jewish reaction and helped lead to organized Jewish counteraction of antisemitism: the Leo Frank case and Henry Ford's antisemitic propaganda campaign. In 1913 American Jews were shocked when Leo Frank, a Jewish factory manager in Atlanta, Georgia, was convicted on flimsy evidence of the murder of one of his female employees. In 1915 Frank was abducted from his jail cell and lynched by a mob. There was never evidence that established that Frank had committed the crime; indeed, seventy years later an eyewitness to the crime came forward to exonerate Frank. But the circumstances surrounding the Frank conviction were those of blatant mob antisemitism reminiscent of the Crusades, during which, as will be recalled, political and religious leaders who sought to protect the Jews were helpless before the fury of the mob.

The notorious Frank case, and its overt antisemitism, was both a result and a harbinger of an upsurge of antisemitic feeling and expression in the first two decades of the new century, and particularly in the 1920s, and resulted in a heightened consciousness on the part of the organized Jewish community.[12] Anti-Jewish expression during this period was rooted in older stereotypes, reinforced by nativist thinking and by economic pressures. Economic antisemitism was certainly part of the agenda of some of the Populists; their movement of protest against capitalism and monopoly at times included railings against Jewish capital, which was identified with the hated Wall Street.

One result of the surge of nativism during the early part of the twentieth century was the fear of foreign leftist radicalism. Bolshevism, often associated with Jews, became a target of the post–World War I so-called Red Scare. The Jewish-Communist nexus thus became, and remained, a permanent part of antisemitic propaganda.

This element of antisemitism was reinforced considerably by the appearance, in 1919, of a U.S. edition of the *Protocols of the El-*

ders of Zion, the notorious forgery that asserted that an international Jewish conspiracy was at work to dominate the world and destroy Christendom and that the Bolshevik revolution was work of this conspiracy. The libel, which found few listeners and believers among most serious Americans, was picked up by none other than Henry Ford, the most prominent industrialist of his time. The *Dearborn Independent*, a magazine owned and published by Ford, launched an antisemitic propaganda campaign without precedent in the United States, in which the libel was reprinted in hundreds of thousands of copies. Ford's propaganda found ready acceptance in rural areas and in small towns, less in urban areas, and a negative reaction among policymakers. The *Protocols* made it possible to believe that Jewish capitalists such as the Rothschilds and Communists such as Leon Trotsky were all part of the same power directorate. This theory of Jewish world conspiracy would thus "explain" the success of the Bolshevik Revolution— and it could act as a warning against allowing the Jews to extend their wealth and power in the United States. Henry Ford's paper became the first trumpet of antisemitism in America in the 1920s.

Although Henry Ford was forced in 1927 to recant his antisemitism, the damage had been done. Red-baiting and nativism set the seal on a conviction that was widely held in the 1920s by people who did not consider themselves Jew-haters. Jews were not seen as individuals; they were attacked as a group for being different and clannish.

The spectacular revival of the Ku Klux Klan in the 1920s—the Klan counted 4 million members at its height in 1924—was the most significant expression of American nativism. Although its primary targets were Catholics and blacks, the Klan went after Jews as well. The significance of the Klan in the history of U.S. antisemitism is that it was the first substantial, organized, mass movement in which antisemitism was used.

The period of the first half of the twentieth century was one in which antisemitism manifested itself in a variety of forms of discrimination. Of greatest concern to Jews was discrimination in higher education—the classic *numerus clausus*, the quota system—established by a number of colleges that were faced with increasing numbers of Jewish applicants. The quota system in its most blatant form became a national issue in 1922 when President A. Lawrence Lowell of Harvard announced that a quota system was under consideration. Although the quota was rejected by the

Harvard faculty, the system survived for many years at many leading colleges. Social discrimination was found in business and the professions as well, where employers specified that Christians were preferred for positions.

The last major burst of antisemitism in the United States came during the 1930s, with an upsurge of ideologically motivated and political anti-Jewish activity. The impact of the Great Depression, combined with the triumph of Nazism in Germany, produced an outpouring of antisemitic propaganda. The old charges of an international Jewish conspiracy, straight out of the *Protocols*, were trotted out again and again throughout the decade. The revival of a native, populist, U.S. antisemitism, fundamentalist and pseudoagrarian, was spearheaded by the likes of Gerald L. K. Smith, whose brand of antisemitism yet resonates among some in rural areas to the present day.

And then there was Father Charles Coughlin, a Catholic priest whose weekly radio broadcasts with an openly antisemitic message reached millions in the 1930s. Coughlin's magazine, *Social Justice*, reprinted the *Protocols* with Coughlin's own commentary. Father Coughlin's campaign paved the way for isolationist organizations such as the America First Committee to attract antisemites to their banners. Remarks terming the Jews the most dangerous force pushing the United States into war were voiced even on the floor of the Congress. And the tensions of the war years themselves, according to national polls, stimulated a considerable amount of antisemitic sentiment. The numbers of Americans professing negative attitudes toward Jews reached their peak—more than 50 percent—during the war years.

The experience in the postwar years has been one in which that antisemitism has lost the ideological strength it had achieved during the preceding decades (even as new expressions of antisemitism were informed by other ideologies), and behavioral antisemitism has been limited for the most part to incidents of antisemitism against individuals and to isolated fringe groups whose memberships declined in number during the 1990s. Of continued concern during the 1990s were racist expressions on the part of some extremist leaders in the African American community. There was little political antisemitism, arguably the single most virulent form of the disease, and discriminatory barriers have continued to fall in all areas of U.S. society, including the corporate world. Perhaps most important, attitudinal surveys have continued to show a steady decline, over a forty-year period from the early 1960s to the early twenty-first century in negative attitudes toward Jews.

Antisemitism continues to exist in the United States, and some manifestations are indeed of concern. Nonetheless, the kind of antisemitism that inhibits the ability of Jews either individually or as a polity to participate in the workings of the society is not a significant factor in American society in the early twenty-first century.

Retrospect and Prospect

In the postwar world the issue of antisemitism, at least in Europe, was in large measure one of Christian contrition. Protestant denominations took great pains to denounce antisemitism; and the Roman Catholic Church, in a development that can be characterized as no less than radical, set into motion a mechanism that resulted in a revision of 2,000 years of Church teachings about the Jews. The Second Vatican Council in 1965 promulgated the watershed document *Nostra Aetate (In Our Time)* that repudiated fundamental antisemitic attitudes of Jewish deicide and the legitimacy of the Jewish religion as a faith community. *Nostra Aetate* rejected the "teaching of contempt" that had long characterized the Catholic Church, repudiated the charge against the Jews of deicide, and, in essence, said that antisemitism must no longer be embedded in Catholic teaching and practice. This seminal Vatican document defined the nature of a new relationship between Catholics and Jews. Whatever difficulties are encountered in Catholic-Jewish relations—and clearly Vatican-Jewish relations were not trouble-free during the 1980s and 1990s—it is not hyperbole to say that there has been more progress in the relationship over the past forty years, particularly with respect to antisemitism, than in the previous 2,000.

Nonetheless, it is clear that antisemitism has not disappeared from Europe. Newer forms of antisemitism invoke classic motifs of Jewish power, Jewish domination, and Jewish control. Virulent anti-Israel rhetoric across Europe (especially in France), neo-Nazi elements in Germany and elsewhere, radical racist skinheads in England and the United States, and, very significantly, attacks on

the legitimacy of the State of Israel—that call into question the legitimacy of Jewish peoplehood itself—all merit careful monitoring and vigorous counteraction.

And finally, there was the question of antisemitism in the Soviet Union (USSR) and today in the states of the former Soviet
Union. The collapse of the USSR brought into sharp focus both
the past and present of antisemitism in the East. Soviet antisemitism after the consolidation of the Soviet regime, principally
under Stalin, was for the most part a conscious state policy, but it
was a policy that exploited the traditional antisemitism of the various parts of the Soviet Union, especially the Ukraine and parts of
Russia. Antisemitic intent in the Soviet Union was usually clear to
all through the use of thinly veiled terms such as *cosmopolitan*,
Zionist, and so on; the word *Jew* was rarely mentioned in propaganda. The government's aim was to eradicate tendencies initiated and supported by "rootless," foreign, traitorous elements,
namely the Jews.

The situation for the Jews in the Soviet Union began worsening toward the end of the 1930s with the great purges, during
which time the government began systematically liquidating
Jewish institutions and leading figures. But the truly bad times—
the *"Shvartzer Yor'n,"* the Black Years—were during the last five
years of Stalin's life, from 1948 to 1953, when the antisemitic line
became the active policy of the government at its highest level.
The murder of Solomon Mikhoels, director of the Jewish State
Theatre in Moscow, touched off what developed into the systematic liquidation of all the Jewish cultural institutions that were left
from the 1930s or that had been established during the war. Early
in 1949 Soviet newspapers opened an anti-Jewish campaign, viciously exploiting for Soviet government aims popular hatred of
the Jews. Events that took place in rapid succession—the arrests
and executions of Jewish writers, artists, and public figures; the
dissolution of the Jewish Anti-Fascist Committee; the Slansky
trial in Czechoslovakia; the dismissal of thousands of Jews from
their jobs; the portrayal of the State of Israel as an instrument of
an anti-Soviet U.S. spy network; and the "Doctors' Plot" of Jews
to murder Stalin—were all part of the antisemitic program of the
Black Years. According to reliable data, Stalin had intended to deport the Jewish population from the principal cities of the Soviet
Union to eastern Siberia; only his death prevented the execution
of this awful plan.

During the Khrushchev and Brezhnev years there was less of the blatant and overt antisemitic activity of the Stalin years, yet antisemitism was always a significant factor in Soviet life. Indeed, it is accurate to say that it was antisemitism entrenched in the institutions of Soviet power that informed and drove the power apparatus on issues that related to Soviet Jews, especially the growing movement (both within and outside the USSR) aimed at freedom for Soviet Jewry.

With the coming of Gorbachev-era glasnost, new fears were expressed regarding the emergence of ethnic-Russian antisemitism. Although the state-sanctioned antisemitism of the Soviet regime was a matter for the past, antisemitism was a common feature of the numerous ultranationalist and neo-Stalinist groups that emerged on the fringe of Russian politics. The radically nationalistic organization Pamyat, for example, views the Jews as being primarily responsible for the crumbling of the Russian empire; Jews are viewed as those who created communism, the satanic evil that good Christian nationalistic Russians must destroy.

Although the data from opinion polls taken in the countries of the former Soviet Union indicate that Jews are not the primary target of grassroots prejudice—ethnic and racial hostility are directed mainly against Chechens, Armenians, and Roma (Gypsies, who are held responsible for crime)—Jews appear likely to be caught up in any social or political convulsions that might arise in the inherently unstable Russian environment. The reelection of Russian president Boris Yeltsin in 1996, although not presaging a completely irenic future, nonetheless assuaged some fears with respect to the security of Russia's Jews. In the Putin era, there remain a number of serious question marks that collectively do not bode well for the future of political stability in Russia. It is difficult to envision a legal framework for the protection of minorities that could be maintained in such circumstances.

Source note: Much of the foregoing material is excerpted, with permission, all rights reserved, from Jerome A. Chanes, *A Dark Side of History: Antisemitism through the Ages* (New York: Anti-Defamation League, 2000).

Antisemitism through the Ages: A Time Line

Jews throughout history have been perceived of and treated as perpetual outsiders and dangers to the societies in which they live. Although the intensity of antisemitism has at times subsided, history teaches that it always returns as well. One compelling proof of the Jew's pariah status throughout history is offered by official antisemitic state policies that entrench discrimination and foster prejudice.

Interspersed in this chronology is a sampling of antisemitic laws, edicts, legal decisions, papal rulings, and other examples of state policy that have been promulgated over the last 2,000 years. They demonstrate the persistence of official antisemitism throughout the world and the need for efforts to eradicate it. (The legal texts are excerpted from Anthony Julius, Robert S. Rifkind, Jeffrey Weill, and Felice D. Gaer, *Antisemitism: An Assault on Human Rights* [New York: The Jacob Blaustein Institute for the Advancement of Human Rights/American Jewish Committee, 2001]. Excerpted and reprinted with permission.)

586 BCE Destruction of the First Temple in Jerusalem and dispersion of the Jews (Babylonian captivity).

Third century BCE Antisemitic themes are popularized by Egyptian priest Manetho.

Second century BCE Under Antiochus IV (Epiphanes), Jews are compelled, under urgings by Jewish Hellenizers in Jerusalem, to reject many of the laws of their fathers. Sanctuary in Jerusalem is defiled.

First century BCE Josephus's Apologetica, *Contra Apionem*.

38 BCE First recorded pogrom against Jews, in Alexandria.

70 CE Siege of Jerusalem by the Romans; destruction of the Temple.

80 CE	Definitive separation between "church" and "synagogue."
135–138 CE	Bar Kochba rebellion against Rome; last gasp of Jewish autonomy.
135 CE	Emperor Hadrian issues anti-Jewish edicts (including prohibition of circumcision) in response to the Bar Kochba rebellion.
321	Christianity becomes the official religion of the Roman state.
325	Council of Nicaea formulates Christian church's policy toward the Jews; anti-Jewish edicts.
400–500	Anti-Jewish measures are promulgated by Emperor Constantine and others, including edicts prohibiting Jewish pilgrimages to Jerusalem and forbidding conversion to Judaism.
414	Bishop Cyril of Alexandria in Egypt stages a pogrom and expels the Jews from this ancient city of learning, the first recorded expulsion of Jews from any city.
425	Office of the Nasi, the temporal and spiritual leader of the Jews, is abolished.
483	Theodosian Code.

The Theodosian Code is a sixteen-volume work containing the imperial edicts of Christian emperors from Constantine (early fourth century) to Theodosius II. Some sections of laws within the Code are excerpted here.

Laws of Constantine the Great (October 18, 315) We wish to make it known to the Jew and their elders and their patriarchs that if, after the enactment of this law, any one of them dares to attack with stones or some other manifestation of anger on another who has fled their dangerous sect and attached himself to the worship of God [Christianity], he must speedily be given to the flames and burned together with all his accomplices. Moreover, if any one of the populations should join their abominable sect and attend their meetings, he will bear with them the deserved penalties.

Laws of Constantius (August 13, 339) This pertains to women, who live in our weaving factories and whom Jews, in their foulness, take in marriage. It is decreed that these women are to be restored to the weaving factories. This prohibition [of intermarriage] is to be preserved for the future lest the Jews induce Christian women to share their shameful lives. If they do this they will subject themselves to a sentence of death.

A law of Theodosius II (January 31, 438) No Jew—or no Samaritan who subscribes to neither [the Jewish nor the Christian] religion—shall obtain offices and dignities; to none shall the administration of city service be permitted; nor shall any one exercise the office of a defender of the city. Indeed, we believe it sinful that the enemies of the heavenly majesty and of the Roman laws should become the executors of our laws. . . . We forbid that any synagogue shall rise as a new building. To these things we add that he who misleads a slave or a freeman against his will or by punishable advice, from the service of the Christian religion to that of an abominable sect and ritual, is to be punished by loss of property and life. On the one hand, whoever has built a synagogue must realize that he has worked to the advantage of the Catholic Church [which will confiscate the building]; on the other hand, whoever has already secured the badge of office shall not hold the dignities he has acquired. On the contrary, he who worms himself into office must remain, as before, in the lowest rank even though he will have already earned an honorary office. And as for him who begins the building of a synagogue and is not moved by the desire of repairing it, he shall be punished by a fine of fifty pounds gold for his daring. Moreover, if he will have prevailed with his evil teachings over the faith of another, he shall see his wealth confiscated and he soon subjected to a death sentence.

553 Emperor Justinian's Novella 146

Christian Emperor Justinian bans rabbinic interpretation, demands use of languages other than Hebrew in the synagogue, and insists on certain articles of belief.

Preface. Necessity dictates that when the Hebrews listen to their sacred texts they should not confine themselves to the meaning of the letter, but should also devote their attention to those sacred prophecies which are hidden from them, and which announce the mighty Lord and Savior Jesus Christ. Ch. I ii. But the Mishnah, or as they call it the second tradition, we prohibit entirely. For it is not part of the sacred books, nor is it handed down by divine inspiration through the prophets, but the handiwork of man, speaking only of earthly things, and having nothing of the divine in it. Ch. II. If any among them seek to introduce impious vanities, denying the resurrection or the judgment, or the work of God, or that angels are part of creation, we require them everywhere to be expelled forthwith; that no backslider raise his impious voice to contradict the evident purpose of God. Those who utter such sentiments shall be put to death, and thereby the Jewish people shall be purged of the errors, which they introduced. Epilogue. This is our sacred will and pleasure, and your Excellency and your present colleague and your staff shall see that it is carried out, and shall not allow the Hebrews to contravene it. Those who resist it or try to put any obstruction in its way, shall first suffer corporal punishment, and then be compelled to live in exile, forfeiting also their property, that they flaunt not their impudence against God and the empire. You shall also circulate our law to the provincial governors, that they learning its contents may enforce it in their several cities, knowing that it is to be strictly carried out under pain of our displeasure.

565   Justinian Code is completed under Emperor Justinian I.

Emperor Justinian I orders the creation of a unified collection of earlier imperial laws, to which he adds his own, one of which is excerpted.

A Law of Justinian: Since many judges, in deciding cases, have addressed us in need of our decision, asking that they be informed what ought to be done with witnesses who are heretics, whether their testimony ought to be received or rejected, we therefore ordain that no heretic, nor even they who cherish the Jewish superstition, may offer testimony against orthodox Christians who are engaged in litigation, whether one or the other of the parties is an orthodox Christian.

589   Council of Toledo declares that children of mixed marriages have to be Christian.

589–694   Councils of Toledo III-XVII (Spain)

This series of Spanish councils inaugurates the period when Spain passes from Arian Christian to Catholic control and begins detailing the laws that would govern Jews under Catholic rule for centuries.

Toledo VI (638) Inflexibilis on safeguarding the faith of Jews: Judaeorum Perfidia. The inflexible perfidy of the Jews seems to shake at last under piety and power from high, since it is manifest that the most excellent and most Christian prince, inspired by the supreme God and ablaze with the fire of faith, decided, together with the priests of his kingdom, to eradicate entirely their prevarications and superstitions. . . . We promulgate with him, therefore, this unanimous decision . . . namely, that anyone who will obtain in the succession of time the crown of the kingdom should not ascend the royal throne before he had promised, among the other terms of his oath, that he would not allow them [the Jews] to violate this Catholic faith and that he would not show favor in any way to their perfidy. . . . Toledo XII (681) On the Confirmation of the Laws that were Promulgated Against the Vileness of the Jews, Following the Ordered List of the Titles of these Laws, which is given in the same Canon: De Judaeorum Autem: We have examined thoroughly, and with great attention to meaning, the laws recently given by the glorious prince concerning the execrable perfidy of the Jews, laws whose regulations are divided among different titles; and, cognizant of the weight of their importance, we have improved their measures. . . . Henceforth they should be maintained irrevocably against their crimes, in due course of justice, as follows: De Commemoratione Priscarum: The law on recalling the ancient laws promulgated against the transgressions of the Jews and on their new confirmation. Item, De Blasphematoribus Sanctae: The Law on those blaspheming against the Holy Trinity. Item, Ne Judaei Aut: That Jews should not remove from the grace of baptism either their sons or their servants. Item, Ne Judaei More Suo Celerbrent: That Jews should not celebrate Pascha according to their custom or practice circumcisions of the flesh, and that they should not turn any Christian from the faith of Christ. Item, Ne Judaei Sabbatha: That the Jews shall not dare to celebrate Sabbath and the other holidays of their rite. Item, Omnis Judaei Diebus: That every Jew should cease from work on Sundays and on the designated days. Item, Ne Judaei more Suo DiJudicent: Jews should not discriminate between foods according to their custom. Item, Ne Judaei Ex Propinquitate: That the Jews should not enter into marriage with close blood relatives, and that they shall not dare to be married without the benediction of a priest. Item, Ne Judaei Religion: That the Jews should not dare defend their sect by insulting our religion, and that they should not move elsewhere in flight from our faith, and that no one should receive them in their escape. Item, Ne Christianus A Judaeo: That a Christian should not accept any sort of gift from a Jew against the faith of Christ. Item, Ne Judaei Libros: That the Jews shall not dare to read those books that the Christian faith repudiates. Item, Ne Judaeis Mancipia: That Christian slaves should not serve Jews or adhere to them. Item, Judaeus Ex Aliis: That a Jew coming from other provinces or territories under our royal rule should not defer presenting himself before the local bishop or priest. Item, De Damnis Sacerdotum: On the punishments of priest and judges who would delay putting into effect the measures instituted in the laws against Jews.

624–628   Jewish communities of Arabia are destroyed by Muhammad.

600–   Pact of Umar
700

This document, composed by Umar I around 637 but subsequently altered, is an early attempt at regulating relations between the Jews and Christians, on the one hand, and Muslims on the other.

This is a letter to the servant of God, Umar, Commander of the faithful, from the Christians of such and such a city. When you [Muslims] marched against us, we asked of you protection for ourselves, our posterity, our possessions, and our co-religionists; and we made this stipulation with you, that we will not erect in our cities or the suburbs any new monastery, church, cell or hermitage; that we will not repair any of such buildings that may fall into ruins, or renew those that may be situated in the Muslim quarters of the town; that we will not refuse the Muslims entry into our churches either by night or by day; that we will open the gates wide to passengers and travelers; that we will receive any Muslim traveler into our houses and give him food and lodging for three nights; that we will not harbor any spy in our churches or houses, or conceal any enemy of the Muslims. . . . that we will not prevent any of our kinsmen from embracing Islam, if they so desire. That we will honor the Muslims and rise up in our assemblies when cap, turban, sandals, or parting of the hair; that we will not make use of their expressions of speech, nor adopt the surnames . . . that we will not ride on saddles or gird on swords, or take to ourselves arms or wear them, or engrave Arabic inscriptions on our rings; that we will not sell wine . . . that we will shave the front of our heads; that we will keep to our own style of dress, wherever we may be; that we will wear girdles round our waists . . . that we will not recite our service in a loud voice when a Muslim is present.

600–1200   The Jews of Angevin England.

This collection of laws contained numerous religious, financial, and social restrictions against Jews.

The Laws of the Church about the Jews (7th C.) I. If any Christian woman takes gifts from the infidel Jews or of her own will and commits sin with them, let her be separated from church a whole year and live in much tribulation, and then let her repent for nine years. . . . But if with a pagan let her repent seven years. II. If anyone shall despise the council of the Nicene Synod and make Easter with the Jews on the fourteenth of the moon, he shall be cut off from the whole church, unless he do penance before his death. III. If any Christian accepts from the infidel Jews their unleavened cakes or any other meat or drink and share in their impieties, he shall do penance with bread and water for forty days. Corpus Juris Canonici. Decretal V. vi (1198) C. III. Jews may keep their old synagogues, may not erect new ones. . . . C. IV. On Good Friday Jews may not keep their doors or windows open. . . . C. V. Christians ought to be excommunicated who serve Jews in their houses. And secular princes ought to be excommunicated who spoil baptized Jews of their goods.

800–900	Reign of Charlemagne

814   Charlemagne's "Capitulary for the Jews"

King Charlemagne, king of the Franks and emperor of the Holy Roman Empire, focuses on financial transactions of Jews in this law.

1. Let no Jew presume to take in pledge or for any debt any of the goods of the Church in gold, silver, or other form, from any Christian. But if he presume to do so, which God forbid, let all his goods be seized and let his right hand be cut off. 2. Let no Jew presume to take any Christian in pledge for any Jew or Christian, nor let him do anything worse; but if he presume to do so, let him make reparation according to this law, and at the same time he shall lose both pledge and debt. 3. Let no Jew presume to have a money-changer's table in his house, nor shall he presume to sell wine, grain, or other commodities there. But if it be discovered that he has done so all his goods shall be taken away from him, and he shall be imprisoned until he is brought into our presence.

1095   The First Crusade is preached by Pope Urban II on 25 November.

1096   The First Crusade. Jewish Rhenish communities are devastated by crusaders

1099   Godfrey of Bouillon and his army capture Jerusalem; the Jewish community is destroyed in a terrible massacre.

1146   Pope Eugenius III calls for a new crusade. Franco-German Jewry is driven out of commerce.

1182   King Phillip Augustus of France issues an edict driving the entire Jewish population from royal domains, confiscating property, converting deserted synagogues into churches, and declaring all debts to Jews from Christians to be null and void.

1190   Anti-Jewish activity shifts to England when Richard I
        decides to take part in the Third Crusade. In January,
        most of the Jews in the port town of Lynn are massa-
        cred. In February and March, massacres in Norwich,
        Stanford, Lincoln, and York.

1215   The Fourth Lateran Council extends anti-Jewish en-
        actments of previous councils: special taxes on Jewish-
        owned lands, the prohibition of Jews having more
        than one synagogue in a town, and most significantly,
        the rule that Jews must dress as distinguishable from
        Christians.

        *The Fourth Lateran Council is the largest ecumenical
        church gathering ever and represents a high-water mark in
        the authority of the papacy under Innocent III.*

        Canon 68: In some provinces a difference in dress distin-
        guishes the Jews or Saracens from the Christians, but in cer-
        tain others such a confusion has grown up that they cannot
        be distinguished by any differences. Thus it happens at times
        that through error Christians have relations with the women
        of Jews or Saracens, and Jews and Saracens with Christian
        women. Therefore, that they may not, under pretext of error
        of this sort, excuse themselves in the future for the excesses of
        such prohibited intercourse, we decree that such Jews and
        Saracens of both sexes in every Christian province and at all
        times shall be marked off in the eyes of the public from other
        peoples through the character of their dress. . . . Moreover,
        during the last three days before Easter and especially on
        Good Friday, they shall not go forth in public at all, for the
        reason that some of them on these very days, as we hear, do
        not blush to go forth better dressed and are not afraid to
        mock the Christians who maintain the memory of the most
        holy Passion by wearing signs of mourning. This, however,
        we forbid most severely, that any one should presume at all
        to break forth in insult to the Redeemer. And since we ought
        not to ignore any insult to Him who blotted out our dis-
        graceful deeds, we command that such impudent fellows be
        checked by the secular princes by imposing them proper
        punishment so that they shall not at all presume to blas-
        pheme Him who was crucified for us. Canon 69: Since it is ab-
        surd that a blasphemer of Christ exercise authority over
        Christians, we on account of the boldness of transgressors
        renew in this general council what the Synod of Toledo (589)
        wisely enacted in this matter, prohibiting Jews from being

given preference in the matter of public offices, since in such capacity they are most troublesome to the Christians. Canon 70: Some [Jews], we understand, who voluntarily approached the waters of holy baptism, do not entirely cast off the old man that they may more perfectly put on the new one, because, retaining remnants of the former rite, they obscure by such a mixture the beauty of the Christian religion. . . . We decree that such persons be in every way restrained by the prelates from the observance of the former rite, that, having given themselves of their own observance. Holy Land Decrees: . . . We command also that Jews be compelled by the secular power to cancel interest, and, till they have done so, intercourse with them must be absolutely denied them by all Christians under penalty of excommunication.

1217   Introduction of the Jew-Badge in England by King Henry III (Oxford, 30 March)

Many laws require Jews to wear distinguishing dress when living among Christian and Muslims.

The King To The Sheriff Of Worchester We order you to have published and observed throughout your bailiwick that all Jews wear upon the fore part of their upper garment, wherever they walk or ride, within or outside the village, two white tables made of white linen or parchment so that, by a sign of this kind, Jews can be patently distinguished from Christians.

1242   The Inquisition of Paris condemns the Talmud; the Talmud is burned.

1246   Orders of Confiscation (France)

The property of Jews in France (and elsewhere) is sometimes confiscated by the crown, as this law describes.

Laws Enacted at Saint-Germain-en-Laye 1. We order you to return to those to whom they belong all those Jews held captive who do not belong to us and not to seize anything from them. 2. However, from those held captive who are our Jews, since we wish to have from them as much as possible, you should seize goods and, indicating to us the sum which you are able to realize therefrom, you should cause that sum to be carefully and safely guarded and preserved. 3. We further order, concerning captive and other Jews of your seneschalsy or Jews who live in those areas under our jurisdiction, that you cause them to be forbidden by person and goods from henceforth presuming to extort usury. Rather, they should earn their sustenance from another source. 4. We also order and command you not to compel anyone to repay debts to the Jews and to receive nothing of debts which Christians owe to Jews.

1200–
1300
German laws.

These sets of laws in Germany force Jews to set themselves apart by their dress.

Provincial Council of Breslau (1267) We also decree and ordain that Jews shall resume the horned hat, which at one time they were accustomed to wear in these parts, and presumed in their temerity to put aside, so that they should be clearly discernible from Christians. Schwabenspiegel Article 214, 10. The Jews shall wear hats that are pointed; thereby they are marked off from the Christians, so that one shall take them for Jews.

Las Siete Partidas ("The Seven-Part Code") (Castile).

These laws are part of a much larger code. Composed in the thirteenth century, they do not take effect until the fourteenth century. Once enacted, they are applied throughout Spain and in territories possessed by Spain (including Louisiana, Florida, and Puerto Rico).

Title XXIV. Concerning the Jews: Law VII. What Penalty a Christian Deserves Who Becomes a Jew Where a Christian is so unfortunate as to become a Jew, we order that he shall be put to death just as if he had become a heretic; and we decree that his property shall be disposed of in the same way that should be done with that of heretics. Law VIII. No Christian Man or Woman shall live with a Jew We forbid any Jew to keep Christian men or women in his house, to be served by them; although he may have them to cultivate and take care of his lands or protect him on the way when he is compelled to go to some dangerous place. Moreover, we forbid any Christian man or woman to invite a Jew or a Jewess, or to accept an invitation from them, to eat or drink together, or to drink any wine made by their hands. . . . Law IX. What Penalty a Jew Deserves Who Has Intercourse with a Christian Woman Jews who live with Christian women are guilty of great insolence and boldness, for which reason we decree that all Jews who, hereafter, may be convicted of having done such a thing shall be put to death. Law XI. Jews Shall Bear Certain Marks in Order That They Be Known Many crimes and outrageous things occur between Christians and Jews because they live together in cities, and dress alike; and in order to avoid the offenses and evils which take place for this reason, we deem it proper and we order that all Jews male and female living in our dominions shall bear some distinguishing mark upon their heads so that people may plainly recognize a Jew or a Jewess; and any Jew who does not bear such a mark, shall pay for each time he is found without it ten maravedis of gold; and if he has not the means to do this he shall publicly receive ten lashes for his offence.

1249	Pope Innocent IV issues papal bull against the "blood libel."

1275	Edward I of England enacts the Statute of Judaism, prohibiting the Jews' chief source of income, money-lending, as well as all intercourse between Jews and Christians, and calling for capital punishment for Jewish "blasphemy" and for forced conversion sermons.

1288	France sees the first mass burning at the stake of Jews under Inquisition directives.

1290	Edict to expel Jews from England. Jews are given three months to settle their affairs. Sixteen thousand Jews are expelled from the realm, most finding refuge in France.

1304	Capitation tax at Segovia (29 August 29)

King Ferdinand issues this law, which requires payment from Jews for the death of Jesus.

We, Ferdinand, by the grace of God, king of Castile, etc., etc. To the Jews of the Jewry of Segovia, and all other Jewries of the towns and places within the said diocese, to whom this my order or a copy of it signed by a Notary Public, cometh, health and grace. Know ye, that the bishop and dean have complained to me, and say, that you will not pay nor account with them, nor to their order, the thirty deniers each of you have to give in memorial of the death of our Lord Jesus

Christ, when the Jews crucified him, and intreat me to order what I deem right. You are bound to pay the same in gold, and I consider it just that you pay the amount in the correct coin. Therefore I command that you give and pay the same, and annually make payment thereof to the bishop, dean, and chapter, aforesaid, or any of them, or the persons that receive for them, thirty deniers of the current coin, each of you well and truly, in such manner that there be no deduction therefrom. And should they require assistance for the fulfillment hereof, I command the councilors, magistrates, alcaldes, judges, and all other officers, or any of them, to whom this my order, or a copy of it duly authenticated, cometh, to accompany and assist them in such manner that what I command be fulfilled. Given at Palencia, 29th August 1304.

1306   Laws enacted at Paris (18 August).

Another confiscation decree in France.

Philip, by the grace of God king of the French, to the overseers of Jewish affairs in the bailliage of Orleans and to the bailiff of that area, greetings: We command you and each of you to have all lands, houses, vineyards and other possessions, which the Jews of the said bailliage held as their own at the time of their arrest, sold at public auction for a just price on our behalf. This should be done as quickly as possible. . . . You should cause all this to be announced throughout the entire bailliage without delay.

1313   Restrictions by the Provincial Council of Zamora (Spain)

A panoply of restrictions on vocation, social relations, religious practice, and so on.

Constitution: 1. Thirty days are allowed to all Jews that now do or hereafter may reside in our province, for the execution hereof. That in criminal, civil, and all other causes, they shall not oppose nor defend themselves by the privilege they have; saying that as no Jew was summoned against them in the cause, they cannot be condemned; nor may they claim that or any other privilege to the prejudice of the Christian faith, nor presume to obtain such similar privileges. Therefore we obtain, that in criminal, and all other causes, the testimony of the Jews against Jews shall be valid as heretofore; but not of a Jew against a Christian, nor, as is proper or just, shall his testimony be received. Those persons that desire to place Jews above Christians, and do not observe these and all other constitutions made against the Jews, whether they be ecclesiastic, layman, or secularized clergy; may the curse of Almighty God, of St. Peter and St. Paul, whose constitutions they are inclined to break, and the curse of St. Iago come upon them. The ordinary prelates shall compel and oblige them to observe this. Those persons who act contrary shall receive from the holy church the punishment the sin deserves. 2. Henceforth Jews shall hold no post or dignity from kings, or any secular prince, and within the aforesaid time they shall resign those they now hold. 3. They are not to be admitted into frequent association with Christians, lest from the intimacy, they adopt their errors which they do not understand. 4. That they do not serve as witnesses against Christians, nor claim as hitherto the benefit of the laws. 5. That no Christian women, either temporarily or otherwise, act as wet nurses, or rear their children. 6. They are not to appear in public, from the Wednesday of Passion Week until Saturday; and on Good Friday are to close their doors and windows the whole day, not to mock the sorrow of Christians for the passion. 7. The Jews and Jewesses wear an ostensible sign, that they may be distinguished and separate among Christians, which is right, practiced in other states. 8. Notwithstanding their learning and reputation, they are not to practice medicine with the Christians. 9. They are not to invite Christians to their feasts, that Christians do not eat with Jews; particular they are not to eat their meat or drink their wine. 10. They are annually to pay tithes on their landed property, and the houses they occupy, the same as Christians did before they belonged to Jews. 11. Synagogues that have been newly erected or enlarged, shall be restored to their former state between this date, and the next great festival of the resurrection; this term is peremptorily fixed, and if at its expiration the Jews have not executed it, the judges, alcaldes, communities, and universities of the cities, towns, and places where synagogues have been recently erected and elevated, are to fulfill and have this ordinance executed, in virtue of holy obedience under the penalty of Constitution 1. 12. They are not to practice usury, nor exact, nor take any interest from Christians, as is prohibited by the constitutions of Pope Clement V, enacted at the council of Vienne; and any person who acts contrary, or attempts to hide it, incurs the penalties ordained by the said council. 13. On Sundays and other Christian holidays, they are not to work publicly for themselves or other persons.

1320	"The Shepherd's Crusade" claims the lives of hundreds of Jews in France.
1348	The "Black Death" sparks anti-Jewish calumnies.
1348–1349	Antisemitic activities in Germany, sparked by the Crusades, reach their culmination. Jews are enclosed in special quarters, the ghettos.
1394	Expulsion of Jews from the Kingdom of France.
1410	The charge of desecrating the host is brought against the Jews of Segovia; torture and death follow.
1412	Legislation passed in Segovia prohibits Jews from engaging in handicrafts; dealing in wine, meat, and bread; or acting as brokers. Jews are to keep strictly to their quarters and all social intercourse with Christians is forbidden. (See 1304 "Capitation tax.)
1415	Pope Benedict XIII issues papal bull in Spain decreeing the prohibition of study of the Talmud and censorship of the Talmud.

Following the disputation at Tortosa, one of the Jewish-Christian debates that rabbis were compelled to attend, Pope Benedict XIII issues this bull.

1. To prohibit generally all persons, without distinction, publicly or privately, to hear, read, or teach the doctrines of the Talmud; ordering that within one month there be collected in the cathedral of every diocese, all copies that can be found of the Talmud . . . and every other writing that has directly or indirectly any relation to such doctrine; and the diocesans and inquisitors are to watch over the observance of this decree, visiting the Jews personally or by others, within their jurisdictions every two years, and punishing severely every delinquent. . . . 3. That no Jew may make, repair, or under any pretence have in his possession any crucifix, chalices, or sacred vessels, nor bind Christians' books in which the name of Jesus Christ or the most Holy Virgin Mary is written. Christians who give any of these articles to Jews . . . are to be excommunicated. 4. No Jew may exercise the office of judge, even in causes that may occur among his people. 5. All syn-

agogues recently built or repaired are to be closed. Where there is one, it may remain, provided it is not sumptious . . . but should it be proved that any one of the said synagogues has at any time been a church, it is immediately to be closed. 6. No Jew may be a physician, surgeon, druggist, shop- keeper, provision dealer, or marriage maker, or hold any other office, whereby he has to interfere in Christians' affairs; nor may Jewesses be midwives, or have Christian nurses; nor Jews have Christians to serve them, or sell to, or buy pro- visions of them, or join them at any banquet, or bathe in the same bath, or be stewards or agents to Christians, or learn any science, art, or trade in their schools. 7. That in every city, town, or village where there are Jews, barriers shall be ap- pointed for their residence apart from Christians. 8. That all Jews or Jewesses shall wear on their clothes a certain red and yellow sign, of the size and shape designated in the bull, men on the breast of the outward garment, and women in front. 9. That no Jew may trade, or make any contract; thus to avoid the frauds they practice, and the usuries they charge to Christians. 10. That all Jews and Jewesses converted to the Catholic faith . . . may inherit from their unconverted par- ents and relatives; declaring null any testament, codicil, last- will or donation INTER VITO they may make to prevent any of their property devolving to Christians. 11. That in all cities, towns, and villages, where there may be the number of Jews the diocesan may deem sufficient, three public ser- mons are to be preached annually; one on the second Sunday of Advent; one on the festival of the Resurrection; and the other on the Sunday when the Gospel, "And Jesus ap- proached Jerusalem," is chanted. All Jews above twelve years of age shall be compelled to attend to hear these ser- mons. The subjects are to be the first to show them that the true Messiah has already come, quoting the passages of the Holy Scripture and the Talmud that were argued in the dis- putation of Jerome of Santa Fe; the second to make them see that the heresies, vanities, and errors of the Talmud, prevent their knowing the truth; and the third, explaining to them the destruction of the Temple and the city of Jerusalem, and the perpetuity of their captivity, as our Lord Jesus Christ and the other prophets had prophesied. And at the end of these sermons this bull is to be read, that the Jews may not be ig- norant of any of its decrees.

1421   The *Wiener Gesera*, the expulsion of Jews from Austria.

1453   Muslim conquest of Constantinople.

1479   Spanish kingdom unites following the marriage of Isabella and Ferdinand.

1480   The Inquisition is established in Spain.

1483   Tomas de Torquemada is appointed to direct the Inquisition (inquisitor-general).

1492   Spanish Catholics defeat Muslims in the Iberian Peninsula. Catholic monarchs expel all Jews from the Spanish kingdom; the edict is signed on 31 March. By 30 July not a single Jew remains in the realm.

           Edict of Expulsion from Spain

           After consolidating Spain under their rule, Ferdinand and Isabella order the expulsion of the ancient Spanish Jewish community. An estimated 40,000–100,000 Jews are forced to leave Spain.

           Whereas, having been informed that in these kingdoms, there were some bad Christians who judaized and apostatized from our holy Catholic faith, the chief cause of which was the communication of Jews with Christians; at the Cotes we held in the city of Toledo in the year of 1480, we ordered the said Jews in all the cities, towns, and places in our kingdoms and dominions, to separate into Jewries and place apart, where they should live and reside, hoping by their separation alone to remedy the evil. Furthermore, we have sought and given orders, that inquisition should be made in our said kingdoms, which, as is known, for upwards of twelve years has been, and is done, whereby many guilty persons have been discovered, as is notorious. And as we are informed by the inquisitors, and many other religious, ecclesiastical, and secular persons, that great injury has resulted and does result, and it is stated, and appears to be, the participation, society, and communication they held and do hold with Jews, who it appears always endeavor in every way they can to subvert our holy Catholic faith, and to make faithful Christians withdraw and separate themselves therefrom, and attract and pervert them to their injurious opinions and belief, instructing them in the ceremonies and observances of their religion, holding meetings where they read and teach them what they are to believe and observe according to their religion; seeking to circumcise them and their children; giving them books from which they may read their prayers; and explaining to them the fasts they are to observe; assembling with them to read and to teach the histories of their law; notifying to them the festivals previous to their occurring, and instructing them what they are to do and observe thereon; giving and carrying to them from their houses unleavened bread and meat slaughtered with ceremonies; insulting them what they are to refrain from, as well as in food as in other matters, for the due observance of their religion, and persuaiding them all they can to profess and keep the law of Moses; giving them to understand, that except that, there is noother law or truth, which is proved by many declarations and confessions, as well of Jews themselves as of those who have been perverted and deceived by them, which has greatly rebounded to the injury, detriment, and opprobrium of our holy Catholic faith. Notwithstanding we were informed of the major part of this before, and we knew the certain remedy for all these injuries and inconveniences was to separate the said Jews from all communication with Christians, and banish them from all our kingdoms, yet we were desirous to content ourselves by ordering them to quit all the cities, towns, and places of Andalusia, where, it appears they had done greatest mischief, considering that would suffice, and that those other cities, towns and places would cease to do and commit the same. But as we are informed that neither that nor execution of some of the said Jews, who have been guilty of the said crimes and offenses against our holy Catholic faith, has been sufficient for a complete remedy to obviate and arrest so great an opprobrium and offence to the Catholic faith and religion. And as it is found and appears, that the said Jews, wherever they live and congregate, daily increase in continuing their wicked and injurious purposes; to afford them no further opportunity for insulting our holy Catholic faith, and those whom until now God has been pleased to preserve, as well as those who have fallen, but have amended and are brought back to our Holy Mother Church, which, according to the weakness of our human nature and the diabolical suggestion that continually wages war with us, may easily occur, unless the principal cause of it be removed, which is to banish the said Jews from our kingdoms. . . . Therefore we, by and with counsel and advice from some prelates and high noblemen of our kingdoms, and other learned persons of our council, having maturely deliberated thereon, resolve to order all the said Jews and Jewesses to quit our kingdoms, and never to return or come back to them, or any of them. Therefore we command this our edict to be issued, whereby we command all Jews and Jewesses, of whatever age they may be, that live, reside, and dwell in our said kingdoms and dominions, as well natives as those who are not, who in any manner or for any cause may have come to dwell therein, that by the end of the month of July next, of the present year 1492, they depart from all our said kingdoms and dominions, with their sons, daughters, man-servants, maid-servants, and Jewish attendants, both great and small, of whatever age they may be; and they shall not presume to return to, nor reside therein, or in any part of them, either as residents, travelers, or in any other manner whatever, under pain that if they do not perform and execute the same, and are found to reside in our kingdoms and dominions, or should in any manner live therein, they incur the penalty of death, and confiscation of all their property to our treasury, which penalty they incur by the act itself, without further process, declaration, or sentence. And we command and forbid any person or persons of our said kingdoms, of whatsoever rank, station, or condition they may be, that they do not presume publicly or secretly to receive, shelter, protect, or defend any Jew or Jewess, after the said term of the end of July, under pain of losing all their property, vassals, castles, and other possessions; and furthermore forfeit to our treasury any sums they have, or receive from us. And that the said Jews and Jewesses during the said time, until the end of the said month of July, may be the better able to dispose of themselves, their property, and estates, we hereby take and receive them under our security, protection, and royal safeguard; and insure to them and their properties, that during the said period, until the said day, the end of the said month of July, they may travel in safety, and may enter, sell, barter, and alienate all their moveable and immoveable property, and freely dispose thereof at their pleasure. And that during the said time, no harm, injury, or wrong whatever shall be done to their persons or properties contrary to justice, under the pains those persons incur and are liable to, that violate our royal safeguard. We likewise grant permission and authority to the said Jews and Jewesses, to export their wealth and property, by sea or land, from our said kingdoms and dominions, provided they do not take away gold, silver, money, or other articles prohibited by the laws of our kingdoms, but in merchandise and goods that are not prohibited. And we command all the justices of our kingdoms, that they cause the whole of the above herein contained to be observed and fulfilled, and that they do not act contrary hereto; and they afford all necessary favor, under pain of being deprived of office, and the confiscation of all their property to our exchequer.

1496–1497   Expulsion from Portugal; mass forced conversion.

1500–   Series of expulsions from cities and principalities in
1600   Germany and Austria.

Austrian Emperor Ferdinand I Johannes Purgoldt's law book.

Book VIII, Article 102. In all respects the Jews shall be different, in their dwellings, clothes, and other things. Their houses shall be separated from those of the Christians, and all of them shall be together, and ropes shall be drawn across the streets. Their clothes shall also be separate from the clothes of the Christians; males shall not wear kogeln but higher hats of felt. Men shall also wear boots, and go without wooden shoes; the women with wound veils and with wide windows on their cloaks, and without wooden shoes.

1551   *Austrian law enacted by Ferdinand I at Vienna (1 August).*

We, Ferdinand, by the grace of God King in Hungary and Bohemia etc. It has come to us frequently and credibly to what an extent the Jews, whom we have mercifully admitted and permitted to dwell and live in a number of places of our principalities and lands, practice indecent intolerable usury, damage and injury on our Christian people and subjects; that furthermore they also indulge in many other ways in all sorts of evil, scandalous and vicious actions to the disgrace, defamation and disparagement of our sacred Christian name, belief, and religion. These scandalous evil actions are said to flow in good part from the fact that the Jews in numerous localities dwell and move about among the Christians without any distinguishing marks and without any difference in clothes and costume and thus cannot be distinguished from Christians nor recognized as Jews. Therefore, it is due and proper to us as a Christian governing Lord and Prince, by virtue of our office, to take appropriate account of this. . . . Hence, we order that there be observed a distinction between Christians and Jews in clothing and costume and, as is done in numerous countries, the Jews be marked and recognized by a certain sign. . . . Thus we decree and order . . . that all Jews, settled in our hereditary principalities and lands or now and then sojourning in them on business, shall begin within one month from the publication of this our general decree to use and wear publicly an uncovered a sign, by which they are to be distinguished and recognizable from Christians: namely on the outer coat or dress over the left breast a yellow ring, circumference and diameter of the circle as herein prescribed and not narrower nor smaller, made of yellow cloth (notwithstanding any previous enactments or exemptions which are hereby revoked).

1542 Martin Luther publishes "Concerning the Jews and Their Lives." In it he renews old charges of the past, perpetuating patterns that have become familiar during the Reformation: Jews are usurers; they are parasites on Christian Society; Jews consort with Satan. He advocates burning synagogues and expelling Jews from their territories.

1555 Pope Paul IV orders that Jews be confined to ghettos.

1569 Expulsion from Papal States.

1648–1649 *Gezeroth Tah v'Tat.* Tens of thousands of Jews are massacred at the hands of Ukrainian leader Bogdan Chmielnitski.

1670 Jews are expelled from Vienna.

1600– Restrictions on Jews in many Muslim lands, including
1700 Yemen.

In this document, the Yemeni Imam al–Mahda excoriates the Jewish leaders in Yemen and exhorts them to convert to Islam. This speech, as related by a Jewish historian, follows the plundering of Jewish homes by Yemeni forces. A later Imam expels the Jews from Yemen to Mauza in the region of Tihama.

O you filthy, despicable and indolent people! I know the wickedness and evil which you have harbored in your heart against us since the day you came to our land. You think evil of our kingdom and our prophet. You are anxiously awaiting the time of our visitation and downfall, with the advent of your false-messiah. . . . You have sinned in the times of Moses your prophet, until your God was furious with you and He dispersed your fathers from His land and scattered them in all the countries until this very day. Yet you did not hearken to the Lord of your prophets, nor did you obey Him. You also dealt deceitfully with our prophet Muhammad, the seal of the prophets, and you betrayed him. . . . Do you think that your kingdom will be reestablished, so that you may dominate all the world and corrupt it as your fathers did? It is better for you to hearken to our words and believe in our prophet, not to deny him, so that we may become one nation. [If you don't obey] you shall risk your lives, and you shall descend to the terrible fire of Hell, the place where Jews and all the rebels and unbelievers in our prophet and his teaching go. But [if you obey] you shall be worthy of dwelling in the land, enjoying life full of pleasure, peace and tranquility. Moreover, you shall inherit a good portion in paradise, where you shall delight in abundance of marvelous orchards, streams of honey and buttermilk, with the beautiful maidens. . . .

1700–
1800   Edict against the Jews (Rome).

This excerpt illustrates the early modern church's restrictions on Jewish behavior, just one of a range of legal restrictions.

Article 31: Jews and Christians are forbidden to play, eat, drink, hold intercourse, or exchange confidences of ever so trifling a nature with one another. Such shall not be allowed in palaces, houses, or vineyards, in the streets, in taverns, in neither shops nor any other place. Nor shall the tavern-keeper, inn-keeper, nor shop proprietor permit any converse between Jews and Christians. The Jews who offend in this matter shall incur the penalties of a fine of 10 scudi and imprisonment; Christians, a similar fate and corporal punishment.

1700   Johann Eisenmenger publishes *Entdeckes Judentum* (*Judaism Unmasked*), an "encyclopedia of antisemitism."

1753   The "Jew Bill" (Jewish Naturalization Bill) is passed by Britain's Parliament but repealed that year.

1760   Founding of the Board of Deputies of British Jews, among the first Jewish communal organizations in modern times.

1762   Petition dismissed by Rhode Island court.

Jews and other religious minorities often face inequality before the law in the American colonies.

The petition of Messrs. Aron Lopez & Isaac Elizar, Persons professing the Jewish Religion, praying that they may be naturalized on an Act of Parliament made in the thirteenth year of his late Majesty's Reign, George the Second, having been duly considered, and also the act of Parliament therein referr'd to; this Court are unanimously of Opinion that the said Act of Parliament was wisely designed for increasing the number of Inhabitants in the plantations, but this Colony being already so full of People that many of his Majesty's good Subjects, born within the same have removed & settled in Nova Scotia & other Places, cannot come within the Intention of the said act. Farther by the Charter granted to this Colony it appears that the free & quiet Enjoyment of the Christian Religion and a Desire of propagating the same were the principal Views with which the Colony was settled, & by a Law made & passed in the year 1663, no Person who does not profess the Christian Religion can be admitted free of this Colony. This Court, therefore, unanimously dismiss the said Petition as absolutely inconsistent with the first principles upon which the Colony was founded & a Law of the same now in full Force.

1782   Russian central authorities rule that burghers and merchants must reside in towns and not in villages, the first step to banish Jews from villages.

Toleranzpatent issued by Austria's Emperor Josef II.

1789	Abbé Gregoire in France publishes *Sur la Regeneration Physique, Morale, et Politique des Juifs.*
1790	Enactment of the Bill of Rights in the United States; the First Amendment to the Constitution guarantees freedom of religion, prohibiting the "establishment" of religion and protecting the "free exercise" of religion.
1791	Jews of France are emancipated during the Enlightenment.
	The Pale of Settlement is established in Russia by decrees (beginning in 1786) of Catherine II; all Jews must live in this geographical area.
1700–1900	Some writers characterize Jews as a "race," and the myth of the "Aryan race" is developed.
1802	Alexander I ascends to the Russian czar's throne with the establishment of a special committee to study the "Jewish question."
1803–1873	Chronology of Romanian laws against Jews.

The Romanian Constitution of 1866 limits Jewish civil rights, stating "only Christians may obtain naturalization" (Article VIII). These laws limit Jewish economic rights and expel Jews.

1803: Alexander Monize, ruler of Moldavia, forbids Jews to rent farms. 1804: Alexander Monize forbids Jews to buy farm products. 1817: Code Cahmachi forbids Jews of Romania to acquire real property. 1818: Code of John Caradja of Wallachia repeats the ancient church laws against allowing Jews to witness against Christians. 1819: Code of Kallimachor of Moldavia gives civil rights to Jews, who, however, may not own land. 1831: Fundamental law of Moldavia, chapter 3, section 94, orders all Jews and their occupations to be registered; Jews not of proved usefulness are to be expelled. 1839:

Tax of sixty plasters per annum placed on Jews of Moldavia. 1850: No Jew is allowed to enter Romania unless possessed of 5,000 plasters and of known occupation. 1861: Circulation of Romanian ministry preventing Jews from being innkeepers in rural districts. 1864: Jews are excluded from being advocates/lawyers. 1868: Jews are excluded from medical profession. 1869: Jews are not allowed to be tax farmers in rural communes. 1869: Jews are prevented from being apothecaries, except where there are no Romanian apothecaries. 1873: Law forbids Jews to sell spiritual liquors in rural districts (Julius, Rifkind, Weill, and Gaer).

1814–1815   The Congress of Vienna instructs the German states to grant citizenship rights to Jews.

1835   Delineation of the Pale of Settlement (April).

In 1791, Catherine the Great issues a decree barring Jews from certain areas in the Russian Empire. The area in which Jews are allowed to live becomes known as the Pale of Settlement. Nicholas I officially delineates the Pale of Settlement in April 1835. It is abolished in 1917.

3. A permanent residence is permitted to the Jews; (a) In the provinces: Grodno, Vilna, Volhynia, Podolia, Minsk, Ekaterinoslav. (b) In the districts: Bessarabia, Bialystok. 4. In addition to the provinces and districts listed in the preceding section, a permanent residence is permitted to the Jews, with the following restrictions: (a) in Kiev province, with the exception of the provincial capital, Kiev; (b) in Kherson province, with the exception of the city of Nikolaev; (c) in Tavaria province, with the exception of the city of Sebatopol; (d) in the Mogilev and Vitebsk provinces, except in the villages; (e) in Chernigov and Poltava provinces, but not within the government and Cossack villages, where the expulsion of the Jews has already been completed; (f) in Courland province permanent residence is permitted only to those Jews who have been registered until the present date with their families in census lists. Entry for the purpose of settlement is forbidden to Jews from other provinces; (g) in Lithland province, in the city of Riga and the suburb Shlok, with the same restrictions as those applying in Courland province . . . 11. Jews who have gone abroad without a legal exit-permit are deprived of Russian citizenship and not permitted to return to Rus-

sia. 12. Within the general area of settlement and in every place where the Jews are permitted permanent residence, they are allowed not only to move from place to place and to settle in accordance with the general regulations, but also to acquire real estate of all kinds with the exception of inhabited estates, the ownership of which is strictly forbidden to Jews. . . . 23. Every Jew must be registered according to the law in one of the legal estates of the realm. Any Jew not complying with this regulation will be treated as a vagrant.

1840 The Damascus affair, a charge of "ritual murder."

1844 Karl Marx publishes his essay "On the Jewish Question," making the identification between Jews and capitalism, much to the discredit of the Jews.

1858– The Mortara affair in Italy, the kidnapping of a Jewish
1859 child, sanctioned by the papacy.

1862 General Ulysses S. Grant, at the time a Union commander, issues "General Orders Number 11" on 17 December, expelling Jews "as a class" from the territory under his jurisdiction. (President Lincoln revokes this order a few weeks later, primarily because of constitutional strictures against any agency of the federal government singling out any group for special treatment.)

General Grant blames the Jews in his department (Kentucky, Tennessee, and Mississippi) for illegal cotton trading during the U.S. Civil War. Only a handful of Jews are involved in the trade, but Grant expels all Jews from the area under his control.

The Jews, as a class violating every regulation of trade established by the Treasury Department and also department orders, are hereby expelled from the department within 24 hours from receipt of this order. Post commanders will see to it that all of this class of people be furnished passes and required to leave, and any one returning after such notification will be arrested. . . . No passes will be given these people to visit headquarters for the purpose of making personal application of trade permits.

1871   Canon August Rohling, a professor at the Imperial University of Prague, publishes *Talmudje* (*The Talmud Jew*), a book based on the theme of ritual murder, claiming that Jews are authorized by their religion to destroy the lives, honor, and property of all Gentiles.

1873   German journalist Wilhelm Marr publishes the pamphlet *Der Sieg des Judentums Uber das Germametum* (*The Victory of the Jews over Germandom*). Marr is credited for coining the term *antisemitism*. In 1879 he introduces the *Antisemiten-Liga* (League of Antisemites), the first organization anywhere to carry such a title.

1877   The Saratoga Springs Hotel bars a prominent Jewish banker from staying there, one of the first instances of social antisemitism in the United States.

1879   Antisemitic articles by H. von Treitschke.

1881   Assassination of Czar Alexander II by revolutionary terrorists, one of whom is a Jew. Reactionary newspapers immediately begin whipping up antisemitic sentiment, and the result is a wave of pogroms in some 160 cities throughout Russia.

1882   The 1881 assassination of the czar is used as the pretext for the passage of the May Laws (Russia, 3 May), severe anti-Jewish economic legislation.

          A two-year spate of pogroms began in Russia in 1881. Alexander III, following the policy of "isolation and assimilation," enacts the May Laws.

          1. As a temporary measure and until the revision of the laws regulating their status, Jews are forbidden to settle hereafter outside of cities and towns. Exception is made with regard to Jewish villages already in existence where the Jews are engaged in agriculture. 2. Until further order all contracts for the mortgaging or renting of real estate situated outside of cities and towns to a Jew, shall be of no effect. Equally void is any power of attorney granted to a Jew for the administration or disposition of property of the above-indicated nature. 3. Jews are forbidden to do business on Sundays and Christian

holidays; the laws compelling Christians to close their places of business on those days will be applied to Jewish places of business. 4. The above measures are applicable only in the governments situated within the pale of settlement.

The May Laws bring discrimination to the Russian military when the tsarist minister of war issues the following regulation to decrease the number of Jewish doctors in the military because doctors possess the rights of army officers, a privilege otherwise unattainable for Jews.

First, to limit the number of Jewish physicians . . . in the Military Department to five percent of the general number of medical men. Second, to stop appointing Jews on medical service in the military districts of Western Russia, and to transfer the surplus over and above five percent to the Eastern districts. Third, to appoint Jewish physicians only in those contingents of the army in which the budget calls for at least two physicians, with the proviso that the second physician must be a Christian. It is necessary to stop the constant growth of the number of physicians of the Mosaic [Jewish] persuasion in the Military Department, in view of their deficient conscientiousness in discharging their duties and their unfavorable influence upon the sanitary service in the army.

A chronology of antisemitic laws in Russia in the late nineteenth century includes the following issued under Alexander III and his successor, Nicholas II.

1882: An order by the governor-general of St. Petersburg shuts down the business of fourteen apothecaries. 1886: A senatorial decision sets forth that no Jew can be elected to a vacancy on the board of an orphan asylum. 1886: A circular of the minister of finance and a senatorial decree introduce rigorous restrictions concerning Jews engaged in the liquor traffic, permitting them to sell liquor only from their own homes and owned property. 1887: A senatorial resolution states that Jews who graduated from a university outside Russia do not belong to the privileged class possessing the universal right of residence by virtue of their diplomas and therefore must not settle outside the Pale of Settlement. 1887: An imperial sanction prohibits Jews from settling in Finland. 1889: Jews must obtain a special permit from the minister of justice to be elected to the Bar. 1891: An order forbids non-Christians from acquiring real estate in the provinces of Akmolinski, Semirietchensk, Uralsk, and Turgai. 1892: In accordance with a proposal of the Imperial Council, the mining industry in Turkestan is closed to Jews. 1894: The minister of the interior decrees that Jews that have graduated from a veterinary college are no longer to be admitted to the service of the state. 1895: A senatorial decision asserts that rabbis possess no right of residence beyond the Pale of Settlement. 1895: A circular of the minister of war instructs the Cossack authorities in the Caucasus and the Don Territory that Jews visiting the Don, Kuban, and Terek provinces for the sake of the medicinal waters are to be turned back (Julius, Rifkind, Weill, and Gaer).

1883   *L'Antisemitique*, a French antisemitic weekly begins publishing. It continues for more than a year.

1886   Eduard Drumont's book *La France Juive*, arguing that Jews are an inferior race, goes through over 100 printings.

1894   The trial, conviction, and sentencing of Captain Alfred Dreyfus by a French court. Alfred Dreyfus is retried and pardoned in 1899 and fully acquitted in 1906.

1897   The convening of the first Zionist Congress in Basel, Switzerland.

1898   Émile Zola, responding to the Dreyfus affair, publishes *J'accuse*.

1903   Czar Nicholas II makes no secret of his membership in the antisemitic Black Hundreds that organized pogroms in 1903 and more severe ones two years later.

1905   The antisemitic forgery *The Protocols of the Elders of Zion* is published by the press of the czar under the auspices of the czar's secret police.

1905   A twentieth-century Yemenite version of the Pact of Umar is enacted.

        This decree, modeled on the original seventh-century Pact of Umar, stipulates the nature of relations between Muslims and non-Muslims in Muslim lands.

This is a decree which the Jews must obey as commanded. They are obliged to observe everything in it. They are forbidden to disobey it. . . . That is that these Jews are guaranteed protection upon payment of the jizya by each adult male. . . . In this way their blood is spared, and they are brought in the pact of protection. They may not avoid it. It is incumbent upon each individual to pay it. . . . They are not to assist each other against a Muslim. They may not build their houses higher than Muslim homes. They shall not crowd them in their street. They may not turn them away from their watering places. They may not belittle the Islamic religion, nor curse any of the prophets. They shall not mislead a Muslim in matters pertaining to his religion. They may not ride on saddles, but only sit sidesaddle. They may not wink or point to the nakedness of Muslim. They may not display their Torah except in their synagogues. Neither shall they raise their voices when reading, nor blow their shofars loudly. Rather a muffled voice will suffice. . . . It is their duty to recognize the superiority of the Muslim and to accord him honor.—Sulayman b. Yihya Habshush, Eshkolot Mererot

1911   A conference of associations of Russian nobles demands that Russia be rid of Jews and proceeds to call forth "experts" who claim that Jews need Christian blood for the observance of their religion.

1911– 1913   Trial of Mendel Beilis in Russia (Kiev) on a charge of "ritual murder."

1913   Leo Frank, a Jewish factory manager in Atlanta, Georgia, is arrested and later convicted on flimsy evidence of the murder of one of his female employees. In 1915 he is abducted from his jail cell and lynched by a mob. (Seventy years later an eyewitness to the crime comes forward and exonerates him.)

1916   Madison Grant, paralleling the pseudoscientific themes popularized in European antisemitica, publishes *The Passing of the Great Race,* which condemns the Jews for mongrelizing the United States.

1919   The first appearance of a U.S. version of *The Protocols of the Elders of Zion*. The *Dearborn Independent*, a magazine owned and published by industrialist Henry Ford, launches an antisemitic propaganda campaign unprecedented in the United States.

Pogroms in the Ukraine and Poland; abolition of Jewish community organizations and institutions in Russia.

1920   The Nazi Party in Germany issues its twenty-five-point program that asserts that no Jew could be a member of the *Volk*, the German people. In the same year, the German Nationalist's People's Party takes a formal stand against "the predominance of Jewry in government and public life." *The Protocols*, just translated into German, sells an astounding 120,000 copies.

1924   The Ku Klux Klan, enjoying a spectacular revival in the United States, reaches its height with 4 million members.

The U.S. Immigration Act of 1924 establishes a national origins quota system that discriminates against Eastern European—largely Jewish—immigration.

1924–   Adolph Hitler writes *Mein Kampf*, in which he develops
1925   his anti-Jewish ideas into an all-embracing schema.

1930   The South African Quota Act severely restricts immigration of Jews to South Africa.

Fearing an influx of Jewish immigrants, the South African government institutes a quota policy in which immigrants are placed in one of two tiers. Those from some European countries are allowed unfettered immigration, whereas Jews are limited to extremely small numbers or banned entirely. When fascism arises in Europe in the 1930s, additional Jews seek to emigrate to South Africa, including many from Germany, who would ordinarily be considered immigrants from a more "desirable" country.

1930s   Father Charles Coughlin, the "radio priest," reaches millions of Americans with his openly antisemitic message. His magazine, *Social Justice,* reprints the *Protocols* with Coughlin's commentary.

Iraqi government enacts laws marginalizing Jews.

As anti-Jewish agitation increases during the 1930s in Europe, the Middle East, and North Africa, the Iraqi government takes steps to marginalize Jews. Jewish employees of state industries are dismissed, and limitations are placed on the number of Jewish students allowed in secondary and post-secondary schools. In 1935, Zionist activity in Iraq is declared illegal. In 1941, a pogrom in Baghdad results in the deaths of 900 Jews. The following report, prepared by an official at a Jewish school in Baghdad on 3 October 1934, illustrates the beginning of this trend.

I am pained to inform you that for the last few months a movement of hostility against the Jews has been taking shape around us and is becoming more accentuated from day to day. It began with the more and more systematic dismissal of Jewish employees from government service. After tens of lower and middle senior employees, the secretary of the Ministry of Public Works and the assistant Director of Posts and Telegraph, both Jews, were dismissed after so many others had been previously sacrificed. These continual dismissals have greatly alarmed our Community, which has met to study the situation and see in what measure it can react. Some have advised a mass protest; others have suggested the need to still remain silent. No solution was adopted and the situation remains unchanged. Furthermore, in secondary and superior schools, *a numerus clausus* has been established for Jewish pupils, whose number may not exceed 10 percent of the non-Jewish students, even though the Jewish population of Baghdad (80,000) is one fourth of the total population. Jewish businessmen would have sent funds to Palestine with the aim of undertaking certain commercial transactions. These transfers of money have encountered diverse opposition and multiple hindrances. The Jewish newspapers from Palestine and Europe have been placed on the index and their entry into Iraq is forbidden. On the list is *The Jewish Chronicle, l'Univers Israelite,* and the *Paix et Droit.* The result of this is that we are ignorant of everything going on in the Jewish world.

1933	Adolf Hitler comes to power in Germany as chancellor on 30 January, becoming the *führer* (leader) in 1934. German decree authorizes the elimination of Jews from the civil service. In the next decade, over 400 anti-Jew laws and decrees would be passed.
1935– m1945	Nazi era laws are enacted, including the Reich Citizenship Law, which codifies that German citizenship is not a matter of an individual right but derives from membership in the German *Volk*. The same year the Nuremberg laws, which define legally the National Socialist antisemitic agenda, are passed, legitimizing racialist antisemitism and transmuting "the purity of German blood" into a legal category.

The following laws demonstrate Nazi measures to cut off the Jew from German society, and throughout Europe and other areas conquered by Germany and the Axis powers. Similar laws are forced upon or appropriated by other countries during World War II. These laws begin with loss of citizenship and end with genocide.

The Reich Citizenship Law (September 15, 1935) Article II: (1) A citizen of the Reich is only that subject, who is of German or kindred blood and who, through his conduct, shows that he is both desirous and fit to serve faithfully the German people and Reich. (2) The right to citizenship is acquired by the granting of Reich citizenship papers. (3) Only the citizen of the Reich enjoys full political rights in accordance with the provisions of the Laws. The Fuehrer and Reichs Chancellor Adolf Hitler The Reichs Minister of the Interior Frick

Law for the Protection of German Blood And German Honor (September 15, 1935) Thoroughly convinced by the knowledge that the purity of German blood is essential for the further existence of the German people and . . . by the inflexible will to safeguard the German nation for the entire future. The Reichs Parliament (Reichstag) has resolved upon the following law unanimously which is promulgated herewith: Section 1. Marriages between Jews and nationals of German or kindred blood are forbidden. Section 2. Relations outside marriage between Jews and nationals of German or kindred blood are forbidden. Section 3. Jews will not be permitted to employ female nationals of German or kindred blood in their household. . . . Section 4.1. Jews are forbidden to hoist the Reich's . . . national flag and to present the colors of the Reich. Section 4.2. On the other hand they are permitted to present the Jewish colors. The exercise of this authority is protected by the State.

First Regulation to the Reich's Citizenship Law (Germany, 1935) Article 2: (2) An individual of mixed Jewish blood is one who is descended from one or two grandparents who, racially, were full Jews, insofar that he is not a Jew according to Section 2 of Article 5. Full-blooded Jewish grandparents are those who belonged to the Jewish religious community. Article 4: (1) A Jew cannot be a citizen of the Reich. He has no right to vote in political affairs, he cannot occupy a public office. (2) Jewish officials will retire as of 31 December 1935. If these officials served at the front in the World War, either for Germany or her allies, they will receive in full, until they reach the age limit, the pension to which they were entitled according to last received wages; they will, however, not advance in seniority. Article 5: (1) A Jew is anyone who descended from at least three grandparents who were racially full Jews. (2) A Jew is also one who descended from two full Jewish parents, if: (a) He belonged to the Jewish religious community at the time this law was issued or who joined the community later. (b) He was married to a Jewish person, at the time the law was issued, or married one subsequently. (c) He is the offspring from a marriage with a Jew, in the sense of section 1, which was contracted after the Law for the protection of German blood and German honor became effective (RGB1, I, page 1146 of 15 Sept. 1935). (d) He is the offspring of an extramarital relationship, with a Jew, according to section 1, and will be born out of wedlock after July 31, 1936. . . . The Fuehrer and Reichs Chancellor Adolf Hitler The Reich Minister of the Interior Frick The Deputy of the Fuehrer R. Hess Reich Minister without Portfolio.

Decree governing the Introduction of the Nuremberg Racial Laws in the Province Of Austria (May 20, 1938) On the basis of Article II of the Law of March 13, 1938, governing the Reunion of Austria with the German Reich (Reichsgesetzblatt I page 237), the following is decreed: Section 3. The exclusion of Jews from public offices which they occupy at the time this decree goes into effect will be specially regulated.

Fourth Decree Relating to the Reich Citizenship Law (July 25, 1938) Section 1. Licenses (Bestallungen) of Jewish physicians terminate as of September 30, 1938. Section 3. (1) A Jew whose licenses have terminated and to whom a permit in accordance with section 2 has not been granted are forbidden to practice the art of healing. (2) A Jew who has been granted a permit in accordance with section 2 may, aside from his wife and his children born in wedlock, treat only Jews.

Fifth Decree Governing Reich Citizenship Law (September 27, 1938) Article I: Elimination of Jews from Corps of Lawyers: Section 1. The profession of lawyer is closed to Jews. In so far as Jews are still lawyers they are eliminated from the Corps of Lawyers in accordance with the following regulations: a) In the old Reich territory: The licenses of Jewish lawyers are to be revoked as of November 30, 1938; b) In the Province of Austria: Jewish lawyers are to be stricken from the list of lawyers at the latest by December 31, 1938, by order of the Reich Minister of Justice.

Decree Concerning the Utilization of Jewish Property (December 3, 1938) Article I: Business Enterprises: Section 1. The owner of a Jewish business enterprise (Third Decree of June 14, 1938, under the Reich's Citizenship Law Reichsgesetzblatt 1938, Part I, page 627) can be ordered to sell or dispose of his business within a fixed period of time. Certain conditions can be applied to this regulation. Section 2. Par. 1. For Jewish business enterprises whose owners have been compelled, in accordance with Section 1 of this Decree, to sell or to liquidate the business, a Trustee can be appointed for continuing temporarily the business and for effecting the sale or liquidation. . . . Par. 4. The cost of the administration by the Trustee has to be paid by the owner of the business. Article II: Farming and Forestry Real Estate and Other Property: Section 6. A Jew can be ordered to sell within a fixed period, in whole or in part, his agricultural or forestry business, his other agricultural or forestry property, his other real property or other parts of his property. Such an order can be made under certain conditions.

Regulations for the Execution of the Decree Concerning the Utilization of Jewish Property: Article I: 2 (1) The "Decree concerning the utilization of Jewish property" alters the former legal status, especially in that the elimination of Jews from Jewish concerns, from the ownership of real estate, and from other important property assets, can also be effected by compulsion Article II: Elimination of Jews from Business Concerns: Section 7. If in the case of a permit for the desemitization of a business concern conditions are also made regarding the transfer of shares of stock and other securities, a special permit according to Section 12 of the Decree is not necessary. Article III: Elimination of Jews from the Ownership of Real Estate: 1 (1) Regarding the elimination of Jews from the ownership of real estate, the Decree of December 3,

1938, establishes two important new rules, namely: In section 7 the general prohibition against Jews acquiring real estate, rights similar to real estate and rights in real estate (mortgages, "Grundschulden," etc.); and in Section 8 the obligation upon Jews to apply for a permit to enable them to dispose of their real estate or rights similar to real estate. 9. I [the Minister of Internal Affairs] have expressed in general my approval to the Reich's Minister of Finance that Jewish real property taken instead of cash as payment of the "Jewish atonement fine" will be transferred to the ownership of the Reich.

Implementation Order No. 1 for the Regulation of October 26, 1939 for the Introduction of Forced Labor for the Jewish Population in the Government-General (German Occupied Poland, December 11, 1939) Pursuant to S 2 of the Regulation for the introduction of Forced Labor for the Jewish population of October 26, 1939 (Verordnungsbl. G.G.P., p6), I order the following: 1. As from January 1, 1940, it is forbidden for all Jews within the Government-General of the Occupied Polish Territories to move their place of residence or lodging, without the written permission of the local German Administrative Authority, beyond the limits of the community of their place of residence, or to cross the border of this community and to move away after giving up their permanent residence or lodging. 2. All Jews moving into, or transferred into, the Government-General are required to register immediately with the mayor of the locality when they have taken up residence, but no later than 24 hours after entering the Government-General, and to inform the local Judenrat of their presence. The Judenrat will record this information in writing and submit it to the Mayor on the Monday of each week, against written acknowledgment. 3. After having obtained accommodation, all Jews referred to in S 2 must comply with the requirements of S 1. 4. All Jews within the Government-General are forbidden to enter or use pathways, streets and public squares between the hours of 9:00 P.M. and 5:00 A.M. without written authority specifying the times and places, issued by the local German authorities. Orders by local German authorities containing more severe restrictions are not affected by this regulation. 5. The restrictions of S 4 do not apply in cases of public or personal emergency. 6. Jews contravening the regulations under S 1 through 4 will be sent immediately to prolonged hard forced labor. This does not affect punishment provided by other orders. 7. The orders under S 1 through 6 do not apply to Jews who have moved under the provisions permitting them to do so in accordance with the law setting out an "Agreement between the German Reich Government and the Government of the U.S.S.R. concerning the transfer of the Ukrainian and Byelorussian population out of the area belonging to the Zone of Interest of the German Reich." 8. The public announcement of these instructions will be carried out by the Mayors according to orders by the sub-district Commander (Kreishauptmann) or the City commander (Stadthauptmann). The Judenraete will be instructed by the Mayors. 9. These orders are effective immediately.—Higher SS and Police Leader (Hoeherer SS-und Polizeifuehrer) in the Government-General of the Occupied Polish Territories Krueger SS Obergruppenfuehrer.

German Regulation for the Use of Railroad by Jews in the Government-General (Poland and surrounding occupied areas, January 26, 1940) 1. The use of the Railroad by Jews is prohibited until further notice. 2. This does not apply to journeys for which there is an order in writing from the Governor General, his office, or of a District Commander. Policies Concerning Treatment of Jews in the Government-General (April 6, 1940) In order to preserve uniformity in dealing with all Jewish affairs, it is necessary to reach an understanding concerning the basis on which our future work will be built up. On taking over the department of Jewish affairs in the Office of the Governor General, I am therefore turning to the advisers in this field and would like to outline briefly the attitude that will be appropriate in confrontation with Jewry. This will at the same time indicate the targets at which we must aim (Basic Working Principles 1–9). These working principles are roughly as follows: 1. Spatial separation between Poles and Jews. In the decision whether a person is a Jew or a non-Jew, the sole essential factors are his racial origins and blood and his acceptance of Judaism (through marriage of a non-Jew with a Jew): not simply membership in a religious community. 2. A full Jew (Volljude)—unlike in the Nuremberg Laws—is a person who has two or more Jewish grandparents or is married to a Jew and does not dissolve this connection. 3. As a matter of principle Jews are to work for Jews; for instance, only Jews are to be used for the building of accommodations for Jews. 4. The Jews are to establish their own social insurance system and are not to pay contributions to non-Jewish insurance schemes, nor make claims on non-Jewish facilities. 5. The property and funds of such Jewish organizations will be under the protection of the German Administration. The same applies to Jewish welfare establishments. 6.

It should be considered whether, as a temporary measure, the Polish Red Cross may be used by Jews if Jews had up to now supported and helped this institution. 7. All measures must be directed at the target that later the whole of Jewry will be concentrated in a specific district and in one area of Jewish settlement, as a self-supporting society under the control of the Reich. 8. Preparation of a plan for the resettlement of 400,000 Jews who will enter the area of the Government-General after May 1, 1940. 9. Creation of archives on Polish Jews and Jews in general (newspaper reports, regulations, laws, culture, races, health care, etc.) In addition you are requested to answer the following questions, as far as possible, in accordance with the situation in your district:—In which districts and which sub-districts do the largest number of Jews live at the present time, and what percentage do they form of the general population in those areas (with maps, if possible)?—Which areas are the least valuable economically as regards the nature of the soil? How large are they? Where are they situated (map)?—Which areas are least closely populated, how large are they, how many people live there at the present time? Why are they so sparsely populated? What nationalities live there (numbers!)? To what extent would it be possible to resettle the non-Jewish nationalities? Is the area suited for a purely Jewish colony?—What property is still in Jewish hands? Where is the Jewish property and of what does it consist? What additional means would have to be supplied for the settlement of the 400,000 Jews who will arrive here after May 1, 1940?—What proposals can you make for the accommodation of the deportees? What possibilities of work are there for the deportees in the various districts (preferably in public services)? What temporary arrangements—camps, etc.—are still available at the present time?—What has been done up to now in order to prevent as far as possible the likelihood of infection or disease being passed on to non-Jews? What is the position concerning health and hygiene among the Jews in the area of the Government-General, particularly where living conditions are cramped and close contact between Jews and non-Jews cannot be avoided? In addition, I request a report on all plans for work and the dispatch of a record of all measures taken up to now by your office in any Jewish affairs. Dr. Gottong Head of Department for Jewish Affairs Government-General.

Anti-Jewish laws in Vichy-controlled France (during World War II) Law of 3 October 1940: Article I. For the purposes of the present law, a Jew is one who has three grandparents of the Jewish race; or who has two grandparents of that race, if his or her spouse is Jewish. Article II. The availability and exercise of the following public functions and duties are denied to Jews: Head of State, member of the government, the Conseil d'Etat, the national council of the Legion of Honor, the Cour de Cassation . . ., the courts of appeal, courts of first jurisdiction, justices of the peace, etc. Law of 4 October 1940: Foreign nationals of the Jewish race may, from the promulgation date of the present law, be interned in special camps by a decision of the prefect of the department of their residence. A commission charged with the organization and administration of these camps shall be constituted within the Ministry of the Interior. . . . Foreign nationals of the Jewish race may at any time be assigned a forced residence by the prefect of the department in which they reside.

Ban on Jewish Emigration from the Government-General (November 23, 1940) Memorandum to District Governors in the Government-General: In a Decree of October 25, 1940, the Reich Security Main Office (Reichssicherheitshauptamt) has informed me of the following: "Owing to the fact that the emigration of Jews from the Government-General still further considerable reduced the already shrinking opportunities for emigration for Jews from the Altreich, the Ostmark (Austria) and the Protectorate of Bohemia and Moravia, contrary to the wish of the Reich Marshal, I request that no such emigration be considered." "The continued emigration of Jews from Eastern Europe [to the West] spells a continued spiritual regeneration of world Jewry, as it is mainly the Eastern Jews who supply a large proportion of the rabbis, Talmud teachers, etc., owing to their statements. Further, every Orthodox Jew from Eastern Europe spells a valuable addition for these Jewish organizations in the United States in their constant efforts for the spiritual renewal of United States Jewry and its unification. It is United States Jewry in particular, which is endeavoring, with the help of newly immigrated Jews, especially from Eastern Europe, to create a new basis from which it intends to force ahead its struggle, particularly against Germany." "For these reasons it can be assumed that after a certain number of emigration permits have been issued, creating a precedent for Jews from the Government-General, so to speak, a large part of the entry visas, (which are) mainly for the United States, will in future only be made available for Jews from Eastern Europe." I fully accept the point of view of the Reich Security Main Office and request that you will not pass on to the office here for decision any more applications by Jews to emigrate. Such applications of course have to be rejected here. I empower you to reject without further investigation any applications by Jews from the Government-General for permission to emigrate. It is requested that applications to emigrate shall be forwarded here only if they involve Jews holding foreign citizenship. As there is no further question of emigration by Jews from the Government-General as a matter of principle, there is also no need for a Jew to receive a permit to visit the Reich for the purpose of obtaining a visa from a foreign consulate in the German Reich. It is requested that even applications by Jews for the issuing of a permit for the purpose of obtaining a visa from a foreign consulate in the Reich should also be rejected.

Heydrich's Guidelines (Soviet Union, July 2, 1941) Reich Secret Document. In the following I make known briefly the most important instructions given to me by the Einsatzgruppen and Kommandos of the Security Police and the SD, with the request to take note of them. . . . 4) Executions All of the following are to be executed: Officials of the Comintern (together with professional Communist politicians in general); top- and medium-level officials and radical lower-level officials of the Party, Central Committee and district and sub-district committees; people's Commissars; Jews in Party and State employment, and other radical elements (saboteurs, propagandists, snipers, assassins, inciters, etc.) insofar as they are, in any particular case, required or no longer to be required, to supply information on political or economic matters which are of special importance for the further operations of the Security Police, or for the economic reconstruction of the Occupied Territories. . . .

Regulation on the Introduction of Forced Labor of the Jewish Population (August 16, 1941). Pursuant to Article 8 of the Fuehrer's edict on the Admininistration of the newly occupied Eastern Territories of July 17, 1941, I order the following: Article I: Male and female Jews aged from their completed 14th to completed 60th year, residing in the newly occupied Eastern Territories, are liable for Forced Labor. The Jews will be collected in Forced Labor groups for this purpose. Article II: 1) Any person evading Forced Labor will be sent to prison with hard labor. 2) In the event of several persons conspiring to avoid Forced Labor, or in other especially grave cases, the death penalty may be imposed. 3) Cases will be judged by the Special Courts . . .—The Reich Minister for the Occupied Eastern Territories, signed Rosenberg

Resettlement Order (Government General, July 19, 1942). I herewith order that the resettlement of the entire Jewish population of the Government-General be carried out and completed by December 31, 1942. From December 31, 1942, no persons of Jewish origin may remain within the Government-General, unless they are in collection camps in Warsaw, Cracow, Czestochowa, Radom, and Lublin. All other work on which Jewish labor is employed must be finished by that date, or, in the event that this is not possible, it must be transferred to one of the collection camps. These measures are required with a view to the necessary ethnic division of races and peoples for the New Order in Europe, and also in the interests of the security and cleanliness of the German Reich and its sphere of interest. Every breach of this regulation spells a danger to quiet and order in the entire German sphere of interest, a point of application for the resistance movement and a source of moral and physical pestilence. For all these reasons a total cleansing is necessary and therefore to be carried out. Cases in which the date set cannot be observed will be reported to me in time, so that I can see to corrective action at an early date. All requests by other offices for changes or permits for exceptions to be made must be presented to me personally. Heil Hitler! H. Himmler

Late 1930s Paraguay enacts immigration rules.

The government of Paraguay, after allowing some Jews to enter the country—in particular, those who could work in the agricultural sector and those with capital—issues a decree that "forbids entry of Jews, irrespective of nationality, into Paraguay." In 1938, White Russian immigrants provoke anti-Jewish attacks. Seventeen Jews are expelled from the country as "Communists," and Jewish immigration is thwarted.

1937 Aliens Act is enacted in South Africa, curtailing German Jewish immigration on grounds of "unassimilability." This amendment to the 1930 law allows only those who are considered readily assimilable into South African society to enter, effectively allowing the government to ban Jewish immigrants. The effect of this law is that almost all applications for immigration by German Jews fleeing Europe are denied. Jews are excluded from membership in the National Party, whose 1937 platform urges the complete prohibition of Jewish immigration and the introduction of quotas restricting Jewish participation in economic life.

1938	Kristallnacht, the night of broken glass. More than 7,000 Jewish businesses are destroyed. Some 100 Jews are killed, and thousands are subjected to violence and torments. Thirty thousand Jewish men are arrested and sent to concentration camps.
1939	World War II begins on 1 September.
1939–1941	Formation of ghettos in Poland, followed by massacres and deportations to death-camps; massacres of Jews in occupied USSR.
1941	First "death-camp" established at Chelmno.
1942	The Wannsee Conference of Nazi leadership, at which the coordination with respect to the "final solution," the physical liquidation of the remaining Jews, is effected.
1943	Transports from all over Europe to Nazi death-camps; Warsaw Ghetto uprising; annihilation of most of the ghettos of Europe; Germany is declared *Judenrein* ("empty of Jews").
1946	Pogroms at Kielce, Poland, and other places of mass emigration of Jews during the war.
1948	Establishment of the State of Israel.
	Jewish culture in the USSR is suppressed and leading Jewish intellectuals are shot.
1948–1953	*Schvartzer Yor'n* (the "Black Years") of Soviet Jewry under Stalin.
1949–1953	Purges of Jewish communal leaders in the Soviet Union.

Hundreds of Jewish activists, leaders, and literary figures are arrested, reported missing, or killed. In the following excerpt from Khrushchev Remembers, *Nikita Khrushchev acknowledges that Stalin ordered the death of the prominent Jewish actor, Mikhoels.*

More typical was the cruel punishment of Mikhoels, the greatest actor of the Yiddish theatre, a man of culture. They killed him like beasts. They killed him secretly. Then his murderers were rewarded and their victim was buried with honors. The mind reels at the thought! It was announced the Mikhoels had fallen in front of a truck. Actually, he was thrown in front of a truck. . . . And who did it? Stalin did it, or at least it was done on his instructions. . . . I've tried to give Stalin his due and to acknowledge his merits, but there was no excuse for what, to my mind, was a major defect in his character—his hostile attitude toward the Jewish people.

Stalin diminished the number of Jews in prominent positions in the Soviet hierarchy with a 1942 secret order. From 1937 to 1946, the number of Jews in the Supreme Soviet dropped from 47 (4.1 percent) to 5 (less than 1 percent). The number of Jews in the Soviet of Nationalities dropped during the same period from the 11th highest rank to the 26th. By 1961, the percentage of Jews in the Central Committee had dropped to .3% from almost 25 percent 40 years earlier. A quota system obtained in higher education. In 1948, Jews comprised one-third of the department of sciences at the University of Moscow; in 1964, 20 percent; in the late 1970's out of 500 admissions each year, less than five Jews were admitted. The following account of Milovan Djilas, a Yugoslav political leader familiar with Stalin, illustrates the official dimension to these quotas:

. . .A man of the apparatus of the CC [Central Committee] of the Communist Party of the Soviet Union boasted to me how Zhdanov had cleared all Jews out of the CC apparatus. The Deputy Chief of the General Staff of the Soviet Army, Antonov, was accidentally discovered to be a Jew. Thus his illustrious career came to an end. The struggle against the 'rootless' cosmopolitans in the USSR is in fact a concealed form of the struggle against Jewish intellectuals. During the war, antisemitism was more or less openly expressed in the army. There was a great deal of talk in 1948 in Moscow concerning the Hungarian CC (which, as is known, consisted mostly of Jews). Jews had also been allocated the main role in the Moscow trials. There are no more Jews in the public life of the USSR. They are citizens of a lower, the lowest, order. This same policy is now being applied in Eastern Europe against that handful of martyred people who survived Fascist extermination. And this was, is and will be done regardless of whether the Jews are bourgeois or socialist . . .

**1952–
1953**

The Doctors' Plot and the campaign against cosmopolitanism in the Soviet Union.

An antisemitic propaganda campaign in the Soviet Union climaxes with the doctors' plot and an uprising against cosmopolitanism. The following reports are from the state-controlled Soviet press.

Official Announcement of the Doctor's Plot, Pravda (January 13, 1953). Some time ago, the agencies of state security uncovered a terrorist group of doctors who had made it their aim to cut short the lives of active public figures of the Soviet Union by means of sabotaged medical treatment. . . . The criminals confessed that they took advantage of Comrade A. A. Zhdanov's ailment by incorrectly diagnosing the illness and concealing an infarct of his myocardium and, by prescribing a regime contra-indicated for this serious ailment, killed Comrade A. A. Zhdanov. Investigation established that the criminals likewise cut short the life of Comrade A. S. Shcherbakov by incorrectly employing strong drugs in his treatment, treatment which was fatal to him, bringing about his death. The criminal doctors sought, above all, to undermine the health of leading Soviet military personnel, to put them out of action and to thereby weaken the defense of the country. . . . It has been established that all these homicidal doctors, who had become monsters in human form, trampling the sacred banner of science and desecrating the honor of scientists, were enrolled by foreign intelligence services as hired agents. Most of the participants in the terrorist group (M. S. Vovsi, B. B. Kogan, A. I. Feldman, A. M. Grinshtein, Ya. G. Etinger and others) were connected with the international Jewish bourgeois nationalists organization, "Joint," established by American intelligence for the alleged purpose of providing material aid to Jews in other countries. . . . Article on Cosmopolitanism and the "Doctors Plot" Trud (February 18, 1953). Cosmopolitanism is not just a hostile ideology. Cosmopolitanism is the savage struggle of the doomed classes against new social forces, against everything progressive. . . . It is not pure chance that the cosmopolitans and hardened bourgeois nationalists are given the most foul and filthy tasks by the instigators of war, including murder, espionage, sabotage, wrecking, even the assassination of the best representatives of the Russian nation. New evidence of this is the unmasking, by the organs of State security of the USSR, of a terrorist group of doctor-poisoners, enemies of the people, whose aim was to shorten the lives of active figures of the USSR. Most members of the group—Vovsi, Kogan, Feldman, Grinshtein, Etinger and others—were linked with international Jewish bourgeois nationalist "Joint" organization created by the American intelligence service allegedly to give practical help to the Jews in other countries.

Within a month of Stalin's death on 5 March 1953, an announcement in Pravda acknowledges that the group of doctors had been arrested falsely and had been freed.

1956   Israel's Sinai campaign.

1967   Israel's Six Days' War (June).

Resolution is adopted at the World Islamic Congress on "Jews in Arab countries" (22 September).

Following the 1967 Arab-Israeli war, the World Islamic Congress meets in Jordan and adopts a resolution stating that Jews in Arab lands should be classified as "aggressive combatants."

The congress is certain that the Jewish communities living in Islamic countries do not appreciate the Moslems' good treatment and protection over the centuries. They have encouraged world Zionism and the State of Israel to commit aggression against the peaceful Arabs, usurp their homelands, and violate the Islamic holy places of Palestine. The Congress declares that the Jews residing in Arab countries who contact the Zionist circles of the State of Israel do not deserve the protection and care which Islam provides for the free non-Moslem subjects living in Islamic countries. Moslem Islamic Governments should treat them as aggressive combatants. Similarly, the Islamic peoples, individually and collectively, should boycott them and treat them as deadly enemies.

1968   The government of Iraq Law No. 10 (14 February)

This law is enacted shortly after the 1967 Arab-Israeli war.

Article I Paragraph (6) of Article VII of Law No. 12 of 1951 as amended shall be cancelled and substituted by the following: 1. When this Law comes into force the Land Registration Departments, Waqf authorities and Notaries Public shall abstain from carrying out any transaction of sale of immovable properties belonging to the Jew, and abstain from carrying out on such properties any transactions which involves the transfer, donation, mortgage, liquidation, of joint ownership, selling by execution, making a lien as a security against a debt, bequest, rental for more than one year, causing an attachment or obligation. Also abstain from making any disposition of transaction which would result in such properties being transferred from the Jew's ownership even if the transaction is based on an irrevocable power of attorney. . . . Article II (a) If the Minister of the Interior issues the necessary permit in accordance with any of the paragraphs 5, 6 and 7 of this Article, he may decide that the amounts due to the Jew be deposited in one of the banks. Each time, these amounts shall not be disbursed without the approval of the Minister or anyone who is authorized by him. (b) The provisions of paragraph (a) above shall apply to all other transactions and dispositions which would result in sums being payable to a Jew as a consideration, excluding salaries and wages which do not exceed 100 Iraqi dinars per month. The official and semi-official departments, companies and establishments should not pay the amounts due to any Jew in respect of such transactions or dispositions, but inform the Minister of the Interior thereof. Written in Baghdad on the 16th of Thi-l-qiada 1387, 14th of February 1968. Ministers, Prime Minister, President of the Republic

Mid-late   Antisemitism of the New Left in the United
1960s   States and in Western Europe.

1968   Wave of antisemitism in Poland; emigration of most of Poland's remaining Jews.

1970   Law of expropriation of Jewish property is passed by the Revolutionary Command Council of Libya (21 July).

Libya passes laws to recover money supposedly stolen by former Italian colonists, to which is appended an additional law claiming the property of Libyan Jews (called "Israelis").

In the Name of the People The Revolutionary Command Council In view of the constitutional notice dated 2 Shawal 1389, corresponding to December 11, 1969, and law no. 6 of 1961 making the assets of certain Israelis subject to sequestration. . . . Article 1. The funds and properties of the persons subject to the sequestration provided for law no. 6, of 1961 and law no. 57 of 1970 and whose names are listed in the attachment shall be restituted to the state. . . . The Revolutionary Command Council: Qadhdhafi, Mch. Magareif, Abdussalam Gallud, Moh. Gedei, Dr. Giuna Scriha, Moh. Rabihi. Promulgated on 18 Gemadi 1390, corresponding to July 31, 1970

1975   "Zionism Equals Racism" resolution is passed by the United Nations General Assembly (repealed in 1991).

1970s   Antisemitism in Argentina

Antisemitic incidents, both governmental and popular, have occurred in Argentina since the beginning of the twentieth century when Jews started immigrating there in large numbers. The government-sponsored media at one time were filled with antisemitic references, and religious restrictions hindered Jewish practice, such as a 1943 ban on kosher meat and Jewish publications ordered by Minister Martinez Zuviria, who also authored best-selling antisemitic works. Police and government officials implemented harsh policies toward the Jews, such as the secret police under General José Félix Uriburu in the 1930s. Also, government officials either explicitly or tacitly approved anti-Jewish violence, as in the pogrom of 1919, in which hundreds of Argentine Jews were killed, and the repression and kidnappings of the 1970s and 1980s. In the late 1970s, a talk show host on state-controlled television baits a Jewish guest and challenges his loyalty to Argentina: "If the Jews have been persecuted for 4,000 years, there must be some reason for it, don't you think? Why is it Jews are so greedy? Why are there no poor Jews? What are you first, Argentine or Jew?"

1919: A pogrom known as the Semana Tragica by police forces and right-wing agitators against Jews results in approximated 700 deaths, injury, and damage to Jewish communal property. 1943: Anti-Jewish laws are enacted, including bans on kosher meat and Jewish publications. The *New York Times* reports that "alarm and even terror are beginning to spread in the Jewish quarter because for some time all gatherings of Colonel Peron's followers have been a signal for some action against Jews" (28 November 1945) 1976: The military government issues the Act for the Process of National Reorganization. The act vows "to establish the validity of Christian moral values . . . to ensure national security by eradicating subversion and the factors that abet it; [and to establish] an international place for Argentina in the Christian and Western world." The repression that results from this law targets a disproportionate number of Jewish victims. 1977: Argentine president Videla states that "a terrorist is not just someone with a gun or bomb but also someone who spreads ideas that are contrary to Western and Christian civilization" (Julius, Rifkind, Weill, and Gaer).

Early 1980s	Wave of antisemitic incidents in France.
1991	Antisemitic riots in Crown Heights section of Brooklyn, New York, in August.
1994	Bombing of Jewish Communal Building in Buenos Aires, Argentina.

The bomb attack against the AMIA building, the Argentine Jewish community's central body, kills eighty-five people. (A previous terrorist attack in 1992 had killed twenty-nine at the Israeli embassy in Buenos Aires.) Investigations into the bombing of the AMIA building reveal likely complicity and involvement of local police officers. Among the arrested is the head of the provincial police force's grand auto theft division and a close adviser to the provincial police chief. Buenos Aires police also are accused of Jewish cemetery desecration and an attempted bombing. Responding to the lack of progress of the investigation, the UN's Committee on the Elimination of Racial Discrimination in 1997 urges Argentina "to take all measures within its power to expedite the ongoing proceedings in connection with the 1992 and 1994 antisemitic attacks." Yet it was not until September 2001, seven years after the attacks, that twenty Argentine men went on trial. During the ongoing trial suspicions were voiced about the possible collaboration of politicians, members of the judiciary, and police offices in obstructing the investigation. As of 2004 there has been no resolution of the case. A new government in Argentina has pledged to bring the matter to closure.

2000 The Second Intifadah (renewed violence on the West Bank) begins, signaling new manifestations of anti-Zionist rhetoric and antisemitic behavior, primarily in Europe.

Palestinian Authority television broadcast (13 October)

The following excerpt is from the broadcast of a sermon by Dr. Ahmad Abu Halabiya, member of the Palestinian Authority Fatwa Council.

Have no mercy on the Jews, no matter where they are, in any country. Fight them, wherever you are. Wherever you meet them, kill them. Wherever you are, kill those Jews and those Americans who are like them—and those who stand by them—they are all in one trench, against the Arabs and the Muslims—because they established Israel here, in the beating heart of the Arab world, in Palestine. They created it to be the outpost of their civilization—and the vanguard of their army, and to be the sword of the West and the crusaders, hanging over the necks of the monotheists, the Muslims in these lands. They wanted the Jews to be their spearheads. . . .

2001 Speech of Syrian president welcoming Pope John Paul II (May).

Syrian president Bashar al-Assad made the following statements at a ceremony welcoming Pope John Paul II to Syria on May 5.

[T]here are those who persist in keeping mankind on the path of the agony and torture [suffered by Jesus]. . . . We witness [Israelis] murdering the principle of equality by claiming that God singled them out and desecrating the holy places of Islam and Christianity in Palestine. . . . They are trying to damage and destroy all the principles of the monotheistic religions with the same mentality that led them to betray and torture Jesus and with the same mentality that led them to kill the prophet Muhammad.

The Syrian minister of defense on 5 May 2001 states on LBC television that "if every Arab killed a Jew, no Jews would remain."

Notes

1. The Hasmonean dynasty ruled for approximately 130 years, from the conquest of Jerusalem from the Syrian Greeks in 164 BCE by the Hasmonean Judah the Maccabee.

2. See the discussion at the beginning of Chapter 1 on the definition of antisemitism.

3. Urban's silence was an expression of another well-known pattern—nonintervention and therefore implicit sanction—that was established early on.

4. Voltaire. *Dictionnaire Philosophique/A Philosophical Dictionary*, ed and transl. by Peter Gay (New York: Harcourt Brace & World, 1962) *passim*.

5. *Tah v'Tat*, as these massacres are known by Jews, refers to the years "18 and 19"—5418 and 5419—in the traditional Jewish calendar.

6. The term *Dreyfus affair* refers to the decade-long controversy.

7. *The Proud Tower: A Portrait of the World before the War: 1890–1914* (New York: Macmillan Publishing Co., 1966), 175.

8. Tuchman, *op. cit.*, 176.

9. An excellent review and analysis of the Dreyfus affair for the general reader is Barbara Tuchman's chapter "Give Me Combat!" in her book *A Proud Tower* (New York: Macmillan Publishing Co., 1966

10. Tuchman, *op. cit.*, 184.

11. The Bill of Rights—the first ten amendments to the U.S. Constitution—includes, in the first amendment, the "religion clauses": Congress shall make no law respecting an establishment of religion or prohibiting the free exercise thereof. Analysts note that, although there are occasional tensions between "establishment" and "free exercise," the two clauses are not in competition but complement and reinforce one another.

12. One significant expression of this consciousness was the founding of the Anti-Defamation League of B'nai B'rith in 1913.

3

Biographical Sketches

The history of and literature on antisemitism consist in large measure of the individuals who have either been responsible for antisemitic expression and behavior or those who have been instrumental in its counteraction. Antisemites and anti-anti-semites include well-known names—for example, Hitler, Stalin, and Torquemada—but for the most part the names in this chapter are either not well known or are known to historians and social scientists from other arenas. The following sketches represent a mere sampling of the personalities that defined, expressed, or articulated antisemitism through the ages. (For context and background, see Chapter 2.)

Ambrose (339–397)

One of the most significant of the early church fathers, Ambrose, bishop of Milan, was born in Trier in what is now western Germany. He defended the belief in the divinity of Jesus Christ against the Arians, who argued that, in Christian theology, only God the Father was entirely divine. Ambrose's sermons and piety inspired Augustine, whom Ambrose converted to Christianity.

Although Ambrose seems not to have known Jews personally, his violent diatribes against Jews grew out of the synagogue burning and pillaging instigated by the bishop of Callinicum on the Euphrates in 388. Emperor Theodosius I ordered the perpetrators punished and the stolen objects restored, instructing the bishop to pay for the rebuilding of the synagogue. In his Epistle 40 to the emperor, Ambrose asserted that to have the synagogue built with either public or Christian money was tantamount to permitting the enemies of Christ to triumph over Christianity. Ambrose's purported reason for not setting fire to the synagogue in Milan was that God had spared him that task, as it had been struck by lightning.

Antiochus IV (Epiphanes) (215BCE?–164BCE?)

Antiochus IV (known as Epiphanes), a Syrian Greek ruler of the Seleucid dynasty, is a classic example of a leader who engaged in anti-Jewish activity that did not result strictly from antisemitism.

Educated in an atmosphere of religious tolerance, which he had inherited from Alexander the Great, from the Persians, and, most importantly, from his own father (Antiochus III, who had shown special favor to the Jews), Antiochus IV ascended the throne at a time of conflict with Egypt and Rome and internecine religious power struggles in Judea.

In 174 BCE, for purely financial reasons, Antiochus IV replaced the pious high priest in Jerusalem, Onias III, with Jason, a committed Hellenist who instituted or permitted many pagan practices without any compulsion by Antiochus. Three years later, in 171 BCE, Antiochus dismissed Jason as high priest and replaced him (again, because Antiochus needed money for his increasingly expensive wars) with Menelaus, who was backed by the highly assimilated and financially powerful Tobiad family. Menelaus inaugurated his tenure by murdering Onias III, Jason's brother, and proceeded aggressively to advance the Hellenization of Judea.

In 170–169 BCE—while Antiochus was in Egypt battling his foes, the Ptolemies—Jason, the deposed high priest, seized Jerusalem. Antiochus, who could not afford unrest and civil war, intervened in Palestine, and with Menelaus as aide and instigator, he proceeded to loot the Temple and murder Jews.

In 168 BCE, following a false rumor that Antiochus had died, Jason again attempted to return and seize power in Jerusalem with the support of the majority of the Jews, who sympathized with the Ptolemies. Jason succeeded in expelling Menelaus and his Tobiad supporters, who begged Antiochus for help. Antiochus, who was conducting a military campaign in neighboring Egypt, complied. Abetted yet again by the Jewish Hellenizers in Jerusalem, Antiochus ordered the elimination of the Temple sacrifice and the observance of the commandments of the Torah, intensifying the uprising against him, which now included the Maccabean revolt, celebrated on the Jewish holiday of Hanukkah. The historical record suggests that the Maccabees' real struggle was not so much against Antiochus IV as against the Jewish Hellenizers in Jerusalem who were prosecuting an agenda of Hellenization.

Antiochus did not issue decrees against Jews in neighboring Syria and Asia Minor (where most Jews at the time lived), but only in Judea where civil unrest prevailed, suggesting that his motivation was not antisemitic but political in nature. His actions in Judea were driven for the most part by the power struggle among Jewish Hellenizers, which forced his hand. Numerous Jews in Judea were killed during the reign of Antiochus IV, but what motivated Antiochus was not religious or ethic anti-Judaism but civil unrest and international pressures. He therefore did not fit the classic pattern of antisemitism.

Apion (First Century CE)

Apion, the first-century Greek rhetorician of Egyptian origin, played a leading role in spreading anti-Jewish propaganda and provoking anti-Jewish agitation in Alexandria. So intense were his attacks against Jews that the Jewish historian Josephus felt compelled to write his classic counterargument, *Contra Apionem* (*Against Apion*).

Apion's five-volume *History of Egypt* is filled with imaginary excesses about Jews and others. He added his own gloss on the antisemitic fulminations of earlier writers, appropriating the Egyptian historian Manetho's idea that Jews were expelled from Egypt because they were lepers. Apion insisted that the tenets of their religion obliged Jews to hate the rest of mankind. Once yearly, his canard went, they seized a non-Jew, murdered him, and tasted his entrails, swearing during the meal to hate the nation of which the victim was a member.

During an outbreak of anti-Jewish violence under the government of Flaccus, when the Jewish community was forced to fight for its existence, Apion served as one of the leading and most popular rabble rousers among the Alexandrian mob. He tried to show that the Jews were foreigners, acting to the detriment of Egyptians and thus had no right to consider themselves citizens.

Thomas Aquinas (1125–1274)

St. Thomas Aquinas, the most important of the Christian medieval theologians, was the foremost Aristotelian philosopher in the Christian world of the High Middle Ages. Aquinas's main work, *Summa Theologica,* serves as an introduction to all questions of doctrine. Highly dialectical in nature, *Summa* is the Aristotelian masterpiece nonpareil.

In 1270–1271, Aquinas expressed his opinion on the Christian attitude to Jews in a small treatise, *De Regimine Judaeorum,* a series of answers to questions posed by the Duchess of Brabant, such as whether it was lawful for a Christian prince to exact money from Jews by means of taxes, since the money was earned as a result of usury. Aquinas answered that while Jews were destined to perpetual slavery—sovereigns consequently could treat their goods as their personal property—rulers were not permitted to deprive Jews of all that was necessary to sustain life.

Aquinas advocated that Jews should be compelled to wear a distinguishing badge that would make them recognizable to Christians. He vehemently condemned, however, the baptism of Jewish infants against their parents' wishes, as violating natural justice.

Aquinas interdicted, as a general principle, the use of force against non-Catholics to convert them to Christianity. Citing Augustine, he declared that man is capable of doing certain things against his will, but faith is given only to him who desires it.

Augustine (354–430)

Augustine, the major Christian theologian of the early Western Church and one of the most significant of the church fathers, was born in Tagaste, a city near what is now Constantine, Algeria. His most important works are the *Confessions,* one of the first great autobiographies of Western literature and a classic of early Christian literature, in which he described his early life and spiritual struggles; and the *City of God,* which espoused a religious philosophy of predestination. Augustine's philosophy was based on the anti-Aristotelian notion that the "material" in the world is fundamentally debased.

Augustine took the Jews to severe task for not having accepted the divinity of Jesus, when they should have been the first to acknowledge him. Their rejectionism, according to Augustine, condemned Jews to live in blindness, error, and exile. Elaborating on the views of St. Paul, he taught that the Catholic Church replaced the old Israel as God's chosen people.

Augustine argued, however, that the Jews should be spared, for they still have a role in the salvific plan of Christianity. Although they merit death for the crime of deicide, the Jews should be preserved—and indeed loved—as witnesses to Christian truth but under conditions of reprobation and misery. He regarded Jewish devotion to the law as itself a kind of sacrament. As God's work of redemption has been enacted through their history—Jesus was born a Jew—Augustine insisted that the people of Israel could not be dismissed entirely. Their continued abject existence, however, served to vindicate the claims of Christianity.

The legacy of Augustine's teaching about the Jews—they should survive but not thrive—is ambivalent. Opposed to the vicious diatribes of other church fathers, such as John Chrysostom and Ambrose, Augustine's position required an end to all violent assaults against synagogues, Jewish property, and Jewish persons. Jews were henceforth exempt from the church-sanctioned, state-sponsored campaign to obliterate religious difference. Historians suggest that Augustine's teaching on the special place of Israel and the Jews in Christian redemption protected Jewish communities in Europe for centuries. Augustine's relatively benign attitude toward the Jews, however, is still rooted in Christian supersessionism that ultimately served as a foundation for later antisemitism.

Dietrich Bonhoeffer (1906–1945)

A German Lutheran pastor and theologian, Dietrich Bonhoeffer was imprisoned at the Buchenwald concentration camp and executed by the Nazis on 9 April 1945. He risked his life in helping Jews escape Nazi persecution. He maintained that "the Church is only a Church, when she exists for those outside herself," and proclaimed its unconditional obligation toward the victims of every social system, even if they do not belong to the Christian community.

During his short life, Bonhoeffer welcomed a rapprochement of Christianity and humanism in the face of modern tyrannies. He abjured any dualistic separation of church and world, nature and grace, the sacred and the profane and called for a concrete ethic founded on Christology, a doctrine centered around the person and work of Jesus Christ.

The son of a professor of psychiatry and neurology at the University of Berlin, Bonhoeffer studied theology in the German capital and spent a year as an exchange student at New York's Union Theological Seminary. He came under the influence of Karl Barth's "theology of revelation" and rebelled against the academicism of the age. The beginnings of Bonhoeffer's ministry coincided with the rise of the Nazi Party in Germany. Indeed, from the first days of the Nazi accession to power in 1933, he was involved in protests against the regime, and joined the Confessing Church, the anti-Nazi voice within the larger German church. Bonhoeffer's protests against antisemitism dated from the early 1940s, when the Confessing Church began its activities in the rescue of Jews.

Bonhoeffer taught theology first in Berlin and then in the unofficial seminaries of the Confessing Church. He was on a lecture tour of the United State at the outbreak of World War II and immediately returned to Germany. Soon after, he joined a group of conspirators working for the overthrow of the Nazi regime. Bonhoeffer's rescue efforts on behalf of Jews resulted in his arrest in 1943. He was hanged shortly before the downfall of Hitler. His prison writings are remarkable for the richness of cultural and spiritual life they display, as well as for the profound theological themes they develop.

Bogdan Chmielnicki (1595–1657)

Bogdan Chmielnicki (some historical references transliterate the name as "Khmelnitski"), the leader of the Cossack and Ukrainian peasant uprising against Polish rule in 1648, conducted a campaign to rid the region of its Jews, resulting in the destruction of hundreds of Jewish communities and the murder of an estimated 100 to 300 thousand Jews (Margolis and Marx, 1927, 556).

In the course of Chmielnicki's campaigns, his followers acted savagely against the Jews. His atrocities are infamously known by Jews as *G'zeroth Tah v'Tat* (the decrees of '48 and '49). In the annals of the Jewish people, he is branded as "Chmiel the Wicked," one of the most sinister oppressors of Jews in history.

Most of the Chmielnicki massacres, part of the Ukrainian peasant rebellion and uprising against their Polish Catholic overlords, took place during the months of May to November 1648. At the beginning of the uprising, the Jewish communities east of the

Dnieper River were destroyed. Some Jews converted to Christianity to save their lives, but the overwhelming majority accepted martyrdom. Many were seized by the Tatars and sold into slavery.

John Chrysostom (347?–407?)

John Chrysostom, one of the most celebrated of the early Christian church fathers, proved to be the most viciously antisemitic. His hate-filled sermons belie the name he was given by later generations, Chrysostom, "the golden mouthed."

John was born in Antioch, Syria (now Turkey), to pagan parents. His eight homilies against the Jews painted the synagogue as a den of evil, the representation and source of all vice and heresy. Deicide and dispersion served as the cornerstone of his antisemitic theology. Chrysostom's attacks were directed against not only the teachings of Judaism but most especially the Jewish way of life. In his *First Homily against the Jews,* he characterizes Jews as dogs and drunkards who, unfit for work, are fit only for slaughter. These sermons exceed those of the other church fathers in depth and extent of their cruelty and viciousness, contributing greatly to the formation of anti-Jewish propaganda imagery down the centuries.

Father Charles Coughlin (1891–1971)

A Canadian-born Roman Catholic clergyman, Father Coughlin, known as the "radio priest," used his spellbinding oratory to foment antisemitism in the Depression-era 1930s United States.

Upon his ordination in 1926, Father Charles Coughlin was assigned to the lower-middle-class Detroit suburb of Royal Oak. In his mellow brogue, he presided over a radio program, "The Golden Hour from the Shrine of the Little Flower," initially broadcasting a message of brotherly love. The Depression gave him the opportunity, however, to ventilate his wider-ranging political, economic, and social views.

In January 1930, he first warned his listeners of a Communist conspiracy within the United States, a plot he linked to the prevalent social evils of divorce, birth control, and free love. He then singled out big business, particularly "international bankers" (a code word at the time for Jews), who, he argued, were compounding the national danger by starving honest workers. By the late spring of 1931, his "Golden Hour" reached twenty-six states, from Maine to Colorado. Two years later he was attracting between 30 to 40 percent of the American listening audience.

Early in 1934 President Roosevelt ordered Secretary of the Treasury Henry Morgenthau Jr. to publish a list of individuals and groups that had invested heavily in silver in anticipation of the U.S. withdrawal from the gold standard. One of these was Coughlin's "Radio League of the Little Flower," which had accumulated holdings of nearly 500,000 ounces of silver. Outraged at his exposure, the compromised Catholic cleric lashed out at an alleged conspiracy head by "Morgenthau and his Jewish cohorts."

Coughlin's antisemitic rhetoric became ever more strident and menacing in mid-1939. He accused Roosevelt and his New Deal planners of softening the United States for the "international bangsters" (Coughlin's neologism)—"the Kuhn-Loebs, the Rothschilds, the Baruchs and the scribes and Pharisees." He spoke of "Shylocks" in London and on Wall Street undermining the United States. Following Roosevelt's landslide 1936 election, an infuriated Father Coughlin went on the air to declare that the "Jewish conspiracy" behind communism and the New Deal was making democracy impossible in the United States. A year later, he publicly praised the Italian Fascist dictator Mussolini and supported Hitler's imperial ambitions.

In the summer of 1937, extracts from the vicious Czarist canard, *The Protocols of the Learned Elders of Zion*, together with articles perpetuating the Shylock myth of the Jew as unscrupulous moneylender and ruler of international banking, began appearing in successive issues of Father's Coughlin nationally distributed magazine, *Social Justice.*

By spring 1939, some fifty to seventy-five Coughlin-inspired and -sanctioned antisemitic rallies were taking place in New York each week, arousing a serious upsurge in physical violence against Jews. As soon as World War II broke out, he expressed considerable sympathy for the Nazis. In 1942, the U.S. government barred *Social Justice* from the mails, and his church superiors silenced his radio program.

Father Coughlin's aggressive antisemitic populism and broadcast acumen proved a dangerous mix of religious prejudice and racial hatred, at odds with a vision of American democratic pluralism.

David Duke (1951–)

David Duke, an American political extremist, has sought to "mainstream" racism and antisemitism in the United States. Ever since the 1970s, Duke has encouraged Ku Klux Klan (KKK) members to "get out of the cow pastures and into the hotel meeting rooms." Increasingly following his own advice, over the years he has mastered the use of code words and has disguised his reactionary ideas behind more mainstream conservative-sounding rhetoric.

Duke started out as a small-time leader of a campus white supremacist organization at Louisiana State University in the early 1970s. In 1974, he assumed the position of grand wizard of the Ku Klux Klan but sought to demystify his title by renaming himself "national director" and by referring to cross burnings as "illuminations." In 1980, Duke resigned from the KKK and formed the Association for the Advancement of White People (NAAWP), a "political organization" to promote the cause of White Rights.

Duke's attempts at running for political office have largely fallen flat. Except for his election to the Louisiana state legislature in 1989, his bids for governor of Louisiana and U.S. senator from Louisiana, as well as for president of the United States in 1988 and 1992, have been failures. Although he has been repudiated by the national leadership of the Republican Party, he has served as party chairman for the St. Tamany Parish in Louisiana. Duke did receive approximately 55 percent of the white vote in Louisiana in his 1991 gubernatorial race (Chanes, 1995, 22).

In his 1998 self-published autobiography, *My Awakening*, Duke wrote of Jews that "they thoroughly dominate the news and entertainment media in almost every civilized nation; they control the international markets and stock exchanges; and no government can resist doing their bidding on any issue of importance." In a 13 May 1990 interview, quoted a year later in the *San Francisco Examiner* (13 November 1991), he stated, "The Jews are trying to destroy all other cultures . . . as a survival mechanism . . . the only Nazi country in the world is Israel."

A decades-long denier of the Holocaust (the mass murder of 6 million Jews during World War II), Duke said in a March 1985 interview:

> Did you ever notice how many survivors they have? . . . Every time you turn around, 15,000 sur-

vivors meet here, 400 survivors convention there. I mean, did you ever notice? Nazis sure were inefficient weren't they? Boy, boy, boy! . . . You almost have no survivors that ever say they saw a gas chamber or saw the workings of a gas chamber. . . . They'll tell these preposterous stories that anybody can check out to be a lie, an absolute lie.

In January 2000 Duke announced the formation of a new racist organization, the National Organization for European American Rights (NOFEAR), whose purpose is to "defend the civil rights of European Americans." In keeping with the stated goals and political ideology of NOFEAR, Duke has appeared at various pro-Confederate flag, anti-immigrant, and racist rallies.

Louis Farrakhan (1933–)

Louis Abdul Farrakhan, the African American nationalist leader and an apostle of the late Elijah Muhammad and head of an American Muslim sect that preaches black separatism, moral rearmament, and economic self-reliance, has generated widespread controversy. Although he articulates the anger and aspirations of many of the African American underclass left behind in the progress generated by the civil rights movement, Farrakhan's rhetoric has a distinctly antiwhite and antisemitic message. Regarded by some as an eloquent black spokesman and by others as a racist demagogue, he remains one of the more divisive figures in American racial politics.

Louis Farrakhan was born Louis Eugene Walcott in 1933 to Caribbean immigrants in New York and grew up in the Roxbury section of Boston. He made his living as a guitar-playing calypso and country singer until Malcolm X, the chief spokesman of the Chicago-based Elijah Muhammad, recruited him into the Nation of Islam. As a Black Muslim, Louis Eugene Walcott discarded his "slave" name and styled himself Louis X and finally Louis Farrakhan.

As head of the Nation of Islam, a breakaway from the more moderate Black Muslim group headed by Elijah Muhammad's son, Farrakhan organized the 1995 Million Man March, ranked as the largest-ever civil rights march in the nation's capital. He followed the Million Man March by launching his World Friendship Tour during which he dismissed all charges of slavery in the

Sudan and praised the "wise Islamic leadership" of dictator Hassan al-Turabi. In Nigeria he spoke approvingly of Sani Abacha, Nigeria's dictator who had hanged the internationally renowned author, Ken Saro-Wiwa.

In 2001, Farrakhan organized a sequel to the Million Man March, the Million Family March in the shadow of the Washington Monument. His incendiary, hate-mongering rhetoric has alienated him from the mainstream, however, and made his attempts at respectability insincere.

Although not significant in terms of antisemitic impact on the general American population, Farrakhan exemplifies the dynamic in which substantial numbers of people—in this case black Americans who are attracted to his legitimate message of economic self-reliance and empowerment—will put aside the racism and antisemitism of a leader if his message in areas of immediate concern is appealing.

Henry Ford (1863–1947)

Henry Ford, the industrial genius and legendary auto magnate who perfected the mass production of motorcars before World War I, was a reclusive man with strong antisemitic prejudices. He opposed social and cultural change, including Hollywood movies, out-of-home childcare, government regulation of business, labor unions, and immigration from Eastern Europe.

Between 1920 and 1922 Ford published a series of four paperbound books entitled *The International Jew: The World's Foremost Problem*. These amounted to a collection of antisemitic articles from his privately owned newspaper, the *Dearborn Independent*. *The International Jew* was based largely on the notorious late-nineteenth-century forgery, *Protocols of the Learned Elders of Zion*, concocted by the Russian secret police. *The International Jew* was translated into sixteen languages, and millions of copies were circulated. The book ultimately became a significant conduit in the United States for propagating toxic fabrications about Jewish designs to control the world.

Some of Ford's greatest damage was in serving as an inspiration to Adolf Hitler. In 1922 when the Nazis were yet to achieve power, Hitler adorned his office with a large portrait of Henry Ford and kept a copy of Ford's *International Jew* on his desk. In 1923, Hitler told a reporter from the *Chicago Tribune*, "We look to

Heinrich Ford as the leader of the growing Fascist movement in America" (Baldwin 2003, 185). Whether Ford helped bankroll Hitler remains uncertain. Circumstantial evidence indicates that he did, but not surprisingly, no documentation has survived.

In 1927, in response to intense public pressure, Ford publicly apologized for having published antisemitic propaganda in his newspaper, the *Dearborn Independent*.

Ford died in 1946, at age eighty-two, without ever sending back the Nazi medal, the German Eagle, conferred on him by Hitler in 1938 on the occasion of the magnate's seventy-fifth birthday. To his dying day, a largely unrepentant Ford claimed that Jewish bankers had caused World War II.

Abraham H. Foxman (1940–)

Abraham H. Foxman, national director of the Anti-Defamation League since 1987, is a highly visible leader in the American Jewish monitoring and counteraction of antisemitism.

Born in Poland in 1940, Foxman was rescued from the Nazis as an infant by his Polish Catholic nursemaid, who baptized him and raised him as a Catholic during the war years, thereby saving his life. His real parents survived the war and eventually reclaimed their son.

In addition to his leadership in program development on antisemitism and human rights, Foxman has focused attention on the heroic efforts of Christian rescuers of Jews and has taken the lead in developing education programs about the Holocaust.

Count Joseph-Arthur de Gobineau (1816–1882)

Called "the father of modern racism," Count Joseph-Arthur de Gobineau was a nineteenth-century French diplomat, writer, ethnologist, and social thinker whose theory of race-determinism had an enormous influence upon the subsequent development of social theory and practices—and of antisemitism—in Western Europe.

A member of an aristocratic French royalist family, Gobineau was well educated in languages and became secretary to the writer and statesman Alexis de Tocqueville during the latter's brief term as foreign minister in 1849. Gobineau then embarked on his own diplomatic career, which took him to posts in Bern, Hanover, Frankfurt, Tehran, and Rio de Janeiro.

In his four-volume *Essai sur l'inegalite des races humaines* (*Essay on the Inequality of Human Races*), written between 1853 and 1855, Gobineau advanced the theory that the fate of civilization is determined by racial composition, that Aryan societies flourish as long as they remain racially free of "lesser" strains, and that the more a civilization's racial character is diluted through miscegenation the more likely it is to lose its vitality and creativity and sink into corruption and immorality.

Gobineau's theories, now discredited, were the products of his historical, anthropological, and ethnological studies and were part of a general European interest in biological and sociological determinism. His work was not well received in France but widely appreciated in Germany, especially by such cultural titans as Wagner and Nietzsche, as well as the Germanized Englishman Houston Steward Chamberlain, through whom Gobineau unwittingly gave German racialism its ideological basis.

Gobineau's racist thought was not strictly antisemitic. He was not anti-Jewish and rated the contribution of the Jews to history and culture very highly, although he viewed the Teutons, the purest whites, as the highest branch of the Aryans. Nonetheless, his racialist theories were crucial in creating an atmosphere in which antisemitism flourished in nineteenth- and twentieth-century Europe, ultimately becoming embedded in the institutions of power and leading to the Holocaust.

David Harris (1949–)

Since 1990 David A. Harris has been the executive director of the American Jewish Committee (AJC), the New York–based human relations organization founded in 1906. (The AJC has been a leading agency in the counteraction of antisemitism.)

Harris is the author of four books and the coauthor of a fifth. He appears regularly on radio and television and has testified on several occasions before the U.S. Congress and the United Nations. Under his leadership, the AJC has moved aggressively from an emphasis on U.S. domestic issues into the arena of international affairs.

Rabbi Marvin Hier (1939–)

Rabbi Marvin Hier is the founder and dean of the Simon Wiesenthal Center and its Museum of Tolerance in Los Angeles. Under his leadership, the center, named after the famed Nazi hunter and numbering a fairly sizable constituency with offices on four continents, is today a visible Jewish human rights advocacy group.

The Museum of Tolerance, the educational arm of the center that opened in February 1993, is designed to challenge visitors to confront bigotry and racism and to understand the Holocaust in both historic and contemporary contexts.

Hier is the founder of Moriah, the center's documentary film division and the recipient of two Academy Awards: the first in 1997, as coproducer of *The Long Way Home,* the story of the plight of tens of thousands of refugees who survived the Holocaust; the second in 1981, as coproducer and cowriter for *Genocide,* a documentary on the Holocaust that had a wide international impact.

Adolf Hitler (1889–1945)

The Austrian-born genocidal ruler of Germany between the years 1933 to 1945, Adolf Hitler ranks among history's most horrific figures. Guided by concepts of racial elitism, rooted in traditional German *Volk* ideology, he established a brutal totalitarian regime under the German National Socialist (Nazi) banner. Hitler's drive for empire, which resulted in the devastation of World War II and the state-sponsored mass murder of European Jewry (the Holocaust), ended only with Nazi Germany's total military defeat in 1945.

The elements of the myth of the Jew conceived by Hitler were previously used by German and Austrian racialist antisemites during the nineteenth century, as well as in different forms in works such as *The Protocols of the Learned Elders of Zion,* a Czarist-era antisemitic forgery. According to the racialist antisemitic view, the Jews are an incurably evil race whose ultimate aim is to destroy the superior "Aryan (Anglo-Saxon) race" and dominate the world. Hitler insisted, far more than did his antisemitic predecessors, on the danger of "sexual contamination" by Jews and dehumanizingly identified them with microbial infection, calling for commensurate techniques of extermination.

Hitler organized the "Beer Hall Putsch" on 8–9 November 1923 in Munich, aimed at the capture of the Bavarian government, but the putsch was suppressed by the authorities. He served nine months of his five-year sentence in the fortress prison, where he wrote *Mein Kampf,* a crude and extended elaboration of racial antisemitism that underscored his persistent theme that the violent struggle for life governs the relationships of both individuals and nations and in which he developed his anti-Jewish agenda and program.

In the last free election of the Weimar Republic, more than 17 million people—one-third of the German population— voted for the Nazis, Hitler's racist party (Bullock, 1961, 224). On 30 January 1933, Hitler became chancellor of the German Republic. One of history's greatest tyrants thus came to power legally, exploiting the letter of the law to successfully subvert it and working for the systematic "purification" of the German Reich of Jews. The Nuremberg Laws (1935) created the "legal" definition of the Jew and the artificial and deadly distinction between German and Jew, and many anti-Jewish measures were enacted. The Nuremberg Laws marked the elimination of the Jews from the German economy, educational system, and places of public accommodations. Kristallnacht—"the night of broken glass" that was the premeditated expropriation and destruction of German-Jewish property on 9–10 November 1938—was followed by the first mass imprisonment of German-Jewish men.

Hitler was the person who planned the systematic extermination of the Jews of Europe, the largest and most intricate state-sponsored genocide in history. He took the decision, attracted a dedicated cadre of followers, and created the required bureaucratic scheme to implement his infernal plan, finding sympathizers and supporters in the many millions in the German-speaking world and later all across Europe.

Under the cover of World War II, which he instigated and initiated, Hitler and the Nazi apparatus set up concentration and annihilation camps in Europe for the destruction of Jewry. By the end of the war, some 6 million Jews, in addition to homosexuals, Gypsies, communists and many other "undesirables," had been burned, gassed, and shot by Hitler's followers.

Hajj Amin al-Husseini (1893–1976)

Hajj Amin al-Husseini, an anti-Zionist and anti-Jewish Muslim clerical leader, used his position as mufti (expounder of Muslim law and leader of the Muslim community) of Jerusalem during the period of the British mandate to foment anti-Jewish riots in Palestine and to spread antisemitic propaganda across the Middle East. During World War II, he collaborated with the Nazi regime.

In 1920 al-Husseini was sentenced to ten years imprisonment by a British military court for inciting Arab mob violence in the Jewish quarter of Jerusalem but managed to flee to Transjordan. Amnestied in 1921 by mandate high commissioner Herbert Samuel, he returned to Palestine a year later. In an effort to assuage him, Samuel's administration was instrumental in nominating al-Husseini as mufti of Jerusalem. Within a short time al-Husseini was appointed president of the Muslim Supreme Council and of the religious courts, a position that enabled him to appoint preachers in the mosques and judges in the Muslim courts, whom he shrewdly directed to propagate violent opposition to Jewish life in Palestine.

By 1936 al-Husseini became the dominant figure of the Arab Higher Committee, which included leaders of all six existing Arab political groups in Palestine. Overriding the objections of more moderate members of the committee, he launched the "Arab Revolt" in April 1936 against the British and the Jews.

Once the British realized that he was not merely anti-Jewish but anti-English as well, al-Husseini was removed as head of the Muslim Supreme Council. In October 1937 he fled to Lebanon. From Beirut and Damascus, he continued to direct anti-Jewish terrorism in Palestine. In 1938 his bands killed 297 Jews and wounded 427 (Schechtman, 1965, 73). Some of his Arab opponents, mainly from the rival Nashashibi clan, were attacked and murdered as well.

With the outbreak of World War II, al-Husseini moved to Baghdad, where in May 1941 he induced Iraqi prime minister Rashid Ali to launch an anti-British coup, with promised Axis support. When this armed movement failed, the mufti fled first to Tehran, then to Italy, and finally to Nazi Germany.

In Berlin, al-Husseini became active in support of Hitler's plan to annihilate European Jewry, collaborating eagerly with the Nazi war machine, organizing sabotage in Arab countries under

Allied rule, and rallying political support for Nazi Germany among Muslims in Axis-occupied countries.

After the collapse of the Nazi regime, Al-Husseini continued to operate from Europe, playing an important part in militarily organizing the Arabs in Palestine during the crucial years of 1947–1948. After the 1948 Israeli war of independence and the birth of the State of Israel, the Arab Higher Committee moved to Egyptian-held Gaza and al-Husseini was appointed president of the National Assembly. His subversive activities culminated in the murder of moderate King Abdullah of Jordan in July 1951, which resulted in large measure from his machinations.

Pope Innocent IV (d. 1254)

Innocent IV was the Roman Catholic pope who decreed the burning of the Talmud (the massive compendium of Jewish law and tradition; next to the Hebrew Bible the central repository of Jewish normative tradition). He completed the policy of his predecessor, Gregory IX, whose antisemitism included the order impounding the Talmud for an examination of its contents, the intervention against the Jews of Castile and Portugal in 1231, and the condemnation in Germany of the employment of Christian servants by Jews in 1233.

Soon after his accession in 1244, Innocent IV wrote to the king of France to warn him of a number of Jewish "abuses": the continued study of the Talmud and the employment of Christian wet nurses. In 1247 Innocent relented somewhat, swayed by the pleas of the Jews that they could neither study nor teach the Bible without the help of the Talmud. His advisers, however, secured Innocent's thoroughgoing condemnation of the Talmud and the call for its burning in 1248. Although he condemned the blood libel against the Jews in 1249, Innocent IV approved the archbishop of Vienna's expulsion of the Jews in 1253.

St. John/Gospel of St. John (d.100CE?)

The four Gospels, Matthew, Mark, Luke, and John, the primary source for facts about the historic Jesus, were written well after Paul's mission to the gentiles and are heavily marked by the supersessionist teachings that sought to replace Judaism with Christianity. John's Gospel, however, with its frequent critical and derogatory mention of the "Jews," is considered to be the most antisemitic.

The picture of Jesus in the first three, Synoptic, Gospels is drawn from a similar perspective, yet each emphasizes different things, contradicting some of the details of the other two. John's Gospel stands apart from the three synoptics because it tends to be more theological, offering a belief that Jesus was the pre-existent *Logos* (Word), which had taken on human form and lived among the people—the Incarnation—concealing his true nature from all but those who saw him through the eyes of faith.

All the Gospels present a negative picture of the Jews and of Jesus' relationship with them. The Gospel of Matthew gives a consistently denigrating picture of the Jews, calling them a "viper's brood" and showing them enunciating the terrible curse against themselves—"His blood be upon us and our children" (Matt. 27: 25)—which was to echo so appallingly through the centuries. The Gospel of John identifies the Jews as sons of the devil, thus beginning a process of demonization in statements, not extant in the other gospels, attributed to Jesus himself:

> I know that you are descended from Abraham, but you are bent on killing me because my teaching makes no headway with you. . . . Jesus said, "If God were your father you would love me, for God is the source of my being and from him I come. . . . Your father is the devil and you choose to carry out your father's desires. He was a murderer from the beginning, and is not rooted in the truth. . . . You are not God's children that is why you do not listen" (John 8: 37–45).

John's Gospel, branding the Jews as the sons of the devil, set the stage for further elaboration, and over time the Jews became the very incarnation of evil. Denigrated as liars, deceivers, corrupters, horned beasts, treacherous poisoners, and killers, the Jews became, through Christian scripture, associated down the ages with any new verbal or visual characterization of the devil.

Martin Luther King Jr. (1929–1968)

Martin Luther King Jr., the eloquent minister and towering symbol of the struggle for civil equality in the United States, devoted his life to the fight for full citizenship rights of the poor, disadvantaged, and racially oppressed. A *philosemite,* King defended Jews at a time of an increase of antisemitism and anti-Zionism emerging from the African American community.

In 1954 King accepted his first pastorate at the Dexter Avenue Baptist Church in Montgomery, Alabama. A year later, Rosa Parks, a Montgomery resident, defied the ordinance mandating segregated seating on city buses. King's successful organization of the year-long Montgomery bus boycott catapulted him into national prominence as a leader of the growing civil rights movement. In 1957, he became founding president of the Southern Christian Leadership Conference (SCLC), one of the principal civil rights groups in the United States.

A follower of Gandhi's doctrine of nonviolent civil disobedience, King organized the massive March on Washington (28 August 1963) where, in his brilliant "I Have a Dream" speech, he challenged the nation to act in a spirit of morality. That same year, in his classic "Letter from Birmingham Jail," he wrote: "We can never forget that everything Hitler did in Germany was 'legal' and everything the Hungarian freedom fighters did in Hungary was 'illegal.' It was 'illegal' to aid and comfort a Jew in Hitler's Germany. But I am sure that, if I had lived in Germany during that time, I would have aided and comforted my Jewish brothers even though it was illegal." In 1964 King won the Nobel Prize for Peace and was the first African American chosen by *Time* magazine as its Man of the Year.

King spoke out about a rising tide of black antisemitism that marked the late 1960s. In "Of Riots and Wrongs against Jews" in the Winter 1964–1965 issue of *American Judaism,* he wrote: "I solemnly pledge to do my utmost to uphold the fair name of the Jews. Not only because we need their friendship, and surely we do, but mainly because bigotry in any form is an affront to us all"(74).

King recognized the deeper relations of economics and poverty to racism and called for a society to resconstruct itself, with a new set of values. Along with demands for civil and voting rights legislation and for a meaningful poverty budget, he spoke out against the Vietnam War and in favor of the rights of Soviet Jewry. Upon receiving the American Jewish Committee's American Civil Liberties Medallion in May 1965, King called for protests against antisemitism in the Soviet Union, arguing once again that the greatest danger is from the silence that encourages evil to flourish.

In a 1968 speech he gave at Harvard University, King, addressing anti-Zionism, spoke out against political and moral hypocrisy, in effect equating anti-Zionism with antisemitism. (This speech was among the first in which the question of anti-Zionism was addressed.) Ten days before his assassination, he addressed the Rabbinical Assembly of America (the rabbinical body of Conservative Jews) and declared: "We have made it clear that we cannot be the victims of the notion that you deal with one evil in society by substituting another evil. We cannot substitute one tyranny for another and the Black man to be struggling for justice and then turn around and be antisemitic is not only a very irrational course but it is a very immoral course, and wherever we have seen antisemitism we have condemned it with all our might."

King's murder on 4 April 1968 in Memphis marked an irrecoverable loss for U.S. civil rights, for the counteraction of antisemitism, and for black-Jewish relations.

Martin Luther (1483–1546)

Martin Luther, the father of Protestantism, is the founder of Lutheranism, one its major branches. On 31 October 1517—a nodal point in Western history—he nailed a list of ninety-five theses, or propositions, to the door of the Church of Wittenberg, questioning, among other things, the right of the pope to forgive religious sins by the sale of indulgences (partial remissions of sins to those who made monetary donations to the Church).

At first, Luther condemned the persecution of the Jews and recommended a more tolerant policy toward them, based on the spirit of true Christian brotherhood. He spoke out against the preachers who exaggerate the Jews' misdeeds against Christ.

Luther had a deep and abiding love of the Hebrew Bible and accepted the Hebrew language as the only one adequate for the expression of religious truth and sentiment. Noteworthy is his German translation of the Bible as an outstanding event in German religious and literary history.

Luther directly examined the Jewish question, first in his 1523 pamphlet *Das Jesus Christus ein geborener Jude sei* (*That Christ was born a Jew*). He argued that the Jews, who stemmed from the same stock as the founder of Christianity, had actually been right in refusing to accept the "papal paganism" presented to them as Christianity.

In part, his polemics against the use of images in churches got Luther branded as a "half-Jew" by church authorities. Initially some Jews, assuming Luther to be a philosemite, naively regarded his anti-idolatrous innovations as a harbinger of his return to Judaism itself.

When Jews resisted accepting his message of Protestantism, however, Luther grew increasingly and, indeed, vociferously hostile. In 1526 Luther complained of the Jews' stubbornness in clinging to their traditional interpretation of scriptures. His repeated attacks on usury began to assume an antisemitic bias, and he frequently complained about Jews who were stubborn and stiff-necked, equating them with the devil. His invective turned increasingly poisonous. He began repeating the accusations of medieval anti-Jewish polemics and subjecting Jews to a torrent of vile abuse, characterizing them as "venomous and virulent," "thieves and brigands," and finally "disgusting vermin" (*Encyclopedia Judaica*, vol. 11, 585). In addition to reviling Jews, he made practical suggestions for their disposition, ranging from forced labor to outright banishment.

As many Protestant rulers of the times relied on his political advice, Luther's views resulted in the expulsion of the Jews from a number of German principalities, including Saxony in 1543. His virulent anti-Jewish views helped to inspire later centuries of European antisemitism, culminating in the Nazi Holocaust.

Manetho (305BCE?–285BCE?)

Manetho, the third-century Egyptian priest and historian, was the earliest known popularizer of antisemitic themes, which laid an ancient groundwork for later animosity.

In the third century BCE, Egypt's sizable Jewish community, centered in Alexandria, then regarded as a second Athens, had become the heart of the Diaspora. Jewish refusal to accept the religious and social standards of the day was resented by the strongly Hellenized Egyptians, transforming Alexandria into a center of antisemitism in the ancient world. The Alexandrenes took vigorous exception to the emphasis placed by Jews on such events as the Exodus from Egypt, which wounded national sensitivities. Animosities were further aggravated by the equivocal status of the Jews poised between successive conquering minorities and the oppressed native majority. Manetho, an Alexandrene, capitalized on and exploited these sensitivities.

Manetho taught, among other things, that Jews were originally lepers who, upon expulsion from Egypt, became a tribe of
misanthropic wanderers. His theme of the leprous origins of the
misanthropic Jews became a constant in the litanies of pagan antisemitism.

Wilhelm Marr (1818–1904)

Wilhelm Marr, the radically antisemitic nineteenth-century German nationalist, coined the word *antisemitism* to replace *Judenhass*
("Jew-hatred"). The new term, sounding scientifically neutral,
was a way of secularizing traditional Judeophobia. Hostile to religion, Marr, a journalist who championed the modern, wished to
give Jew-hatred a new legitimacy, to remove it from what he regarded as the musty realm of religion and to locate it in the
pseudoscientific category of race.

In his pamphlet, "The Victory of Jewry over Germandom"—
in effect, the first antisemitic bestseller in history—Marr outlined
the threat, drawing upon the prevailing scientific mindset of the
nineteenth century, which racial theories pervaded. Marr argued
that Jews have a biologically destructive mission, to subjugate
and undermine the German and Aryan race. Marr's concept of
antisemitism was essentially a secularization of the Jews' demonization in Christian theology.

Marr, regarded as the "patriarch of antisemitism," despised
Christianity but denigrated Judaism even more and designated it
as the vehicle that, by "inventing" Christianity, imposed the alien
Semitic yoke of moral restraint upon European culture.

Now that Jews were regarded as a race, argued Marr, their
assimilation into Western culture was impossible. Conversion
would be ineffectual, as the Jews' difference lay in their blood; ultimately their biological alienation signified that their evil nature
could only be expunged with their physical elimination.

Karl Marx (1818–1883)

Political philosopher and economic theorist Karl Marx ranks
among the most important thinkers of the nineteenth century. His
writings, such as *The Communist Manifesto* (1848, written with
Frederick Engels) and *Das Kapital* (1864), form the foundation-
stone of Marxism and communism. Few writers in modern history have rivaled Marx's influence on world affairs.

Marx, the grandson of a rabbi and the descendant of talmudic scholars, was converted to Protestantism by his father. As an adult his attitude toward Jews and Judaism was marked by a powerful strain of ideological "self-hatred." Although Marx favored the political emancipation of the Jews, he used strong and indeed vituperative anti-Jewish language to present his view. Regarding Jews as synonymous with bourgeois capitalism, he wrote in "The Jewish Question" the Jew's nationality is that of the merchant. Marx reinforced his reductionist view by arguing that the secular basis of Judaism is practical need and self-interest, and that Deity of the Jews is money.

Marx's derogatory references to Jews, his symbol of financial power and capitalist mentality, mark his private correspondence. Yet his Jewish origins became a powerful catalyst of antisemitic propaganda. The Russian anarchist Mikhail Bakunin, Marx's rival in the First International (the organization dedicated to improving the life of the working class), used anti-Jewish outbursts while attacking Marx. In the first half of the twentieth century, Fascist and Nazi regimes used Marx's ancestral Judaism as a means of bolstering antisocialism and anti-semitism.

Martin Niemoller (1892–1984)

A prominent German anti-Nazi theologian and pastor, Martin Niemoller founded the *Bekennende Kirche* (Confessing Church), a symbol of clerical resistance to Hitler during World War II, in 1933.

Before beginning theological studies at Munster, he served as a naval officer and commander of a German U-boat in World War I. In 1931 he became pastor at Dahlem, a fashionable suburb of Berlin. Two years later, as a protest against interference in church affairs by the Nazis, Niemoller founded the *Pfarrernotbund* (Pastors' Emergency League), which helped combat rising discrimination against Christians of Jewish background. As founder and a leading voice of the Confessing Church, within the larger Evangelical (Lutheran and Reformed) Church of Germany, Niemoller was influential in building clerical opposition to Hitler's efforts to bring German churches under the control of the Nazis.

In 1937 Niemoller was arrested by the Gestapo, Hitler's police, and eventually sent to the Sachsenhausen and then to the Dachau concentration camps. He was moved in 1945 to the Tyrol, where Allied forces freed him at the end of World War II. In 1945 Niemoller wrote his famous lines about the wages of moral indifference:

> First they came for the Communists,
>> and I didn't speak up,
>> because I wasn't a Communist.
>
> Then they came for the Jews,
>> and I didn't speak up,
>> because I wasn't a Jew.
>
> Then they came for the Catholics,
>> and I didn't speak up,
>> because I was a Protestant.
>
> And then they came for me,
>> and by that time
>> there was no one left
>> to speak up for me.
>
> (Niemoller Speeches, *Time*, 1945)

This quote has endured as the most dramatic articulation of the consequences of indifference to racist expression against any group.

After the war, Niemoller became convinced of the collective guilt of the Germans in unleashing war and genocide. He was responsible to a large extent for the Evangelical Church's declaration of German complicity in 1945 with the *Stuttgarter Schuldbekenntnis* (Stuttgart Confession of Guilt).

In later years, increasingly disillusioned with the prospects for world demilitarization, Niemoller became a controversial pacifist. He lectured widely in favor of international reconciliation and against armaments and sought contacts with Eastern-bloc countries.

Origen (185?–254)

Origen, the third-century Christian biblical scholar and theologian of Alexandria, Egypt, propagated, as did many of the church fathers, a theology demonizing the Jews, conceptualizing them as part of a diabolic trinity, the Devil–Antichrist–Jew, in contradistinction to the pure image of the Father–Son–Holy Spirit.

Origen presented as fact that the Jews nailed Christ to the cross and therefore deserve requisite punishment. This idea is part of a general early Christian defamation that charges Jews with the crime of deicide, with national degeneration at the time of Jesus, a people essentially rejected by God, and that attributes their exile among the nations as God's fit chastisement of the Jews for the crucifixion of Christ.

Origen's demonization of Jews grew out of emerging gentile Christianity's need to differentiate itself from ancient Israel. The literal meaning of Jewish texts and historical events was subverted, read as a mere harbinger of Christian history. The more they de-Judaized Jesus, the more easily could they demonize the Jews.

Philip II (Augustus) (1165–1223)

The king of France between the years 1180 and 1223, Philip II, know as Philip Augustus, consolidated power at the expense of feudal lords and doubled the size of the royal domain. He detested Jews, an attitude informed by stories of the blood libel that were gaining currency during this era.

Soon after his accession in 1180, Philip Augustus ordered the imprisonment of all Jews in his kingdom; only a large ransom freed them. To bolster his treasury before going to war, Philip in 1182 ordered the expulsion of the Jews from his kingdom. Synagogues were converted into churches, Jewish real estate was confiscated and most of it sold on behalf of the royal treasury, and debtors were absolved of their obligations to Jews if they paid the treasury one-fifth of the monies owed.

Philip II persecuted Jews even beyond the borders of his kingdom. In 1190 he attacked the Jewish community of Bray-sur-Seine in Champagne, killing almost 100 people. He authorized the return of the Jews to his kingdom in 1198 for purely financial reasons.

Robert M. Shelton (1930–2003)

For nearly three decades, Robert M. Shelton led the United Klans of America, one of the largest and most notorious factions of the racist Ku Klux Klan (KKK). A former factory worker, he was an adept organizer and rode a tide of Klan infighting to become the leader of the largest Klan group.

The United Klan was directly linked to such crimes as the bombing of the 16th Street Baptist Church in Birmingham, Alabama, that killed four black girls; the death of a civil rights worker, Viola Liuzzo, on her way to Montgomery; and the firing into the houses of National Association for the Advancement of Colored People (NAACP) officers.

Shelton's KKK activism came to an end when Morris Dees, founder of the South Poverty Law Center, won a pivotal lawsuit that bankrupted the organization. Dees represented the mother of Michael Donald, a black teenager who was beaten to death by Klansmen and hanged from a tree in Mobile, Alabama. In 1987 a federal jury awarded her a $7 million judgment (Anti-Defamation League, 2004). Similar suits effectively put an end to the United Klans of America.

Joseph Stalin (1879–1953)

Joseph Stalin, the Bolshevik revolutionary who became the autocrat of the Soviet Union between the years 1928 and 1953, embodied the murderous cruelty and organized paranoia of state totalitarianism. His attitude toward Jews veered from the cynical to the calamitous and indeed genocidal.

Stalin had to deal with the "Jewish question" in Russia throughout his entire career, given the endemic nature of anti-semitism in that country, and his actions during his dictatorship of the Soviet Union had a profound influence on the fate of the Jewish people. As the author of the 1913 Lenin-approved essay "Marxism and the National Question," Stalin denied the Jews any national status and adhered to Lenin's concept of their unavoidable progressive assimilation and disappearance.

As commissar of nationalities in the first Soviet government (1917–1923), however, Stalin was responsible for the policy of fostering Yiddish cultural and educational activity, Jewish administrative institutions, and agricultural settlement. He even gave the formal permit to a young theater troupe, Habimah, in Moscow. As late as 1931 he came out strongly against antisemitism, characterizing it as a most dangerous vestige of cannibalism, a sentiment he allowed to be published in the Soviet Union in 1936.

Nonetheless, during the bloody purges he orchestrated in the mid- to late 1930s, Stalin liquidated the Yiddish school system, publications, research institutions, and theaters, as well as many of its leaders. During his rapprochement with the Nazi Germany (1939–1941), he extradited to Berlin German Communists who fled to the Soviet Union, many of them Jews, and suppressed in the press and radio any mention of Nazi antisemitic atrocities, which left the Jews unwarned and unprepared for the mass killings unleashed by the Nazi SS in the first year after their invasion of Russia on 22 June 1941. Stalin's attitude toward Jews was similar to his attitude toward other minority and ethnic groups in the Soviet Union: contempt.

In 1942, he established the Jewish Anti-Fascist Committee, which enlisted worldwide Jewish support for the Soviet war effort. Composed of leading Soviet Jews, the committee was allowed to exploit Jewish hopes and fears and even to use Jewish historical and nationalist rhetoric. When the committee had finished serving its purpose, it was disbanded. Eventually many of its members were shot.

In the postwar era Stalin pursued a two-track policy toward Jews. During 1947 and 1948, he resolutely supported the establishment of a Jewish state in Palestine, a policy clearly directed against Britain's position in the Middle East. The internal repression of Soviet Jews mounted, however—an ominous prelude to the "black years" of Soviet Jewry—with the 1948 camouflaged assassination of Solomon Mikhoels, the gifted Yiddish actor and de facto head of Soviet Jewry.

From 1948 until his death in 1953, Stalin displayed an extremely hostile and indeed paranoid attitude toward everything Jewish. He embarked on a course of complete liquidation of the last remaining Jewish institutions in the Soviet Union. Mass arrests of leading Jewish writers and artists followed. These purges were accompanied by a vituperative campaign of the Soviet press against Western-oriented "cosmopolitans," a code word for Jews.

In mid-1952, a closed trial was held against members of the former Anti-Fascist Committee and other leading personalities in Jewish cultural life, culminating in the execution of twenty-six leading Jewish personalities in the Soviet Union on 12 August 1952. This event has come to be known as the Night of the Martyred Poets. The Doctor's Plot, staged under Stalin's supervision in 1952, was designed to set in motion a genocidal campaign, the exile to Siberia, and eventual elimination of the Jews of the Soviet Union. Only his death on 5 March 1953 prevented this mass atrocity.

Stalin's personal hostility toward Jews extended to his own family: it is known that he strongly disapproved of his children's marriages to Jews.

Marc D. Stern (1950–)

Marc D. Stern, assistant executive director of the American Jewish Congress (AJCongress) and codirector of its Commission on Law and Social Action, is a leading authority on church-state and religious liberty issues. His legal expertise has been instrumental in helping the American Jewish community—and the larger community—successfully resist attempts to weaken First Amendment protections, especially the separation of church and state.

Stern has prepared briefs and conducted litigations on a range of issues, chiefly in the area of religious liberty and civil rights and has drafted legislation for Congress and state legislatures and testimony for Congressional committees. He has taken the lead role in coalitions assembled by the AJCongress that have produced guidelines utilized by government to clarify contentious church-state issues in U.S. society. These guides include *Religion in the Public Schools, Religion in the Federal Workplace,* and *Public Schools and Religious Communities: A First Amendment Guide.*

Tomas de Torquemada (1420–1498)

Tomas de Torquemada, a monk in the Roman Catholic Dominican order (founded in 1216) and confessor to Queen Isabella and King Ferdinand, was appointed grand inquisitor in Spain in 1483. Torquemada's religious fanaticism and intolerance played a major role in the expulsion of the Jews from Spain in 1492.

Torquemada, born in Valladolid, Castile, entered the Dominican Order (popularly known as *domini canes*—"watchdogs of the Lord"—because of their leading role in the Inquisition) at the age of fourteen and soon took his place among the strictest members of his monastery. He came into contact with Queen Isabella in 1469 and soon became her confessor. He was confessor as well to King Ferdinand, affording him influence over the royal couple—especially on the queen—that effectively made him a powerful factor in Spanish politics. His request to Pope Sixtus IV to establish a unified national Spanish inquisition was granted in 1478. Under Torquemada's implacable direction, the Inquisition began to operate on an enormous scale. Many suspected "Judaizers" among the *Conversos* (the so-called Marranos) were arrested and imprisoned to wait in their turn to be tried, tortured, and often burned by the courts of the Inquisition.

During the sixteen years of Torquemada's bloody rule of the Holy Office, a virtual reign of terror gripped the million or so Jews and *Conversos* of Spain. A large number perished at his direction, as did Moorish and Christian heretics. He burned 2,000 heretics and imprisoned 100,000 others (Margolis and Marx 1927, 468). Many were left in prison. Thousands were reported to have remained firm under the torture and fire of the *auto-da-fe* ("the act of faith").

Torquemada, having determined the impossibility of suppressing "Judaizing" among the *Conversos*, called for the removal of the source of the Jewish "contagion." He campaigned vigorously at the Spanish court for exile and on 31 March 1492, Ferdinand and Isabella signed the edict of expulsion. After hundreds of years of residency, the Jews were driven out of Spain. Torquemada has gone down in history as a symbol of religious and ideological extremism, of cruel persecution, and of inhuman interrogation.

Voltaire (1694–1778)

Voltaire, the French writer and philosopher, personified the Enlightenment and its struggle against traditional religion, the divine rights of kings, and the infallibility of the Church. Born in Paris and educated in a Jesuit college, Voltaire's original name was François-Marie Arouet. He was one of the Age of Reason's most famous champions of free thought and political and religious liberty. Voltaire created the climate that made the emancipation of the Jews possible but also prepared the ground for a particularly pernicious form of secular antisemitism.

Voltaire's antisemitism stemmed from his profound hatred for the Catholic Church, and it led him to concentrate a good deal of his wrath on the Hebrew Bible and its followers, the Jews. In writing about the Jews, Voltaire ascribed their religious fanaticism (as he viewed it) as racially based and predicted that the Jews would be a danger to the human race.

References

Anti-Defamation League. 2004. *Extremisim in America.* http://www. adl.org. Accessed August 2004.

Baldwin, Neil. 2003. *Henry Ford and the Jews: The Mass Production of Hate.* New York: Perseus Books Group/Public Affairs.

Bullock, Alan. 1961. *Hitler: A Study in Tyranny.* New York: Bantam Books (originally published by New York: Harper and Brothers, 1953).

Chanes, Jerome A. 1995. *Antisemitism in America: Outspoken Experts Explode the Myths.* New York: Carol Publishing Group/Birch Lane Press.

Margolis, Max, and Alexander Marx. 1927. *History of the Jewish People.* Philadelphia: The Jewish Publication Society of America.

Niemoller: Speeches, 1945, reprinted in *Time,* 28 August, 1989.

Schechtman, Joseph B. 1965. *The Mufti and the Fuehrer.* New York: Thomas Yoseloff.

4

The State of Antisemitism: A Country-by-Country Survey

The material presented in this chapter provides the student, scholar, journalist, public affairs professional, public official, and general reader with an overview of the nature and extent of antisemitism around the world in the first decade of the twenty-first century. The chapter begins with a country-by-country survey of antisemitism. Please note that this is not a comprehensive survey of countries; countries are not included in this survey if they are not significant in terms of geopolitical influences on antisemitism or if antisemitism is not an issue. Population figures for each country are from the *American Jewish Year Book* (New York: American Jewish Committee, 2002). Included at the end of the chapter are brief essays on a number of discrete topics that reflect significant developments in contemporary antisemitism.

Western Europe

A wave of antisemitic attacks against Jews and Jewish institutions, often perpetrated by young Arabs and Muslims, spread over much of Western Europe in 2002 in the wake of the second Intifada. A growing anti-Israel animus has also marked the European political left, including the media and academics.

In France, for example, there were more anti-Jewish incidents in 2002 than in any year since the Holocaust. The relatively weak initial response of European governments against the rise of anti-semitism has been followed by a growing awareness on the part of governments, and by the European Union, of the dangers to their societies of an antisemitic resurgence.

Austria

Population: 8 million
Jewish population: 10,000
Form of government: federal state with two legislative houses
Legal system: civil law with Roman law origin; judicial review of
       legislative acts by the Constitutional Court; separate
       administrative and civil/penal supreme courts
Capital: Vienna

Recent Developments.   Austria has in recent years been in the forefront of Far Right extremism in Europe, resulting in part from the electoral success in recent years of Jorg Haider's Freiheitliche Partei Österreichs; Freedom Party of Austria (FPO). In November 2002, however, the FPO's standing suffered when it won a mere 10 percent of the popular vote, down from an unprecedented 27 percent it had garnered in the 1999 elections, at which time the FPO had joined Austria's coalition government. That success had led to a sharp nationwide rise in antisemitic threats, and some attacks.

Haider's popularity among associations of ultraright-wing male students had by 1999 expanded into the ranks of young workers, a traditional bastion of the Social Democrats. In a nation with a strong preference for stability and predictability, however, Haider's antics in 2003—friendly meetings with Saddam Hussein, to take one example—considerably damaged his standing with voters.

Historical Legacy.   Jews have lived in Vienna for a millennium. During the late Middle Ages, Austrian antisemitism earned the country the title of "the bloodstained land." Under the Hapsburg Empire, particularly during the rule of Franz Joseph II, assimilation was encouraged, and Jews were admitted into the army. The latter years of the nineteenth century, however, saw the fateful emergence of Catholic religious antisemitism.

The *Anschluss*, the incorporation of Austria into Hitler's

Third Reich in 1938, was an early step that culminated in the Holocaust. The official Austrian narrative of its role during World War II is as "the first victim of Nazism," although the populace enthusiastically welcomed the Nazi takeover of Vienna.

A 1995 law establishing a restitution fund for victims of Nazism dictated that the money was not to be construed as "compensation" for Austrian Nazi activity but as a "recognition" of Austrian survivors. The depth of "denial" found in Austria is unmatched anywhere in Europe.

Belgium

Population: 10.2 million
Jewish population: 31,500
Form of government: federal constitutional monarchy with a
     parliament composed of two legislative chambers
Legal system: civil law influenced by English constitutional
     theory; judicial review of legislative acts
Capital: Brussels

Recent Developments.   Belgium is second to France in serving, in 2002, as a host country for Western Europe's most virulent outbreak of antisemitism in recent history. Much as its neighbor to its immediate south, Belgium is home to a growing, poorly integrated, and increasingly radicalized Arab community. The pro-Palestinian policy of the Brussels government has served to complicate a difficult situation.

Although Belgium adopted legislation against Holocaust denial in 1995, it remains a center of neo-Nazis publishing and is the headquarters of VHO, Europe's main distributor of such literature. Since 1996 this Belgium-based publishing firm has used American- and German-based funds to distribute Holocaust-denial texts in print and on-line in French, German, Dutch, and English.

In October 2000 and April 2001, Belgium, driven by its own ethnic and linguistic rivalries and by an increasingly politicized Muslim immigrant community, experienced an uncommon spurt of antisemitism, which effectively shattered the tranquility that Belgian Jews had enjoyed since the end of World War II.

Left-wing, Muslim-inspired antisemitism has not thus far led to a corresponding upsurge of extreme right-wing hatred, although elements of right-wing extremism can be found.

Antisemitism and racism in Belgium are viewed in the context of intraethnic strife in the country. Decentralization has made inroads in Belgian political life: in 2001 the government took steps in distributing power in the country's three regions: Flemish Flanders, French Wallonia, and bilingual Brussels.

Historical Legacy. Antisemitism was most virulent in the 1930s, when Jewish inhabitants comprised largely immigrants, exiles, and political refugees. Fascists, such as the Flemisch Vlaams National Verbond (Flemish National Union) attacked Jews in election campaign and later cooperated with the Nazis, resulting in the deportation of 25,000 Belgian Jews to Nazi death camps.

After the 1967 Six Days' War, left-wing anti-Zionism took on a distinct antisemitic coloration. The Belgian left condoned Palestinian terrorism. On the right, Holocaust denial increased markedly during the 1976–1991 period.

Extremist Groups. The Vlaams Blok is the largest nationalist party, representing Far Right interest in Flanders and Brussels. Adopting Jean-Marie Le Pen's National Front platform, it has enjoyed growing electoral success since 1991, garnering 15 percent of all Flemish votes and double that in Antwerp.

In Francophone Belgium, the Front National Belge (FN), the Front Nouveau de Belgique (FNB), and Referendum (REF) represent the right-wing extremism, although these groups are largely marginalized and fragmented.

Neopagan groups have been restructuring and realigning themselves in recent years within the Far Right. They profess opposition to Judeo-Christianity, to the globalization of the economy led by the United States, and to the Americanization of society.

Manifestations. The vast majority of antisemitic acts in Belgium have been committed by Muslims, with vandalism of businesses, synagogue attacks, and graffiti daubings taking place in 2002.

Assessment. Despite (or because of) the high profile of antisemitism in Belgium, the country has made efforts to counter the phenomenon of intensified extremism. Since 2000, the numbers of anti-Fascist demonstrations have increased, as have legal complaints and proceedings against Far Right leaders. The *cordon sanitaire,* an agreement between all the democratic parties to isolate the Far Right politically in Wallonia, has been reinforced.

Denmark

Population: 5.3 million
Jewish population: 7,000
Form of government: parliamentary state and constitutional
    monarch with one legislative house
Legal system: civil law system; judicial review of legislative acts
Capital: Copenhagen

Recent Developments.   Turmoil in the Middle East has spilled
over into the streets of Copenhagen. Palestinians, in the name of
solidarity, have demonstrated in the heart of the nation's capital,
burned Israeli and American flags, brandished firearms, and attacked police and civilians.

Anti-immigrant rhetoric is spreading in Denmark and giving
rise to an upsurge of extreme right-wing groups, who peddle
xenophobia but who have not incorporated antisemitism as a significant part of their hate-filled ideology.

Danish Jewry, of which one-third are Polish Jews and their
children, appears well integrated and for the most part enjoys
equal access to social services and amenities. More visible minorities, however, have increasingly felt discriminated against,
particularly in the realms of employment, leisure activities, and
police surveillance.

Historical Legacy.   Denmark achieved heroic status during
World War II for its rescue operation in which more than 90 percent of its Jewish population crossed the sea to neutral Sweden.
More recently, Denmark's status as a paragon of courage and
principle has been somewhat dimmed by research indicating that
between 1940 and 1944 twenty-one stateless Jewish refugees were
sent to their doom in Nazi Germany, a move instigated by a nar-
row-minded, corrupt, and antisemitic segment of Danish bureau-
cracy. After the war, these morally comprised civil servants—now
mostly deceased—rose to prominent positions in the Danish police force and legal system.

Finland

Population: 5.1 million
Jewish population: 1,500
Form of government: multiparty republic with one legislative
    house

Legal system: civil law system based on Swedish law
Capital: Helsinki

During World War II, despite Finland's status as a Nazi ally, no anti-Jewish legislation was enacted, and Jews fought in the national army.

Minor threats have been made against the Jewish community when there have been crises in the Middle East, although Finland's pro-Arab orientation since the 1967 Six Days' War has in itself not affected Jews domestically.

France

Population: 60 million
Jewish population: 600,000
Form of government: Republic with a two-house legislature
Legal system: Civil law with indigenous concepts and review of
    administrative but not legislative acts
Capital: Paris

Recent Developments.   Jean-Marie Le Pen, the founder of the Far Right anti-immigration National Front, won a surprise second-place finish in the 2002 election, knocking Prime Minister Lionel Jospin off of the ballot. President Jacques Chirac won an 82–18 percent margin in the 5 May election, the widest margin of victory ever in a French presidential election.

The year 2002 marked a spike in antisemitic propaganda and incidents across France. Indeed, no country in Europe exemplifies the close link between Middle East geopolitics and antisemitic expression more than does France. The second Intifada radicalized Muslims, who constitute nearly 10 percent of the French population and are the nation's largest minority.

In 1999 there were sixty reported antisemitic incidents in France. In 2000 they jumped tenfold to 603. Acts of anti-Jewish violence spurted from nine in 1999 to 116 in 2000. In 2002 attacks ranged from vandalism of Jewish schools and houses of worship to cemetery bombings, drive-by shootings of Jewish commercial establishments, synagogue torchings, and campus harassments and assaults. Most are committed by disaffected local Muslim youth from the Maghreb (Morocco, Algeria, Tunisia) countries.

The lack of a concerted government response to antisemitic agitation was troubling until France proposed legislation to counteract antisemitism. French police initially displayed reluctance to counter Muslim-inspired attacks, as opposed to those emanating from the extreme right. Calls for "death to the Jews" in Paris were not met with strong countermeasures. Authorities customarily use the Middle East crisis and France's own pro-Arab tilt as exculpation for a lack of action. (French diplomacy is considered by many analysts to be generally biased against Israel and, on occasion, descends to scatology in describing the Jewish state.)

Historical Legacy. Antisemitism is a thread running through French history. From the time of the Crusaders; through the Enlightenment, nineteenth-century racialism, the Dreyfus affair; to the twentieth and twenty-first centuries, antisemitism has been a factor in French history.

The Enlightenment of the eighteenth century gave rise to a form of secular antisemitism; Jews were identified as a grasping, moneyed class with a penchant for religious obscurantism and reaction. The Dreyfus affair, which began in 1894 and effectively polarized French society for a decade, was both cause and effect of intense antisemitic agitation in France. The 1930s saw a resurgence of antisemitism nourished by mass immigration of Jews from Nazi-ruled Germany and from eastern Europe, at a time when severe U.S. immigration restrictions made western Europe the destination of choice for politically and economically harassed Jews.

Antisemitism reached its apogee during the Vichy regime of wartime France, which introduced severe anti-Jewish legislation and aided the Germans in identifying and arresting Jews. Seventy thousand men, women, and children—a quarter of the Jewish population—died in Nazi concentration and death camps.

The Six Day War (1967) led to a Gaullist about-face in the Middle East. The Arabs were to be wooed, Israel to be kept at a distance. More recently, the growth of Holocaust denial, the rise of the French extreme right, and Muslim radical fundamentalism have aggravated an already complex situation.

Extremist Groups. The Front National (NF) led by Jean-Marie Le Pen is the leading extremist group on the right; the Nouvelle Resistance, a group founded in 1991, is slightly to the right of the NF. The Research and Study Group for European Civilization (GRECE) is a racist think tank headed by Alain de Benoist that attempts to introduce Far Right extremism into mainstream thought. The 1,500-member Charlemagne Hammerskins, a Satanist skinhead group based in Toulon and closely allied with British neo-Nazis, is devoted to the memory of Hitler.

France is the home of a number of religious Far Right groups with a proclivity for conspiracy theories, including Christianity-Solidarity (Chretienté-Solidarité), allied with Fraternity of St. Peter (Fraternité Sainte Pierre), composed of fundamentalists who remain faithful to the Vatican. Knights of Notre Dame (Chevaliers de Notre Dame) and Catholic Counter-Reform (Contre-reforme catholique) still exist in France as do such influential antisemitic figures as Holocaust denier Robert Faurisson, Marxist-turned-Islamicist Roger Garaudy, and entertainer Brigitte Bardot.

Recent Manifestations.   The range of antisemitic incidents recorded in France in 2002 was noteworthy; the following incidents were selected from those in the first one-third of the year. On 1 January 2002 a classroom of the Jewish Ozar Ha Torah school in Creteil, a Paris suburb, was destroyed by a fire ignited by a Molotov cocktail. Less than a week later, rocks and fire-bombs were thrown at a synagogue in Gousainville, a Paris suburb. On 23 January, rocks shattered the windows of a bus from the Sinai school in Sarcelles, yet another Paris suburb. On 14 March 2002 a Jewish day-care center in Pierrefitte was vandalized with antisemitic inscriptions scrawled on the wall, and a gang of young Arabs insulted and physically attacked two sixteen-year old Jews. Later that month, Toulouse was the scene of a drive-by shooting by hooded individuals at the show window of a kosher butcher shop. On 31 March a pregnant Jewish woman and her husband were attacked in a Lyon suburb, requiring her hospitalization.

April 2002 was a full-blown crisis month with a fusillade of firebombs and Molotov cocktails thrown at synagogues across France. Jews were assaulted in the streets of Paris, and antisemitic graffiti were found on the "Wall of Peace" on the Champ de Mars, close to the Eiffel Tower.

The number of attacks against Jews in France is relatively larger than in other European countries, stemming in part from a growing Muslim population, which comprises a tenth of the population and is vocally and ideologically aligned with an extreme anti-Western politics.

Legal Remedies.   In December 2002, the French National Assembly and Senate unanimously adopted legislation making it an "aggravated crime" to commit acts of violence on the basis of ethnic, racial, or religious background. The legislation, ordering special penalties for such crimes, was a direct response to the more than 400 attacks on Jews and Jewish institutions between the fall of 2000 and the spring of 2002.

Germany

Population: 83 million
Jewish population: 100,000
Form of government: multiparty republic with two legislative houses
Legal system: civil law system with indigenous concepts; judicial review of legislative acts in the Federal Constitutional Court
Capital: Berlin

Recent Developments. The second Intifada triggered a dramatic increase in antisemitic acts by both radical Islamists and right-wing extremists. Desecration of synagogues, cemeteries, and Holocaust memorials surged. In recent years the total number of extreme right-wing crimes has reached its highest point since World War II.

Neo-Nazis infiltrate the German army in order to receive military training and to recruit activists and sympathizers; they cultivate, as well, an elaborate prisoner-support network in East German jails aimed at recruiting activists. Polls indicate that 16 percent of potential army volunteers identity with extreme right-wing parties.

A dramatic spike in German hate sites is visible on the Web. White Power and neo-Nazi skinhead music, often inciting to murder, use the Internet as a favored site. By 2000 the number of Web sites operated by German right-wing extremists had increased twenty-five fold since 1996.

Historical Legacy. Modern German antisemitism, closely tied to nationalism and racism and involving a rejection of liberalism, modernism, and Jewish emancipation, developed in the last quarter of the nineteenth century, following the nation's unification, and continued into the twentieth. The German traditional national *Volk* ideology, combined with nineteenth-century racialist theories, resulted in an antisemitism that was embedded in German institutions. This ideology became a central component of Nazism.

Germany's defeat in World War I was explained by the extreme right as an act of Jewish betrayal. Militaristic and antide-mocratic movements provided the subsoil out of which Nazism emerged. Immediately upon gaining power, the Nazis imple-mented their antisemitic program, eliminating the civil, property, and basic human rights of Jews and forcing them into social iso-lation and emigration. The November 1938 nationwide pogrom, Kristallnacht, added the public use of force to legislative discrim-ination.

The Nazi program culminated in the Holocaust, the state-sponsored genocide that resulted in the annihilation of six million European Jews.

After the defeat of the Nazis, the Allies sought to undo racism and antisemitism in the Federal Republic of Germany. Since 1960 anti-Jewish incitement has been a criminal offense. In 1985, denial of the Holocaust was criminalized as well. The fall of the Berlin wall and the reunification of Germany led to coopera-tion of far rightists in both East and West Germany, which, al-though still a marginal phenomenon, is increasingly worrisome.

Greece

Population: 11 million
Jewish population: 5,000
Form of government: multiparty republic with one legislative
     house
Legal system: based on codified Roman law; judiciary divided
     into civil, criminal, and administrative courts
Capital: Athens

Recent Developments.   In the wake of the socialist government decision in May 2000 to abolish religious affiliation of state-issued identity cards, the Jewish cemetery in Athens was desecrated—more than fifty tombstones, the Holocaust memorial, and the building used for burial services were daubed with Nazi Schutzstaffel (SS) swastikas, symbols, and slogans such as "Hitler was right."

In Salonika (Thessaloniki), whose 50,000 Jews were deported and murdered during the Nazi occupation of Greece, the neo-Nazi organization Chrissi Avgi (Golden Daybreak) in recent years repeatedly daubed swastikas and antisemitic slogans on the site of the Holocaust memorial and on the Monastirioton Synagogue.

Historical Legacy. Jews have lived in Greece since the third century BCE. In the late fifteenth century, several thousand arrived in the country after their expulsion from Spain. Jewish success in intellectual and commercial life coupled with support for the Ottoman Empire vexed Christian Orthodox Greeks, who during the nation's War of Independence (1821–1829), massacred several thousand Jews.

A tense economic climate followed the exodus of Greeks from Asia Minor and their resettlement on the Greek mainland in the first third of the twentieth century, culminating in the burning of the Jewish district of Kampel in Salonika (Thessalonika) in 1931.

Nazi troops occupied Greece in 1941 and deported 65,000 Jews (92 percent of the nation's Jews) to their deaths. Antisemitism continued after World War II, often finding a home in PASOK, the Greek socialist party. Israel was compared to the Nazis in prosocialist papers, and state-controlled radio called for the boycott of Jewish shops. In recent years, Greek diplomatic relations with Israel have improved intercommunal relations.

Ireland

Population: 3.8 million
Jewish population: 1,500
Form of government: democratic republic with a directly elected
    though largely titular president and a two-chamber
    parliament
Legal system: based on English common law, substantially
    modified by indigenous concepts
Capital: Dublin

Recent Developments. Antisemitism is rare and when it surfaces is largely expressed via verbal abuse.

Ireland's economic growth in the late 1990s witnessed its dramatic shift from a nation of emigration to one of immigration. In 1990, thirty-one individuals requested asylum; in 2000, the number sprang to 10,000. Immigration has spawned xenophobic sentiments with occasional verbal and physical attacks on refugees and asylum seekers. A distinct growth in the frequency of racially motivated incidents in the greater Dublin area has been reported in recent years.

Historical Legacy. Jews have lived in Ireland since the seventeenth century, but the majority arrived in the 1880s, mainly from Lithuania. By the early twentieth century some 4,000 Jews lived in Dublin, Cork, and Limerick, with a number attaining high professional and communal status.

In 1904, Father John Creagh, a priest of the Redemptorist Order, incited the local population in Limerick against "blood-sucking" Jewish money lenders and traveling peddlers. He precipitated the Limerick pogrom, a two-year trade boycott of Jewish businesses, accompanied by intimidation, abuse, harassment, and beatings.

Attempts to settle Jewish refugees in neutral Ireland before, during, and after World War II met with consistent government opposition. Prime Minister Eamon de Valera spoke disparagingly of Jews and never uttered a word of condemnation against German genocide.

Italy

Population: 58 million
Jewish population: 30,000
Form of government: republic with two legislative houses
Legal system: civil law; appeals treated as new trials; judicial
      review under certain conditions in Constitutional Court
Capital: Rome

Recent Developments. After years of post–World War II tranquility, Italy has experienced a surge of antisemitic activity and a growing legitimacy of racist stereotypes. The year 2000 saw a 30 percent increase in antisemitic manifestations over the previous year, which itself had experienced a spike in racist incidents. Uncritical sympathy for the Palestinian cause has created a radically anti-Israel mood, aggravated by growing Muslim militancy in Italy.

Legal Developments. Italy's Mancino Law prohibits incitement of racial hatred and religious discrimination. Most right-wing antisemites circumvent the law by declaring their opinions orally during concerts and interviews or by masking their antisemitism as anti-Zionism, as is customary among their left-wing counterparts.

In 2001 the Italian parliament passed a law establishing Holocaust Memorial Day "in memory of the extermination and persecution of the Jewish people and Italian soldiers and politicians in the Nazi camps," which has received wide national press and broadcast coverage. Nevertheless, 37 percent of Italians believe it is time for the Jews to put the Holocaust behind them and stop acting like victims, 10 percent insist that genocide is mentioned too often, and a further 10 percent altogether deny the mass murder of the Jews during World War II.

Historical Legacy. Jews have lived continuously in Italy for over 2,000 years. Times of relative tolerance have alternated with periods of severe repression. From the middle of the sixteenth century onward, papal attitudes toward Jews became increasingly more ambiguous and problematical. The 1861 unification of Italy brought Jews full civil and political rights.

The Fascist era (1922–1945) saw a distinct evolution of antisemitic policy from an initial indifference to Jewish matters, to openly anti-Jewish legislation by 1938 that deprived Jews of their rights, and culminating in 1943 with the deportation of more than 8,500 Jews to Nazi concentration camps.

The Netherlands

Population: 16 million
Jewish population: 28,000
Form of government: Constitutional monarchy with a parliament
    consisting of two legislative houses
Legal system: civil law incorporating French penal theory
Capital: Amsterdam; seat of government: The Hague

Recent Developments. The Netherlands, the most densely populated country in Europe, has grown by a million people in the last decade, partly the result of immigration from Third World countries.

Traditional Dutch liberalism has been consistently critical of the policies of the government of Israel and largely sympathetic and supportive of Palestinians. Although few antisemitic incidents have been reported, Amsterdam Jews report a marked hostility toward them from the large North Africa community. Soon after the outbreak of the second Intifada, Moroccan immigrants in Amsterdam chanted, "Hamas, Hamas, all Jews to the gas."

In recent years the Netherlands has been the site of several meetings of European extreme right-wing activists. Neo-Nazi groups have gathered to commemorate Hitler's seizure of power on 39 January 1933 as well as to organize a memorial service for Rudolf Hess, waving flags bearing runic symbols resembling swastikas. Dutch extremists continue to have a negligible influence, however, on mainstream political life.

Historical Legacy. The Netherlands served as haven for Jews fleeing the Spanish Inquisition and for centuries was one of the most liberal countries in Europe with respect to granting rights to Jews. During World War II, however, Holland was a major gathering point for the annihilation of Jews. Of the 140,000 Jews who lived in the Netherlands at the outset of the war, 107,000 were deported to Nazi concentration camps; only 5,000 returned. The 65 percent wartime murder rate outpaced that of any other Western European nation.

Holland's self-declared "rescuer" image has come in for intense reexamination, with recent scholarship revealing a preponderance of Dutch wartime collaboration.

Legal Measures. In May 2001 the Amsterdam Higher Court of Justice fined French Holocaust denier Robert Faurisson for asserting that Anne Frank's diary was a forgery, a vigorous response that the court followed, as well, in a ruling against Belgian denier Siegried Verbecke and a flea market merchant who sold *Mein Kampf.*

Norway

Population: 4.5 million
Jewish population: 1,000 (mainly in Oslo)
Form of government: constitutional monarchy with one legislative
    house
Legal system: mixture of customary, civil, and common law
    traditions; Supreme Court renders advisory opinions to
    legislative when asked
Capital: Oslo

Recent Developments. Anti-immigrant sentiment has strengthened xenophobic attitudes in Norway, a largely Evangelical Lutheran country. The Progress Party, the nation's third largest, proffers immigration as the explanation for all of Norway's travails. In September 2000 opinion polls showed the Populist Party reaching an approval rating of 34.3 percent compared to 22 percent for the governing Labor Party.

Although antisemitism plays a role in Norwegian Far Right politics, it has not been central to these politics.

Historical Legacy.   Racism and antisemitism have had proponents in Norway since the beginning of the twentieth century. In the 1930s the national Union Party, led by Vidkun Quisling, advocated racist ideas. Upon his assumption of the office of president of Nazi-occupied Norway in 1942, 760 Jews were deported to concentration camps; only 24 returned. A spate of swastika daubing in early 1960 led to the passage of measures combating antisemitism.

Spain

Population: 40 million
Jewish population: 15,000
Form of government: constitutional monarchy with two legislative
    houses
Legal system: civil law system with regional applications
Capital: Madrid

Recent Developments.   Middle East violence in recent years has radicalized the half million Muslims in Spain, mostly immigrants from the Maghreb (Morocco, Algeria, and Tunisia). Attacks on the Jewish community—vandalism of the Madrid Synagogue and desecration of the Barcelona Holocaust memorial—occurred soon after Muslims called for pro-Palestinian demonstrations.

Right-wing extremists, increasingly led by university graduates, have directed much of their ire against immigrants.

Historical Legacy.   After the expulsion of Jews in 1492, Spain remained officially without Jews until 1689, when a new constitution implicitly revoked the edict, allowing private religious practice.

During the civil war of 1936–1939, the small Spanish Jewish community, caught between the warring sides, largely fled the country. General Francisco Franco remained officially neutral during World War II but sympathized with the Axis powers. Yet, the Spanish government issued passports to some 11,000 Sephardic Jews in Nazi-occupied Europe and allowed a further 35,000–45,000 Jews to pass through Spain en route to other destinations. After the war, Spain provided shelter to Nazis and their collaborators.

In 1982, Judaism, together with Islam and Protestantism, was granted equal legal status with Catholicism.

Sweden

Population: 8.9 million
Jewish population: 18,000
Form of government: constitutional monarchy and parliamentary
    state with one legislative house
Legal system: civil law influenced by customary law
Capital: Stockholm

Recent Developments.   Sweden's embrace of high technology—the Internet, mobile phones, and the manufacture of telecommunications equipment—has recently improved its sluggish economy. Yet despite economic advances, Sweden remains one of the world's largest producers of White Power music, race hate videos and compact discs, and neo-Nazi skinhead merchandise.

Reaction in Sweden to Middle East upheaval and the second Intifada, although less vehement than in some other European nations, is still palpable. Pro-Palestinian demonstrations have resulted in several violent antisemitic incidents in recent years.

Holocaust awareness has grown in Sweden, especially in 2000 when Sweden hosted the Stockholm International Forum on the Holocaust, attended by forty-five heads of state who declared that the destruction of European Jewry "challenged the foundation of civilization."

Historical Legacy.   In 1782 Sweden permitted Jews to settle in the country without converting to Christianity. A century later, in 1879, Swedish Jews were emancipated. During the early Nazi period, anti-Jewish attitudes influenced the government's restrictive immigration policy, although at the height of World War II, Sweden made efforts to rescue Jews. Many Danish Jews were saved by Swedes. Nonetheless, antisemitism in the upper levels of Sweden's "blue"—those with ties to Swedish royalty and other Swedish aristocracy—has long been a factor in the social fabric of the society.

A violent neo-Nazi skinhead culture that emerged in the first half of the 1980s has become the main nucleus of today's racist subculture. Arab news outlets, such as Radio Islam, have spread vitriolic antisemitic propaganda and Holocaust denial.

Switzerland

Population: 7.2 million
Jewish population: 18,000
Form of government: federal state with two legislative houses
Legal system: civil law system influenced by customary law;
    judicial review of legislative acts, except with respect to
    federal decrees of general obligatory character
Capital: Bern (administrative); Lausanne (judicial)

Recent Developments. Manifestations of popular antisemitism initially declined with the global settlement of dormant accounts, Jewish assets held in Swiss banks since before World War II, only to resurge with the outbreak of violence in the Middle East. Many anti-Israel demonstrations are marked by the use of antisemitic slogans, often invoking violence and murder. Hani Ramadan, the leader of the Geneva Islamic Center and the grandson of Egypt's fundamentalist Muslim Brotherhood founder Hassan al-Bana, has called for jihad against Israel.

Anti-Israel sentiment is also evident on the left, which accuses Israel of racism and colonialism and even at times denies its right to exist. Many use the Middle East as a pretext for anti-semitism, a pretext convenient for expressing anti-Jewish sentiment deriving from the debate over bank accounts of Holocaust victims, dormant since the end of the war, which resulted in a $1.25 billion fund to be distributed to entitled beneficiaries.

The Swiss continue to have difficulty in comprehending their nation's moral culpability during World War II, especially its behavior toward Jewish refugees. Although a majority supports findings that Swiss immigrant policy was biased against Jews during the war, the government justifies this policy as a result of the circumstances of the period and therefore no apologies are deemed necessary. In September 2002 Swiss voters rejected the Solidarity Fund referendum, designed to aid Holocaust and racial persecution victims. The Conference of Swiss Bishops asked forgiveness, however, for its attitude toward Jews during the Holocaust, and the Geneva canton expressed its regrets to victims and their families.

Skinheads, whose numbers have multiplied more than three-fold in recent years, are heavily equipped with sophisticated, illegal weapons and turn increasingly to the Internet to incite violence. New recruits, as young as thirteen, are more radical and prone to violence; they still lack organizational structure and charismatic leadership, however.

In recent years, Holocaust deniers and Nazi sympathizers have been dealt with gingerly, almost all receiving suspended sentences.

Historical Legacy.   Swiss Jews were the last in western Europe to acquire complete emancipation. During World War II, more than 30,000 refugees, mostly Jews, were refused asylum and forced to return to Nazi-controlled countries. The cost of the up-keep of the 24,000 who were admitted was imposed on the Swiss Jewish community.

In the 1980s antisemitic incidents, apart from activities of small neo-Nazi groups, occurred mainly as a reaction to events in the Middle East.

United Kingdom (UK)

Population: 60 million
Jewish population: 280,000
Form of government: constitutional monarchy with two legislative
    houses
Legal system: common law tradition with early Roman and
    modern continental influences; no judicial review of acts of
    Parliament
Capital: London

Recent Developments.   Tension in the Middle East increased the number of anti-Zionist and antisemitic incidents; in 2000 such occurrences surged by 50 percent. Although the UK's Muslim population is overwhelmingly South Asian, it contains active cells of such Arab violent groups as Hizbollah and Hamas. The most active Islamist group is al-Muhajiroun (the Emigrants), which denies the Holocaust and often calls for the outright killing of Jews.

Open expressions of antisemitism have become nearly re-spectable in London's political and diplomatic salons. As was re-ported in numerous press reports in 2002, at a private dinner hosted by Lord Black of Crossharbour, owner of the *Daily Tele-graph,* the French ambassador to Britain, Daniel Bernard, referred to the Jewish state as "that shitty little country Israel," the pre-sumed cause of world's troubles, and asked "why should the world be in the danger of World War III because of those people?"

Analysts suggest that this incident, although minor, was not trivial in that it reflected the transmuting of anti-Israel rhetoric into an antisemitic anti-Zionism.

Legal Development.   The effective enforcement of the Race Relations Act of 2000 has helped lower overt extreme right-wing antisemitic propaganda.

Historical Legacy.   Individual Jews were present in the British Isles in Roman times, but organized settlement of Jews began after the Norman conquest of 1066. Massacres of Jews occurred in many English cities in 1190, most notably in York. The medieval settlement of Jews ended with their expulsion by King Edward I in 1290.

The current English Jewish community dates from 1656. By the early nineteenth century, Jews had achieved virtual economic and social emancipation. The influx of Jewish refugees from Russia between 1881 and 1914 led to antisemitic agitation in both parliament and in the streets of English cities.

The rise of fascism and Nazism encouraged the growth of the British Union of Fascists and the Imperial Fascist League, which led to street battles between racist right-wingers on the one hand and Jews and leftists on the other.

The United Kingdom severely limited Jewish immigration to Palestine, a policy known as the White Paper, effectively assuring that many refugees during World War II would remain stranded in Europe and die in the Holocaust.

Vatican City

See discussion under Special Topics.

Eastern Europe

Extreme right-wing nationalists and Nazi apologists continue to pose a problem with respect to antisemitism, although their influence may be on the decline. Arab and Muslim populations are small, and the pro-Palestinian, anti-Israel sentiment so pronounced in Western Europe does not have equal resonance in most Eastern European countries.

Deeply rooted popular antisemitism is embedded in the countries of the former Soviet Union, although the state-sponsored antisemitism no longer exists. The involvement of the Russian Orthodox Church in the production and distribution of antisemitic material is a growing concern.

In contradistinction to Western Europe, antisemitic violence does not possess an Arab/Muslim connection and often appears with no clear pattern or motivation.

Belarus

Population: 10 million
Jewish population: 26,000
Form of government: authoritarian republic with two legislative
    bodies (the legal status of the Stalinist government of
    Alexander Lukashenko is controversial).
Legal system: civil law
Capital: Minsk

Recent Developments.   Antisemitism has shown a steady decline in recent years. President Aleksandr Lukashenko, whose authoritarian government and state-controlled economy are highly controversial, has reiterated his support for the fight against racism and antisemitism. Although desecration of synagogues, cemeteries, and Holocaust memorial sites has continued over the years, criminal perpetrators have been prosecuted.

The Belarus branch of the neo-Nazi Russian National Unity Party has branches in more than ten cities, the most active in Minsk and Vitebsk. Its distribution of antisemitic material remains largely unhindered by the authorities. The bookshop chain of the Russian Orthodox Church has sold some antisemitic books that include chapters on the *Protocols of the Elders of Zion.*

Belarus's newly established law, About the Freedom of Confessions and Religious Organizations, which codifies religious persecution, has met with the condemnation of the U.S. State Department for its violations of international principles of religious freedom.

Historical Legacy.   Jews have lived in Belarus for more than 500 years. At the turn of the twentieth century, Jews comprised 14 percent of the population, forming the majority in the region's principal towns.

During the Holocaust, Belarussian Jewry was virtually destroyed. Since the collapse of the Soviet Union, the rights of the remaining remnant have been fully respected.

Bulgaria

Population: 8 million
Jewish population: 5,000
Form of government: parliamentary democracy with one
    legislative body
Legal system: civil and criminal law based on Roman model
Capital: Sofia

Recent Developments.   Since the collapse of the Communist
regime, the rights of the Jewish community have been fully respected. Antisemitism remains largely marginal, and ultranationalist organizations have a largely insignificant following.

Typical targets of racist attacks are Romas (Gypsies), ethnic
Turks, and Asians. Bulgaria has an estimated 500,000–800,000
Roma, a transnational people who have become the orphans of
post-Communist transition. Only 7–8 percent of Roma children
attend secondary school compared to 54 percent of ethnic Bul-
garians. Without adequate social welfare, many turn to begging,
crime, and prostitution, reinforcing traditional stereotypes and
creating a vicious circle of violence and counterviolence.

Bulgarian-Israeli relations are good, evidenced by President
Petar Stoyanov's four-day official visit to Israel in 2000, resulting
in mutually beneficial cooperation.

Historical Legacy.   During World War II, Bulgaria was a Nazi
satellite state with persecution of the Jews modeled after the
Nuremberg Laws. Twelve thousand Jews from Bulgarian-occu-
pied territories in Greece and former Yugoslavia were deported to
Nazi death camps with the authorization of the Bulgarian government and King Boris III. In the spring of 1943, Bulgarian Jews
were rescued, just in time, because of domestic and international
pressure. This pressure led King Boris III to postpone and later revoke their deportation.

Croatia

Population: 4.4 million
Jewish population: 2,000
Form of government: multiparty republic with one legislative
    house
Legal system: based on civil law system
Capital: Zagreb

Recent Developments. Although concern regarding the reha-
bilitation of the wartime Nazi puppet state and its leadership continues, the ongoing consolidation of the democratic reforms put
into motion after the death in 1999 of nationalist strongman
Franjo Tudjman is encouraging.

Historical Legacy. Under the pro-Nazi Ustashe regime, many
tens of thousands of Serbs, Jews, and Roma (Gypsies) perished in
such concentration camps as Jasenovac. In 1956, the Croatian Liberation Movement (HOP) was founded in Argentina by Ante
Pavelic, leader of the Ustashe movement and the wartime Nazi
puppet state of Croatia, and found legitimacy in independent
Croatia in 1993. President Franco Tudjman wrote in the late 1980s
that the number of Jews who died in the Holocaust was exaggerated but later, under intense international pressure, apologized
for his remarks.

Czech Republic

Population: 10.5 million
Jewish population: 5,000–15,000
Form of government: multiparty republic with two legislative
　　houses
Legal system: civil law based on Austro-Hungarian codes; legal
　　code modified to bring it in line with Organization on
　　Security and Cooperation in Europe (OSCE) obligations and
　　to eliminate Marxist-Leninist legal theory
Capital: Prague

Recent Developments. Although the Czech Republic is home
to an estimated 5,000 skinheads, the Jewish community has seen
little overt antisemitism. Xenophobia, racism, and hate crimes,
particularly against Roma (Gypsies), who suffer disproportion-
ately from poverty, disease, and illiteracy, raise concern, however.
Worrisome as well is the growing general dissatisfaction with the
state of the economy and its spillover xenophobic and antisemitic
effects.

　　The government's desire to proceed with Holocaust restitution and its effort to counter antisemitism have met with wide
praise.

Historical Legacy. The flourishing Jewish community of the interwar period, which numbered 118,000, was nearly entirely an-

nihilated during the Holocaust. The 1952 Moscow-orchestrated show trials of Rudolf Slansky and other top Communist Party officials, several of whom were Jewish, bore clear antisemitic overtones.

Since the collapse of the Communist regime, the right of the small Czech Jewish population has been respected.

Estonia

Population: 1.36 million
Jewish population: 3,000
Form of government: multiparty republic with single legislative body
Legal system: based on civil law system; no judicial review of legislative acts
Capital: Tallinn

Recent Developments. The Baltic nation's complicity in the crimes of the Holocaust exerts a negative impact on Jewish-Estonian relations. Annual commemorations of World War II events continue to have antisemitic overtones. The education ministry declared that Holocaust education is unnecessary.

Historical Legacy. The Jewish community was founded by conscripts in the army of Czar Nicholas I (1825–1855). In the 1930s, the pro-Fascist group Omakaitse rapidly gained influence and assisted the Nazi invasion in 1941, engaging in the roundup and slaughter of Jewish men. The Estonian *Selbstschutz* ("self protection units") collaborated with the Nazis in shooting of thousands of Jewish men, women, and children. Additionally, the Nazis used Estonians in the running of concentration camps.

Hungary

Population: 10.4 million
Jewish population: 90,000
Form of government: parliamentary democracy with one legislative house
Legal system: rule of law based on Western model
Capital: Budapest

Recent Developments. In the first such agreement since the mid-nineteenth century, in 1999, the national government and the

Jewish community signed a formal agreement promoting the "political and social and economic stability of Hungarian Jewry" and acknowledging its contributions to "the moral and intellectual progress" of the nation. The agreement pledges the government to commemorate the Holocaust and to introduce Holocaust education into the school curriculum.

Much of extremist activity is focused precisely against Holocaust memory and education, as well as Jewish claims for wartime compensation. Frequent reference is made to the "communist holocaust," in which Jewish leaders were allegedly involved. Istvan Czurka's Justice and Life Party (MIEP) and its newspaper, *Magyar Forum*, have become centers of xenophobic and veiled antisemitic rhetoric. Although the number of neo-Nazis is small, their visibility in public demonstrations on national holidays or anniversaries linked to World War II is notable.

Historical Legacy.   Until the early 1940s, Hungary, in comparison to other eastern European countries, was widely perceived as something of a haven for Jews, despite widespread social antisemitism; the Horthy regime's exclusion of Jews from certain positions in civil service, law, and medicine; and the adoption in 1920 of a *numerus clausus* law that restricted the admission of Jews to universities.

The Nazi invasion of Hungary in March 1944 led to the destruction of nearly 600,000 Hungarian Jews with considerable collaboration by local authorities.

Under communism, anti-Zionist agitation became a regular feature of the press, although generally milder than in neighboring Soviet satellites. Since the collapse of Communist rule, Hungary has restored the rights of its largely secular Jewish population, the largest in Eastern Europe outside of the former Soviet Union.

Latvia

Population: 2.4 million
Jewish population: 12,000
Form of government: multiparty republic with a single legislative
     body
Legal system: based on civil law system
Capital: Riga

Recent Developments. President Vaira Vike-Freiberga denounced Latvian Nazi war criminals, stressing the need to try them without regard to the statute of limitations, a marked change from a hesitant and ambiguous government policy regarding veterans of Latvian Nazi SS divisions. Some explain this shift as the result of the nation's eagerness to enter the North Atlantic Treaty Organization (NATO) and the European Union. In the early 1990s many World War II criminals were pardoned by the post-Soviet Latvian government.

Historical Legacy. Jews have lived in the territory of Latvia since the mid-seventeenth century. On the eve of World War II, Latvian Jewry totaled over 90,000, most of whom were murdered by the Nazis and their Latvian collaborators. At the end of the war only 320 Jews survived in Latvia. The current Jewish community consists largely of immigrants from various regions of the former Soviet Union.

Lithuania

Population: 3.7 million
Jewish population: 7,000
Form of government: parliamentary democracy with a single
    legislative body
Legal system: based on civil law system
Capital: Vilnius

Background. The government shows increasing willingness to come to grips with Lithuania's wartime past, although bureaucratic delays have impeded the prosecution of war criminals. Extreme right-wing parliamentary groups continue to advocate legitimizing the Lithuanian regime set up by the Nazis in 1941. Equally troubling is the general public's continued exoneration of national collaboration during the Nazi period.

The Lithuanian Catholic Church has been forthright in condemning antisemitism.

But Jewish cemeteries have been desecrated in Vilnius, Kaunas, Psaualis, and Kelme. Nazi flags and antisemitic slogans have appeared in Lithuania on 20 April, the anniversary of Hitler's birthday.

Historical Legacy. Lithuanian Jewry, one of the oldest such communities in Europe, played a significant role in the development of religious thought and secular Yiddish culture. Its capital, Vilnius (or Vilna), commonly known as the Jerusalem of Lithuania, was a notable center of rabbinic thought and of scholarship, publishing, literature, and social activism.

On the eve of World War II, Lithuanian Jewry numbered 250,000. One of the hardest hit by Nazi mass murder, only 12 percent of prewar Jewry survived.

After Lithuania regained independence in 1990, the wartime genocide was officially denounced, various Jewish public and state organizations were reestablished, and government funding was allocated for Jewish cemeteries and sites of mass murder.

Poland

Population: 38.6 million
Jewish population: 5,000–15,000
Form of government: parliamentary democracy with two
        legislative houses
Legal system: mixture of Napoleonic civil law and holdover
        Communist legal theory; changes being gradually
        introduced as part of broader democratization process
Capital: Warsaw

Recent Developments.   Patterns of ethnic prejudice continue to be structurally present in Poland, despite efforts over the past two decades to promote tolerance and cultural pluralism and to expose acts of discrimination. Deeply ingrained anti-Jewish stereotypes continue to go largely unacknowledged. Antisemitism is present both in the mainstream and on the fringe, the latter consisting in part of an extreme right wing boasting an estimated 15,000 activists with a widely developed social and cultural network. Synagogue and cemetery desecrations continue in large and small Polish cities.

Poland's legal and penal code has recently made provisions against hate speech and Holocaust denial. The judicial system nonetheless is often highly reluctant to use the law against perpetrators of hate crimes. The Roman Catholic Church in Poland continues to be deeply ambivalent about Christian-Jewish relations and antisemitism. Ultraconservative clerical circles, associated with the right-wing, xenophobic Radio Maryja, promote an antiminority model of Polish national identity in which antisemitic propaganda plays a central role.

Revelations during 2001 with respect to the wartime Jedwabne massacre of 1,600 Jews by Poles challenged long-held and deeply ingrained perceptions of Poles as victims and not as perpetrators of atrocity. In 2001 the Polish Episcopate publicly apologized for the sins committed against the Jews in Jedwabne and elsewhere, an apology tempered by prejudicial statements made by Cardinal Glemp and Father Henryk Jankowski, a Gdansk priest and ally of former prime minister Lech Walesa. The rightwing Polish press continues to engage in either denial or exculpation by linking revelations about Jedwabne with property claims advanced by "the international Jewish lobby."

Having said this, the fact remains that Poland, partly under pressure from the West and as a condition for joining NATO, has made enormous strides—the most significant in Europe in recent years—in terms of its relations with Jews.

Historical Legacy.   During the Middle Ages, Poland served as a haven for Jews fleeing persecution and antisemitism in Germany. After the partition of Poland between Russia, Prussia, and Austria-Hungary in 1795, intercommunal relations deteriorated. The rise of modern Polish nationalism intensified antisemitism by portraying the Jews as the religious, economic, and existential "other." During the interwar period (1918–1939), hostility to Jews was actively supported by the Catholic Church and by a wide section of Polish society, eventually leading to economic boycott and violence.

On the eve of World War II, Poland had 3.5 million Jews, the largest such community in Europe and comprising one-fifth of the world's Jews. The destruction of over 90 percent of Polish Jewry during the Holocaust by the Nazis and their collaborators essentially brought one thousand years of Jewish life in Poland to an end. Postwar hopes of improved relations with the miniscule saved remnant were thwarted by the murder of some 2,500 Jews, culminating in the 1946 pogrom in Kielce, which claimed forty-two lives.

Romania

Population: 23 million
Jewish population: 14,000
Form of government: constitutional republic with a multiparty
   system

Legal system: formerly mixture of civil law system and
   communist legal theory; now based on the constitution of
   France's Fifth Republic
Capital: Bucharest

Recent Developments. A dwindling, mainly elderly Jewish
population faces no immediate serious threat. The surprising
electoral success of the Greater Romania Party (PRM), led by former dictator Nicolae Ceausescu's hagiographer Cornelius Vadim
Tudor, is troubling. Tudor's ties with France's Jean-Marie Le Pen
have caused alarm. Since PRM's electoral success, the pro-An-
tonescu school of Holocaust and World War II revisionism has
gained considerable ground.

Historical Legacy. In the nineteenth and early twentieth
century, Romania was widely considered one of Europe's most
antisemitic countries. In 1923, following intense foreign pressure,
citizenship was reluctantly granted to Jews. Antisemitism reemerged as a potent influence in the late 1920s with the establishment of the Fascist Legion of Archangel Saint Michael (also
known as the Iron Guard and the All for the Country Party) led
by Corneliu Zelia Codreanu.

   On 14 September 1940, General (later Marshal) Ion Antonescu, with the help of the Iron Guard, organized the National
Legionary State. A part of the Jewish population was deported to
the Trans-Dniester (Transnistria) killing fields. Further atrocities
were committed by the Romanian army against the Jewish population in the occupied territories—a total of some 20,000–25,000
Jews were burned alive in Odessa on 23 October 1941 on the orders of Antonescu. Some 250,000–300,000 Romanian Jews perished under Romanian jurisdiction during World War II.

   Several Jews were prominent in the immediate postwar Romanian Communist Party, but at no point was its leadership composed of a majority, or even a plurality, of Jews. Neonationalism
reached a new peak under Nicolae Ceausescu, who condoned but
did not officially endorse antisemitism.

   In recent years many Romanian intellectuals have joined
forces with the Jewish community in fighting xenophobia.

Russia

Population: 144 million
Jewish population: 335,000

Form of government: federal multiparty republic with a bicameral
legislative body
Legal system: based on civil law system; judicial review of
legislative acts
Capital: Moscow

Recent Developments. Antisemitism has been used as a
weapon in the political battles within Russia, particularly by the
Communist Party and its parliamentary faction, which accuses
the government of selling out to the Jews. Although legislation
against antisemitism and extremism is on the books, parliamentary members take advantage of their protected status to make
racist remarks, and Russian authorities do not always react with
sufficient rigor in bringing antisemitic criminals to justice. The
weekly Communist newspaper *Zavtra* (*Tomorrow*) is the most influential of the anti-Jewish media.

Some 25 million Muslims live in Russia, mainly in the northern Caucasus, Tatarstan, and Bashkirstan. Extremist Islamic tendencies, as well as Muslim antisemitism and anti-Zionism, have
intensified during the war in Chechnya. The Russian Federal Security Service in 2000 uncovered cells of the radical Muslim
Brotherhood movement, which coordinates its activities with
Middle East Islamic terrorist organizations, in half of Russia's administrative regions.

Historical Legacy. The October Revolution (1917) brought to an
end a long history of institutionalized antisemitism in Czarist
Russia and seemingly accorded the Jewish minority equal rights.
But the rise of Stalin in the late 1920s marked increasing persecution and repression of minorities.

During the Nazi occupation of the Soviet Union during
World War II, approximately two million Jews were killed. In the
postwar years, Stalin's institutionalized anti-Jewish campaign intensified, culminating in the execution of major Jewish figures in
the arts.

Khrushchev's policy of de-Stalinization during the 1950s was
not devoid of its anti-Jewish elements. During the Brezhnev era
anti-Zionist propaganda campaigns were aimed at countering
Jewish emigration sentiment. Glasnost and the eventual breakup
of the Soviet Union brought in their wake a resurgence of ultranationalist and antisemitic groups emerging on the fringe of
Russian politics.

Slovakia

Population: 5.4 million
Jewish population: 3,000
Form of government: multiparty republic with one legislative
   house
Legal system: civil law system based on Austro-Hungarian codes;
   legal code modified to comply with the obligations of
   Organization on Security and Cooperation in Europe
   (OSCE) and to eliminate Marxist-Leninist legal theory
Capital: Bratislava

Recent Developments.   The small, aging Slovak Jewish community has been confronted by ultranationalist forces, seeking to re-
habilitate Catholic priest Jozef Tiso, leader of the wartime pro-
Nazi Slovak state responsible for the deportation of the nation's
Jews to death camps. The Slovak Catholic Church, although trying to appear sympathetic to the Jewish tragedy, sides with much
of Tiso's clerical Fascist legacy.
   President Rudolf Shuster has condemned the Tiso pro-Nazi
regime and was the first Slovak head of state ever to visit Israel,
where he apologized for his nation's deeds during the Holocaust.
   In March 2000, the participants of the European Conference
of Rabbis had to enter the presidential palace in Bratislava by a
side-door entrance owing to a noisy neo-Fascist demonstration;
this, after the meeting had been transferred from Vienna in
protest against Jorg Haider's electoral victory in Austria.
   In late 2000 some 5,000 copies of *Mein Kampf* were published
in two volumes with a thirty-page commentary, stressing the
book's violent racism and antisemitism. Violent attacks on Roma
(Gypsies) by skinheads continue to plague the nation.

Historical Legacy.   For a thousand years Slovakia was part of
the Hungarian kingdom. In 1918 it became part of Czechoslovakia, one of the more economically and democratically advanced
interwar nations in Eastern Europe. The more favorable economic
position of the Jews and their mother tongue, either Hungarian or
German, led to a spike in Slovakia of anti-Semitism, however.
   During World War II, the pro-Nazi Tiso not only acceded to
Hitler's demand of the deportation of the 137,000 Slovakian Jews
but also paid Nazi Germany 500 marks for every Jew deported.
Seventy-two thousand Jews perished in the death camps; another

forty thousand died in the deportation from the southern part of the country, which was occupied during the war by Hungary.

Ukraine

Population: 49 million
Jewish population: 135,000
Form of government: multiparty republic with a single legislative body
Legal system: based on civil law system; judicial review of legislation
Capital: Kiev

Recent Developments.   In contrast to Russia, antisemitism has played a much weaker role in Ukrainian political and economic rivalries in the last decade. Russia, rather than the Jews (who play a much more modest role in Ukrainian political and economic life), is blamed for the nation's worsening economic and social situation. Racism is moderated by Ukraine's aspirations to be accepted into NATO.

Antisemitism is fueled by economic instability, political immaturity of the population at large, and the weakness of governing institutions. Vandalism of Jewish sites has declined in Ukraine, however, in comparison to the early days of independence. As in other states of the former Soviet Union, the shift toward democracy has been accompanied by a marginal ultranationalist movement.

Historical Legacy.   Intolerance in Ukraine, where Jews have lived for nearly a thousand years, is traceable to the establishment of the early Russian Church. In 1648, the Chmielnitski uprising against Polish-Russian overlords claimed tens of thousands of Jewish lives, the worst pre-Holocaust disaster to have befallen east European Jewry. In the eighteenth and nineteenth centuries, *Haidamaki*, groups of peasants, launched more limited but in some respects even more vicious attacks against local Jewish communities.

During the civil war that followed the Bolshevik revolution, thousands of Jews were murdered in pogroms by anti-Red forces, who regarded all Jews as Communists. Local collaboration of the Ukrainian population with German Nazis in widespread Holocaust crimes assured the nearly total annihilation of the nation's Jews.

Africa

Ethiopia

Population: 66 million
Jewish population: 100
Form of government: federal republic with two legislative houses
Legal system: currently transitional mixture of national and
     regional courts
Capital: Addis Ababa

Ethiopia, with a tiny Jewish population, has long been a flash point for Jewish issues. Most of the Falashas (Ethiopians who practice Jewish traditions) were airlifted to Israel during the 1980s and 1990s. The fate of the Falash Mura (Ethiopian Christians who retain a generational tie to Judaism) is uncertain.

South Africa

Population: 43.5 million
Jewish population: 85,000
Form of government: multiparty republic with two legislative
     houses
Legal system: based on Roman-Dutch law and English common
     law
Capital: Pretoria

Recent Developments.   Right-wing extremist groups have increasingly posed little threat to the Jewish community. South Africa is home to 850,000 Muslims, however, and the second Intifada has led to a spike in antisemitism, particularly among extremist groups. The extremist Muslim view of Israel and the Jews first came to the fore during the Lebanon war in 1982 and has remained part of the South African scene ever since.

The African National Congress (ANC) successfully proposed a parliamentary motion to adopt the Stockholm Declaration in which, at an international gathering in the Swedish capital in January 2000, forty-six countries committed themselves to Holocaust memory and education. The debate in parliament was the first ever of its kind.

Historical Legacy.   The ban of Jewish settlement in the Cape Colony introduced during the rule of the Dutch East India Company (1652–1795) was abrogated by the Batavian administration (1803–1806). Jews achieved enfranchisement only with the British occupation of South Africa in 1902. Jewish immigration—largely from Lithuania, in response to the discovery of gold and diamonds in the late nineteenth century—generated considerable opposition. Antisemitism in the 1920s culminated in the 1930 Quota Act, which virtually ended immigration from Eastern Europe; and in the 1937 Aliens Act, which kept out German Jews seeking a haven from Fascist oppression.

Close ties between South Africa and Israel in the 1970s complicated the Jewish community's relationship with the majority black population, who increasingly sympathized with the Palestinian cause. Since the normalization of South Africa politics in the postapartheid era, antisemitic incidents have been confined to the Far Right and Islamist groups.

Arab/Islamic Countries

With the outbreak of the second Intifada in 2000, there has been in the Arab and Islamic worlds a pronounced increase in state-sponsored and popular antisemitism, even in such countries as Egypt and Jordan, with which Israel is formally at peace. Holocaust denial, blood libels, and canards about Jewish involvement in the 11 September 2001 attacks against the United States are widespread.

Antisemitism permeates the media, schools, and government-run organizations. What makes Arab and Islamic antisemitism difficult to parse is that anti-Jewish hatred in the Middle East and in the larger Islamic world of South and East Asia is often a manifestation of a wider hostility to Western democratic values and culture.

Afghanistan

Population: 27.7 million
Jewish population: 50
Form of government: interim regime
Legal system: The Bonn Agreement calls for a judicial
    commission to rebuild the justice system in accordance with
    Islamic principles, international standards, the rule of law,
    and Afghan legal tradition
Capital: Kabul

Jews have lived in Afghanistan since antiquity. A century ago they numbered 40,000, but since 1948 a mass emigration to Israel has left only a few families in Kabul and Herat.

The terrorist attacks in the United States on 11 September 2001 set off a chain reaction that resulted in the fall of the radical Islamist Taliban regime and produced Afghanistan's first orderly change of government in decades. Anti-Zionist and anti-Jewish agitation diminished with the disappearance of the Taliban.

Algeria

Population: 32.3 million
Jewish population: 100
Form of government: multiparty republic with two legislative
    bodies
Legal system: socialist, based on French and Islamic law
Capital: Algiers

Recent Developments.   Algeria has continued to suffer from the chronic and endemic violence of the past decade that has taken 200,000 lives. The Armed Islamic Group and the Salafist Group for Preaching and Combat have attacked civilians and military targets and have espoused radical anti-Zionism. Although Jews are not the primary targets of these groups, antisemitism emerges in the context of their deep hostility to the West as a whole and to France and the United States in particular. Violence between militant Islamists and government forces has increased the vulnerability of the few remaining Jews in Algeria.

Historical Legacy.   During the nineteenth century, traditional Christian antisemitism was introduced into parts of the Muslim world, including Algeria, by European clerics and missionaries.

Following the 1894 Dreyfus affair, the leading French antisemite, Edouard Drumont, was elected as the representative in the French Parliament for Algiers. Although the antisemitic movement of the time was short-lived, Nazi propaganda in the 1940s caused its resurgence. Under the Vichy regime, Jews were treated with contempt by the French authorities, who applied the antisemitic Vichy laws in all their severity.

In 1960, during anti-French riots, the Great Synagogue of Algiers was destroyed, Jewish areas were attacked repeatedly, and synagogues and cemeteries were desecrated. After Algeria gained independence from France in 1962, most of the country's 140,000

Jews emigrated. Algerian Jews, almost universally Gallicized, were viewed by Muslims not only as Zionists, and therefore enemies of Arab national aspirations, but also as Europeans. The 1967 Six Days' Israeli-Arab War led to further looting, attacks, and desecrations.

Bahrain and Other Gulf States

Population (Bahrain): 700,000
Jewish population (Bahrain): 20
Form of government (Bahrain): constitutional monarchy
Legal system (Bahrain): generally Islamic law and English
    common law
Capital (Bahrain): Manama

With the exception of Bahrain, Gulf societies evolved without Jewish communities. Antisemitic images were largely imported to the Gulf States by westerners, who introduced such antisemitica as *The Protocols of the Learned Elders of Zion*. The continuous identification of the Gulf societies with Arab and Palestinian issues has encouraged the persistence of a belief in demonic images of Jews.

There is little antisemitism directed at the small Bahraini Jewish community, which enjoys a close relationship with the regime.

In the late nineteenth century, Jews from Iraq, India, and Iran settled in Bahrain, where they engaged in commerce and made their living from handicrafts. In 1947–1948, before the establishment of the State of Israel, antisemitic riots broke out and the synagogue was destroyed. Most of the Jews subsequently emigrated, but a tiny community remains.

Egypt

Population: 70 million
Jewish population: 200
Form of government: republic with one legislative house
Legal system: based on English common law, Islamic law, and
    Napoleonic codes; judicial review by Supreme Court and
    Council of State
Capital: Cairo

Recent Developments. The Egyptian media's longstanding hostility to Israel and Jews took an even more ominous turn with the new thirty-part television series, *Horseman without a Horse*, based on the infamous antisemitic forgery, *The Protocols of the Learned Elders of Zion*. As part of an intensified psychological warfare campaign against Israel, the *Protocols* appears to be gaining an ever-stronger foothold in the Arab world in general and in Egypt in particular. (The producer and actor of the series insisted his research revealed that nineteen of the twenty-four protocols have been put into practice.) Egyptian mainstream media have made an unprecedented number of references to Israel as a Nazi model state and to Zionism as pure racist ideology.

In early 2001 Egyptian and other Arab film producers decided to make a movie version of Syrian defense minister Mustafa Tlas's book, *The Matzah of Zion*, which is based on a blood libel.

Historical Legacy.   Prior to 1948 the Jewish community in Egypt numbered nearly 70,000. During the 1948–1949 Israeli War of Independence, hundreds of Jews were arrested, killed, or maimed in bombings of Jewish neighborhoods, and Jewish-owned property and businesses were confiscated.

In 1952 attacks on Jewish establishments caused millions of pounds worth of damage. After the 1956 war with Israel, 3,000 Jews were interned and thousands of others, whose property was confiscated, were given a few days to leave the country. After the Six Days' War of 1967, hundreds of Jews were arrested and tortured. By the mid-1970s only 350 Jews remained in Egypt, with the figure today at around 200. Official and semi-official anti-Zionist policies; sanctioned antisemitism.

The 1979 peace treaty between Israel and Egypt enabled Jews to establish links with Israel. But rising anti-Israel hostility, often tinged with raw antisemitism, has cast a pall on the handful of Jews in Egypt.

Iran

Population: 64 million
Jewish population: 25,000
Form of government: Islamic republic with one legislative house
Legal system: constitution codifying Islamic principles of
        government
Capital: Tehran

Recent Developments.   Tension in the Middle East has further intensified harsh anti-Zionist propaganda expressed by the Iranian Shi'ite leadership. As is the case throughout the Arab world, the distinction among Jews, Israel, and Zionism is blurred. In April 2001, Iran's leader, Ayatollah Khamenei, addressing an international conference in Tehran, spoke of the "close collaboration of the Zionists with Nazi Germany" and referred to "the exaggerated numbers of Jews killed in the Holocaust," a claim, as he put it, "fabricated to solicit the sympathy of world public opinion and . . . justify the atrocities of the Zionists."

The arrest in 2000 of thirteen Jews charged with spying for Israel and the conviction and imprisonment of ten of them continued to instill a sense of insecurity among Iranian Jews, who suffer discrimination in employment, housing law, and education. Yet more Jews live today in Iran than in any other Muslim country; most enjoy a relative sense of stability.

In recent years Iran has become a center for the dissemination of Holocaust revisionist views. Many Holocaust deniers have been welcomed and given opportunities to lecture at Iranian universities. The *Tehran Times* appears especially obsessed with Holocaust denial, insisting that there "is no documentary evidence for the gassing of even one human being in a German camp."

Historical Legacy.   Throughout their millennium-long history in the region, Iranian Jews have experienced several periods of intense persecution and discrimination. Between 1613 and 1662, many Jews were forced to convert; their property was looted, and those who dared resist were murdered. Hundreds as well were murdered at the end of the eighteenth century in the northern city of Tabriz as a result of a blood libel.

The golden era of Iranian Jews, lasting from 1963 to 1979, during which they enjoyed cultural and religious autonomy under Shah Mohammed Reza Pahlavi, came to an abrupt end with the ascendancy of the extremist clerical regime. The 1979 Islamic revolution forced 50,000 Jews to flee Iran. Shi'ite religious leaders have continued their implacable enmity toward Israel and Zionism.

Iraq

Population: 24 million
Jewish population: 75
Form of government: As of mid-2004, governmental structure yet
    to be determined
Legal system: based on Islamic law
Capital: Baghdad

Recent Developments. Unremitting anti-Zionism and anti-Americanism have marked Iraq's foreign policy since the establishment of the State of Israel. Saddam Hussein, dictator of Iraq until 2003, repeatedly asserted, "An end must be put to Zionism." Iraq's second-highest official described Jews as "the sons of monkeys and pigs" and called for the destruction of the Jewish state.

It is early to say whether the United States invasion of Iraq in 2003, and subsequent efforts at installing democratic governmental structures, will have an impact on the anti-Zionist stance of Iraq's leadership. Analysts suggest that the ethnic and religious configuration of the new government will have an impact on this issue.

Arabic translations of classic antisemitic texts such as *The Protocols of the Learned Elders of Zion* and Hitler's *Mein Kampf* are widely available in Iraq.

Historical Legacy. Iraqi Jewry was once one of the largest and most important Jewish communities in the Middle East. A sovereign Iraq, which acquired independence in 1932 from Britain, institutionalized discrimination against Jews, however. In a major pogrom unleashed a month after the anti-British, pro-Nazi Rashid Ali revolt in May 1941, 129 Iraqi Jews were murdered, hundreds were wounded, and Jewish property was looted and destroyed. In August 1948 many Jews were imprisoned on charges of "Zionism" and some executed. More than 120,000 Iraqi Jews, after being stripped of their citizenship and assets, left for Israel in the early 1950s.

During the Six Day War of 1967, Jews were subject to severe restrictions. Some 300 Jewish business owners and community leaders were arrested and tortured for "espionage" or for "economic support for Israel." In 1971 the Ba'ath party conducted the public hanging of thirteen young Jews and executed many others.

Jordan

Population: 5.2 million
Jewish population: none
Form of government: constitutional monarchy with two legislative
    houses
Legal system: based on Islamic law and French codes
Capital: Amman

The Jordanian Writers Association works closely with other professional associations in Jordan to combat normalization with Israel. At its meeting in May 2001, it reiterated alleged parallels between Zionism and Nazism, Jewish exploitation of the Holocaust, and the exaggerated numbers of Jews annihilated during World War II. It also praised such Holocaust deniers as Roger Garaudy and Robert Faurisson and proposed establishing an Arab Committee of Historical Revisionism.

Jordan shares much of its history with Israel. The area comprising Jordan (then known as the Transjordan) was established in 1920 within the British mandate of Palestine. After the War of Independence of 1948–1949, Jordan annexed the West Bank, administering it until Israel gained control of the area in the Six Days' War (1967). In 1970–1971, Jordan was wracked by a civil war, a struggle that ended with the expulsion of the Palestine Liberation Organization (PLO) from Jordan. In 1988 King Hussein renounced all Jordanian claims to the West Bank in favor of the PLO. Six years later, Jordan and Israel signed a full peace agreement.

Lebanon

Population: 3.6 million
Jewish population: 75
Form of government: multiparty republic with one legislative
    house
Legal system: Ottoman law and Napoleonic Code
Capital: Beirut

Lebanon continues to be occupied by 30,000 Syrian troops, ensuring that Damascus has a firm hand over Lebanese domestic and foreign policy. Following lengthy talks between Beirut and Jerusalem, Israeli troops abruptly withdrew from Lebanon in 2000.

In 1929 there were an estimated 5,000 Jews in Beirut. As one of twenty-three minorities in Lebanon. they were treated with tolerance and enjoyed complete religious, economic, and legal freedom. Lebanese Jews were not adversely affected by the establishment of the State of Israel in 1948. Indeed, the number of Jews increased to an estimated 13,000 after 1948 because of the emigration of Jewish refugees from Syria and Iraq; these emigrants either remained in Lebanon or crossed into Israel. Jewish emigration from Lebanon began after the Six Days' War in 1967 and reached a peak during the civil war, which broke out in 1975.

Libya

Population: 5.2 million
Jewish population: 50
Form of government: socialist state with one policymaking body
Legal system: Italian civil law and Islamic law
Capital: Tripoli

Libya has engaged in state-sponsored terrorism; numerous examples include the explosion of Pan Am Flight 102 over Lockerbie, Scotland, in December 1988. International relations in the 1990s were dominated by the consequences of the bombing of the U.S. airliner; the United States accused Libyan nationalists of the deed and imposed a trade embargo on Tripoli, endorsed by the UN in 1992. Libya handed over the bombing suspects for trial in the Netherlands, and UN sanctions were suspended, but most U.S. sanctions remained in place.

The year 2003 marked the thirty-second year of dictatorial rule by Colonel Muammar Qaddafi. He remains an implacable opponent of Israel and denies the right of Jews to live in Israel, arguing that those who immigrated after 1948 should return to their countries of origin. He invariably uses the term *Israeli* and *Jew* interchangeably. Although a champion of the Palestinian cause, he saw fit in the 1990s to deport them from Libya.

Libyan Jews were subjected to Italian racial laws in 1936. During World War II, the Jewish quarter of Benghazi was sacked and 2,000 Jews were deported. In November 1945, more than 100 Jews were murdered in anti-Jewish riots in Tripoli.

Most of the 38,000 Libyan Jews emigrated to Israel before Libya achieved independence in 1951. During the 1967 Six Days' War, 118 Jews were killed amid widespread destruction of Jewish property. When Qaddafi assumed power in 1971, all Jewish property was seized without compensation.

Morocco

Population: 30 million
Jewish population: 5,800
Form of government: constitutional monarchy with two legislative
    houses
Legal system: based on Islamic law and French and Spanish legal
    systems
Capital: Rabat

King Hassan II, a moderate ruler, died in July 1999 after thirty-eight years on the throne and was succeeded by his eldest son, Sidi Muhammad, who took the name Muhammad VI.

The Jewish community of Morocco, which dates back more than 2,000 years, has experienced various waves of both tolerance and discrimination. The worst outbreaks of antisemitic violence occurred during the Middle Ages, when Jews were massacred in Fez in 1033 and in Marrakesh in 1232. Following the establishment of the French protectorate in 1912, Jews began to enjoy greater equality. Under the Vichy regime, Jews suffered discrimination, but King Muhammad V did much to ensure that they were not deported.

By 1948 there were some 270,000 Jews in Morocco; thereafter the population decreased rapidly. The establishment of the State of Israel provoked numerous attacks on Jewish individuals and premises. In June 1953, forty-three Jews were murdered, and violence persisted until Morocco gained independence in 1956.

After the 1967 Six Day War, many middle-class Jews emigrated because of worsening conditions, including a virulent antisemitic and anti-Israel press campaign.

Pakistan

Population: 145 million
Jewish population: 100–200
Form of government: interim military regime
Legal system: based on English common law with provisions to
    accommodate Pakistan's status as an Islamic state
Capital: Islamabad

Background. Pakistan's 7,500 religious seminaries (*madrassas*), with a student body of nearly a million drawn from the dire poor, function as incubators for the birth, growth, and development of Islamic martyrs. Those situated near the border with Afghanistan, especially in the lawless North-West Frontier Province, have become an assembly line for jihad (holy war). They are taught a form of militant Islam that is strongly anti-American and anti-Zionist.

In 1992, India established diplomatic relations with Israel, prompting the Pakistani media to repeatedly refer to the "Zionist threat on our borders."

Historical Legacy.   The creation of Pakistan in 1947 brought a revocation of Jewish communal rights and political representation. Following the establishment of Israel in 1948, violent attacks were unleashed against Pakistan's small Jewish community of approximately 2,000, resulting in large-scale emigration, mostly to India. Anti-Israel rhetoric, a constant in Pakistan's history, has reached a crescendo since the 11 September attacks and the outbreak of the second Intifada.

Saudi Arabia

Population: 22.8 million
Jewish population: none
Form of government: monarchy
Legal system: Islamic law; some secular codes as well
Capital: Riyadh

Saudi Arabia's ruling family's adherence to the strict form of Wahabbi Islam informs the ways in which it relates to the external world. The kingdom has maintained a strong anti-Israel position since the creation of the State of Israel. Saudi Arabia's reputation suffered from the 11 September 2001 terrorist attacks, as fifteen of the nineteen suicide bombers were identified as Saudis, as is Osama bin Laden, the leader of the al-Qaeda terror network. Limited Saudi aid has been given to U.S. antiterrorist activities and to the war in Afghanistan.

Although demonstrations are usually forbidden in Saudi Arabia, several were held in 2001 to attack Israel and the United States. The more than 5 million foreign workers residing in Saudi Arabia are subject to severe forms of discrimination. Non-Muslims are barred from visiting Mecca and its holy sites. English-language programs that aim to promote Islam among foreign workers regularly seek to discredit both Judaism and Christianity. Strong ambivalence toward the U.S. military presence and anti-Western sentiment is often expressed through religious rhetoric.

Sudan

Population: 36 million
Jewish population: none
Form of government: federal republic with one legislative body
Legal system: Based on English common law and Islamic law
Capital: Khartoum

For more than half of the twentieth century Britain ruled Sudan, generally in partnership with Egypt, until Sudan achieved independence in 1956. Since then the country has fluctuated between ineffective parliamentary government and unstable military rule. The non-Muslim population of the south has engaged in ongoing resistance and rebellion against the Muslim-controlled government of the north, leading to famines and the displacement of some four million people.

Sudan, which denies the legitimacy of the State of Israel and opposes peace between Arabs and Jews, has in recent years become a center of Islamic extremism with ties to al-Qaeda. Militant Islamist groups such as Islamic Jihad, Hamas, and Hizbollah have received military training as well as political support in Sudan.

Until 1948 a small number of Jews lived in the Sudan. Following the establishment of the State of Israel, most chose to leave the country. During the late 1970s, the Numeiri government was the only Arab state, apart from Morocco and Oman, that staunchly supported both the visit of the Egyptian president, Anwar Sadat, to Israel and the Camp David Accords. In the mid-1980s, Sudanese leader Jaafar Numeiri assisted the emigration of Jews from Ethiopia to Israel.

Syria

Population: 17 million
Jewish population: 200
Form of government: autocratic regime controlled mainly by the
     president's religious sect, the Alawites
Legal system: based on Islamic law and civil law system; special
     religious courts
Capital: Damascus

Background.   Bashar al-Assad succeeded his father, the long-standing dictator Hefz el-Assad, as president in 2000 and reaffirmed Syria's hard-line attitude toward Israel. Although cautious criticism of the government and the Ba'ath party was initially permitted, by mid-2001 dissidents were arrested and the state-run media attacked reform elements.

In an address welcoming Pope John Paul II to Damascus, Syrian president Bashar al-Assad condemned Jews for considering themselves "the chosen people" and "superior to other nations." In an effort to solicit the pope's sympathy and support, he sought to demonstrate that Muslims and Christians alike had been targeted by Jews since the time they had allegedly betrayed and tortured Jesus Christ and had presumably made a similar attempt against Muhammad. In response to the international uproar his remarks aroused, Assad noted that no one can accuse the Semitic Arabs of being antisemites.

The Syrian press frequently promotes Holocaust denial and equates Zionism with Nazism. Syrian textbooks exalt anti-Zionism and martyrdom as virtues. Supporting terrorist activities against Israelis a common theme, although the term *terror* itself is never used in this context—such activities are sanitized as operations against military targets.

The book *Matzah of Zion,* in its eight printing in Syria, propagates the age-old antisemitic blood libel that accuses Jews of preparing unleavened bread, the traditional Passover staple, from the blood of Arab children.

Historical Legacy.   The Jewish community, which dates back to the third century BCE, prospered under the Ottomans, who conquered Syria in 1516. Three centuries later, the Damascus affair (1840), which involved the first use of doctrinaire European antisemitism in the Muslim world, rocked the relative calm of the Jews in the region.

In 1947, there were about 30,000 Jews in Syria. Hostility toward Israel led to officially orchestrated riots in Aleppo and Damascus with numerous dead and wounded. Fifteen thousand Jews fled; a further 10,000 left during periods when emigration restriction were temporarily lifted.

During the 1960s the Ba'ath regime subjected Syrian Jews to strict supervision. The situation improved a bit in the 1970s, and in 1992 the Assad regime announced that Jews could leave Syria provided their destination was not Israel. By 1995 virtually all Jews who wished to leave had done so.

Tunisia

Population: 10 million
Jewish population: 1,500
Form of government: multiparty republic with one legislative
     house
Legal system: French civil and Islamic law
Capital: Tunis

Despite their fairly liberal treatment during various periods of Tunisian history, Jews have generally felt vulnerable to the effects of Arab nationalism and the threat posed by militant Islamists. The 2002 bombing of the synagogue on the island of Djerba and the deaths of European tourists indicated the spread of Islamic extremism and al-Qaeda in Tunisia.

Tunisia was occupied by France in 1830, and a French protectorate was established in 1881. The Jews largely benefited from the French presence. During World War II, the brief German occupation of Tunisia led to the establishment of forced-labor camps for thousands of Jews.

Following independence in 1956, the situation of Tunisian Jewry was tolerable, but anti-Jewish rioting broke out during the Six Days' War in 1967, resulting in the destruction of Jewish shops and damage to the Great Synagogue in Tunis.

Turkey

Population: 67.3 million
Jewish population: 20,000
Form of government: multiparty republic with one legislative
    house
Legal system: derived from various European continental legal
    systems, with remnants of the Ottoman system
Capital: Ankara

Recent Developments.   The 2002 election of the Justice and Development Party and its advocacy of Islam created some concern about a fundamentalist tilt in secular Turkey. Nonetheless, the party leadership is viewed by most analysts as a moderating force; they expect that Turkey can provide the Middle East with an Islamic imprimatur for liberal change. In late 2003, however, the bombings of two Istanbul synagogues raised serious concerns.

The European Union's 2002 refusal to consider Turkey as a potential member aggravated a tense situation, leading to fears that the Eurasian nation would look east for its future political and social development. Turkey continues to walk a fine line between control of terrorist elements and suppression of political dissent, which creates unease in European capitals.

Since the outbreak of the second Intifada, mass protests have taken place at universities and mosques at which Israel was cursed and its flag burned.

Historical Legacy.   The present-day Jewish community largely traces its origin to the Sephardim expelled from Spain in 1492. Under the Ottoman Empire, Jews enjoyed relatively comfortable conditions; when necessary, police quelled outbreaks of violence resulting from the spread of blood libels.

As part of the Treaty of Lausanne, the Turkish republic, created in 1923 from the Turkish remnants of the Ottoman Empire, provided equal rights for Jews. During World War II, Turkey imposed some discriminatory measures against non-Muslims, yet it served as a corridor of safe passage for many Jews fleeing Nazi Europe.

Since the 1960s, antisemitic articles have appeared in the Turkish press, particularly in Islamicist publications. Since 1986, there have been several attacks on synagogues in Turkey.

Yemen

Population: 18 million
Jewish population: 1,000
Form of government: multiparty republic with two legislative
   houses
Legal system: Based on Islamic law (Ottoman law), English
   common law, and tribal law
Capital: Sanaa

The hard-to-patrol mountainous hinterlands of Yemen have served as a refuge for terrorist fugitives and followers of Osama bin Laden, whose ancestors are Yemeni.

Yemeni Jews, renowned for their skills as silversmiths and jewelers, were traditionally prevented from owning land and were subject to other restrictions. During the Ottoman period, Jewish men were forced to grow side locks, and Jews were prohibited from wearing bright colors, building homes above a certain height, or riding animals. In 1905 a new law required Jewish orphans under the age of thirteen to be converted to Islam.

Before the establishment of the State of Israel in 1948, some 16,000 Jews managed to escape to Palestine. Between June 1949 and July 1950, a further 43,000 Jews were airlifted to Israel in an operation dubbed "Operation Magic Carpet."

Asia and Australasia

Australia

Population: 19.5 million
Jewish population: 120,000
Form of government: federal parliamentary state with two
    legislative houses
Legal system: based on English common law
Capital: Canberra

Recent Developments.   As is the case in most British Commonwealth nations, antisemitism is not a significant issue in the Australian populace. The country is, however, home to a large Arabic-speaking community and has seen the acceleration of Middle East violence spark a dramatic increase in antisemitic incidents. Pro-Palestinian demonstrations in Melbourne and Sydney occasioned the burning of Israeli and American flags as well as being the occasion for antisemitic speeches by such extreme right-wing activists as Jack King.

As of 2002, vandalism, harassment, assault, and synagogue desecration jumped 47 percent over the previous year and soared 62 percent higher than the average over the previous ten years.

Right-wing extremists have increasingly used the Internet as the preferred and unregulated mode of antisemitic transmission. Extreme left-wing groups demonize Israel in language often nearly indistinguishable from that of the Far Right.

Virtually all of Australia's antisemitic organizations promote Holocaust denial of one kind or another, usually employing it as the central plank in their platforms. They perceive the nation's ethnic communities, particularly those from Central and Eastern Europe, as fertile ground for recruitment and appeal to them by Holocaust revisionism. Growing cooperation between Muslim and right-wing extremists is particularly salient in the area of Holocaust denial.

Historical Legacy.   Jews have been a presence in Australia since British colonization in 1778. They have figured prominently in public and have experienced little or no institutionalized discrimination.

During the period from 1933 to 1945, informal restrictions, guided by a conscious desire to minimize the number of Jews entering the country, were placed on those fleeing the ravages of Nazi Europe. Nevertheless, some 40,000 Jewish refugees entered the country during the Nazi period and during the 1950s.

China

Population: 1.28 billion
Jewish population: 3,000–3,500
Form of government: single-party people's republic with one
      legislative house
Legal system: Civil code in effect since 1987
Capital: Beijing

China has for many years sided with the Arab world in the Arab-Israeli conflict. More recently, a thaw in Sino-Israeli relations has developed.

There have been small Jewish populations in China for centuries—most recently a substantial community of refugees from Nazi-occupied lands during World War II—and antisemitism has not been an issue.

The island of Hong Kong and adjacent islets were ceded by China to the British in 1842. A joint Chinese-British declaration, signed on 19 December 1984, paved the way for the entire territory to be returned to China, a transfer that occurred on 1 July 1997.

Antisemitism has not been an issue for the Jewish community of Hong Kong.

India

Population: 1.04 billion
Jewish population: 5,600
Form of government: multiparty federal republic with two
      legislative houses
Legal system: based on English common law
Capital: New Delhi

Background.   India faces problems of massive overpopulation, environmental degradation, extensive poverty, and ethnic and religious strife. Tensions over the disputed territory of Kashmir coupled with terrorist attacks against India by Muslim extremists have brought India and Pakistan to the brink of war.

Facing similar threats from a politicized Islamic world, India has drawn closer to Israel, with which it has had diplomatic relations for over a decade.

Historical Legacy.   Jews trace their origin in India as far back as 175 BCE. In 1730 Baghdadi Jews began settling in Bombay, but they did not become a presence until 1832 when David Sassoon arrived and began a commercial and philanthropic dynasty that drew Jews from throughout the Ottoman Empire.

Indian Jewry once numbered between 30,000 and 50,000, but the emergence of both an independent Israel and India, with its then pronounced pro-Arab tilt, spelled the community's dramatic decline. Fearful of anti-Jewish expression and of an economic downturn, most Indian Jews left for Israel, and others went to other English-speaking countries.

Indonesia

Population: 213 million
Jewish population: 200–500
Form of government: multiparty republic with two legislative houses
Legal system: based on Roman-Dutch law, substantially modified by indigenous concepts
Capital: Jakarta

Although there are few Jews living in Indonesia, the country is nonetheless important as the world's most populous Muslim nation. Until 2002 Indonesia was relatively unmarked by religious radicalism. In recent years, however, radical Islam has become a presence in Indonesia.

Israel

Population: 6.4 million
Jewish population: 5.2 million
Form of government: multiparty republic with one legislative house
Legal system: mixture of English common law, British Mandate regulations, and (in personal-status matters) Jewish, Christian, and Muslim legal systems
Capital: Jerusalem

Tension within Israel and between Israel and the Arab states over the last five and a half decades has clearly influenced and often exacerbated antisemitism around the world. The antisemitic face of anti-Zionism is often indistinguishable from antisemitism.

Japan

Population: 127 million
Jewish population: 2,000
Form of government: constitutional monarchy with a national Diet (parliament), consisting of two legislative houses
Legal system: modeled after European civil law system with English-American influence; judicial review of legislative acts in the Supreme Court
Capital: Tokyo

Background.   Bank failures and a shrinking gross domestic product have put into question Japan's expected role as an international engine of growth. Even in financially more robust times, the development of commercial ties between Tokyo and Jerusalem has never reflected Japan's economic strength, owing to Japan's wariness of the Arab boycott.

Historical Legacy.   A small number of Jewish merchants appeared in Japan in the mid-nineteenth century, subsequent to the arrival of Commodore Matthew C. Perry of the U.S. Navy in 1853. The Jewish population grew in the early twentieth century with the passage of refugees from the Russian revolution through Siberia and Kamchatka and during the late 1930s from Nazi Germany. In 1940, 5,000 Jewish refugees from Poland and Germany arrived in Kobe, subsequently leaving for the United States and Shanghai.

Antisemitic literature continues to be published in Japan. In the mid-1980s, Holocaust-denying books attained best-sellerdom.

Malaysia

Population: 22.6 million
Jewish population: 50–100
Form of government: federal constitutional monarchy with two legislative houses
Legal system: Based on English common law
Capital: Kuala Lampur (but transferring to Putrajaya by 2012)

In the months after 11 September 2001, Malaysia arrested dozens of suspected Islamic militants. In June 2002 Prime Minister Mahathir bin Mohammad, who had been Malaysia's ruler since 1981 and had frequently expressed anti-Zionist and even antisemitic remarks, announced he would step down in 2003. Before he did, however, he delivered an address replete with antisemitica to an international conference. Generally speaking, however, antisemitism has not been a significant issue in Malaysia.

New Zealand

Population: 3.8 million
Jewish population: 4,000
Form of government: constitutional monarchy with one legislative house
Legal system: Based on English Common Law
Capital: Wellington

The settlement of Jews in New Zealand dates from the establishment of British sovereignty in 1840. Jews have occupied important positions in New Zealand, including that of prime minister and chief justice. There have been six Jewish mayors of Auckland and two of Wellington. Unlike similar societies, such as Australia and Canada, there were no Fascist groups in New Zealand during the 1930s, although antisemitism manifested itself on a small scale among some owners of small farms and businesses who sought a scapegoat for their economic difficulties during the 1930s and later.

Latin America

Radical and extremist groups have taken advantage of the region's economic crises, lack of credibility of traditional institutionism, and corrupt, ill-equipped security organizations to spread racist hatred, rendering Jewish communities potentially vulnerable.

The pro-Palestinian tilt in the policies of many Latin American countries contributes to a climate that makes antisemitic attitudes and acts more acceptable. Chiles's Palestinian community of 400,000, the largest outside the territories under Palestinian Authority jurisdiction, and Venezuela's influential 1.3 million Arab community, as well as sizable Arab/Muslim populations in various other nations in the region, are significant in this regard.

Argentina

Population: 37.5 million
Jewish population: 200,000
Form of government: federal republic with two legislative houses
Legal system: mixture of U.S. and Western European legal
     systems
Capital: Buenos Aires

Recent Developments.   Economic chaos and collapse triggered a severe political crisis at the end of 2001. The Argentine Jewish community, the largest in Latin America, was adversely affected by the economic mayhem, prompting emigration to Europe, North America, and Israel. There was little antisemitic fallout, however, from the economic crisis.

An Iranian defector's sealed testimony revealed that Tehran organized and carried out the bombing of the Jewish Community Center in Buenos Aires in 1994 that claimed eighty-five lives and paid then-president Carlos Saul Menem $10 million to cover it up. Iran had cultivated President Menem because of his Muslim ancestry and connection to Argentina's small but influential Syrian-Lebanese community.

The rapid growth of neo-Nazi Internet activity in Latin America is sobering. Indeed, one of Argentina's main ultraright-wing nationalist movements, Partido Nuevo Triunfo (New Triumph Party; PNT), led by Alejandro Biondini, evolved from an Internet publication and now provides links to 300 extreme right-wing sites around the world.

Historical Legacy.   The legacy of the Spanish colonial period, and indeed of the Inquisition in Spain, informed a tradition of intolerance in Argentina. In the early years of the twentieth century, however, Jews were among the beneficiaries of generally unrestricted large-scale immigration, thought imperative for the country's modernization. Nonetheless, nativist opposition led a pogrom in January 1919, the so-called "Tragic Week," one of the most serious episodes of anti-Jewish violence in the nation's history.

The 1930s saw an upsurge of antisemitism, part of a wider xenophobia, that drew on ideas from European Fascist sources and that was abetted by Nazi Germany's diplomatic corps in Buenos Aires.

Argentina became a haven for Nazi war criminals seeking to escape Europe in the immediate postwar years.

Bolivia

Population: 8.5 million
Jewish population: 600
Form of government: multiparty republic with two legislative
    houses
Legal system: based on Spanish law and Napoleonic Code
Capital: La Paz (administrative); Sucre (judicial)

Bolivia broke away from Spanish rule in 1825. Much of its subsequent history has consisted of a series of hundreds of coups and countercoups.

Presidential balloting in August 2002 resulted in the election of Gonzalo Sanchez de Lozada, a millionaire mining executive who grew up in the United States and speaks Spanish with an accent, to the nation's highest office. Bolivia continues to face deep-seated poverty, social unrest, and drug production.

Skinhead posters, featuring Hitler's face decorated on either side with swastikas and eagles and urging people to counter the "plague of the Jews and their accomplices: capitalists, neoliberals and communists," have appeared in the main cities in recent years.

Brazil

Population: 172 million
Jewish population: 160,000
Form of government: multiparty federal republic with two
    legislative houses
Legal system: based on Roman codes
Capital: Brasilia

Recent Developments.   The fallout of the second Intifada spurred a rise in antisemitic incidents.

Brazil, which leads Latin America in the number of antisemitic Web sites, is home to various extremist groups, although discrimination on the basis of sex, race, religion, and nationality is unconstitutional. Isolated skinhead episodes do not constitute a viable group threat and have usually resulted in immediate police reaction and condemnation.

Brazil perceives itself as a racial democracy with equality for all regardless of skin color; yet many blacks experience racial discrimination in housing, employment, and education. The nation's indigenous people are also a main target of xenophobic sentiment. Although contemporary Brazil has few overt antisemitic movements, the popular television comedy *Escolinha do Barulho* (*Cool School*), which reaches millions of young Brazilians, depends primarily on the use of stereotypical characters, among the most notorious of whom is Samuel Blaustein, "the miserly Jew."

Historical Legacy.   Conversos (New Christians) fleeing the Portuguese Inquisition were among the first Europeans to settle in then Dutch-controlled parts of Brazil, especially Recife. Most Brazilians, who had very little contact with Jews, viewed antisemitism as the creation of upper-class elites.

Modern Brazilian antisemitism dates from the 1930s when the Vargas nationalist regime pursued a nativist policy and tolerated the virulently antisemitic campaign of the Brazilian Integralist Party. Government policy, which clearly sided with the Axis powers, banned the entry of European Jews fleeing from Nazism.

Chile

Population: 15.5 million
Jewish population: 21,000
Form of government: multiparty republic with two legislative
    houses
Legal system: based on code of 1857 derived from Spanish law
    and subsequent codes influenced by French and Austrian
    law; judicial review of legislative acts in the Supreme Court
Capital: Santiago

Recent Developments.   Chilean Jews are largely well integrated into society and occupy important positions in the professions and the arts. The outbreak of the second Intifada occasioned scattered outbreaks of antisemitism, largely the work of Arab and Muslim extremists, as well as the Palestine embassy in Chile. The Chilean Palestinian community, numbering 300,000 strong and one of the largest in the world, presses leading political figures to condemn Israel and encourages neo-Nazi groups to join their anti-Zionist activity. Notable among the latter is Patria Nueva Sociedad (PNS), whose antisemitism serves as a common denominator with radical Moslem organizations.

Some fear that Chile may be one of the Latin American countries most vulnerable to an Islamicist terrorist attack because the nation has no antidiscrimination laws to curb extremist activity.

Historical Legacy. Jewish immigration to Chile, largely from Russia, eastern Europe, and the Balkans, increased significantly in the beginning of the twentieth century. Jews from Germany and Austria arrived in restricted numbers before and during World War II. Chileans of German descent formed pro-Nazi parties that tried unsuccessfully to overthrow the government in 1938. The last wave of Jews arrived in Chile from Hungary after the 1956 uprising.

Cuba

Population: 11 million
Jewish population: 1,500
Form of government: unitary socialist republic with one legislative house
Legal system: based on Spanish and American law, with large elements of Communist legal theory
Capital: Havana

The 1990s saw a visible revitalization of Jewish life in Cuba. As the regime loosened restrictions on religion, Cubans of all persuasions discovered or rediscovered their ancestral faiths. A steady stream of people began to acknowledge their Jewish ancestry and seek affiliation with the Jewish community. Despite the demographic challenge symbolized by emigration to Israel, and the uncertainty surrounding the political and economic future, a Cuban Jewish renaissance continues. Antisemitism is not an issue in Cuba.

Although the foreign policy of Fidel Castro toward Israel has had its ups and downs, he has pursued a consistently benign approach toward the local Cuban Jewish community. He maintained diplomatic relations with Israel after the 1967 Six Day War, when the entire Communist bloc broke relations with the Jewish state. At the United Nations World Conference Against Racism, Racial Discrimination, Xenophobia, and Related Intolerance, held in Durban, South Africa, in 2001, Castro encouraged the African and the Muslim/Arab groups to press their grievances, engaging in vicious anti-Israel propaganda.

Ecuador

Population: 13.5 million
Jewish population: 1,000
Form of government: multiparty republic with one legislative
  house
Legal system: based on civil law system
Capital: Quito

In the 1990s social unrest caused political instability and several changes of heads of state. In a controversial move to help stabilize the economy, the U.S. dollar replaced the sucre as the national currency in 2000.

Nazi graffiti have appeared in various Quito neighborhoods, as well as on the walls of the Einstein Jewish School. Widespread antisemitism is not, however, an issue.

Mexico

Population: 100 million
Jewish population: 40,000
Form of government: federal republic with two legislative houses
Legal system: mixture of U.S. constitutional theory and civil law
  system; judicial review of legislative acts
Capital: Mexico City

Recent Developments.   President Vicente Fox and his center-right Partido Accion Nacional (PAN) have encouraged a pluralistic approach to cultural, religious, and ethnic diversity. Extreme right-wing publications continue, however, to traffic in Holocaust denial and extreme anti-Zionist rhetoric. The second Intifada has led to vandalism of Jewish schools and a hate campaign organized by Fawzi Yossif, the representative of the Palestinian authority in Mexico. Notwithstanding these manifestations, antisemitism has not been a serious issue in contemporary Mexico.

Historical Legacy.   Antisemitism in contemporary Mexico was initially prompted by debates surrounding immigrant policies during the late 1920s. The Anti-Jewish National League founded in 1930 and the Honorable Traders, Industrialists, and Professionals lobbied the government to restrict Jewish immigration. In the 1930s, racial antisemitism dominated Far Right groups such as the Mexico Revolutionary Action and its paramilitary units, the Golden Shirts.

The financial crisis of 1982 and the social upheaval caused by the 1985 earthquakes in Mexico City led to expressions of anti-Jewish sentiment in the media. Articles in the influential daily *Excelsior* accused Jewish factory owners of profiting from the disaster and letting their workers die while saving themselves and their property.

Panama

Population: 2.9 million
Jewish population: 9,250
Form of government: multiparty republic with one legislative
    house
Capital: Panama City

The Jewish community in Panama, one of the larger such communities in Latin America, has been in existence for nearly 150 years. Antisemitism has not been a significant issue.

Paraguay

Population: 5.8 million
Jewish population: 1,000
Form of government: multiparty republic with two legislative
    houses
Legal system: based on Argentine and Roman law and French
    codes
Capital: Asunción

A thirty-five-year military dictatorship of Alfredo Stroessner was overthrown in 1989. During 2001 Paraguay faced a series of political and socioeconomic challenges, primarily stemming from corruption scandals and ineffective economic policies that threatened to overwhelm the country's weak democracy and fragile economic system.

Antisemitic neo-Nazi groups have been active in Paraguay.

Uruguay

Population: 3.3 million
Jewish population: 25,000
Form of government: republic with two legislative houses
Legal system: based on Spanish civil law system
Capital: Montevideo

The 1990s brought a general upturn in the economy, but an out-break of foot-and-mouth disease in 2001 damaged Uruguay's important meat-export industry. The economy was also hit hard by economic crises in neighboring Brazil and Argentina, which adversely affected exports and tourism. Uruguay's political and labor conditions are among the freest in the world.

Antisemitic graffiti periodically appear in various public places, including on the Holocaust memorial in Montevideo.

Venezuela

Population: 24.6 million
Jewish population: 22,000
Form of government: multiparty republic with a unicameral
    legislature
Legal system: based on organic laws as of July 1999
Capital: Caracas

Appealing to the urban poor and the downwardly mobile middle class, President Hugo Chavez Frias has generated much opposition from the business, military, and upper class but remains firmly in power.

The second Intifada has had a significant impact on Venezuela's large and influential community of 1.3 million Arabs. Radical language used by Arab organizations, directed at delegitimizing the State of Israel is often antisemitic, comparing Israeli soldiers to Nazis

North America

Middle East violence has had considerable impact on antisemitic attitudes, although to a lesser extent than in Western Europe and the Islamic world. Hate-filled rallies, false ascription of inordinate Jewish political power, verbal assaults, vandalism, and calls for disinvestment from Israel mark an increasingly hostile atmosphere on North American college campuses but find little resonance elsewhere.

A 2002 poll revealed that as many as 17 percent of Americans held "unquestionably antisemitic" views and that a surprising 44 percent of foreign-born Hispanics held hardcore anti-Jewish beliefs. The 17 percent figure, while seemingly dramatic, represented the continued decline in antisemitic attitudes that has characterized the United States. A spike in Canadian antisemitic incidents in the first six months of 2002 followed a 35 percent increase in the five-year period from 1996 to 2001.

Canada

Population: 31 million
Jewish population: 365,000
Form of government: multiparty parliamentary state with two
    legislative houses
Legal system: based on English common law, except in Quebec,
    where a civil law system based on French law prevails
Capital: Ottawa

Recent Developments.   In some areas of Canada antisemitic incidents have doubled since the outbreak of the second Intifada. At pro-Palestinian rallies in Montreal, Toronto, and Ottawa, participants chanted "Kill the Jews" and carried placards equating the Star of David with the Nazi swastika.

Muslim terrorist groups such as Hizbollah, Hamas, and al-Qaeda are reportedly active in Canada. Security intelligence authorities consider Islamic terrorists, who blend into local immigrant communities, to be Canada's primary security threat. The Royal Canadian Mounted Police have uncovered apparent plots among Egyptian immigrants to bomb Israeli diplomatic offices in Ottawa and Montreal.

Although the Canadian white supremacist scene is scattered and largely leaderless, it is garnering new members through the Internet. In the year 2000 it saw a sharp rise in support in Quebec due to the increasing militancy of Parti Quebecois hardliners.

Historical Legacy.   The bulk of Canadian Jewry is descended from twentieth-century immigrants, from eastern Europe and Russia in the first half of the century and more recently from North Africa and the Middle East.

Canada's refusal to admit refugees fleeing from Nazism before and during World War II is a well-documented chapter in national indifference: "None is too many"—World War II prime minister MacKenzie King's government's assertion with respect to admitting Jewish refugees—summed up the Canadian government's stance.

The threat of Quebec separatism in the mid-1970s drove tens of thousands of English-speaking Jews to leave Montreal and to move principally to Ontario, making Toronto home to the largest Canadian Jewish community. Although the emigration of Jews from Quebec was not the result of expression of antisemitism, Jewish fears of anti-Jewish animus in large measure fueled the exodus.

United States of America

Population: 289 million
Jewish population: 5.7 million
Form of government: federal republic with two legislative houses
Legal system: based on English common law; judicial review of
    legislative acts
Capital: Washington, D.C.

Background.   Although most antisemitism in the United States is limited to hate propaganda, extremist organizations occasionally employ threats, violence, and vandalism. Smaller racist and white supremacist groups, which promote Holocaust denial, have succeeded via the Internet in reaching an audience disproportionate to their size.

Middle East tensions continue to spill over on U.S. campuses, with anti-Zionist rhetoric having increased. Harvard University president Lawrence Summers asserted in a speech at Harvard in September 2002, "Profoundly anti-Israel views are increasingly finding support in progressive intellectual communities," giving rise to "actions that are antisemitic in their effect if not in their intent."

Black-Jewish tensions and antisemitism emerging from the black community, once a serious concern of American Jews, have eased.

Historical Legacy.   The United States is a country in which antisemitism, whatever its manifestations, did not take firm root in the institutions of society as it did in Europe. The history of a pluralist America is that of a country that did not carry the "baggage" of a pre-Enlightenment past in which Jews were defined— legally and therefore socially—as outsiders and therefore alien, as different and therefore deviant.

The long tradition of democratic pluralism in the United

States has been marred by a history of prejudice. Racist antisemitism emerged the 1890s in response to large-scale Jewish immigration from eastern Europe. By the 1920s, the U.S. Congress passed restrictive immigration laws in the form of national origin quotas, with the result that the United States was unavailable as a refuge for a significant number of Jews fleeing Nazi Europe.

The 1920s and 1930s in the United States were marred by distinct anti-Jewish prejudice in many sectors of society. The 1940s, a period of social cohesion as the nation went to war, witnessed high levels of attitudinal antisemitism and continuing high levels of bias in employment, housing, and higher education.

Beginning in the 1950s and continuing to the present, there has been a gradual but steady diminution of both behavioral and attitudinal antisemitism in the United States, with levels of Jewish security—the ability of Jews to participate in the society at any level without fear of anti-Jewish animus—very high whatever antisemitism may be present.

During the latter part of the 1980s and continuing into the 1990s, the number of incidents of antisemitic vandalism and harassment rose around the country. Afrocentric anti-Zionism and anti-Jewish sentiments were a major source of anxiety. Slanderous charges of Jewish control of the media and entertainment, of participation in the slave trade, allied with vociferous propaganda by the Nation of Islam and the violence directed against Hasidim in Crown Heights, Brooklyn, aggravated intercommunal tensions.

Notwithstanding these tensions, the situation in the United States in the 2000s is one in which antisemitism continues on its decline and Jewish security remains strong. Although these are the realities, a strong majority of American Jews asserts when polled that antisemitism is a "serious" problem in the United States.

Assessment. Overall, in the United States the distinction between antisemitism, which continues to manifest itself albeit at low levels, and Jewish security, which is strong because of the pluralist and democratic nature of the society, is an important one. Jewish security—the ability for Jews to participate in the society at any level—has not been compromised because of anti-Jewish animus.

(For attitudinal surveys on American antisemitism, and for audits of antisemitic activity in the USA, see Chapter 5.)

Special Topics

Antisemitism in the Muslim World

For a full treatment of Islam and the Jews, see Chapter 2 and the appropriate bibliographic references.

In recent years, the growth, expansion, and virulence of antisemitism in the Muslim and Arab worlds have reached alarming proportions. From the Atlantic to East Asia, the myth of the all-powerful Jew harboring ambitions of world domination, and other expressions of antisemitism, are now part of the daily discourse in many parts of the Muslim world. Indeed, substantial Muslim minority communities in the West have bought into antisemitic canards, demonizing Jews as a sinister, immoral people, involved in blood rituals and international cabals.

Muslim Judeophobia often hides behind the disingenuous claim that Arabs cannot, by definition, be branded as antisemites because they themselves are designated as Semites. It ought be clear, however, that the term *antisemitism* is, as we have discussed, used to describe Jew-hatred.

It is often said that antisemitism is a relatively new phenomenon in Arab and Muslim culture. Although it is true that the *dhimmi*—the protected, albeit second-class—status of the Jew in the Muslim world never resulted in the period of Classical Islam in confinement in ghettos, prohibition of land ownership, and other restrictions, Jews have in the 1,400 years of Islamic history been subjected to varying degrees of humiliation and occasionally to popular violence. In the eleventh and twelfth centuries, matters took such a turn that the Jewish philosopher Maimonides referred bitterly to the "nation of Ishmael, who persecutes us severely and who devises ways to harm us and to debase us."

Until the twentieth century and the advent of Zionism and the birth of the State of Israel, the Muslim attitude to Jews was for the most part one of contempt for an inferior minority, rather than the blend of hatred, awe, and jealousy that characterized the relationship between Christians and Jews. The situation for Jews in Muslim/Arab lands was never as bad as it was in Christendom at its worst, but never as good as in the West at its best.

The Koranic image of the Jew is often tainted by anti-Judaism, by harsh passages in which the Jews are branded as enemies of Islam, possessing a malevolent and rebellious spirit. Jews, it is stated, need to be humiliated "because they had disbelieved the signs of God and slain the prophets unrightfully" (Sura 2: 61/58). Their "just" penalty was their transformation into apes and swine. The Koran further insists that Jews knew that Mohammed was the true prophet but rejected him out of sheer jealousy, deceitfulness, and treachery, evil characteristics that have earned them "degradation in this world" and a "mighty chastisement" in the world to come. (See Chapter 2 for a further elaboration of the theological underpinnings of Muslim-Jewish relations.)

In the twentieth century, Islamic Judeophobia has been blended with the most vicious strains of Western antisemitism. Arab propagandists lifted the Czarist-inspired canard, *The Protocols of the Learned Elders of Zion*—which provides a complete conspiracy theory of history in which satanic Jews relentlessly strive for world domination—and adapted it to their political needs. The *Protocols* has thus been resurrected and published in numerous editions throughout the Arab and Muslim world.

Additionally, the blood libel, the calumny that Jews require the blood of non-Jews, especially children, for ritual purposes, so central to medieval Christianity, has now been "Arabized." Syrian defense minister Mustafa Tlas, in his now much-reissued "classic" book, *The Matzah of Zion*, wrote, "The Jew can kill you and take your blood in order to make his Zionist bread." Egypt, officially at peace with Israel for more than two decades, sanctions the articulation and indeed advocacy of the blood libel against Jews on the part of its government-sponsored press and media. The libel has as well been part of the rhetoric of the Saudi ruling family.

Radical Muslim clerics and spokesmen borrow liberally from the pages of Nazi propaganda, viewing Jews as rapacious and monstrous and calling for their total annihilation. Caricatures drawn from the Nazi propaganda newspaper, *Der Stürmer,* depict Jews as scheming, vindictive, and money-grubbing, with hooked noses, blood-dripping talons, and world-devouring lust and ambition. They have borrowed, as well, the apocalyptic, totalitarian, and pseudomessianic aspirations to world hegemony that Nazi Germany fostered.

Muslim antisemites do not balk at the moral obscenity of linking Zionism to Nazism, depicting Israeli soldiers with the crimes of the German SS units of World War II who implemented the Holocaust. This calumny is also coupled with Muslim denial of the Holocaust, even though the historical record provides evidence of the support and collaboration of some of the most powerful Arab clerics and leaders in the destruction of European Jewry, most egregiously exemplified in the vigorous advocacy of Hitler's program on the part of the mufti of Jerusalem, Hajj Amin al-Husseini.

The United Nations

The United Nations (UN) was established in 1945 in the wake of World War II for the purpose of maintaining international peace and security and bringing about cooperation among nations in the economic, social, cultural, and humanitarian spheres.

The UN was instrumental in the process leading to the creation of the State of Israel, as well as in its ongoing struggle for survival. Israel was not literally "created" by the UN partition resolution of 19 November 1947, although the resolution served as an important link in a chain of events that eventually brought the state into being. Under international law, Israel emerged as an independent state from the throes of the War of Independence of 1948 when it proved its viability as a legal unit by meeting the four cumulative conditions of statehood: nation, territory, government, and independence.

In recent years, however, the agencies of the United Nations have displayed systemic bias against the Jewish state. For example, the United Nations Commission on Human Rights annually adopted five anti-Israel resolutions, and the first two UN World Conferences on Women's Rights—in Mexico City (1975) and Copenhagen (1980)—explicitly called Zionism a form of racism.

UN Resolution—"Zionism Is Racism"

On 10 November 1975, on the thirty-seventh anniversary of Kristallnacht, the orchestrated destruction of Jewish life and property in Nazi Germany, the United Nations General Assembly passed Resolution 3379, which "determines that Zionism is a form of racism and racial discrimination." At bottom it was the oil power of Arab states and Soviet pressure that facilitated passage of the resolution. Seventy-two countries, consisting of the Arab states, Third World nations, and the Soviet bloc, voted for the resolution, thirty-five voted against, and thirty-two abstained.

The road to Resolution 3379 began in December 1973, when the African nation of Burundi amended a UN resolution condemning South Africa by adding the words "Zionism" and "Israeli imperialism." The resolution passed by eighty-eight for, seven against, and twenty-eight abstaining. Two years later, in the summer of 1975 in Mexico City, the first UN Conference on Women's Rights linked Zionism with colonialism and declared that the achievement of international cooperation and peace required the elimination of hostile ideologies such as apartheid and Zionism.

In August 1975 the nonaligned movement of nations, which typically took anti-U.S. and pro-Soviet positions, met in Lima, Peru, and condemned Zionism as "a danger to world peace." Two months later, Cuba, Libya, and Somalia introduced a draft resolution condemning Zionism as racism to the UN General Assembly's Third Committee, which oversees resolutions related to social, cultural, and humanitarian issues. The Third Committee passed the resolution on 17 October 1975. The draft resolution then moved to the General Assembly on 10 November. In view of the fact that the outcome had already been determined by the vote in the Third Committee, there was little debate and less question that Resolution 3379 would pass. It quoted Resolution 77 of the Organization of African Unity, passed only three months before, "that the racist regime in occupied Palestine and the racist regimes in Zimbabwe and South Africa have a common imperialist origin, forming a whole and having the same racist structure and being organically linked in their policy aimed at repression of the dignity and integrity of the human being."

In his denunciation of Resolution 3379, U.S. ambassador to the UN Daniel P. Moynihan proclaimed, "The USA declares that it does not acknowledge, it will not abide by, it will never acquiesce in this infamous act." Israel ambassador Chaim Herzog said, "For the issue is not Israel or Zionism. The issue is the continued existence of this organization, which has been dragged to its lowest point of discredit by a coalition of despotisms and racists."

Repeal of Resolution 3379

Sixteen years later, on 16 December 1991, the United Nations General Assembly voted overwhelmingly to revoke Resolution 3379. One hundred eleven nations voted in favor of repealing the resolution; twenty-five nations, mostly Islamic and hard-line Communist, voted against. Thirteen nations abstained, and seventeen, including Egypt, which by then had recognized Israel, Kuwait, and China, did not take part in the voting.

President George H. W. Bush had called for the repeal in September 1991 in a speech to the General Assembly. U.S. embassies around the world were instructed to place maximum pressure to secure the appeal. A total of eighty-five countries, or just more than half of the 166 members in the United Nations, cosponsored the repeal resolution, including the former Soviet Union and all its former Communist allies in Eastern Europe that had voted for the resolution in 1975.

Ultimately, the repeal vote reflected the shifting political currents of those years, particularly in the aftermath of the Persian Gulf War, which split the Arab and Islamic worlds, and the changes in the former Soviet bloc, fostered by the collapse of communism.

The Road to Durban

In December 1997, the United Nations announced plans for a third World Conference against Racism, Racial Discrimination, Xenophobia, and Related Intolerance (WCAR). The UN General Assembly contemplated a forward-looking conference, led by former Irish president, Mary Robinson, the UN High Commissioner for Human Rights, focusing on confronting and reversing a host of disturbing contemporary manifestations of racism. In 1999 the General Assembly's Third Committee decided that the conference should be held in Durban, South Africa, in 2001 and should be preceded by regional meetings in Strasbourg, France; Santiago, Chile; Dakar, Senegal; and Tehran, Iran, during the fall of 2000 and the winter of 2001.

The Asian Preparatory Meeting, which convened in Tehran from 19 to 21 February 2001, marked a sharp departure from the spirit of tolerance that was evident at the first three regional meetings. Iran, the host government, did not recognize Israel and repeatedly called for its elimination. Jewish nongovernmental organizations (NGOs) were effectively excluded from participation, and no Israeli delegates attended. Australia and New Zealand, two outspoken supporters of Israel in the Asia group, were also excluded from participation in the meeting. Indeed, the day the conference opened, the Iranian government placed an article in the *Tehran Times* denying the Holocaust. The Declaration and Plan of Action agreed to by the delegates in the discriminatory atmosphere of Tehran amounted to a declaration by the states present of their intention to use the conference as a propaganda weapon attacking Israel.

Fresh from their triumph in Tehran, the Muslim delegates further politicized the two-week final preparatory meeting at the UN in Geneva, held from 21 May to 1 June by delegitimizing the moral argument for Israel's existence as a haven for Jews. They sought to brand Israel as a racist state, casting doubt on whether there was a place for it in the community of nations. Their attempt to deny the unique status of the Holocaust was, in effect, a move to deny the magnitude of the crime perpetrated against the Jews of Europe and a further effort at eroding the legitimacy of the State of Israel.

Commissioner Mary Robinson's failure to speak out forcefully at Tehran and in Geneva against the hateful language contributed to the crisis that threatened to thwart a constructive conference. It is noteworthy that although Robinson was an avowed champion of women's rights, in deference to her Tehran hosts she did not call for elevating the status of women in Islamic society. At bottom, analysts suggest that Robinson caved in to the antiglobalization sentiment of the developing world and its convenient use of Israel as a vicarious target for anti-American and anticolonial sentiment. Following a similar pattern of bias during her years as high commissioner, she effectively mollified the Arab/Islamic bloc by voicing criticism of Israeli policies and the slanted media images emanating from the second Intifada, in which Israelis were consistently portrayed as oppressors and the Palestinians as innocent victims. Indeed, instead of condemning the attempt at politicization by the Muslim lobby in Durban and its transparent effort to revive the Zionism-is-racism label that the UN General Assembly had adopted in 1975 and repealed in 1991, Robinson legitimized it, effectively knocking the conference off track in Tehran and completely derailing it in Geneva.

The Durban Debacle

The WCAR held in Durban, South Africa, from 31 August through 8 September 2001, attended by 14,000 participants representing 3,900 NGOs and fifteen heads of states, had two components, an NGO conference and the main, governmental conference.

The Muslim and Arab NGOs thought it opportune to make use of the South African venue of the conference to resurrect the antiapartheid coalition of Third World states against Israel. Employing invidious comparisons and outright antisemitica, they hoped to create Israel as the next embodiment of "apartheid" evil, one that the international community would be obligated to dismantle.

The NGO conference, dominated by anti-Israel rhetoric, re-sulted in a final declaration incorporating all the extremist anti-Zionist and antisemitic language demanded by the Arab lobby. Respected Western human rights NGOs, such as Human Rights Watch, the Lawyers Committee for Human Rights, and Amnesty International, did little to denounce the activities of the radicals in their midst. At Durban, copies of the notorious Czarist antisemitic forgery, *The Protocols of the Learned Elders of Zion,* published in Iran with a new introduction describing Israel as a "deadly cancerous tumor," were openly on sale, as were Holocaust-denial materials and an array of Nazi-inspired cartoons depicting hook-nosed Jews with fangs dripping with blood.

On 3 September 2001, the United States and Israel withdrew from the United Nations World Conference against Racism, protesting the drafting of a final document that condemned Zionism as "based on racial superiority" and that singled out Is-rael as a racist, apartheid state guilty of crimes against humanity. The Durban draft resolution recapitulated and further intensi-fied the notorious "Zionism Is Racism" resolution that had been adopted by the General Assembly more than a quarter century before.

U.S. secretary of state Colin Powell referred to the hateful language in the drafts and specifically instructed State Depart-ment officials to return home. Representative Tom Lantos (D-CA), a Holocaust survivor, who had been part of the U.S. contingent, summed up the proceedings by saying that "extreme elements" had "hijacked" the conferences for their own purposes.

Despite the tidal wave of antisemitic propaganda made eas-ier by the well-established tradition of using the UN's human rights apparatus against Israel, the Arab/Muslim lobby ulti-mately did not succeed in its aim of pushing through a Durban declaration that would have made Israel an international pariah. Steadfast support of the United States, and later backing of Israel by the more moderate European Union, made the difference. The final declaration adopted by the conference, even though it made mention of "the suffering of the Palestinian people under foreign occupation," was a far cry from the hate-filled document up for discussion at the start of the conference. Offensive references to Israeli "genocide," "ethnic cleansing" and "racism" were re-moved as were the sections aimed at undermining the signifi-cance of the Holocaust.

The Vatican (Vatican City)

Population: 850
Jewish population: none
Form of government: ecclesiastical
Legal system: ecclesiastical
Capital: Vatican City

Vatican City, the independent papal state, is the smallest sovereign entity in the world. Within its medieval and Renaissance walls lies a miniature nation. The ecclesiastical governance of the Roman Catholic Church, the Holy See, is a function of the Vatican.

Historically, the antiliberal bent of the modern papacy engendered insensitivity to human rights. Pope Gregory XVI's 1832 encyclical *Mirari Vos* against the "evils" of "shameless lovers of liberty" and his successor Pius IX's 1864 "Syllabus of Errors" were affirmations of antiliberalism. Even the more moderate Leo XIII's *Rerum Novarum,* issued in response to the challenge of unionization of the working class, was framed in a classic Thomist context not friendly to liberal or human rights ideals. In the twentieth century, Pope Pius XI's 1931 encyclical *Quadregesimo Anno* proposed an organic notion of society rooted heavily in a medieval Catholic social vision inimical to liberalism and social justice. For him as for his successor, Nazism was preferable to communism, which was viewed as a direct threat to the church, further triggering an antiliberal ecclesiastical stance with devastating consequences during the Holocaust.

The contemporary Vatican attitude toward Judaism has undergone considerable change—openness is now official church policy. Following the watershed of Vatican II and *Nostra Aetate* (1965), which shaped the contours of the relationship between Catholics and Jews and rejected "teachings of contempt," Pope John Paul II in the 1980s specifically and forthrightly condemned antisemitism. The pope's condemnation was followed by the 1989 papal document on racism, *The Church and Racism,* specifically repudiating antisemitism, and by the 1990 Polish bishops' pastoral letter on antisemitism. These and other declarations marked a significant change in the Christian stance toward Jews that had characterized the previous 2,000 years.

There are, however, fault lines, if not fissures, in Vatican policy and action. The 1982 papal meeting with PLO leader Yasser Arafat; the 1987 meeting with UN secretary-general Kurt Waldheim (allegedly a Nazi collaborator during World War II), followed a year later by the papal defense of the conduct of Austrian and German churches during the Nazi period; and papal homilies on supersessionism muddied the waters of reconciliation. A joint Catholic-Jewish team of scholars set up to study wartime Vatican archives collapsed in 2002 amid angry recriminations regarding inaccessibility. Responding to criticism that Pius XII, the wartime pope, did not do enough to oppose the Holocaust and yet whose candidacy for sainthood in the Catholic Church is under way, the Vatican was to release, but did not, in 2003 some diplomatic documents from the tenure of the previous pope, Pius XI, who reigned from 1922 to 1939. A full accounting of the role of the Vatican in Nazi Germany and occupied Europe remains yet to be offered. Finally, the long-awaited Vatican document on the Holocaust, antisemitism, and the Church, *We Remember: A Reflection on the Shoah* (1998), raised as many questions as it answered.

5

Documents and Statistics

Surveys and Statistics

Antisemitism in Europe

Anti-Semitism Index

Since 1964, the Anti-Defamation League has conducted a series of public opinion surveys in the United States to measure levels of anti-Semitism in the country. An index of 11 questions was developed by researchers at the University of California to be used in these public opinion surveys to provide an analytical tool for identifying which respondents have a propensity to be more prejudiced toward Jews.

This index of 11 questions was employed for the first time in Europe in September 2002. As in the United States, those respondents who agreed with six or more of the statements listed below were considered "most anti-Semitic."

Before answering the index questions, respondents were read the following statement: "I am now going to read out another series of statements, again some of them you will agree with and some of them you will not. Please say which ones you think are probably true and which ones you think are probably false."

The following are the eleven statements that constitute the anti-Semitism index.

1. Jews don't care what happens to anyone but their own kind.
2. Jews are more willing than others to use shady practices to get what they want.
3. Jews are more loyal to Israel than to this country.
4. Jews have too much power in the business world.
5. Jews have lots of irritating faults.

6. Jews stick together more than other Italians (Spanish, Dutch, Swiss, Austrians).
7. Jews always like to be at the head of things.
8. Jews have too much power in international financial markets.
9. Jews have too much power in our country today.
10. Jewish business people are so shrewd that others do not have a fair chance to compete.
11. Jews are just as honest as other business people. (Considered prejudiced if answered "probably false" to this statement.)

- The data indicate that one out of five respondents, *21 percent*, are characterized as "most anti-Semitic."
- Of the five countries surveyed, Spanish respondents harbor the most anti-Semitic views while Dutch respondents harbor the fewest anti-Semitic views.
- *34 percent* of those surveyed in Spain are considered "most anti-Semitic, *23 percent* of those polled in Italy are considered "most anti-Semitic," *19 percent* of Austrians are considered "most anti-Semitic," *22 percent* of Swiss respondents are considered "most anti-Semitic," and *7 percent* of Dutch respondents are considered "most anti-Semitic."
- A majority, 56 percent, responded that it is "probably true" to characterize Jews as being more loyal to Israel than to their own country.
- Nearly three-quarters of Spanish respondents, 72 percent, believe that Jews are more loyal to Israel than to Spain.
- 40 percent of the respondents believe that Jews have too much power in the international financial markets.
- Again, 71 percent, of those surveyed in Spain believe that Jews have too much power in the international financial markets—almost twice the overall average.
- 40 percent say that Jews have too much power in the business world, with 63 percent of Spanish respondents saying this is "probably true."
- Nearly two-thirds, 63 percent, of respondents believe that Jews stick together more than other people in the country.
- 29 percent believe that Jews do not care what happens to anyone but their own kind.
- 16 percent of respondents overall believe that Jews have lots of irritating faults.
- However, despite the fact that only 7 percent of Spanish respondents say that they come into contact with Jews, 32 percent of them believe that Jews have lots of irritating faults.
- 29 percent of respondents in all five countries believe that

Jews always like to be at the head of things.
- 9 percent of respondents believe that Jews have too much power within their particular country.
- 18 percent of all respondents believe that Jewish business people are so shrewd that others do not have a fair chance to compete.
- 11 percent believe that Jews are not as honest as other business people.

Attitudes Toward Jews

The results of this survey reconfirm previous results which point to a new form of anti-Semitism taking hold in Europe. This new anti-Semitism is fueled by anti-Israel sentiment and questions the loyalty of Jewish citizens.

A majority, 56 percent, believe that Jewish citizens in their respective countries are more loyal to Israel than to the country they live in.

53 percent of those surveyed believe that the recent outbreak of violence against Jews in Europe is a result of anti-Israel sentiment, while 17 percent believe it is a result of anti-Jewish feelings. 9 percent feel that both are contributing factors.

Almost two-thirds, 64 percent, say they are either "very" or "fairly" concerned about the recent outbreak of violence against Jews.

21 percent of Italian respondents say they are "very concerned" about the recent outbreak of violence directed at Jews. 46 percent say they are "fairly concerned," while 30 percent are "fairly unconcerned" or "not concerned at all" about the violence directed at Jews.

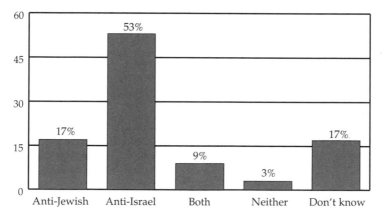

Figure 5.1

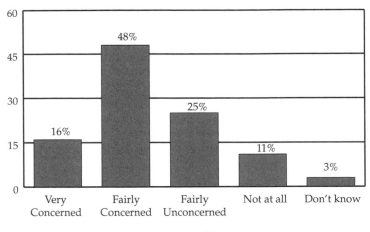

Figure 5.2

A majority, 57 percent, think that their governments are doing enough to ensure the safety and security of Jewish citizens.

Thirty percent of Spanish and Italian respondents do not think that their government is doing enough to ensure the safety and security of its Jewish citizens—the highest percentage among the countries surveyed.

Do you think your government is doing enough to ensure the safety and security of its Jewish citizens?

A plurality, 42 percent, believe that anti-Jewish feelings have remained the same over the last five years, while 35 percent think they have increased.

However, by a margin of 35 percent–14 percent, respondents are more likely to say that anti-Jewish feelings have increased as opposed to decreased.

Overall, 44 percent of respondents believe there is a possibility of an increase in anti-Jewish feelings within their respective countries over the next few years.

Swiss and Dutch respondents (52 and 49 percent respectively) are most likely to believe that anti-Jewish feelings could rise within their borders.

Table 5.1

	Austria	Italy	Netherlands	Spain	Switzerland
Very concerned	16%	21%	13%	13%	17%
Fairly concerned	48%	46%	46%	38%	47%
Fairly unconcerned	25%	20%	27%	26%	25%
Very unconcerned	6%	10%	12%	18%	9%
Don't know	5%	3%	2%	5%	2%

Table 5.2

	Austria	Italy	Netherlands	Spain	Switzerland
Yes	74%	44%	55%	39%	74%
No	15%	30%	19%	30%	9%
Don't know	11%	26%	25%	30%	16%

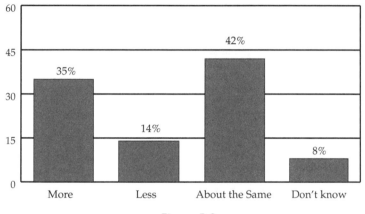

Figure 5.3

Do you see any possibility of an increase in anti-Jewish feeling around the country in the next few years? Percentage responding "Yes."

A majority, 53 percent, believe that it is "very" or "fairly" likely that there could be a serious increase in anti-Jewish feeling around the world in the next few years.

When asked the same question in the United States, 63 percent of respondents felt it was likely that there could be a serious increase in anti-Jewish feeling around the world in the next few years.

Nearly half of all respondents, 49 percent, say that Jews still talk too much about what happened to them in the Holocaust.

Respondents in Spain, 57 percent, and Austria, 56 percent, are most likely to feel that Jews still talk too much about the Holocaust.

69 percent say that most people in their country are prejudiced against other ethnic groups, even if they don't admit to it in public.

Source: Anti-Defamation League. "European Attitudes toward Jews: A Five Country Survey." http://www.adl.org/adl.asp. Accessed June 2004.

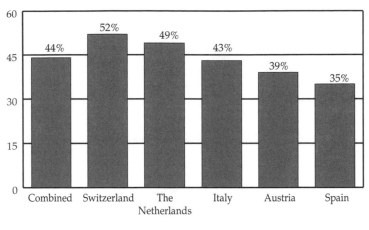

Figure 5.4

Anti-Semitism in America 2002

Note: The following is an excerpt from the survey. The entire text may be viewed at http://www.adl.org/adl.asp.

Highlights from a May 2002 Survey Conducted by the Marttila Communications Group and SWR Worldwide for the Anti-Defamation League, Including Poll Results from 1992 and 1998; June 11, 2002

Methodology

Over the past ten years, the Marttila Communications Group—a Boston-based public opinion research firm—has conducted three national surveys (1992, 1998 and 2002) for the Anti-Defamation League (ADL) to measure and monitor levels of anti-Semitism in the United States.

In this latest survey, conducted jointly with the polling firm of SWR Worldwide, 1,000 Americans age 18 and older were interviewed on the evenings of April 26–May 6, 2002, by trained professionals working from a central, monitored location.

Respondents were selected from all American households using a random probability sampling procedure which included unlisted telephone numbers. An oversample of 300 African-Americans and 300 Hispanic-Americans was carried out to increase the reliability of the results obtained within these important subgroups; Hispanics were also given the opportunity to be interviewed in Spanish. The margin of error in a poll of this size is plus or minus three percent, but is higher for subgroups (the margins of error for the African-American and Hispanic-American samples, for example, are plus or minus 5.7%).

In addition, *for the first time this yea*r, two additional surveys were conducted among 800 college students and 500 college faculty to measure anti-Semitic propensities on U.S. college campuses. Interviews with college undergraduates were conducted between April 26–May 3, 2002. Interviews with college undergraduate faculty were conducted between May 1–31, 2002. The margin of error in the student survey is plus or minus 3.4%; the margin of error in the faculty survey is plus or minus 4.4%.

2002 ADL Poll Context

The most recent ADL polls of the general public, college students and college faculty were conducted in April and May of 2002.

The terrorist attacks of September 11th were still fresh in the minds of the American people and the United States' war on terrorism continued to be front-page news throughout the country.

The violence in the Middle East, which had been going on for more than a year, had reached a particularly dangerous moment with a series of suicide bombings in Israel. In response, the Israeli military had begun sending its troops into Palestinian territories on a regular basis. One of Israel's most widely publicized military actions—in the town of Jenin on the West Bank—had just been completed when the ADL survey commenced.

According to the 2002 ADL polling results, a majority of Americans (59%) had come to believe that the United States had entered "a new and dangerous era" as a result of the events of September 11th. Most (68%) said they believed there would be another major terrorist attack against the United States within the year.

The explosive events in the Middle East were very much on the minds of the American people. Nearly three-quarters (71%) of Americans said they were following events in the region, with a third saying they were paying very close attention to the escalating Israeli-Palestinian conflict.

The Anti-Semitism Index

To provide an analytic tool for identifying which Americans have a propensity to be more prejudiced toward Jews, all three national surveys conducted over the past ten years (1992, 1998 and 2002) have relied upon an anti-Semitism index developed for ADL nearly 40 years ago.

The index was developed and first used in conjunction with a 1964 ADL survey conducted by researchers at the University of California. The index assigns respondents to one of three categories based on the number of times they agree with 11 statements made about American Jews. These 11 statements are included within a longer list of statements about Jews.

While there have been slight changes over the years in the wording of the 11 statements to keep them relevant and contemporary, the basic structure of the index has been retained throughout all three national surveys.

In 2002, as in 1992 and 1998, respondents are grouped as follows:

1. **Not Anti-Semitic:** People who agree with none or one of the statements are considered essentially free of prejudicial attitudes toward the Jewish community.
2. **Middle:** People who agree with between two and five of the statements are considered to be neither prejudiced nor unprejudiced—that is, not completely prejudice-free in their attitudes toward Jews, but not an audience to be deeply worried about.
3. **Most Anti-Semitic:** The people who agree with six or more of the statements are considered the most anti-Semitic group of Americans, and have been isolated for special analysis and demographic identification.

The 11 statements that constitute the index are listed [in the next section]. While at least one or two of the statements are arguably ambiguous in their nature, they have been included in the current study because they have been part of the research since 1964.

No public opinion index is a perfect tool for measuring accurately a phenomenon as complex as anti-Semitism. The real purpose of the index is in its role as a social sleuth—to help identify those demographic groups which have a propensity to hold more anti-Semitic views than the public at large. In other words, the index is most useful in answering the question, "Which groups of Americans tend to be anti-Semitic?" rather than the question, "How many Americans are anti-Semitic?" In this context, the index has been highly successful in identifying those demographic groups most likely to hold anti-Semitic views and uncovering the underlying beliefs that foster anti-Semitism.

Index Statements

The index statements, which are included within a longer list of positive and neutral statements about Jews, are introduced to respondents as follows: "I am going to read a list of statements about Jews. For each one, please tell me whether you think that statement is probably true or probably false."

The following are the 11 statements that constitute the anti-Semitism index. As noted earlier, agreement with 0–1 of these statements is considered "not anti-Semitic," agreement with 2–5 statements is considered "middle," and agreement with 6–11 statements is considered "most anti-Semitic."

1. Jews stick together more than other Americans.
2. Jews always like to be at the head of things.
3. Jews are more loyal to Israel than America.
4. Jews have too much power in the U.S. today.
5. Jews have too much control and influence on Wall Street.
6. Jews have too much power in the business world.
7. Jews have a lot of irritating faults.
8. Jews are more willing than others to use shady practices to get what they want.
9. Jewish businesspeople are so shrewd that others don't have a fair chance at competition.
10. Jews don't care what happens to anyone but their own kind.
11. Jews are [not] just as honest as other businesspeople.

I. Anti-Semitism in the United States

Anti-Semitic propensities have increased in the United States since 1998, reversing a steady decline in anti-Jewish feeling in the U.S. over the past ten years.

During the past year, there has been a significant amount of news coverage about increased anti-Semitism throughout Europe and the Arab world. Also reported have been specific acts of anti-Semitism in the United States. Many reporters and analysts have speculated that anti-Semitic feelings in the U.S. may have increased during this period of global upheaval.

The 2002 ADL survey confirms that there has been an increase in anti-Semitic propensities in the U.S. since 1998. In 2002, 17% of Americans—or approximately 35 million adults—hold views about Jews which are unquestionably anti-Semitic. This compares to 12% who fell into the most anti-Semitic category in 1998 and 20% in 1992 (an earlier ADL survey conducted in 1964 found 29% of Americans to hold anti-Semitic views).

The 2002 increase can be explained by two factors: a slight increase in anti-Semitic propensities among whites (9% in 1998 to 12% in 2002) and a more sophisticated analysis since 1998 of anti-Semitic propensities in the Hispanic community.

New research conducted by ADL in 2001 uncovered—for the first time—that Hispanic-Americans who were born outside of the U.S. are much more likely to hold anti-Semitic views than Hispanics born in the United States.

This new information about higher levels of anti-Semitism among foreign-born Hispanics means that levels of anti-Semitism reported in 1998 were probably somewhat understated. This is because the ADL researchers at the time were not fully aware of the striking differences in attitudes between U.S.-born and foreign-born Hispanics.

In 2002, as a result of the insights gained from the 2001 research, more sophisticated screening and sampling was done to ensure an appropriate mix of U.S.-born (37%) and foreign-born (63%) Hispanics. In addition, Hispanics were given the opportunity to be interviewed in Spanish.

Positive Images of Jews

While there has been an increase in levels of anti-Semitism in the United States, it should be emphasized that more than 80% of Americans fall into the "not anti-Semitic" or "middle" categories, with nearly half of all Americans (48%) essentially free of prejudicial attitudes toward Jewish Americans.

As mentioned earlier in this report, the 11 Anti-Semitism Index statements were included within a longer list of positive and neutral statements about Jews. While much of this report focuses on negative stereotypes about Jews, it is important to point out that an overwhelming majority of Americans accept virtually all of the positive statements about Jews that were presented in the 2002 survey. It is significant that none of the negative statements are accepted as widely as the positive statements.

For example, 80% of Americans surveyed in 2002 believe that Jews place a strong emphasis on the importance of family life; 69% believe that Jews have contributed much to the cultural life of America; and 58% believe that because of their own history of fighting discrimination, Jews have a special commitment to social justice and civil rights. In addition, 53% believe that Jews have played a vital role in making sure the U.S. is a positive, moral force in world affairs.

Concern about Rising Anti-Semitism

Reporting of anti-Semitic incidents in the U.S. and around the world has clearly had an impact upon American attitudes. When asked whether there is more, less or about the same amount of anti-Jewish feeling in America today as there was ten years ago, 22% of Americans say there is more. This is nearly double the response from 1998, when only 11% of Americans said there was more anti-Jewish feeling in America.

Further, 37% of Americans say they see a possibility of an increase in anti-Jewish feeling around the country in the next few years, an increase of 12% from 1992—the last time this question was asked.

While Americans are concerned about rising anti-Semitism in the U.S., they are even more concerned about an increase in anti-Jewish feeling around the world. In response to the question "How likely do you think it is that there could be a serious increase in anti-Jewish feeling around the world in the next few years," 63% said they felt such an increase in global anti-Semitism was likely. When this question was last asked in 1998, only 45% saw a potential for an increase in anti-Jewish feelings around the world.

According to the 2002 poll results, a majority of Americans believe that the United States has entered a dangerous new era in the country's history. Clearly, Americans foresee an increase in religious and ethnic tensions as part of this new era.

II. The Impact of Education
Less educated Americans continue to be more likely to hold anti-Semitic views.

A regression analysis of the 2002 survey results confirms one of the most important findings from the 1992 and 1998 surveys: that education is a very strong predictor of anti-Semitism. Simply put, the more educated a person is, the less likely he or she is to accept anti-Semitic beliefs.

For example, only about one-in-ten (12%) college graduates and those with postgraduate degrees falls into the most anti-Semitic category, while nearly one-in-four (23%) high school graduates is in the most anti-Semitic group.

As a person's educational level increases, his or her tendency to hold anti-Semitic views decreases by 15%.

As further evidence of the positive impact of education, anti-Semitic propensities among college students and faculty members were found in 2002 to be the lowest of any demographic cohort studied during ADL's ten years of research on the topic.

III. Perceptions of Jewish Power
Stereotypes about Jewish power in the U.S. have replaced many of the classic ethical stereotypes previously attributed to Jewish Americans and are now fostering anti-Semitic beliefs.

When ADL first began polling the American public about issues of anti-Semitism in 1964, the predominant negative stereotypes about Jews dealt with issues of honesty and business ethics. Over time, these traditional stereotypes have been rejected by most Americans and replaced by concerns about Jewish power in the U.S.

In the 2002 survey, 20% of Americans said they agreed with the statement: "Jews have too much power in the U.S. today." This is an increase of 4% from a national survey conducted in 2001, and a 9% increase from the 1998 survey. Nearly three-quarters (72%) of those who fall into the most anti-Semitic category believe that Jews have too much power in the U.S. today.

Similarly, more Americans appear to be concerned about the power Jews hold in the business world. In 2002, nearly a quarter of all Americans (24%) said they agreed with the statement: "Jews have too much power in the business world." This is an increase of 3% since 2001 and 8% since 1998. African-Americans and Hispanic-Americans are nearly twice as likely to agree with this proposition.

The regression analysis of the 2002 data also confirms that concerns about Jewish power have become key drivers of contemporary anti-Semitic beliefs in the United States. The analysis shows that if a person believes that Jewish Americans have too much power in the U.S., his or her propensity to be anti-Semitic increases by 17%.

IV. Opinions of Israel and U.S. Policy in the Middle East

Negative attitudes toward Israel and concerns that American Jews have too much influence over U.S. Middle East policy are emerging as factors responsible for fostering anti-Semitic beliefs.

One of the more important findings from the analyses of the 1992 and 1998 ADL surveys was that Americans' opinions about Israel did not appear to affect their attitudes toward Jews.

For example, the previous polling—conducted during two contentious moments in the U.S.-Israeli relationship—found that upper-educated Americans were highly critical of the Israeli governments at that time. However, these upper-educated Americans were also the least anti-Semitic of all Americans. For this leadership cohort, critical judgments about Israel did not have any influence on their feelings about Jews.

Further, the in-depth analyses of the 1992 and 1998 data found that critical judgments about Israel did not foster anti-Semitic beliefs among Americans in general, even among those who fell into the most anti-Semitic category. The most anti-Semitic Americans have always been more critical of the Israeli government, but the previous analyses revealed that these negative feelings about Israel were a consequence of their anti-Semitic beliefs rather than a cause of them.

The 2002 survey tells a different story. The regression analysis reveals that—for the first time—attitudes toward Israel are actually fostering anti-Semitic beliefs among some Americans.

Those Americans who believe that Jews have too much influence over U.S. policy in the Middle East, that U.S. policy tilts too much toward Israel, that the U.S. is more likely to be targeted for a terrorist attack because of American support, and who see increased anti-Jewish activity around the country and the world, have a significantly greater likelihood of falling into the most anti-Semitic category. This analysis is illustrated by the following key poll results:

- On whether the Bush administration has been tilting too much toward Israel in its Middle East policies, slightly more than half of Americans (51%) said the U.S. has been tilting too much toward Israel while three-quarters of the most anti-Semitic Americans (73%) said they felt this way.
- And, on one of the key analytic findings that emerged from the 2002 survey, as a driver of anti-Semitic beliefs, the most anti-Semitic Americans were four times as likely (42%) to

believe that American Jewish leaders have too much influence over U.S. foreign policy than Americans holding non anti-Semitic beliefs (11%).

One of the most remarkable findings in the 40 years of ADL research on this topic—and one of the most telling indicators of anti-Jewish prejudice in the United States—has been the question of fundamental Jewish loyalty to the U.S. When this question was first asked in 1964, 30% of Americans said they believed that Jews were more loyal to Israel than to America.

There has been very little variation over the years, with 30% of Americans questioning Jewish loyalty to the U.S. in 1981, 35% in 1992, 31% in 1998, and 31% percent in 2001. In 2002, as in previous years, a third of Americans (33%) said they believe Jews are more loyal to Israel than to the United States.

However, a much larger percentage of people who fall into the most anti-Semitic categories believe that American Jews are more loyal to Israel than to the U.S. In the 2002 survey, nearly three-quarters (74%) of the most anti-Semitic Americans believe this to be the case, while only 7% of the least anti-Semitic Americans accept this assertion.

V. Attitudes of Hispanic-Americans

Hispanic-Americans born outside of the U.S. are much more likely than other Hispanics and other Americans to hold anti-Semitic views.
In both this survey, which included an oversample of 300 Hispanics, and a previous 2001 survey of 1,000 Hispanic-Americans also conducted by ADL, a portrait of two very different Hispanic communities emerges, each holding very different views of Jews and tolerance in general.

The first community is made up of those born in the United States, the second of foreign-born Hispanics. In total, 37% of Hispanics were born in the U.S., while 63% were born in other countries.

There are significant differences in the characteristics of the two communities. Some of these differences include:

- Seventy-eight percent of foreign-born Hispanics speak Spanish at home compared to 20% of those born in the United States. Not surprisingly, over half (54%) of these foreign-born Hispanics receive their news from Spanish language sources.
- A quarter of foreign-born Hispanics have never attended high school, compared to 5% of Hispanics born in the U.S.
- Half of foreign-born Hispanics attend church at least once a week, compared to 38% of U.S.-born Hispanics.

Forty-four percent of foreign-born Hispanics fall into the most anti-Semitic category, while only 20% of Hispanics born in the U.S. fall into this category. As a result, it is only foreign-born Hispanics whose anti-Semitic propensities are significantly above the national average (44% vs. 17%). The anti-Semitic propensities of U.S.-born Hispanics are only slightly above the national average (20% vs. 17%).

It is encouraging to note that once Hispanics have been assimilated into the U.S. population, their attitudes about Jews appear to change significantly.

Perceptions regarding Jewish control, influence and power as well as more traditional canards about Jews, religion and ethical practices appear to be driving anti-Semitism among foreign-born Hispanics.

For example, over half of foreign-born Hispanics (55%) agree with the assertion that "Jews don't care what happens to anyone but their own kind," compared to 26% of Hispanics born in the U.S.

Forty-four percent of Hispanics born outside of the U.S. agree with the assertion that "Jews were responsible for the death of Christ," compared to 26% of those born in the U.S.

Forty-six percent agree with the statement that Jews are "more willing than others to use shady practices to get what they want," compared to 22% of those born in the U.S.

Finally, over half (52%) of foreign-born Hispanics believe Jews have too much power in the business world, compared to 26% of Hispanics born in the U.S.

VI. Attitudes of African-Americans
Anti-Semitic propensities among African-Americans, while still high, have remained stable since 1992.

The 2002 survey confirms the results of the 1992 and 1998 research: that African-Americans remain considerably more likely than whites to hold anti-Semitic beliefs. In the 2002 survey, blacks are nearly three times (35%) more likely than whites (12%) to fall into the most anti-Semitic category.

While there has been a near doubling in the number of African-Americans who fall within the "not anti-Semitic" category since 1992 (14% in 1992 to 23% in 2002), the number of African-Americans who fall into the most anti-Semitic category has remained stable since 1992.

At the same time, however, the 2002 polling makes clear that as education increases, African-Americans—like other Americans—become more tolerant. For example, when asked to respond to the statement, "books that contain dangerous ideas should be banned from public libraries," 60% of blacks with only a high school education agreed with this statement, while only 40% of college-educated blacks agreed. On the statement, "I do not have much in common with people of other races," 24% of high school-educated blacks agreed with this statement, while only 8% of college-educated blacks did. Finally, on the statement, "AIDS might be God's punishment for immoral sexual behavior," 43% of high-school educated blacks agreed. Among college-educated blacks, only 26% agreed.

VII. Anti-Semitism and Intolerance

There is a high correlation between anti-Semitic beliefs and intolerance generally.

The 2002 survey reaffirms one of the most important findings from the 1992 and 1998 surveys—that there is a strong correlation between anti-Semitism and intolerance generally. Americans who fall into the most anti-Semitic category are much more likely to embrace a series of intolerant propositions than those Americans who fall into the least anti-Semitic categories.

Americans who are most likely to have negative attitudes toward Jews are also much more likely than the rest of the population to hold intolerant beliefs about other groups, including immigrants, gays and people of other racial, ethnic and religious backgrounds.

Thus, anti-Semitic propensities are often much more likely to flow from inner beliefs—an individual's basic values or view of the world—than from external events, such as an economic downturn.

Americans who fall into the most anti-Semitic category are twice as likely (40%) as the least anti-Semitic Americans (20%) to agree with the statement: "AIDS might be God's punishment for immoral sexual behavior."

The most anti-Semitic Americans are also three times as likely (30%) than the least anti-Semitic Americans (11%) to agree with the statement: "I do not have much in common with people of other races."

Finally, the most anti-Semitic Americans are nearly twice as likely (54%) as the least anti-Semitic Americans (32%) to agree with the statement: "Books that contain dangerous ideas should be banned from public libraries."

VIII. Anti-Semitism and Age

Age continues to be a slight predictor of anti-Semitic propensities, but is much less of a factor in 2002.

In the 1992 and 1998 surveys, age was one of the most important predictors of anti-Semitic beliefs, with Americans over the age of 65 twice as likely as those under 65 to fall into the most anti-Semitic category. However, the 2002 survey results reveals that age is much less of a factor today than it was in 1992 and 1998.

The current survey shows that adults over 65 remain more likely to fall into the most anti-Semitic category but by substantially lesser margins than they did in 1992 and 1998. Today, seniors are only 13% more likely to fall into the most anti-Semitic category than the rest of the population.

Also, the educational levels of people over 65 are somewhat lower than the rest of the population. The ADL surveys have conclusively demonstrated that increased levels of education produce increased levels of tolerance. Therefore, these educational differences are another factor in accounting for seniors' propensities to hold more anti-Semitic views.

Nevertheless, the 2002 survey shows that age is less of a factor than it ever has been in the ADL research before. Presumably, age will be even less of a factor in future polling.

As one further indication of increased tolerance among seniors, the responses of people over 65 to the questions in the 2002 survey that measure tolerance are not materially different from the rest of the population.

IX. Anti-Semitism on College Campuses
Anti-Semitism on college campuses is virtually non-existent.

While the past year has seen incidents of anti-Semitism on college campuses and campus demonstrations in opposition and support of both sides in the Israeli-Palestinian conflict, ADL's first survey of college students and college faculty finds that levels of anti-Semitism among both groups are extremely low. Importantly, while criticism of Israel is high relative to the national population—especially among college faculty—there is no corresponding evidence of significant anti-Semitic sentiment.

Compared to other Americans, college students and faculty are also significantly more tolerant on issues related to free speech and race.

While more than three out of five faculty members (62%) and a majority of undergraduates (51%) have an unfavorable impression of the current Israeli government, only 3% of undergraduates and 5% of faculty members fall into the most anti-Semitic category.

The current conflict in the Middle East is a prominent issue on college campuses, with 60% of students and 59% of faculty members reporting that the Israeli-Palestinian conflict is important to students at their schools.

Twenty-nine percent of students also report that there have been demonstrations in support of the Palestinian position on their campuses and 26% report that pro-Israeli demonstrations have taken place.

When students and faculty were asked how influential they viewed certain institutions and organizations on campus, the college's administration, faculty and student government were deemed the most influential when it came to affecting social and political attitudes.

Traditional political organizations such as college Democrats or Republicans, human rights groups like Amnesty International and advocacy organizations such as pro-Israeli groups and pro-Palestinian groups are perceived as less influential.

Fewer than one in five students (18%) considers him or herself to be politically active. Of those who report being politically active, the vast majority (60%) are active on both foreign and domestic issues.

X. Ten-Year Lessons

During the past 10 years, the Anti-Defamation League (ADL) has conducted three national surveys (1992, 1998, 2002) to measure anti-Semitic propensities among the American people.

These national surveys were supplemented by a national survey of Hispanic-Americans in 2001 and additional smaller surveys of African-Americans in 1992 and 1998. In addition, during the past decade, ADL has conducted numerous surveys to measure American public reaction to unfolding events in the Middle East.

The totality of this work has produced a very solid analytic foundation to explain some of the root causes of anti-Semitism. At the same time, the ADL research has eliminated from consideration a series of demographic and attitudinal factors that had previously been seen as contributors to anti-Semitic beliefs in the United States.

Predictors of Anti-Semitism

Education

The ADL research has conclusively proven that as educational levels increase, tolerance increases. More educated Americans are much less likely to hold anti-Semitic views than less educated Americans. Moreover, more educated Americans are much more tolerant on a range of issues, including diversity, race relations, alternative lifestyles, women's empowerment and freedom of speech and the press.

Power

Forty years ago, when ADL first began its research into anti-Semitism, the most common negative Jewish stereotypes dealt with issues of Jewish honesty and ethics. Today, the most common negative stereotypes are much more likely to be centered on the issue of Jewish power in the U.S. In fact, for the first time ever, the issue of Jewish power emerged as a driver of anti-Semitic propensities in the 2002 survey. Simply put, Americans who believe that Jews have too much power in the U.S. are statistically more likely to hold anti-Semitic beliefs.

Israel

Until 2002, negative attitudes toward Israel did not appear to be a significant factor in driving anti-Semitic propensities in the United States. Even among the most anti-Semitic Americans, negative views about Israel were much more likely to be a result of personal beliefs than a contributing factor to those anti-Semitic propensities. In contrast, the 2002 survey reveals that negative attitudes toward Israel and a belief that Jews have too much influence on U.S. policies in the Middle East are now driving anti-Semitic beliefs in America.

Race

The 2002 ADL survey confirms earlier research showing that both African-Americans and Hispanic-Americans are much more likely to hold anti-Semitic views than other Americans. In part, these anti-Semitic propensities can be explained by lower levels of education among African-Americans and Hispanic-Americans in comparison to white Americans in particular.

One of the most important findings of the ADL research in recent years is that foreign-born Hispanics are especially likely to hold anti-Semitic views. In fact, this cohort of Americans has more individuals in the most anti-Semitic category than any other demographic sector of the U.S. population.

Tolerance

The three ADL surveys have conclusively proven that intolerance breeds further intolerance. Therefore, if a person is generally intolerant, then he or she is much more likely to hold anti-Semitic views. The ADL research has proven conclusively that the viruses of intolerance travel together.

Age

While age was once a very important predictor of anti-Semitic propensities, the 2002 survey reveals that it is losing its predictive value. Its importance as a predictor of anti-Semitic views is likely to be even less of a factor in future research.

Factors Found Not to Drive Anti-Semitism

Religion

In all three ADL surveys, the regression analysis concluded that religion is not a driver of anti-Semitic propensities in the United States. The current survey shows that Hispanic Catholics are more likely to hold anti-Semitic views. However, as noted earlier, this is largely attributable to the anti-Semitic propensities of Hispanic Catholics born outside of the United States.

Economic Distress

Contrary to a widely held belief regarding the emotional and attitudinal impact of economic distress, regression analyses conducted of the ADL survey results have rejected the notion that economic distress triggers anti-Semitic propensities.

The 1992 survey was conducted during a particularly difficult period in the economic history of the United States, and many questions about the economic impact of the 1992 recession were included as part of that survey. Nevertheless, the analysis concluded that even the severe economic distress of 1992 did not trigger anti-Semitic beliefs.

Political Ideology and Party Affiliation

The 10 years of ADL research have shown that political ideology and party affiliation are not drivers of anti-Semitic propensities.

Source: Anti-Defamation League. "Anti-Semitism in America 2002." http://www.adl.org/adl.asp. Accessed June 2004.

2002 Audit of Anti-Semitic Incidents

Anti-Defamation League of B'nai B'rith

Executive Summary

- In 2002, 41 states and the District of Columbia reported **1,559 anti-Semitic incidents** to the Anti-Defamation League. This marks approximately an **8 % increase** in anti-Jewish incidents from 2001, when the total was 1,432. (The 2000 total had been 1,606.)
- Anti-Semitic activity reported in 2002 included **1,028 acts of harassment** (intimidation and threats directed at individuals or institutions, as well as personal assaults), a **17 % increase over 2001**. As in the past, harassment made up the majority—this year about two-thirds, or 66 percent—of all the incidents reported. Also, **531 acts of vandalism** were reported—the lowest total in 20 years—reflecting a decrease of 4% from the 2001 total of 555 incidents. Over the past three years, vandalism incidents reported annually to ADL have declined by **27 %**. Acts of vandalism include arson, violence against Jewish institutions, cemetery desecration and other forms of property damage. [The predominance of harassment totals over those of vandalism continues an 11-year trend.]
- A total of 106 anti-Jewish incidents were reported on college **campuses** nationwide, a **24% increase** over 2001, when there were 85 incidents reported. After a five-year general trend of decline, campus incidents have **increased for three straight years**. Many of the 2002 incidents grew out of anti-Israel or "anti-Zionist" demonstrations or other actions in which some participants engaged in overt expression of anti-Jewish sentiments, including slurs and threats directed at Jewish students, placards comparing the Star of David to the Nazi swastika, or vandalism of Jewish student property, such as Hillel buildings. (Note: Anti-Israel rallies or other actions were not included as incidents in the *Audit* unless they reflected overt manifestations of anti-Semitism.)
- Higher security awareness by Jewish community institutions and the significant law enforcement activity since September 11, 2001 regarding potential terrorist targets may help account for the continuing decrease in anti-Semitic vandalism incidents.

- The *Audit* does not exist in a vacuum. There are still many groups dedicated to promoting their racist and anti-Semitic worldviews. In addition to their mass mailing and printing of anti-Jewish and racist publications, these extremist groups continue to find in the Internet—a medium that is inexpensive, can provide anonymity, and is almost impossible to regulate—a growing vehicle for their hate. (Note: "General" Internet-related anti-Semitism not aimed at a specific target— e.g., that which is found at ongoing Web sites of hate groups, in chat rooms, message boards, "spam" messages, and the like—is not part of the statistical findings of the *Audit*.)

The Findings

- The states reporting **the most anti-Semitic incidents** in 2002 were **New York** (302, down from 408 in 2001), **California** (223, up significantly from 122), **New Jersey** (171, down from 192), **Massachusetts** (129, nearly unchanged from 126), **Pennsylvania** (101, up from 61), and **Florida** (93, down from 115). Together, these six states (with large Jewish populations and thus the most targets of opportunity) account for 1,019, or nearly two-thirds, of the 1,559 incidents reported (65%).
- A total of **106** anti-Jewish incidents were reported on college **campuses** nationwide, a **24% increase** from 2001, when there were 85 incidents reported. After a five-year general trend of decline, campus incidents have increased for three straight years, rising by more than 50% during that period.

What Is the ADL Audit?

The *ADL Audit of Anti-Semitic Incidents,* published annually since 1979, is an account of overt acts and expressions of anti-Jewish bigotry or hostility. It reflects accurately the number of incidents reported to ADL, and to law enforcement agencies when such figures are made available. It is not, and does not claim to be, a scientific measure of anti-Semitism in all of its forms.

Many incidents reported in the *Audit* are not crimes. For example, distributing neo-Nazi pamphlets or slurs directed against Jewish individuals are both protected free speech. Therefore, there will most likely be discrepancies between the total numbers of anti-Semitic incidents reported in the *Audit* and in official law enforcement bias-crime statistics.

The *Audit* is not only a catalog of anti-Jewish acts that take place in a given year. It seeks also to uncover trends in anti-Semitic activity, especially trends in the types of activity reported, such as changes in the proportion of attacks against Jewish institutions.

A Note on Evaluating Anti-Semitic Incidents

Overt and obvious expressions of anti-Jewish animosity are easiest to categorize as anti-Semitic incidents, and the vast majority of incidents in the *Audit* do reveal such overt expressions of anti-Semitism. Swastikas spray-painted on synagogues or on tombstones in Jewish cemeteries, and epithets like "dirty Jew" directed against people wearing identifiable Jewish clothing (such as yarmulkes), are all clear evidence of anti-Semitism. More difficult to classify are situations in which, for example, a Jewish institution is vandalized without any specific anti-Semitic graffiti. For the purposes of this report, any deliberate and gratuitous destruction of Jewish property (such as broken windows or display cases), brings the act into the sphere of the *Audit*. Therefore, a stone thrown at a synagogue window, even without any markings of definitive anti-Semitic intent, is considered anti-Jewish hostility. While there may not be conclusive evidence to that effect, ADL tries to make reasonable judgments based on likelihood and probability.

- ADL generally counts as anti-Semitic harassment the distribution of neo-Nazi and anti-Semitic materials to individual Jews, or the placing of such items on their property. This also holds true if the material is sent to a Jewish institution or posted in a public area.
- A series of apparently related incidents, such as similar anti-Semitic graffiti painted on neighboring Jewish properties in one night, or a mass mailing of anti-Semitic material to many recipients in a particular neighborhood, counts as one incident, even though many people may be affected.
- ADL also receives complaints of anti-Semitism directed at *non-Jews*. In ADL's view, anti-Semitic slurs, threats or vandalism "mistakenly" carried out against targets thought to be Jewish, or purposefully directed against non-Jews believed to be sympathetic to Jewish causes, are clearly signs of anti-Semitic animus and deserve inclusion in the *Audit*.
- ADL does not include cases of alleged employment discrimination in hiring, firing or promotion, unless the situation includes evidence of overt anti-Semitism. A claim of discrimination in itself, based on inferences of anti-Semitism because of alleged unequal treatment in work assignments or denial of time off for holiday observance, is not considered an incident for the purposes of the *Audit*. Such claims involve a different kind of anti-Semitic problem which, while hurtful to the complainant, are nevertheless distinct from overt expressions of anti-Jewish hostility.

- Expressions of anti-Israel or "anti-Zionist" attitudes, as in demonstrations or programs on campus or in the media, are not counted as anti-Semitic incidents, unless accompanied by overt anti-Jewish statements, threats or actions directed against Jews.

Anti-Semitism and the Internet

Overview
While some bigots mail anti-Semitic letters to or shout hateful slurs at their victims, others transmit their hate electronically. Anti-Semitic propaganda or threats directed to a specific person or institution and received by E-mail, in a chat room, or sent via an instant messaging program are considered anti-Semitic harassment by the *Audit*. These messages are deliberately directed to a particular target in an effort to intimidate.

E-mail messages are essentially electronic letters. Nearly anyone with access to the Internet can send and receive E-mail messages anonymously and free of charge. A mailing list can easily be compiled from public sources such as online E-mail address directories.

Enterprising bigots have E-mailed hate materials to hundreds, if not thousands, of people. Targets of such messages open their E-mail mailboxes and find hate mail just as surprised recipients of anti-Semitic leaflets find printed hate material on their doorsteps. Bigots can easily create numerous E-mail accounts, so even if an E-mail account is deleted because of the hate messages sent using it, another can quickly be opened. As with mass mailings of printed hate literature, anti-Semitic electronic messages such as these are each classified by the *Audit* as one incident, regardless of the number of people they are sent to.

Hate-filled World Wide Web sites and online bulletin board messages are not included as anti-Semitic incidents in the *Audit*. While readers may be offended by such material, it generally does not target them specifically. In addition, Internet users are often not passive recipients of this material, unlike the unsuspecting addressees of E-mail messages.

The Current Picture
In 2002, use of the Internet by extremists continued to develop and expand. There are literally hundreds of Web sites that spread racism and anti-Semitism, as well as expressing Holocaust denial. Virtually every major extremist and racist group based in the United States has some form of Internet presence. Extremists and groups with established hate sites include white supremacist David Duke, the neo-Nazi National Alliance, Matt Hale and the WCOTC, "Identity" Churches, and a host of neo-Nazis, racist skinheads, "Aryan" women's groups and Klan chapters. Holocaust denial groups such as the Institute for Historical Review

and the Committee for Open Debate on the Holocaust, as well as a number of militia groups and conspiracy theorists, are also accessible online.

The Internet has been utilized by anti-Semites and racists to create an electronic community of hate to help further their goals. The anti-Semitic materials that are shared online often spread to a variety of lists and sites—including Islamic extremists. In some cases, materials produced by those on the right have even been reproduced in the mainstream Arab press—notably an essay by David Duke that was subsequently run in *Arab News*, the English-language paper in Saudi Arabia.

The Internet as a medium not only allows communication between individuals and on an individual-to-group level; it can also create an interactive community for extremists. The Internet has allowed groups to plan events together, regardless of the distance between the members, and irrespective of any ideological differences.

Campus Incidents

After a 15% increase in 2000, and an increase of 23% in 2001, the number of anti-Semitic incidents on college campuses in 2002 rose to 106. This represents a further increase of 24% over the previous year, and a rise of 53% in the past three years.

Many of the 2002 incidents grew out of anti-Israel or "anti-Zionist" demonstrations or other actions in which some participants engaged in overt expressions of anti-Jewish sentiments, including name-calling directed at Jewish students, placards comparing the Star of David to the swastika, or vandalism of Jewish student property, such as Hillel buildings. (It should be noted that anti-Israel rallies *per se* were not included as incidents in the *Audit* unless there was a clear manifestation of anti-Semitism during the event.)

Appendix I: Overview of Other Anti-Semitic Activity in the United States, 2002

For a valuable review of extremist groups and activities and of Holocaust denial, see parts A and B of this appendix in the full text of the ADL Audit, *available from the Anti-Defamation League, on the ADL Web site, http://www.adl.org.*

C. Responses to Racism and Anti-Semitism
Legislation/Law Enforcement
As of March 2003, forty-six states and the District of Columbia now have penalty-enhanced hate crime laws. The New Mexico state legislature passed the most recent hate crimes penalty enhancement bill, defining a hate crime and laying out penalties for perpetrators of crimes that are proven by the District Attorney to be motivated by hate. The bill also provides for law enforcement training and reporting. Moreover, the Federal Hate Crime Statistics Act requires the Justice Department to acquire data on crimes which "manifest prejudice based on race, religion, sexual

orientation, or ethnicity" from law enforcement agencies across the country and to publish an annual summary of its findings.

Appendix II: Campus 2002

Throughout 2002, American colleges and universities witnessed a dramatic increase in the frequency and intensity of anti-Israel and anti-Semitic incidents resulting from the "campus Intifada," the organized and increasingly widespread anti-Israel campaign tied to the ongoing violence in the Middle East. This campaign did much to generate a negative atmosphere on many campuses, creating a sense of disquiet and an amount of real fear among many Jewish members of the campus community. Many of the reported cases of anti-Semitic vandalism and harassment, seemingly independent of events in the Middle East, were generated, at least in part, out of this environment.

While most anti-Israel and pro-Palestinian campus events were entirely legal and peaceful, if often uncivil in tone, a substantial number crossed the line into anti-Semitic bigotry and a few degenerated into bias crimes. For instance, participants in pro-Israel rallies and demonstrations at San Francisco State University in May and at the University of Colorado in September were physically threatened by pro-Palestinian crowds, some of whom yelled out: "Hitler didn't finish the job."

Anti-Israel activity on campus created de-facto alliances among domestic extremists on the left and the right, often interacting with extremist Palestinian/Arab/Muslim groups. At the University at Albany (SUNY), for instance, a History Department–sponsored Web site providing linkages to on-line Middle East materials, included a connection to a site run by the Palestinian Authority, which in turn is linked to domestic U.S. hate sites promoting Holocaust denial and *The Protocols*. The International Socialist Organization (ISO), a leftist extremist group with branches on a number of campuses, especially in California, played a leading role in many anti-Israel activities.

The anti-Israel campaign on campus was particularly intense during the months of March through May 2002. This reflected the marked increase in violence following the wave of terrorism that culminated in the 2002 Passover bombing in Israel and the Israeli military incursion into the territories that followed.

Anti-Israel Themes and Tactics on Campus

The anti-Israel coalition has developed over time a number of specific themes as well as discrete organizational and programmatic tactics. These are communicated through such devices as rallies, demonstrations, acts of guerilla theater, flyers, publications, petitions, materials submitted to campus newspapers, films, information tables, lectures, Web sites, etc. To some extent, the Palestinian cause has come to be seen as the "progressive" cause on campus, especially on those campuses with longstanding liberal activist political traditions. The emerging themes include:

1. *The charge that Israel is a brutal neo-colonial occupier of the Palestinians and their land.* In doing so, anti-Israel groups routinely utilize Nazi imagery in order to equate today's Palestinians with the European Jewish victims of the Holocaust and to suggest that today's Israelis are the equivalent of the Nazis of old. Ubiquitous iconography equates Sharon (as was the case with Barak before him) with Hitler and Israeli flags are often overlaid with swastikas or equated to Nazi banners. Anti-Israel publications and Web-based materials often provide gruesome photos of alleged victims of Israeli atrocities and IDF actions (for instance, the battle of Jenin) are described as war crimes and/or crimes against humanity. One way of dramatizing this theme is the use of mock Israeli army checkpoints on campus where students portraying IDF soldiers act out the alleged brutalization of innocent Palestinians.

2. *The divestment (divestiture) campaign.* This campaign, which has surfaced on nearly 60 campuses, deliberately employs the tactics used in the late 1980's by campus activists to target the then-Apartheid regime in South Africa. Just as with South Africa in the 1980s, the current campaign calls on colleges and universities to divest their portfolios of stock in companies that are based in or do significant business with Israel. This is generally done through public petition drives on individual campuses. Major divestment drives have taken place at such campuses as Princeton, MIT, Harvard, Columbia, Michigan, the University of Pennsylvania and the University of California system. More than achieving a financial result (which has been rejected by campus administrations in each and every instance), the campaign seeks to demonize and deligitimate Israel by comparing it to the previous regime in South Africa and by suggesting that Israel is the preeminent current example of a racist Apartheid state.

3. *Anti-Zionism used as a cloak for outright anti-Semitism.* As we have seen, continuing anti-Israel and anti-Zionist agitation often creates an atmosphere conducive to the emergence of outright anti-Semitism. For instance, during the spring 2002 semester, otherwise unattributed anti-Semitic flyers, making highly defamatory claims concerning Jewish Talmudic and rabbinic literature and beliefs, appeared on the campuses of the University of California at Berkeley and the University of California at San Diego. These claims have long been available in the literature of anti-Semitic and extremist hate groups in America. Known anti-Israel activists on campus had been seen posting the flyers. In one infamous case, a flyer advertising an April 8, 2002 anti-Israel rally at San Francisco

State University featured a can of "Palestinian Children Meat" which was "slaughtered according to Jewish rites."

4. *A linkage between the anti-Israel and anti-war movements.* An increasingly heard theme on campus during 2002 linked the then possibility of war with Iraq to feverishly imagined machinations of the Israeli government and the Zionist lobby. "Hands off Iraq" was heard alongside "Justice for Palestine." This theme was made explicit at the October 2002 national Divestment conference held at the University of Michigan and soon surfaced at many "peace" demonstrations across the country.

Source: Excerpted from *2002 Audit of Antisemitic Incidents.* 2002. Anti-Defamation League. Reprinted with permission. All rights reserved.

The Legal Battle against Antisemitism

A survey of legal developments with respect to antisemitism and racism in general is significant not only in terms of understanding which remedies are available—and which are not—but also in fleshing out the picture of antisemitism, racism, and xenophobia.

The basic treaties—indeed, enabling documents—are the International Convention on the Elimination of all Forms of Racial Discrimination, the United Nations Declaration on the Elimination of all Forms of Racial Discrimination, and the Declaration on the Elimination of all Forms of Intolerance and of Discrimination based on Religion or Belief. They are too voluminous to be reproduced in this volume, but they are readily available on-line. Collectively these documents develop the protocols for freedom of thought, conscience, and religion and for the elimination of discrimination based on race and/or religion.

The best sources for treaty texts on-line are http://www.bayefsky. com and http://www.unhchr.ch. The reader is urged to make use of these resources. Treaties and other international protocols, as well as jurisprudence, are organized by topic and subject matter, and full texts are available.

United Nations Treaties and Protocols

This section will not give texts of all of the international instruments and protocols. The reader will, however, find the following summary useful. For a sampling of antisemitic laws, edicts, legal decisions, papal rulings, and other exam-

ples of state policy that have been promulgated over the last 2,000 years, please see Chapter 2.

1. *The United Nations Charter.* The UN Charter, adopted in 1945, sets forth as one of the purposes of the United Nations "respect for the human rights and fundamental freedoms for all, without distinction as to race, sex, language, or religion." This language is reiterated several times in the Charter; the basic legal instrument establishing the United Nations thus stands firm against all forms of discrimination, including antisemitism.

2. *The International Bill of Human Rights.* The International Bill of Human Rights is composed of three instruments: the Universal Declaration of Human Rights, the International Covenant on Civil and Political Rights, and the International Covenant on Economic, Social, and Cultural Rights. The Bill enumerates the protections and rights that states must ensure for all of their citizens, including Jews.

Universal Declaration of Human Rights (1948). The Universal Declaration, the cornerstone document of international human rights, proclaims human rights as a common standard for all peoples and all nations. The declaration affirms (Article 1) that "everyone is entitled to all the rights and freedoms" that are set forth, and that they apply on a non-discriminatory basis. The Universal declaration proclaims that the principle of non-discrimination governs relations between individuals as well as between governments and the governed. It was, in fact, the revelation not merely of unbridled discrimination, but of the way such persecution led to deliberate mass murder—the genocide of the Jews—that in significant part motivated the drafting of the Declaration. References in the Declaration (Article 2) reinforce the world community's commitment to combat all prejudice and intolerance, including intolerance and discrimination based on religious belief, which includes beliefs of the Jewish religion. Finally, language in the Declaration (Article 30), and its legislative history, prohibits the actions of hate-based groups (such as Nazis) or states from engaging in actions aimed at destroying the rights of Jews, Blacks, and others.

International Covenant on Civil and Political Rights. The International Covenant specifies further measures states must take to ensure rights, including the measures needed to prohibit antisemitism. Article 2 of the Covenant obligates states to ensure civil and political rights to all, regardless of "race, colour, sex, language, religion, political or other opinion." The Covenant addresses as well specifically religion. Article 18 affirms the right to believe and the right to manifest those beliefs in four areas—worship, observance, practice, and teaching—thus ensuring the individual's rights are not limited to inner beliefs, but have external aspects that may be visible within the normal life of the society in which he or she is situated. Language specifying religious minorities is especially important with respect to antisemitism. Discrimination against the world's Jewish communities, normally small minorities in the countries in which they are present, is clearly prohibited by the Covenant. Finally, Article 26 calls for equal protection under the law and states that the law must prohibit discrimination on many grounds, including religion and national origin, both of which are aspects of Jewish identity. And Article 27 addresses the protection of minorities in terms of culture, religion, and language. The Jewish people possess an identifiable culture, practice a religion, and use a particular language that is holy to them; plus, the Jews qualify as a minority in any common interpretation of the term: numerical inferiority, non-dominant position, and a common will to preserve its distinctive characteristics.

3. *Racism Convention*. While antisemitism is not specifically mentioned in the International Convention on the Elimination of all Forms of Discrimination (ICERD), the legislative history of the convention demonstrates that antisemitism was very much of concern to the drafters of ICERD and that it was intended to come within ICERD's purview. The only specific mention in the Convention of discrimination, however, is apartheid. The important thing to remember about ICERD is that antisemitism would fall under the Convention's own definition of racial discrimination, whether the Jews are seen as a "race" or as a "national" or as an "ethnic" group.

4. *UN Declarations on Religious Discrimination and Religious Intolerance*. Twin UN declarations were drafted as a response to an outbreak of antisemitic incidents in 1959–1960. The Declaration on the Elimination of all Forms of Intolerance and Discrimination Based on Religion or Belief (1981) contains no specific mention of antisemitism, but it is clear that antisemitism is the referent. Articles 1 and 6 guarantee the free exercise of religion; Article 2 prohibits discrimination on the basis of religion or belief; Article 3 demands that "discrimination on the grounds of religion or belief constitutes an affront to human dignity and a disavowal of the principles of the Charter of the United Nations, and shall be condemned as a violation of the human rights and fundamental freedoms proclaimed in the Universal Declaration of Human Rights. . . ." This declaration clearly includes antisemitism as a concern of the UN's major human-rights instruments, including the Charter and the Universal Declaration.

5. *Regional Meetings*. Prohibitions against antisemitism have been recognized by regional conferences and expert preparatory meetings to the Durban World Conference Against Racism, Racial Discrimination, Xenophobia and Related Intolerance. . . . For example, The General Conclusions of the European Conference Against Racism (2000) contain independent references to antisemitism. In Paragraph 29 of the document, devoted exclusively to antisemitism, the European Conference notes that "combating antisemitism is integral and intrinsic to opposing all forms of racism" and stresses the necessity of developing "effective measures to address the issue of antisemitism in Europe today." Other regional

conferences discussed plans of action (including Holocaust education) in countering antisemitism.

Source: Julius, Anthony, Robert S. Rifkind, Jeffrey Weill, and Felice D. Gaer. August 2001. *Antisemitism: An Assault on Human Rights.* New York: American Jewish Committee/The Jacob Blaustein Institute for the Advancement of Human Rights, 21–30.

The forgoing consists merely of highlights of a few of the more significant international instruments. For full texts, the reader is referred to the Web site of the United Nations High Commissioner on Human Rights: http://www.unhchr.ch; http://Bayefsky.com; and the Web site of the University of Minnesota, link to Human Rights, which retains a comprehensive catalog of documents.

Organization on Security and Cooperation in Europe: Special Meeting on Anti-Semitism (February 2003)

The Organization on Security and Cooperation in Europe (OSCE)— better known as the Helsinki Process—traces its origins to the signing of the Helsinki Final Act in 1975, setting standards for military security, economic and environmental cooperation, and human rights and humanitarian concerns. In 2003 the OSCE convened a Special Meeting on Anti-Semitism—the first of its kind under international auspices— for the purpose of addressing the increase in antisemitic incidents in Europe during 2002. The meeting, held in Vienna, was attended by some seventy-five parliamentarians from seventeen countries.

Among the presentations at the Special Meeting were discussions of legislative initiatives on antisemitism on the part of European countries and a number of declarations. Chief among these was the Resolution on Anti-Semitic Violence in the OSCE Region, a fifteen-point document. Chief among the points: " . . . violence against Jews and other manifestations of intolerance will never be justified by international developments or political issues . . ." (Article 11); and An Action Program: Confronting and Combating Anti-Semitism in the OSCE Region, developed jointly by the USA and Germany.

For the full text of the OSCE Special Meeting on Anti-Semitism, see the Web site http:// www.csce.gov.

Christian Statements on Antisemitism

The Christian faith communities, from the earliest days of the Christian Church, have been a primary source of antisemitism. Of paramount importance, therefore, are the various statements that have emerged from the various Christian communities in recent decades. Offered here are not only statements repudiating antisemitism but also—and even more important—those statements on the relationship of Christianity to Jews and Judaism. It is at the core of the relationship between Christians and Jews that antisemitism either flourishes or is rejected.

The Church Council of the Evangelical Lutheran Church in America, on 18 April 1994, adopted the following document as a statement on Lutheran-Jewish relations:

In the long history of Christianity there exists no more tragic development than the treatment accorded the Jewish people on the part of Christian believers. Very few Christian communities of faith were able to escape the contagion of anti-Judaism and its modern successor, *anti-Semitism*. Lutherans belonging to the Lutheran World Federation and the Evangelical Lutheran Church in America feel a special burden in this regard because of certain elements in the legacy of the reformer *Martin Luther* and the catastrophes, including the *Holocaust* of the twentieth century, suffered by Jews in places where the Lutheran churches were strongly represented.

The Lutheran communion of faith is linked by name and heritage to the memory of Martin Luther, teacher and reformer. Honoring his name in our own, we recall his bold stand for truth, his earthy and sublime words of wisdom, and above all his witness to God's saving Word. Luther proclaimed a gospel for people as we really are, bidding us to trust a grace sufficient to reach our deepest shames and address the most tragic truths.

In the spirit of that truth-telling, we who bear his name and heritage must with pain acknowledge also Luther's anti-Judaic diatribes and the violent recommendations of his later writings against the Jews. As did many of Luther's own companions in the sixteenth century, we reject this violent invective, and yet more do we express our deep and abiding sorrow over its tragic effects on subsequent generations. In concert with the Lutheran World Federation, we particularly deplore the appropriation of Luther's words by modern anti-Semites for the teaching of hatred toward *Judaism* or toward the Jewish people in our day.

Grieving the complicity of our own tradition within this history of hatred, moreover, we express our urgent desire to live out our faith in *Jesus Christ* with love and respect for the Jewish people. We recognize in anti-Semitism a contradiction and an affront to the Gospel, a violation of our hope and calling, and we pledge this church to oppose the deadly working of such bigotry, both within our own circles and in the society around us. Finally, we pray for the continued blessing of the Blessed One upon the increasing cooperation and understanding between Lutheran Christians and the Jewish community.

Source: Evangelical Lutheran Church in America.

Christians and Jews

Christians and Jews live side by side in our American society. We engage one another not only in personal and social ways but also at deeper levels where ultimate values are expressed.

Both the increasingly pluralistic character of our U.S. society and historical events of the twentieth century—including the Holocaust and the establishment of the State of Israel—have posed challenges to the theological assumptions of the American churches as they relate to Jews.

The 199th General Assembly of the Presbyterian Church (U.S.A.) (1987) adopted "A Theological Understanding of the Relationship between Christians and Jews" for study and reflection. Its affirmations propose a foundation for Christian relationships with Jews:

1. The God who addresses both Christians and Jews is the same—the living and true God.
2. The church's identity is intimately related to the continuing identity of the Jewish people.
3. We are willing to ponder with Jews the mystery of God's election of both Jews and Christians to be a light to the nations.
4. As Christians we acknowledge that Jews are in covenant relationship with God, and we consider the implications of this reality for evangelism and witness.
5. As Christians we acknowledge in repentance the church's complicity in proliferation of anti-Jewish attitudes and actions, and we determine to put an end to the teaching of contempt for Jews.
6. We are willing to investigate the continuing significance of the promise of "land," with its associated obligations, and to explore the implications for Christian theology.
7. We act in hope, which we share with Jews, as we both await the final manifestation of God's promise of the peaceable kingdom.

Presbyterians have identified underlying questions that require continuing reflection by Christians. Our response should be made in humility and with a deep respect for others' human integrity and spiritual values.

- What are our understandings of Jesus in a religiously plural world?
- What is the appropriate biblical material to guide reflection about Christians and Jews?
- What are the appropriate content and forms of evangelism among people of other faiths?

Dialogue is the appropriate form of faithful conversation between Christians and Jews. As trust is established, not only questions and concerns can be shared but faith and commitments as well. Christians have no reason to be reluctant in sharing the good news of their faith with anyone. A militancy that seeks to impose one's own point of view on another, however, is not only inappropriate but counterproductive. In dialogue, partners are able to define their faith in their own terms, avoiding caricatures of one another. They are thus better able to obey the commandment, "You shall not bear false witness against your neighbor." It is out of a mutual willingness to listen and to learn that faith deepens and a new and better relationship between Christians and Jews is enabled to grow.

Christians are challenged to review and change attitudes that belittle Jews or fan hatred. We can become aware of those uses of Judaism in preaching and teaching that make it a negative example in order to commend Christianity. We can avoid repetition of stereotypes or nonhistorical ideas about Pharisees and Jewish leadership.

Christians and Jews are each called to the service of God in the world, and Christian witness includes commitment, with others, to human solidarity against injustice and for the unity and integrity of creation.

Both peoples are sensitive to the dimension of the holy. Jews and Christians can cooperate in providing liturgical and theological resources on issues.

Support the search to promote understanding.

- Initiate opportunities to hear the self-understanding of Jews.
- Engage in dialogue with Jewish partners.
- Participate in educational programs designed to foster understanding and better relationships.
- Plan congregational education for Christians and Jews together. Discover activities for all age groups.
- Study materials that explore theological and biblical understandings. Be aware of roots of anti-Semitism that have often come from distortions of Christian faith.
- Seek historical information about past relationships between Christians and Jews.

Support the search for cooperation.

- Teach that authentic Christianity can have no complicity in anti-Semitic attitudes or actions. Work to oppose persecution or denigration of Jews.
- Develop with Jews common opportunities for service and mission to meet human needs and address societal issues of peace and justice.
- Determine appropriate responses to Yom Hashoah, the Holocaust Remembrance Day listed in the Presbyterian calendar.
- Seek common ethical grounds in the Abrahamic faith traditions that enable solidarity on behalf of justice and peace.
- Engage in dialogue with Jewish groups about the State of Israel. Encourage work for reconciliation in the Middle East in as broad a way as possible. Facilitate constructive dialogue and common efforts between Jews, Christians, and Muslims.
- Pray for and encourage those who would break cycles of vengeance and violence, whether of states or resistance movements, of terror or retaliation.

Support the search for faithful witness.

- Participate in common celebration, prayer, and worship with Jews.
- Respond to pastoral needs arising out of the interaction of Jews and Christians in U.S. society.
- Testify by deeds and words to the all-encompassing love of Christ through whom we "who were far off have been brought near" to the covenants of promise.
- Cooperate with other churches to seek the visible Christian unity that makes credible our witness in a pluralistic world.

See General Assembly actions on which this content is based: Christian-Jewish 1987, 1989; Anti-Semitism 1990; Middle East yearly. See also Christian Identity, 1987.

Source: "Christians and Jews," a brochure produced and distributed by the Office of Ecumenical and Interfaith Relations, 1990, Presbyterian Church (U.S.A.), 100 Witherspoon St., Louisville, KY 40202-1396.

Ecumenical Considerations on Jewish-Christian Dialogue

Through dialogue with Jews many Christians have come to appreciate the richness and vitality of Jewish faith and life in the covenant and have been enriched in their own understandings of God and the divine will for all creatures.

Bible-reading and worshiping Christians often believe that they "know Judaism."... This attitude is often enforced by lack of knowledge about the history of Jewish life and thought through the 1,900 years since the parting of the ways of Judaism and Christianity.

In the process of defining its own identity the church defined Judaism, and assigned to the Jews definite roles in its understanding of God's acts of salvation. It should not be surprising that Jews resent those Christian theologies in which they as a people are assigned to play a negative role. Tragically, such patterns of thought in Christianity have often led to overt acts of condescension, persecution, and worse.

Source: World Council of Churches, Ecumenical Considerations on Jewish-Christian Dialogue, 1982. http://www.wcc-coe.org. Accessed 1 March 2004.

Nostra Aetate: Declaration on the Relation of the Church to Non-Christian Religions

Proclaimed by His Holiness Pope Paul VI on October 28, 1965

The central enabling document of the modern Roman Catholic Church with respect to relations with non-Christian religions—including Jews—is Nostra Aetate, *adopted by the Second Vatican Council in 1965.* Nostra Aetate, *among other issues, addresses the "teaching of contempt" and antisemitism.*

1. In our time, when day by day mankind is being drawn closer together, and the ties between different peoples are becoming stronger, the Church examines more closely the relationship to non-Christian religions. In her task of promoting unity and love among men, indeed among nations, she considers above all in this declaration what men have in common and what draws them to fellowship.

One is the community of all peoples, one their origin, for God made the whole human race to live over the face of the earth.(1) One also is their final goal, God. His providence, His manifestations of goodness, His saving design extend to all men,(2) until that time when the elect will be united in the Holy City, the city ablaze with the glory of God, where the nations will walk in His light.(3)

Men expect from the various religions answers to the unsolved riddles of the human condition, which today, even as in former times, deeply stir the hearts of men: What is man? What is the meaning, the aim of our life? What is moral good, what sin? Whence suffering and what purpose does it serve? Which is the road to true happiness? What are death, judgment and retribution after death? What, finally, is that ultimate inexpressible mystery which encompasses our existence: whence do we come, and where are we going?

2. From ancient times down to the present, there is found among various peoples a certain perception of that hidden power which hovers over the course of things and over the events of human history; at times some indeed have come to the recognition of a Supreme Being, or even of a Father. This perception and recognition penetrates their lives with a profound religious sense.

Religions, however, that are bound up with an advanced culture have struggled to answer the same questions by means of more refined concepts and a more developed language. Thus in Hinduism, men contemplate the divine mystery and express it through an inexhaustible abundance of myths and through searching philosophical inquiry. They seek freedom from the anguish of our human condition either through ascetical practices or profound meditation or a flight to God with love and trust. Again, Buddhism, in its various forms, realizes the radical insufficiency of this changeable world; it teaches a way by which men, in a devout and confident spirit, may be able either to acquire the state of perfect liberation, or attain, by their own efforts or through higher help, supreme illumination. Likewise, other religions found everywhere try to counter the restlessness of the human heart, each in its own manner, by proposing "ways," comprising teachings, rules of life, and sacred rites. The Catholic Church rejects nothing that is true and holy in these religions. She regards with sincere reverence those ways of conduct and of life, those precepts and teachings which, though differing in many aspects from the ones she holds and sets forth, nonetheless often reflect a ray of that Truth which enlightens all men. Indeed, she proclaims, and ever must proclaim Christ "the way, the truth, and the life" (John 14:6), in whom men may find the fullness of religious life, in whom God has reconciled all things to Himself.(4)

The Church, therefore, exhorts her sons, that through dialogue and collaboration with the followers of other religions, carried out with prudence and love and in witness to the Christian faith and life, they recognize, preserve and promote the good things, spiritual and moral, as well as the socio-cultural values found among these men.

3. The Church regards with esteem also the Moslems. They adore the one God, living and subsisting in Himself; merciful and all-powerful, the Creator of heaven and earth,(5) who has spoken to men; they take pains to submit wholeheartedly to even His inscrutable decrees, just as Abraham, with whom the faith of Islam takes pleasure in linking itself, submitted to God. Though they do not acknowledge Jesus as God, they revere Him as a prophet. They also honor Mary, His virgin Mother; at times they even call on her with devotion. In addition, they await the day of judgment when God will render their deserts to all those who have been

raised up from the dead. Finally, they value the moral life and worship God especially through prayer, almsgiving and fasting.

Since in the course of centuries not a few quarrels and hostilities have arisen between Christians and Moslems, this sacred synod urges all to forget the past and to work sincerely for mutual understanding and to preserve as well as to promote together for the benefit of all mankind social justice and moral welfare, as well as peace and freedom.

4. As the sacred synod searches into the mystery of the Church, it remembers the bond that spiritually ties the people of the New Covenant to Abraham's stock.

Thus the Church of Christ acknowledges that, according to God's saving design, the beginnings of her faith and her election are found already among the Patriarchs, Moses and the prophets. She professes that all who believe in Christ-Abraham's sons according to faith (6) are included in the same Patriarch's call, and likewise that the salvation of the Church is mysteriously foreshadowed by the chosen people's exodus from the land of bondage. The Church, therefore, cannot forget that she received the revelation of the Old Testament through the people with whom God in His inexpressible mercy concluded the Ancient Covenant. Nor can she forget that she draws sustenance from the root of that well-cultivated olive tree onto which have been grafted the wild shoots, the Gentiles.(7) Indeed, the Church believes that by His cross Christ, Our Peace, reconciled Jews and Gentiles. making both one in Himself.(8)

The Church keeps ever in mind the words of the Apostle about his kinsmen: "theirs is the sonship and the glory and the covenants and the law and the worship and the promises; theirs are the fathers and from them is the Christ according to the flesh" (Rom. 9:4–5), the Son of the Virgin Mary. She also recalls that the Apostles, the Church's main-stay and pillars, as well as most of the early disciples who proclaimed Christ's Gospel to the world, sprang from the Jewish people.

As Holy Scripture testifies, Jerusalem did not recognize the time of her visitation,(9) nor did the Jews in large number, accept the Gospel; indeed not a few opposed its spreading.(10) Nevertheless, God holds the Jews most dear for the sake of their Fathers; He does not repent of the gifts He makes or of the calls He issues—such is the witness of the Apostle.(11) In company with the Prophets and the same Apostle, the Church awaits that day, known to God alone, on which all peoples will address the Lord in a single voice and "serve him shoulder to shoulder" (Soph. 3:9).(12)

Since the spiritual patrimony common to Christians and Jews is thus so great, this sacred synod wants to foster and recommend that mutual understanding and respect which is the fruit, above all, of biblical and theological studies as well as of fraternal dialogues.

True, the Jewish authorities and those who followed their lead pressed for the death of Christ;(13) still, what happened in His passion cannot be charged against all the Jews, without distinction, then alive, nor against the Jews of today. Although the Church is the new people of God, the Jews should not be presented as rejected or accursed by God, as if this followed from the Holy Scriptures. All should see to it, then, that in catechetical work or in the preaching of the word of God they do not teach anything that does not conform to the truth of the Gospel and the spirit of Christ.

Furthermore, in her rejection of every persecution against any man, the Church, mindful of the patrimony she shares with the Jews and moved not by political reasons but by the Gospel's spiritual love, decries hatred, persecutions, displays of anti-Semitism, directed against Jews at any time and by anyone.

Besides, as the Church has always held and holds now, Christ underwent His passion and death freely, because of the sins of men and out of infinite love, in order that all may reach salvation. It is, therefore, the burden of the Church's preaching to proclaim the cross of Christ as the sign of God's all-embracing love and as the fountain from which every grace flows.

5. We cannot truly call on God, the Father of all, if we refuse to treat in a brotherly way any man, created as he is in the image of God. Man's relation to God the Father and his relation to men his brothers are so linked together that Scripture says: "He who does not love does not know God" (1 John 4:8).

No foundation therefore remains for any theory or practice that leads to discrimination between man and man or people and people, so far as their human dignity and the rights flowing from it are concerned.

The Church reproves, as foreign to the mind of Christ, any discrimination against men or harassment of them because of their race, color, condition of life, or religion. On the contrary, following in the footsteps of the holy Apostles Peter and Paul, this sacred synod ardently implores the Christian faithful to "maintain good fellowship among the nations" (1 Peter 2:12), and, if possible, to live for their part in peace with all men, (14) so that they may truly be sons of the Father who is in heaven.(15)

Notes

1. Cf. Acts 17:26

2. Cf. Wis. 8:1; Acts 14:17; Rom. 2:6–7; 1 Tim. 2:4

3. Cf. Apoc. 21:23f.

4. Cf. 2 Cor. 5:18–19

5. Cf. St. Gregory VII, letter XXI to Anzir (Nacir), King of Mauritania (Pl. 148, col. 450f.)

6. Cf. Gal. 3:7

7. Cf. Rom. 11:17–24

8. Cf. Eph. 2:14–16

9. Cf. Lk. 19:44

10. Cf. Rom. 11:28

11. Cf. Rom. 11:28–29; cf. dogmatic Constitution, Lumen Gentium (Light of nations) AAS, 57 (1965) pag. 20

12. Cf. Is. 66:23; Ps. 65:4; Rom. 11:11–32

13. Cf. John. 19:6

14. Cf. Rom. 12:18

15. Cf. Matt. 5:45

Source: Translation of Latin original by the Holy See provided courtesy of Eternal Word Television Network, 5817 Old Leeds Road, Irondate, AL 35210 (http://www.ewtn.com).

Presbyterian Church (USA)—Statement on Violence against Jews

As Stated Clerk of the General Assembly of the Presbyterian Church (U.S.A.), I am writing to express deep concern regarding the escalation of violence against men and women of Israel and the larger Jewish community in many parts of the world. I share with you the following statement condemning violence against Jews:

A Statement Abhoring Violence against Jews

Since 1987, when the 199th General Assembly of the Presbyterian Church (U.S.A.) adopted A Theological Understanding of the Relationship between Christians and Jews for study and reflection, the church has been called to ponder its words, including the statement, "We pledge, God helping us, never again to participate in, to contribute to, or (insofar as we are able) to allow the persecution or denigration of Jews." Today Presbyterians watch with consternation the escalating violence in many parts of the world, including the Middle East. As they do so, one of the concerns that must be addressed is the violence against Jews that is seen both in Israel and around the world.

The world has seen the conviviality of innocent people, gathered to enjoy food, drink, and friendship, shattered by sudden death and injury. A festival of hope and freedom, the Passover, has been distorted by the killing and maiming of celebrants so that the occasion became a symbol of hope diminished.

The Jewish community's felt need for security has been intensified by violence against Jews and Jewish institutions in various parts of the globe, reinforcing once again historic images of insecurity.

Political violence on all sides has undermined fragile trust so that leaders replace talk of peace with the rhetoric and images of war.

None of these can be supported as acceptable expressions of anger and frustration, retribution, tactics in a political struggle, or the acceptable reactions to human wrongs, new or old. No matter how these acts are rationalized, they are not justifiable.

The fear and the pain experienced in the depths of the souls of both Palestinian and Jewish communities cause deep concern and heartfelt pain among people of goodwill. Acts of hate and terror inflicted on innocent children and youth, women and men of Israel and the larger Jewish community must be unequivocally condemned and vehemently abhorred. This is in no way inconsistent with speaking out about the political and military violence of the Israeli government or the militant activities of Israeli settlers. It is possible to speak with Jewish neighbors and fellow citizens about Israel in ways that do not diminish their hope, their security, or their trust. This can only happen when people speak and act with respect for those with whom they agree or disagree.

The time has come to call people living in Europe and North America to cease from hateful acts against Jews that diminish the hope, security, and trust of Jews and Palestinians alike. Even careless words denigrate and lend support to those motivated by the genuine hatred that is manifest in burned synagogues, physical violence against Jews, hostile writing or posted symbols calculated to breed terror. The words of the 1987 General Assembly particularly call our own people in the United States to examine ourselves, lest our attitudes and actions spawn tragic consequences.

Many people throughout the world are alarmed by the expansion of conflict in recent months and weeks. At a time of new efforts to break the cycles of violence, the time has come to call on those most closely involved. Palestinians are called, once and for all, to cease striking terror in the hearts of Israeli Jews by stopping attacks on noncombatants while they are carrying out the activities of their daily lives or the celebrations of their peoplehood. Israelis are called, once and for all, to cease striking terror in the hearts of Palestinians by stopping military operations that assault harmless people and disable Palestinian infrastructures. It is time to stop activities that increase hatred and mutual recrimination and that destroy hope, security, and trust.

Hear the words of A Theological Understanding of the Relationship between Christians and Jews: "Both Christians and Jews are called to wait and to hope in God. While we wait, Jews and Christians are called to the service of God in the world." Our vocation includes "ceaseless activity in the cause of justice and peace."

The Statement can also be found on the Presbyterian Church's Web site at:
www.pcusa.org/pcnews/02196.
Please know of my continued prayer for the people of Israel.
Cordially yours,
Clifton Kirkpatrick
Stated Clerk of the General Assembly
Presbyterian Church (U.S.A.)

Source: Presbyterian Church (USA). http://www.pcusa.org. Accessed 10 February 2004.

Southern Baptist Convention—2003

WHEREAS, Southern Baptists deplore all forms of hatred or bigotry toward any person or people group; and

WHEREAS, Scripture speaks of God's love for the Jewish people, through whom God has blessed the world with His Word and with His Messiah, our Lord Jesus (Romans 9–11); and

WHEREAS, There is a rising tide of anti-Semitism across the globe, which manifests itself in despicable acts of violence and harassment against the Jewish people; and

WHEREAS, Certain government-controlled media outlets throughout the world have cited with approval the virulently anti-Semitic book, *Protocols of the Elders of Zion*, as well as allegations of Jewish rituals of human slaughter; and

WHEREAS, Several recent United Nations–sponsored commissions and conferences have been characterized by statements reflecting a stark anti-Semitism; and

WHEREAS, Populist expressions of anti-Semitism are becoming widespread in some European countries to a degree that has not been seen since World War II; and

WHEREAS, The bloody history of the twentieth century reminds us of the unspeakably evil legacy of anti-Semitism; now, therefore, be it

RESOLVED, That the messengers to the Southern Baptist Convention meeting in Phoenix, Arizona, June 17–18, 2003, denounce all forms of anti-Semitism as contrary to the teachings of our Messiah and an assault on the revelation of Holy Scripture; and be it further

RESOLVED, That we affirm to Jewish people around the world that we stand with them against any harassment that violates our historic commitments to religious liberty and human dignity; and be it finally

RESOLVED, That we call on governmental and religious leaders across the world to stand against all forms of bigotry, hatred, or persecution.

Source: Southern Baptist Church. http://www.sbc.net. Accessed 5 January 2004.

United Church of Christ—1987

We in the United Church of Christ acknowledge that the Christian Church, throughout much of its history, denied God's continuing covenantal relationship with the Jewish people expressed in the faith of Judaism. This denial has often led to outright rejection of the Jewish people and to theologically and humanly intolerable violence.

Faced with this history from which we as Christians cannot, and must not, dissociate ourselves, we ask for God's forgiveness through our Lord Jesus Christ. We pray for divine grace that will enable us, more firmly than ever before, to turn from this path of rejection and persecution to affirm that Judaism has not been superseded by Christianity; that Christianity is not to be understood as the successor religion to Judaism; God's covenant with the Jewish people has not been abrogated. God has not rejected the Jewish people; God is faithful in keeping covenant.

Source: United Church of Christ. http://www.ucc.org. Accessed 2004.

United Church of Christ—2002

Resolution

WHEREAS, when Jesus was asked what was the greatest commandment, he responded quoting Hebrew scripture, "You shall love the Lord your God with all your heart, and with all your soul, and with all your mind. This is the greatest and first commandment. And a second is like it. You shall love your neighbor as yourself. On these two commandments hang all the law and the prophets" (Matthew 22:37–40);

WHEREAS, the shootings that occurred at the Hebrew day care center in California shocked the nation and should be a wake up call for all Christians to denounce anti-Semitism;

WHEREAS anti-Semitism has been deeply embedded in Christian tradition;

WHEREAS anti-Semitism violates Christ's call to love our neighbors as ourselves;

WHEREAS Judaism is the foundation of our faith; and

WHEREAS the delegates to the Sixteenth General Synod (1987) of the United Church of Christ stated, "We in the United Church of Christ acknowledge that the Christian Church has, throughout much of its history, denied God's continuing covenantal relationship with the Jewish people expressed in the faith of Judaism. This denial often has led to outright rejection of the Jewish people and theologically and humanly intolerable violence";

THEREFORE BE IT RESOLVED that we the delegates to Twenty-third General Synod of the United Church of Christ do confess the sin of anti-Semitism and renounce it, knowing that Jews are children of God to be loved as we love ourselves in the way that Christ has commanded us;

BE IT FURTHER RESOLVED that we invite the Justice and Witness Ministries of the United Church of Christ to utilize all rapid response networks to notify conferences that will in turn notify congregations when there is a need to take action against anti-Semitism in a crisis;

BE IT FURTHER RESOLVED that we urge our national representatives to speak out against anti-Semitism in all appropriate circumstances;

BE IT FURTHER RESOLVED that we encourage all churches of the United Church of Christ to build relationships of mutual respect and friendship with their nearby synagogues through interfaith exchanges such as church school, youth and adult education programs, cooperative service projects, and social interactions; and

BE IT FURTHER RESOLVED that the United Church of Christ actively seek and develop relationships of mutual respect and understanding with our Jewish brothers and sisters in all settings of the church.

Funding for this action will be made in accordance with the overall mandates of the affected agencies and the funds available.

—Adopted by the Twenty-Third General Synod

Source: United Church of Christ. http://www.ucc.org. Accessed 10 December 2003.

The Episcopal Church

Resolution Number: 1997-D055

Title: Reaffirm Interfaith Dialogue and Acknowledge Prejudice Against Jews

Legislative Action Taken: Concurred as Substituted and Amended

Final Text:

Resolved, That this 72nd General Convention reaffirm the Episcopal Church's commitment to interfaith cooperation and dialogue with our sisters and brothers of the Jewish faith; and be it further

Resolved, That we commend the Evangelical Lutheran Church in America for the leadership it has given in this area and more particularly its 1994 *Declaration to the Jewish Community*; and be it further

Resolved, That we acknowledge, with regret, our acts of moral blindness and outright prejudice, throughout history and today, that have contributed to the abuse and mistreatment of Jews.

Citation: General Convention, *Journal of the General Convention of . . . The Episcopal Church, Philadelphia, 1997* (New York: General Convention, 1998), p. 216.

EXC021985.27 Urge Christians to End Racism and Religious Bigotry Committee: World Mission

Citation: Executive Council Minutes, Feb. 12–15, 1985, Phoenix, pp. 72–73.

Resolved, That the Executive Council in this 40th Anniversary year of the liberation of the Nazi extermination and concentration camps, encourage all Episcopalians and all people of good will to ponder anew the horror that is racism and religious bigotry and rededicate themselves to purging from their own souls and society all traces of such racism and religious bigotry, including and especially all anti-Semitism; and be it further

Resolved, That in the Lenten and Easter season, all Episcopalians are called to remember, in prayer and action, that God the Father creates all humankind equal, that God the Son enlightens every human who enters the world, and freely gave Himself up as a sacrifice on behalf of all humanity equally, and that God the Holy Spirit goes where He wants, and not in accordance with divisions contrived by humans, and that racism and religious bigotry are utterly incompatible with belief in Christ—a fact all Christians must each reflect in word and deed.

Resolution Number: 1991-D122

Title: Distinguish Between Criticism of Israeli Policy and Expression of Anti-Jewish Prejudice

Legislative Action Taken: Concurred As Submitted

Final Text:

Resolved, the House of Deputies concurring, That the 70th General Convention of the Episcopal Church recognize that a distinction exists between the propriety of legitimate criticism of Israeli governmental policy and action and the impropriety of anti-Jewish prejudice; and be it further

Resolved, That the 70th General Convention of the Episcopal Church deplore all expressions of anti-Jewish prejudice (sometimes referred to by the imprecise word "anti-Semitism"), in whatever form on whatever occasion, and urge its total elimination from the deliberations and affairs of the Episcopal Church, its individual members, its various units. Citation: General Convention, *Journal of the General Convention of . . . The Episcopal Church, Phoenix, 1991* (New York: General Convention, 1992), p.773.

Source: *Journal of the General Convention of the Episcopalian Church.*

6

Organizations

This chapter includes organizations, agencies, educational and research institutions, and other groups, in the United States and in Europe, devoted to the monitoring, assessment, evaluation, historical recording and analysis, and counteraction of antisemitism. The reader is encouraged to visit the Web sites of these organizations for mission statements, further historical data, and in-depth programmatic information of and on these organizations.

U.S. Organizations

American Jewish Committee
165 East 56th Street
New York, NY 10022
(212) 751-4000
http://www.ajc.org

Established in 1906, the American Jewish Committee (AJC) is the oldest human relations organization under Jewish auspices in the United States. It is a membership organization with chapters around the United States and offices in Europe and Israel. The AJC, long committed to research and programming in ethnicity and pluralism, promotes racial, ethnic, and religious coalition-building, and monitors and combats antisemitism and other forms of group prejudice. The AJC publishes the *American Jewish*

Year Book, an annual reference work that is the "document of record" for Jewish life nationally and internationally. The *American Jewish Year Book* is an authoritative source for information on Jewish communal affairs around the world, including anti-semitism. The monthly journal *Commentary* is also published under AJC auspices, albeit with editorial independence.

American Jewish Congress
15 East 84th Street
New York, NY 10028
(212) 879-4500
http://www.ajcongress.org

The American Jewish Congress (AJCongress), founded in 1918, is headquartered in New York with regional chapters around the United States. AJCongress, a pioneer in the use of law and social action to combat prejudice and discrimination, views itself as the "lawyer" of the Jewish community and has participated in many landmark U.S. Supreme Court cases on church-state separation, discrimination, and other communal issues. The American Jewish Congress publishes a semischolarly quarterly, *Judaism,* and a magazine, *Congress Monthly.*

American Jewish Historical Society
15 West 16th Street
New York, NY 10011
(212) 294-6160
http://www.ajhs.cjh.org

The American Jewish Historical Society, located in New York with a branch in Waltham, Massachusetts, identifies as its mission the fostering of awareness and appreciation of the American Jewish heritage and serving as a national scholarly resource for research through the collection, preservation, and dissemination of materials relating to American Jewish history. The society is a good resource for archival and other historical data on antisemitism in the United States.

Anti-Defamation League
823 United Nations Plaza
New York, NY 10017
(212) 490-2525
http://www.adl.org

The Anti-Defamation League (ADL) is the largest and most visible of the "defense" agencies of the Jewish community in the United States. Created in 1913 and headquartered in New York, the ADL's mission is to "stop the defamation of the Jewish people and to secure justice and fair treatment to all citizens alike." The ADL has consistently viewed its role as combating antisemitism and focuses not only on monitoring discrimination against Jews but also on anti-Israel activity, left- and right-wing radicalism, and violations of church-state separation, as well as interfaith work and Holocaust education. The ADL works through a network of regional offices in the United States and has representatives in a number of capitals abroad. The organization publishes and distributes a range of materials on intergroup relations, diversity, and prejudice, especially on the counteraction of antisemitism. The ADL publishes periodic reports on antisemitism (including polling data) in the United States and around the world, legal matters, and interreligious relations.

Jewish Council for Public Affairs
443 Park Avenue South
New York, NY 10016
(212) 684-6950
http://www.thejcpa.org

Established in 1944, the Jewish Council for Public Affairs (JCPA; formerly the National Jewish Community Relations Advisory Council—NJCRAC) is the national umbrella and coordinating body for Jewish public affairs agencies in the United States, comprising thirteen national agencies and more than 200 community relations councils throughout the country. By virtue of its work in the community relations and public affairs arenas, the JCPA has traditionally had significant involvement in the coordination of efforts aimed at monitoring and combating antisemitism and has published periodic "Reassessments" in this area.

Leo Baeck Institute
15 West 16th Street
New York, NY 10011
(212) 722-6200
http://www.lbi.org

The Leo Baeck Institute is devoted to studying the history of German-speaking Jewry from its origins to its destruction by the

Nazis and to preserving its culture. Founded in 1955, the Leo Baeck Institute works through centers in New York, Jerusalem, and London and is an important resource for data on German antisemitism. The institute publishes the *Leo Baeck Institute Yearbook* and an annual *Almanach* (German).

Simon Wiesenthal Center
1399 South Roxbury
Los Angeles, CA 90035
(310) 553-9036
http://www.wiesenthal.com

Established in 1977, the Simon Wiesenthal Center is an international organization, based in Los Angeles, whose stated mission is to "preserve the memory of the Holocaust by fostering tolerance and understanding." The center monitors antisemitism around the world—particularly the activities of hate groups—and produces periodic reports on antisemitism and racism. The center encourages public awareness of the bias and hate incidents and other racist and antisemitic activities. The center's quarterly publication, *Response*, is distributed to its reported 400,000 members. The center's projects include scholarship, education, outreach, and media programs; the centerpiece of the center's programmatic initiatives is the Museum of Tolerance. Offices of the Wiesenthal Center are in New York, Toronto, Miami, Jerusalem, Paris, and Buenos Aires.

Southern Poverty Law Center
P.O. Box 2087
Montgomery, AL 36102
(334) 264-0629
http://www.splcenter.org

The Southern Poverty Law Center (SPLC) was founded in 1971 in order to monitor hate activity in the United States and to engage in litigation against hate groups, including those whose expression is antisemitic. The SPLC has had some notable success in the American courts. Publications of the SPLC include the newsletter *SPLC Report*, published five times a year; and *Teaching Tolerance*, a semiannual publication aimed at educators.

United States Holocaust Memorial Museum
100 Raoul Wallenberg Place, SW
Washington, D.C. 20024
(202) 488-0400
http://www.ushmm.org

The United States Holocaust Memorial Museum, chartered by an act of Congress in 1980 and opened in 1993 in Washington, D.C., is the national institution in the United States for the documentation, study, and interpretation of Holocaust history and serves as this country's memorial to the millions of people murdered during the Holocaust. The museum's primary mission is to advance and disseminate knowledge about the Holocaust, to preserve the memory of the victims of the Holocaust, and to encourage its visitors to reflect upon the moral and spiritual questions raised by the events of the Holocaust as well as their own responsibilities as citizens of a democracy. Its exhibitions, collections, and especially its research center are invaluable to the student and scholar of antisemitism.

YIVO Institute for Jewish Research
15 West 16th Street
New York, NY 10011
(212) 246-6080
http://www.yivo.org

Founded in 1925 in Vilna, Poland, as the Yiddish Scientific Institute and headquartered in New York since 1940, YIVO is devoted to the history, society, and culture of Ashkenazic Jewry and the influence of that culture as it has developed in the Americas. As the only pre-Holocaust scholarly institution to transfer its mission to the United States, YIVO is the preeminent center for the study of East European Jewry and Yiddish language, literature, and folklore. Important to the scholarly mission of YIVO is historical research on antisemitism in prewar central and eastern Europe. YIVO's library is an especially rich resource. YIVO publishes a range of scholarly reports and studies.

Worldwide Organizations

The Coordination Forum for Countering Antisemitism
http://www.antisemitism.org.il

The Coordination Forum for Countering Antisemitism is an Israeli government forum that monitors antisemitic and anti-Jewish activities throughout the world. It coordinates the struggle
against antisemitism with various government bodies and Jewish
organizations around the world and publishes a monthly report,
available on-line.

Members of the forum are the Education and Foreign Ministries of the State of Israel, the Prime Minister's Office/Informa-
tion Centre and Government Secretariat of the State of Israel, the
Jewish Agency, Anti-Defamation League, World Jewish Congress,
B'nai B'rith International, and two research institutes—the
Stephen Roth Institute of Tel Aviv University and the Vidal Sassoon Center of the Hebrew University. The forum convenes periodically to hear updated reports and establish policy on how to
counter different forms of antisemitism.

Institute for Jewish Policy Research
79 Wimpole Street
London W1G 9RY
United Kingdom
http://www.jpr.org.uk

The Institute for Jewish Policy Research (JPR—originally Institute
of Jewish Affairs), a United Kingdom–registered charity headquartered in London, informs and influences policy, opinion, and
decisionmaking on social, political, and cultural issues affecting
Jewish life in the United Kingdom and having international issues, with a special focus on Europe. JPR pursues its mission
through research, analysis, debate, and policy development. With
more than fifty years of research excellence in its former role as
the Institute of Jewish Affairs, JPR possesses a unique authority in
the world of international Jewish public affairs as an independent
think tank and research institute. JPR's research is published in
JPR Reports as well as in *JPR News.* JPR publishes *Antisemitism and
Xenophobia Today* on-line, a constantly updated information
source that can be visited at http://www.axt.org.uk. JPR's aca-

demic journal, *Patterns of Prejudice*, is devoted to examining the causes and manifestations of racial, religious, and ethnic discrimination and prejudice worldwide.

The Stephen Roth Institute for the Study of Contemporary Antisemitism and Racism of Tel Aviv University
P.O. Box 39040
Tel Aviv 69978
Israel

The Stephen Roth Institute is located in the Wiener Library—one of the nonpareil collections of antisemitica and Nazi and extremist literature—at Tel Aviv University. The institute, which began its operations in 1991, maintains an extensive database that monitors antisemitism and racism throughout the world and provides a unique service to researchers and to organizational and public affairs officials worldwide. In conjunction with the Anti-Defamation League and the World Jewish Congress, the institute publishes *Antisemitism Worldwide*, an annual volume tracking developments in this area. *Antisemitism Worldwide* uses the institute's extensive database of statistics and other data on antisemitism. In addition to *Antisemitism Worldwide*, the institute publishes occasional reports and studies on manifestations of antisemitism.

The Vidal Sassoon Center for the International Study of Antisemitism
Hebrew University of Jerusalem
Jerusalem 91905
Israel
http://www.sicsa.huji.ac.il

The Vidal Sassoon International Center (SICSA) was established in 1982 as an interdisciplinary research center dedicated to the accumulation and dissemination of knowledge necessary for understanding the phenomenon of antisemitism. The center engages in research on antisemitism throughout the ages, focusing on relations between Jews and non-Jews, particularly in situations of tension and crisis. SICSA produces an extensive list of academic reports, studies, and monographs on antisemitism. Analysis of Current Trends in Antisemitism (ACTA) is a significant research unit of SICSA and produces valuable reports. The

Felix Posen Bibliographic Project comprises on-line databases in excess of 30,000 items and is an invaluable resource for scholars and students of antisemitism.

World Jewish Congress
501 Madison Avenue
New York, NY 10022
(212) 755-5770
http://www.wjc.org

Headquartered in New York, the World Jewish Congress (WJC) acts as the coordinating arm—and indeed the "address"—for many Jewish communities in Europe. Central to the WJC's mission is the monitoring and counteracting of antisemitism in Europe and exploring those linkages that exist in European antisemitism to the residual effects of the Holocaust.

7

Print and Nonprint Resources

Print Resources

The literature on antisemitism is an extensive one and is expanding. The following list is far from comprehensive; it is intended to provide the researcher with a "road map" to the many resources in this arena. Print resources include works on prejudice and group prejudice in general, in addition to works on the history, psychology, and sociology of antisemitism. Many of the works in this list will provide the student and researcher with additional citations and annotations.

Books, Monographs, and Pamphlets

Adorno, T. W., Else Frenkel-Brunswick, Daniel J. Levinson, and R. Nevitt Sanford. *The Authoritarian Personality.* New York: W. W. Norton, 1950.

A watershed study in social psychology exploring those personality traits that characterize the phenomenon of prejudice, this book identified the important role assumed in the scholarly discussion by psychologists and sociologists. *The Authoritarian Personality* is an essential "way station" for the student and scholar doing research in any aspect of group prejudice, including antisemitism.

Allport, Gordon. *The Nature of Prejudice.* Menlo Park, CA: Addison-Wesley, 1979 (originally published in 1954).

A pioneering work on the social and psychological roots and nature of bigotry. This book is a "must" for anyone engaged in the serious study of any form of individual or group prejudice.

Almog, Shmuel, ed. *Antisemitism through the Ages.* Translated by Nathan H. Reisner. (Translated from *Sin'at Yisrael Ledoroteha,* the Zalman Shazar Center, 1980.) Oxford: Pergamon Press, 1988. Published for the Vidal Sassoon International Center for the Study of Antisemitism, the Hebrew University of Jerusalem.

A substantial collection of scholarly essays exploring many varied facets and arenas of antisemitism. Almog included as well interpretive and historiographical essays; the volume will be useful, therefore, to a range of scholars.

Altschiller, Donald. *Hate Crimes: A Reference Handbook.* Santa Barbara, CA: ABC-CLIO, 1999.

A fine reference work for scholars, journalists, and public officials on an important arena of group prejudice. This work, which emphasizes legal remedies, is a volume in the Contemporary World Issues series.

American Jewish Year Book (AJYB) (annual). New York: American Jewish Committee.

This annual volume is the "document of record" for events, issues, demographics, and personalities in the Jewish world internationally. It contains annual reports, analyses, and assessments of the state of Jewish security in the countries it covers. The *AJYB* is an important first stop for the student, journalist, scholar, and public affairs professional researching any area of contemporary antisemitism. The *AJYB* has been in continuous publication since 1900, making it a useful tool for historians.

Arendt, Hannah. *Antisemitism,* vol. 1, *The Origins of Totalitarianism.* New York: Harvest/HBJ, 1968.

In this short book Arendt kicked off her landmark study of totalitarianism with a highly provocative analysis of the roots and causes of antisemitism.

Baer, Yitzhak F. *Galut.* New York: Schocken, 1947.

A classic in the literature of the underpinnings of antisemitism in classical Christianity by one of the great historians of the Jewish experience. This short, eminently readable book is crucial for anyone exploring the Christian view of Jews and Judaism and the Christian underpinnings of antisemitism.

Baldwin, Neil. *Henry Ford and the Jews: The Mass Production of Hate.* Cambridge, MA: Perseus Books Group/Public Affairs, 2001.

Using the antisemitism of industrialist Henry Ford's *Dearborn Independent* as a vehicle, this book developed a context for understanding the social history—especially the growing antisemitism—of the early decades of the twentieth century in the United States.

Baron, Salo. *A Social and Religious History of the Jews.* 18 vols. New York: Columbia University/Philadelphia: The Jewish Publication Society of America, 1937–1983.

The classic survey and analysis of Jewish history, to the thirteenth century. Scholars will find Baron's voluminous reference notes invaluable in their research on the relations between Jews and non-Jews.

Bat Ye'or. *The Dhimmi: Jews and Christians under Islam.* Rutherford, NJ: Fairleigh Dickinson University Press, 1985.

———. *Islam and Dimmitude: Where Civilizations Collide.* Rutherford, NJ: Fairleigh Dickinson University Press, 2001.

These two books (and other writings) by Bat Ye'or (a pseudonym for an Israeli scholar) are among the finest on the "protected" religions—including Judaism and Christianity—under Islam. These works will explain much of the background of antisemitism under Islam and are most useful for scholars, students, public affairs officials, and journalists.

Belth, Nathan C. *A Promise to Keep: A Narrative of the American Encounter with Anti-Semitism.* New York: Times Books, 1979.

Hidden by the title is the fact that this book is a history of the Anti-Defamation League, one of the leading Jewish "defense"/

human relations agencies. The book is a useful review for the general reader of antisemitism in the United States.

Ben-Sasson, H. H., ed. *A History of the Jewish People.* Cambridge: Harvard University Press, 1976.

The best comprehensive history of the Jews in one volume; serves as background and context for the study of antisemitism. Each era was addressed by the leading historian of that arena. The student and scholar will find Ben-Sasson to be an indispensable companion.

Berger, David, ed. *History and Hate: The Dimensions of Anti-Semitism.* Philadelphia: The Jewish Publication Society, 1986.

This short book contains eight essays, each representing a historical period or geographical and cultural arena, by leading scholars.

Berlin, Naphtali Zvi Yehuda. *Why Antisemitism? A Translation of "The Remnant of Israel" by Rabbi Naphtali Zvi Yehuda Berlin "The Neziv."* Translated and annotated by Howard S. Joseph. Northvale, NJ: Jason Aronson, 1996.

A classic work, by a nineteenth-century Eastern European rabbinic leader, exploring the origins of antisemitism from the perspective of traditional Judaism. Essential for the scholar of the historiography of antisemitism.

Berman, Paul, ed. *Blacks and Jews: Alliances and Arguments.* New York: Delacorte Press, 1994.

A well-written and provocative book on a topic of concern for the last half of the twentieth century and into the twenty-first. The question of black-Jewish relations is inextricable from that of antisemitism emerging from the black community.

Birnbaum, Pierre. *Anti-Semitism in France: A Political History from Léon Blum to the Present.* Translated by Miriam Kochan. Oxford: Blackwell Publishers, 1992. Originally published as *Un Mythe Politique: La "République Juive"* by Librairie Arthème Fayard, 1988.

A well-documented account, by a leading French political scientist, of the origins, history, and effects of antisemitism in France.

————. *The Anti-Semitic Moment: A Tour of France in 1898.* Translated by Jane Marie Todd. New York: Hill and Wang, 2003.

The eponymous "moment" in Birnbaum's book—the period of antisemitic convulsions in France in the wake of the Dreyfus affair—was precisely that, in Birnbaum's view: despite the pervasiveness of antisemitism in France and the complicity of many within the French government, in the end the institutions of the Republic held firm and the antisemites did not take power. This book, not a conventional "history," is an important addition to the literature on antisemitism.

Boonstra, Janrense, Hans Jansen, and Joke Kniesmeyer, eds. *Antisemitism: A History Portrayed.* Amsterdam: Anne Frank Foundation, 1989.

A useful anthology, from European perspectives.

Brown, Michael, ed. *Approaches to Antisemitism: Context and Curriculum.* New York and Jerusalem: The American Jewish Committee and the International Center for University Teaching of Jewish Civilization, 1994.

A most substantial volume, with essays by experts in the field, developing context for the teaching of antisemitism.

Carmichael, Joel. *The Satanizing of the Jews: Origin and Development of Mystical Anti-Semitism.* New York: Fromm International Publishing, 1992.

"Mystical" antisemitism is the irrational hatred that is at the core of anti-Jewish animosity, and Carmichael, in a thoughtful study, traced the history of this irrational core.

Carroll, James. *Constantine's Sword: The Church and the Jews.* Boston: Houghton Mifflin, 2001.

A most readable journalistic account of the history of the relationship of the Catholic Church and the Jews, this book broadened the discussion of Christian-based antisemitism. General audiences will find *Constantine's Sword* readable and indeed entertaining; scholars will find it comprehensive.

Chanes, Jerome A. *A Dark Side of History: Antisemitism through the Ages.* New York: Anti-Defamation League, 2001.

A serious, yet accessible, history of antisemitism. The book focused on setting a historical context for antisemitism and addressed the historical dynamics that resulted in the movement from Christian-based "anti-Judaism" to contemporary antisemitism. Complements Robert Wistrich's *Antisemitism: The Longest Hatred (v. infra).*

————, ed. *Antisemitism in America Today: Outspoken Experts Explode the Myths.* New York: Carol Publishing/Birch Lane Press, 1995.

A "roundtable" on antisemitism in the United States, including history, the psychology of antisemitism, attitudinal and other survey research, international perspectives, antisemitism in the black community, antisemitism of the Right and Left, antisemitism and the law, antisemitism and Christian-Jewish relations, and other perspectives. This book is the only contemporary work of its kind in this arena.

Chazan, Robert. *In the Year 1096 . . . : The First Crusade and the Jews.* Philadelphia: The Jewish Publication Society, 1996.

One of the better works on the anti-Jewish dimensions of the First Crusade. Chazan argued for a nuanced analysis of the destruction of the Rhennish Jewish communities.

Chesler, Phyllis. *The New Anti-Semitism and What We Must Do about It.* New York: Jossey-Bass/John Wiley, 2003.

A popular treatment of the effects of contemporary public events on anti-Jewish activity. Although Chesler's prose is often strident, her bibliography—heavily weighted in popular materials—is useful.

Cohen, Mark R. *Under Crescent and Cross: The Jews in the Middle Ages.* Princeton, NJ: Princeton University Press, 1994.

This superb volume will be valuable as background for anyone exploring antisemitism in the Middle Ages, especially the questions of Jewish coexistence with Christians and Muslims.

Cohen, Naomi W. *Jews in Christian America: The Pursuit of Religious Equality.* Oxford: Oxford University Press, 1992.

This superb work by one of the leading historians of the American Jewish experience is not strictly speaking a work on anti-semitism; but as one of the best books tracking the history of the separation of church and state in the United States, it developed a context for explaining the relative lack of antisemitism embedded in U.S. institutions of power.

Cohen, Susan Sarah. *Antisemitism: An Annotated Bibliography.* **Vols. 1–12.** The Vidal Sassoon Center for the Study of Anti-semitism of the Hebrew University of Jerusalem. New York: Garland Publishing, 1978–.

A useful bibliography of print resources on antisemitism, albeit not as comprehensive as it ought to be. Gaps notwithstanding, Cohen's bibliography, published more-or-less annually, is the only work that systematically cites print resources on an annual basis.

Cornwell, John. *Hitler's Pope: The Secret History of Pius XII.* New York: Viking Penguin, 1999.

A well-researched, controversial biography of Eugenio Pacelli—Pope Pius XII—developed the case that Pacelli as papal envoy and later as pope was useful in the Nazi rise to power and that Pius XII was a de facto collaborator in the Holocaust. This book extended the discussion of Christian antisemitism and is useful in tandem with Kertzer's *The Popes against the Jews* (*v. infra*).

Curtis, Michael, ed. *Antisemitism in the Contemporary World.* Boulder, CO: Westview Press, 1986.

Containing the proceedings of a 1983 conference, Curtis's book is one of the better anthologies on antisemitism. Although clearly dated, there is much that is valuable in this book to the contemporary researcher in history and sociology and to journalists.

Dawidowicz, Lucy. *A Holocaust Reader.* West Orange, NJ: Behrman House, 1976.

An early anthology on the Holocaust, and one of the best, this book nicely complements Dawidowicz's *The War against the Jews.*

———. *The War against the Jews, 1933–1945.* New York: Holt, Rinehart and Winston, 1975.

Among the best of the histories of the destruction of European Jewry. In addition to presenting a superb review of the carrying out of the Holocaust country by country, this book is especially strong on the historical context of antisemitism. In this regard it is important for the student of the history of antisemitism.

Dinnerstein, Leonard. *Uneasy at Home: Antisemitism and the American Jewish Experience.* New York: Columbia University Press, 1987.

Essays illumining varied issues in antisemitism in the United States by a historian of the American Jewish experience.

————. *Anti-Semitism in America.* New York: Oxford University Press, 1994.

A readable, fairly comprehensive, history.

Eitinger, Leo, ed. *The Antisemitism in Our Time: A Threat against us All.* Proceedings of the First International Hearing on Antisemitism Oslo 7–8 June 1983. Oslo: The Nansen Committee (the Norwegian Committee against the Persecution of Jews), 1984.

Historians and psychologists will pay attention to the proceedings of this early conference on international antisemitism. Scholars and public affairs officials contributed papers. Papers by Yehuda Bauer and Leo Eitinger are especially interesting.

Feldman, Louis H. *Jew and Gentile in the Ancient World: Attitudes and Interactions from Alexander to Justinian.* Princeton, NJ: Princeton University, 1993.

This voluminous book is the most comprehensive study of relations between Jew and non-Jew in the ancient world, addressing in detail questions surrounding anti-Jewish expression in the Classical periods. Feldman brings to bear pagan, Jewish, and Christian writings in his analysis, which will be useful to students and advanced scholars both.

Flannery, Edward H. *The Anguish of the Jews: Twenty-Three Centuries of Antisemitism.* Rev. ed. New York: Paulist Press, 1985.

A pioneering work on the history of antisemitism, originally published in 1965, by a Catholic priest who was instrumental in Catholic-Jewish dialogue in the United States.

Forster, Arnold. *Square One: The Memoirs of a True Freedom Fighter's Life-long Struggle against Anti-Semitism, Domestic and Foreign.* New York: Donald I. Fine, 1988.

Numerous factual errors notwithstanding—the editor's "red pencil" ought have been more freely used—this book is a readable narrative by one who was on the "front-lines" in the fight against antisemitism and group prejudice in general and will therefore be useful to student of the counteraction of antisemitism in the United States in the mid-twentieth century. The author's thesis—that not much progress has been made in the struggle—is highly questionable.

Forster, Arnold, and Benjamin R. Epstein. *The New Anti-Semitism.* New York: McGraw-Hill, 1974.

This book is representative of a series of books by Forster and Epstein, who directed the Anti-Defamation League during the decades in which this "defense" agency reached its maturity. The book develops a picture of antisemitism in the late 1960s and early 1970s, even as it does not make the case for a "new" antisemitism, and hampers rather than aids the student by its unfortunate lack of an index. Journalistic in tone and somewhat limited in analysis, the Forster and Epstein books, which had an impact in their time, retain some value for the historian and sociologist.

Friedländer, Saul. *Nazi Germany and the Jews.* Vol. 1: *The Years of Persecution, 1933–1939.* New York: HarperCollins, 1997.

Historian Friedländer, in the first volume of a projected two-volume work, made heavy use of documentary data to ponder a fundamental question: Why did culturally, intellectually, and industrially advanced Germany embark on a program that led to the destruction of European Jewry? This book is an indispensable tool for the serious student of antisemitism and the Holocaust.

Fuchs, Eduard. *Die Juden in der Karikatur: Ein Beitrag zur Kulturgeschichte.* Munich: Albert Langen Verlag, 1921.

This superb volume—long out of print—is the finest, albeit dated, collection of anti-Jewish images and caricatures. Fuchs's extensive commentary is an important contribution to the literature. Students of the history and sociology of antisemitism from the

Renaissance to the early twentieth century will find this volume literally illuminating and of inestimable value.

Gerber, David A., ed. *Anti-Semitism in American History.* Chicago: University of Illinois Press, 1987.

Diverse historical perspectives on antisemitism, including some classic essays. An important volume when it first appeared, the book yet has value for scholars and students of the historical context for antisemitism in the United States.

Gilbert, Martin. *Atlas of the Holocaust.* London: Michael Joseph, 1982.

Gilbert, a historian who has produced a number of "historical atlases," has his best product in this book. Three hundred and sixteen annotated maps trace each phase of the destruction of European Jewry from pre–World War II Europe to the Allied liberation.

Ginsberg, Benjamin. *The Fatal Embrace: Jews and the State.* Chicago: University of Chicago Press, 1993.

The interaction of political history and Jewish security is the topic of this thoughtful book, which will be useful to students and historians of the era.

Glock, Charles Y., and Rodney Stark. *Christian Beliefs and Anti-Semitism.* Vol. 1 in a series based on the University of California's Five-Year Study of Anti-Semitism in the United States. New York: Harper and Row, 1966.

A classic in the field of survey research into antisemitism, distilling the research on the relationship between Christian teachings and antisemitic attitudes. (*V. infra, University of California Five-Year Study of Anti-Semitism in the United States.*)

Glock, Charles Y., Gertrude J. Selznick, and Joe L. Spaeth. *The Apathetic Majority: A Study Based on Public Responses to the Eichmann Trial.* Vol. 2 in a series based on the University of California Five-Year Study of Anti-Semitism in the United States. New York: Harper and Row, 1966.)

An important volume in the literature of survey research. (*V. infra, University of California Five-Year Study of Anti-Semitism in the United States.*)

Goldhagen, Daniel Jonah. *A Moral Reckoning: The Role of the Catholic Church in the Holocaust and Its Unfulfilled Duty of Repair.* New York: Alfred A. Knopf, 2002.

The title says it all. Goldhagen's provocative book is the latest in the genre (cf. Cornwell *supra* and Kertzer *infra*). The value of the book is the seriousness with which the author took documentation; its drawback: its often strident tone.

Gross, John. *Shylock: A Legend and Its Legacy.* New York: Simon and Schuster, 1992.

Theater critic John Gross explored the controversial—and eminently ambiguous—Shakespearean character Shylock in terms of the character's place in the history of antisemitic expression as a cultural, economic, and psychological symbol.

Hay, Malcolm. *The Roots of Christian Anti-Semitism.* Variously published as *Europe and the Jews, The Foot of Pride,* and *Thy Brother's Blood.* New York: Freedom Library Press, 1981. Originally published as *The Foot of Pride.* Boston: Beacon Press, 1950.

The first—and still one of the best—books exploring for the general reader the Christian roots of antisemitism. (Hay was excommunicated by the Roman Catholic Church for his efforts.)

Hecht, Ben. *A Guide for the Bedeviled.* New York: Scribners, 1944.

Written during World War II, this book by a journalist and playwright (*The Front Page*) is a historical curio. This angry book, written in an era in which Jews (and Jewish organizations) felt vulnerable and insecure, will be of interest to social historians.

Hertzberg, Arthur. *The French Enlightenment and the Jews.* New York: Columbia University Press, 1968.

A groundbreaking study at the time it was written—today it is a classic—in the origins of modern antisemitism. An important volume for historians and sociologists of antisemitism.

Hirsch, Herbert, and Jack D. Spiro, eds. *Persistent Prejudice: Perspectives on Anti-Semitism.* Fairfax, VA: George Mason University Press, 1988.

Useful papers for the scholar on historical, religious, and cultural manifestations of antisemitism.

Hobson, Laura Z. *Gentleman's Agreement.* New York: Simon and Schuster, 1947.

A groundbreaking novel, among the first to address social antisemitism and antisemitism in the workplace, the "gentleman's agreement" to exclude Jews. The novel was adapted for the screen (*v. infra* under "Films and Videos" in "Nonprint Resources.").

Iganski, Paul, and Barry Kosmin, eds. *A New Antisemitism? Debating Judeophobia in 21st Century Britain.* London: Profile Books/Institute for Jewish Policy Research, 2003.

Contemporary antisemitism from a British perspective, considered by a roundtable of scholars and public affairs professionals.

Jacobson, Kenneth. "**The Protocols: Myth and History.**" Pamphlet, Anti-Defamation League, New York, 1981.

In an exceptionally concentrated piece, Jacobson traced the background and history of the turn-of-the-twentieth-century Russian antisemitic forgery, *The Protocols of the Learned Elders of Zion.* Scholars will find this pamphlet to be a useful jumping-off point for deeper research on the *Protocols.*

Jaher, Fred Cople. *A Scapegoat in the New Wilderness: The Origins and Rise of Anti-Semitism in America.* Cambridge: Harvard University Press, 1994.

A useful history of the beginnings of antisemitism—meager though it may have been—in the United States.

Jordan, William Chester. *The French Monarchy and the Jews: From Philip Augustus to the Last Capetians.* Philadelphia: University of Pennsylvania Press, 1989.

The instability of the relationship between French Christians and Jews—with economic exploitation, repression, and expulsion of the Jews—through the Capetian era (1179–1328) is richly chronicled by historian Jordan. This marvelously comprehensive book (unfortunately out of print) is essential for students and scholars of medieval history.

Katz, Jacob. *From Prejudice to Destruction: Anti-Semitism, 1700–1933.* Cambridge: Harvard University Press, 1980.

This book is one of the classics of the history of antisemitism. Katz, one of the giants of modern history, blended social and intellectual history in analyzing how negative ideas about Jews became transformed and systematized.

Kertzer, David I. *The Popes against the Jews: The Vatican's Role in the Rise of Modern Anti-Semitism.* New York: Random House, 2001.

A superb study, focusing on the nineteenth and twentieth centuries, of the role played by the Vatican in the development of modern antisemitism.

Kleeblatt, Norman L., ed. *The Dreyfus Affair: Art, Truth, and Justice.* Berkeley: University of California Press, 1987.

This fine anthology discussed those artists and intellectuals who took positions on either side in the Dreyfus affair and explored the remarkable visual culture spurred by the affair, which coincided with the birth of the modern media.

Langmuir, Gavin I. *History, Religion, and Antisemitism.* Los Angeles: University of California Press, 1990 (published with the cooperation of the Center for Medieval and Renaissance Studies).

This book is a serious study of the concepts of religion and antisemitism as they are viewed by sociologists, psychologists, and historians. Langmuir moved from religion to his definition of antisemitism as irrational beliefs about Jews and in the process distinguished between different varieties of Christian antisemitism. An important book, to be used in tandem with the author's *Toward a Definition of Antisemitism.*

———. *Toward a Definition of Antisemitism.* Los Angeles: University of California Press, 1990 (published with the cooperation of the Center for Medieval and Renaissance Studies).

Further explorations by Langmuir. Especially valuable is the author's analysis of the distinctions between "anti-Judaism" and "antisemitism." These two books are important explorations that work with historical contexts for antisemitism.

Lerner, Michael. *The Socialism of Fools: Anti-Semitism on the Left.* Jerusalem: Tikkun Books, 1992.

The author is the editor of *Tikkun,* a leftist magazine of Jewish public affairs. This book will be less useful for its content (meager, indeed) than for its interest to historiographers and historians of sociology of how antisemitism in the 1980s was viewed by proponents of so-called Jewish Renewal.

Lewis, Bernard. *Semites and Anti-Semites: An Inquiry into Conflict and Prejudice.* New York: W. W. Norton, 1986.

This brief volume, by one of the foremost scholars of the history of Islam, is an important review of antisemitism, with a focus on the Muslim world. Indispensable for journalists and public officials for background on the issue.

————. *The Middle East: A Brief History of the Last 2,000 Years.* New York: Simon and Schuster, 1995.

One of the best histories of this arena, providing an invaluable context for antisemitism emerging from the Arab and Islamic world.

————. *The Political Language of Islam.* Chicago: The University of Chicago Press, 1988.

What does the word *jihad* really mean? And so on . . . This short splendid book sets a context for antisemitism in the Islamic world by tracing the development of Islamic political language.

Lindemann, Albert S. *The Jew Accused: Three Anti-Semitic Affairs (Dreyfus, Beilis, Frank) 1894–1915.* Cambridge: Cambridge University Press, 1991.

Modern antisemitism is explored and illumined in three case studies of false accusations—Dreyfus charged with treason, Beilis with "ritual murder," Frank with murder in pursuit of sexual desires—in which antisemitism was used in the pre–World War I generation as a political device to mobilize the masses. This book is a welcome addition to the history of the development of modern antisemitism.

Lipset, Seymour Martin, and Earl Raab. *The Politics of Unreason: Right-Wing Extremism in America, 1790–1970.* Vol. 5 in a series based on the University of California Five-Year Study of Anti-Semitism in the United States. New York: Harper and Row, 1970.

A somewhat dated—and therefore limited but nonetheless valuable—glimpse into this area of antisemitism.

Litvinoff, Barnet. *The Burning Bush: Anti-Semitism and World History.* New York: E. P. Dutton, 1988.

A popular, readable, and generally reliable survey of the history of antisemitism.

Maidenbaum, Aryeh, and Stephen A. Martin, eds. *Lingering Shadows: Jungians, Freudians, and Anti-Semitism.* Boston: Shambala, 1991.

Maidenbaum and Martin's extremely interesting anthology derived from a conference (1989) held on the dynamics of Jungian thought and antisemitism. Historians of psychology, psychoanalysis, and antisemitism will find this volume useful.

Marx, Gary T. *Protest and Prejudice: A Study of Belief in the Black Community.* New York: Harper and Row, 1969.

Vol. 3 in a series based on the University of California Five-Year Study of Anti-Semitism in the United States.

Marx, Karl. *A World without Jews.* Translated from the original German. New York: Philosophical Library, 1959.

Written in 1843 as a lengthy book review, Marx's diatribe against Jewish emancipation—indeed against the very idea of Jewish peoplehood—is a classic of antisemitica.

Miller, Arthur. *Focus.* New York: Reynal and Hitchcock, 1945. Reprinted with an introduction by the author. New York: Penguin Books, 1996.

One of the first treatments in fiction of antisemitism, written during a period of high levels of attitudinal and behavioral antisemitism in the United States. *Focus* is a valuable portrait of the nature of behavioral antisemitism in the 1940s.

Netanyahu, B. *The Origins of the Inquisition in Fifteenth Century Spain.* New York: New York Review Books, 2001.

This massive volume is the most comprehensive—and best—study of the Inquisition. Indispensable for scholars and students of the Inquisition and medieval antisemitism, the book explored the roots of the Inquisition in the context of medieval Jewish history.

Oberman, Heiko A. *The Roots of Anti-Semitism: In the Age of Renaissance and Reformation.* Translated by James I. Porter. Philadelphia: Fortress Press, 1984. Originally published as *Wurzeln des Antisemitismus*, 1981.

This book is a comprehensive review and analysis of European history from the fifteenth to the seventeenth centuries in terms of the development of modern antisemitism. It is useful for historians.

Ostow, Mortimor. *Myth and Madness: The Psychodynamics of Antisemitism.* New Brunswick, NJ: Transaction Publishers, 1996.

This book, the result of a nine-year study of the psychodynamics of antisemitism, uses case-studies, psychoanalytic theory, and historical data to glean insights into bigotry in general and antisemitism in particular.

Parkes, James. *Antisemitism.* Chicago: Quadrangle Books, 1963.

———. *Anti-Semitism: A Concise World History.* Chicago: Quadrangle Books, 1963.

———. *An Enemy of the People: Antisemitism.* New York: Penguin Books, 1945.

Parkes is the author of several classic works on antisemitism, and on Jewish history in general, useful in some areas of historiographical research on antisemitism. *Anti-Semitism: A Concise World History* was one of the first histories of the topic.

Patterson, Charles. *Antisemitism: The Road to the Holocaust and Beyond.* New York: Walker and Company, 1982.

A brief popular treatment.

Pears, Iain. *The Dream of Scipio.* New York: Riverhead Books, 2003.

This richly layered historical novel—set in late-Roman Gaul, fourteenth-century Avignon, and World War II South of France—is one of the few works of fiction that has intelligently sought to unearth the origins of antisemitism by demonstrating the deep roots that antisemitism has in European culture and that has suggested that intellectuals bear much of the responsibility for its propagation.

Pinson, Koppel S., ed. *Essays on Antisemitism.* 2nd ed. New York: Conference on Jewish Relations, 1946.

Historians and historiographers will be fascinated by the essays in this volume, the authors of which are a virtual "Who's Who" of history and social thought of the 1940s. The anthology is divided into "Analytical Studies" and "Historical and Regional Studies."

Poliakov, Léon. *Harvest of Hate: The Nazi Program for the Destruction of the Jews of Europe.* Syracuse, NY: Syracuse University Press, 1954. Originally published as *Bréviare de la haine,* Paris: Calmann-Lévy, Paris, 1951.

One of the earliest books on the Holocaust, most useful for the historiography of antisemitism.

———. *The History of Anti-semitism.* Vol. 1: *From the Time of Christ to the Court Jews.* Translated by Richard Howard. New York: The Vanguard Press, 1965. Originally published as *Histoire de l'Antisémitisme: Du Christ aux Juif de Cour,* Paris: Calmann-Lévy.

———. *The History of Anti-semitism.* Vol. 2: *From Mohammed to the Marranos.* Translated by Natalie Gerardi. New York: The Vanguard Press, 1973. Originally published as *Histoire de l'Antisémitisme: de Mahomet aux Marranes,* Paris: Calmann-Lévy, 1961.

———. *The History of Anti-semitism.* Vol. 3: *From Voltaire to Wagner.* Translated by George Klim. New York: The Vanguard Press, 1975. Originally published as *Histoire de l'Antisémitisme: de Voltaire à Wagner,* Paris: Calmann-Lévy, 1968.

————. *The History of Anti-semitism.* **Vol. 4:** *Suicidal Europe: 1870–1933.* Translated by George Klim. New York: The Vanguard Press, 1985. Originally published as *Histoire de l'Antisémitisme: L'Europe Suicidaire* by Paris: Calmann-Lévy, 1977.

Poliakov's four-volume history is comprehensive and most readable—one of the best. Even though it is dated and flawed, it is an important tool for the student of antisemitism. Out of print for many years, the set is available in most libraries.

Quinley, Harold E., and Charles Y. Glock. *Anti-Semitism in America.* New York: The Free Press, 1979.

At the time it was published, Quinley and Glock represented the best and most up-to-date review of the data on antisemitism in the United States. Although obviously dated, the book—which reported on eight discrete societal arenas—is yet useful.

Reinharz, Jehuda, ed. *Living with Antisemitism: Modern Jewish Responses.* Hanover, NH: Brandeis University Press/University Press of New England, 1987.

This massive anthology of historians writing about antisemitism emphasized not the antisemitic expression but the responses of Jews around the word to antisemitism. It is the only large-scale work of its kind and is a valuable resource.

Rice, Elmer. 1928. *Street Scene. Three Plays* (New York: Hill and Wang, 1965)

This Pulitzer-Prize-winning play was among the first to address the question of intergroup tensions, and specifically urban antisemitism, in working-class neighborhoods.

Rose, Paul Lawrence. *Revolutionary Antisemitism in Germany from Kant to Wagner.* Princeton, NJ: Princeton University Press, 1990.

Historians will find this study of "racialist" antisemitism in Germany useful.

Rosensaft, Menachem Z., and Yehuda Bauer, eds. *Antisemitism: Threat to Western Civilization.* Jerusalem: The Vidal Sassoon International Center for the Study of Antisemitism, the Hebrew University of Jerusalem, 1985.

Notwithstanding some weak papers, the proceedings of this conference—especially the analyses by Hubert Locke, Harry James Cargas, William Korey, and Irwin Cotler—represented important contributions. Students are cautioned to separate out the value of individual papers from the overall slightly hysterical tone set by the conference organizers.

Rubin, Barry. *Assimilation and Its Discontents.* New York: Times Books, 1995.

Rubin's book is a thoughtful historical analysis of the relationship of assimilation and antisemitism.

Rubinstein, William D., and Hilary L Rubinstein. *Philosemitism: Admiration and Support in the English-Speaking World for Jews, 1840–1939.* London: Macmillan Press, 1999.

One of the few books that explore the phenomenon of philosemitism, this one from a modern-era historical perspective.

Samuel, Maurice. *Blood Accusation: The Strange History of the Beiliss Case.* New York: Alfred A. Knopf, 1966.

A popular account of the notorious "ritual-murder" case in early-twentieth-century Russia, by an important writer for general audiences of the last generation.

———. *The Great Hatred.* Boston: University Press of America, 1988.

A classic (first published in 1940) popular work on "Why antisemitism?" by Samuel. This book is useful for those studying how antisemitism was viewed by westerners sixty years ago.

Sargent, Lyman Tower, ed. *Extremism in America: A Reader.* New York: New York University Press, 1995.

A comprehensive anthology of extremism from both ends of the political spectrum—Far Right and Far Left. The book is well organized topically and is most useful.

Sartre, Jean-Paul. *Anti-Semite and Jew.* Translated by George J. Becker. New York: Schocken Books, 1965. Originally published as *Réflexions sur las Question Juive,* Paris: Paul Morihien, 1946.

A classic, and controversial, analysis of the question of "Why antisemitism?" by the Existentialist novelist and philosopher. Sartre's provocative suggestion was that the very existence of the Jew as a causal factor of antisemitism removed antisemitism from general categories of intergroup conflict.

Schäfer, Peter. *Judeophobia: Attitudes toward the Jews in the Ancient World.* Cambridge: Harvard University Press, 1997

The question Schäfer asked was a simple one: what did the Greeks and Romans think about Jews and Judaism; and, via this question, can we locate the origin of antisemitism in the ancient world? This superb book—there is none like it—will be invaluable to students and scholars in history and sociology.

Selznick, Gertrude J., and Stephen Steinberg. *The Tenacity of Prejudice: Anti-Semitism in Contemporary America.* Vol. 4 in the University of California Five-Year Study of Anti-Semitism in the United States. New York: Harper and Row, 1971.

The Tenacity of Prejudice is one of those books that deserve the characterization "classic." Selznick and Steinberg summed up the research of the Berkeley Studies, which developed a scale of antisemitic attitudes and beliefs.

Silberman, Charles. *A Certain People: American Jews and Their Lives Today.* New York: Summit, 1985.

This readable survey of American Jewish life represents the "transformationalist" position on American Jewry, *viz.* that the Jewish community is strong and secure and that antisemitism is at a low.

Stember, Charles Herbert, et al. *Jews in the Mind of America.* New York: Basic Books, 1966.

This collection of essays was the first roundtable on American antisemitism, pulling together what were the available data for that era. It remains among the very best of the explorations of antisemitism in the United States. Dated, but a classic.

Stern, Kenneth S. *Holocaust Denial.* New York: American Jewish Committee, 1993.

This monograph is a useful country-by-country review of one of the arenas of contemporary antisemitism, "Holocaust revisionism"—denial of the Holocaust.

Tobin, Gary A., with Sharon L. Sassler. *Jewish Perceptions of Anti-Semitism.* New York: Plenum Press, 1988.

A flawed but nonetheless useful study, one that explores not antisemitism per se but how American Jews *perceive* antisemitism. (Cf. in this regard chapter 1 of Chanes, *Antisemitism in America Today* (*v. supra*).

University of California Five-Year Study of Anti-Semitism in the United States. Vols. 1–5. New York: Harper and Row, 1966–1970.

Known as the Berkeley Studies, this series summarized the available research of the time into a comprehensive review of the various arenas of antisemitism. The Berkeley Studies set the standard for contemporary study of antisemitism. See entries for Glock and Stark, Lipset and Raab, Gary Marx, Selznick and Steinberg, and Glock, Selznick, and Spaeth.

Wang, Lu-In. *Hate Crimes Law.* Deerfield, IL: Clark Boardman Callaghan, 1994 (annually updated).

A reference resource on U.S. federal and state legislation enacted to address bias-motivated hate-crimes. This work is an essential resource for law enforcement and other public affairs officials, journalists, law students and lawyers, and researchers.

Wistrich, Robert S. *Antisemitism: The Longest Hatred.* New York: Pantheon, 1991.

The best recent short history of antisemitism, with excellent regional surveys and a section on Jews in Islamic lands and Muslim antisemitism. Wistrich's bibliography is especially useful.

———, ed. *Anti-Zionism and Antisemitism in the Contemporary World.* New York: New York University Press, 1990.

The often-nuanced relationship between anti-Israel activity, anti-Zionism, and antisemitism is explored in detail by fifteen leading scholars, who analyze in this unique anthology anti-Zionism of the Left, Muslim and Third World anti-Zionism, and Western anti-Zionism.

————. *Hitler and the Holocaust.* New York: Oxford University Press, 2003.

A fine work exploring a well-mined arena. Journalists and scholars will find this book useful.

Reports and Studies

Governmental and International Documents and Reports

Declarations on Racial Discrimination and Religious Intolerance

These twin United Nations declarations, adopted in 1960, specifically condemned antisemitism.

The International Bill of Human Rights

The International Bill of Human Rights adopted by the United Nations, composed of the Universal Declaration of Human Rights (1948), the International Covenant on Civil and Political Rights (1966), and the International Covenant on Economic, Social, and Cultural Rights (1966), specified the protections and rights that states must ensure for all of their citizens, including Jews.

The United Nations Charter

Adopted in 1945, Article 1 of the Charter, the basic legal instrument establishing the United Nations, stood firm against all forms of discrimination.

U.S. Congress, House Committee on Foreign Affairs, Subcommittee on International Security, International Organizations, and Human Rights, 103rd Cong., 2nd Sess. *Global Dimensions of Anti-Semitism: Hearings.* 8 February 1994.

These hearings constitute a comprehensive review and analysis of antisemitism around the world.

U.S. Congress, Senate Foreign Relations Committee, European Affairs Subcommittee, 106th Cong., 1st Sess. *Anti-Semitism in Russia: Hearings.* 24 February 1999.

A comprehensive review of antisemitism in Russia and the FSU.

Nongovernment Reports

ACTA—Analysis of Current Trends in Antisemitism. Jerusalem: The Vidal Sassoon Center for the Study of Antisemitism of The Hebrew University of Jerusalem.

A series of occasional papers exploring various facets of anti-semitism.

ADL in the Courts: Litigation Docket (annual). New York: Anti-Defamation League.

A useful annual report of legislation and litigation, produced by a leading human relations agency.

AJC in the Courts (annual). New York: American Jewish Committee.

A useful annual report of litigation and legislation on civil and human rights, hate-crimes, church-state separation, and other issues related to antisemitism and group prejudice.

Anti-Semitism and Prejudice in America: Highlights from an ADL Survey, November, 1998. New York: Anti-Defamation League, 1998.

This poll, one of a series conducted by the Marttila Communication Group/Kiley and Co., Inc., for the Anti-Defamation League, presents valuable data.

Anti-Semitism in America, 2002: Highlights from a May 2002 Survey. New York: Anti-Defamation League, 2002.

One of a series of attitudinal surveys conducted under the auspices of the Anti-Defamation League, this poll, conducted by the Marttila Communication Group and SWR Worldwide—notwithstanding some flaws in the survey design—presents valuable data for the student, scholar, public affairs official, and journalist.

Antisemitism World Report (annual, to 1998). London: Institute for Jewish Affairs.

The Institute of Jewish Affairs (now the Institute for Jewish Policy Research) produced, from 1992 on, an authoritative country-by-country report on developments on the antisemitism front. (The *Antisemitism World Report,* no longer published in book form, is available over the Internet. See below, "Nonprint Resources.")

Antisemitism Worldwide (annual). Tel Aviv: Tel Aviv University, The Stephen Roth Institute for the Study of Contemporary Antisemitism and Racism.

This annual volume, produced by Tel Aviv University in conjunction with the Anti-Defamation League and the World Jewish Congress, contains much useful data.

Audit of Anti-Semitic Incidents (annual). New York: Anti-Defamation League.

For some two decades the Anti-Defamation League has been reporting on incidents of antisemitic expression—including violence and vandalism—in the United States. Although this audit reflects only one "index" of antisemitism, it is nonetheless a useful indicator for journalists, public officials, and scholars.

Bútorová, Zora, and Martin Bútora. *Attitudes toward Jews and the Holocaust in Independent Slovakia.* Working Papers on Contemporary Anti-Semitism No. 23. New York: American Jewish Committee, 1995.

Survey conducted by the Center for Social Analysis.

Catterberg, Edgardo, and Norma Vanoli. *Argentine Attitudes toward Jews.* Working Papers on Contemporary Anti-Semitism No. 19. New York: American Jewish Committee, 1994.

This paper reports on an attitudinal survey conducted in Argentina on attitudes toward Jews.

Chanes, Jerome A., and Melanie Schneider. *Anti-Semitism on the Campus: A Report.* New York: National Jewish Community Relations Advisory Council, 1990.

The only discrete study of this topic. (Cf. in this regard Jeffrey Ross and Melanie Schneider, "Antisemitism on the Campus," in *Antisemitism in America Today: Outspoken Experts Explode the*

Myths, ed. J. A. Chanes [New York: Carol Publishing/Birch Lane Press, 1995].)

Cohen, Renae. *Attitudes toward Jews in Poland, Hungary, and Czechoslovakia: A Comparative Survey.* Working Papers on Contemporary Anti-Semitism No. 6. New York: American Jewish Committee, 1991.

Survey conducted by Penn and Schoen.

Epstein, Simon. **"Cyclical Patterns of Antisemitism: The Dynamics of Anti-Jewish Violence in Western Countries since the 1950s."** *ACTA—Analysis of Current Trends in Antisemitism No. 2.* Jerusalem: The Vidal Sassoon Center for the Study of Antisemitism, 1993.

This report suggested possible explanations for the recorded "waves" of antisemitic incidents.

European Attitudes toward Jews: A Five Country Survey. New York: Anti-Defamation League, 2002.

A poll, conducted by First International Resources and commissioned by the Anti-Defamation League, of attitudes toward Jews in the Netherlands, Austria, Italy, Spain, and Switzerland.

Fire and Broken Glass: The Rise of Antisemitism in Europe. New York: Lawyers Committee for Human Rights, 2002.

The adequacy—or inadequacy—of governments to address antisemitism in Europe is the focus of this report, which outlined the scope of European antisemitism and the efforts aimed at monitoring and confronting the issue.

Golub, Jennifer. *British Attitudes toward Jews and other Minorities.* Working Papers on Contemporary Anti-Semitism No. 14. New York: American Jewish Committee, 1993.

Survey conducted by Gallup of Great Britain.

———. *Current German Attitudes toward Jews and Other Minorities.* Working Papers on Contemporary Anti-Semitism No. 17. New York: American Jewish Committee, 1994.

Survey conducted by the Emnid Institute.

————. *What Do We Know about Black Anti-Semitism?* Working Papers on Contemporary Anti-Semitism No. 3. New York: American Jewish Committee, 1990.

One of the first of the analyses of African American attitudes toward Jews, this report, derived from Tom Smith's data, is invaluable.

Golub, Jennifer, and Renae Cohen. *What Do Americans Know about the Holocaust?* Working Papers on Contemporary Anti-Semitism No. 11. New York: American Jewish Committee, 1993.

Poll conducted by the Roper Organization.

————. *What Do the British Know about the Holocaust?* Working Papers on Contemporary Anti-Semitism No. 12. New York: American Jewish Committee, 1993.

Poll conducted by Gallup of Great Britain.

————. *What Do the French Know about the Holocaust?* Working Papers on Contemporary Anti-Semitism No. 15. New York: American Jewish Committee, 1994.

————. *What Do Australians Know about the Holocaust?* Working Papers on Contemporary Anti-Semitism No. 21. New York: American Jewish Committee, 1994.

————. *Knowledge and Remembrance of the Holocaust in Poland.* Working Papers on Contemporary Anti-Semitism No. 22. New York: American Jewish Committee, 1995.

————. *Current Austrian Attitudes toward Jews and the Holocaust.* Working Papers on Contemporary Anti-Semitism No. 24. New York: American Jewish Committee, 1995.

These papers report on and analyze polling data on attitudes toward Jews in the respective countries.

Gordon, Murray. *The "New Anti-Semitism" in Western Europe.* New York: American Jewish Committee, 2002.

A useful report on recent trends in Europe, culled from journalistic sources.

Gutkov, Lev, and Alex Levinson. *Attitudes toward Jews in the Soviet Union: Public Opinion in Ten Republics.* Working Papers on Contemporary Anti-Semitism No. 10. New York: American Jewish Committee, 1992.

————. *Attitudes toward Jews in the Commonwealth of Independent States.* Working Papers on Contemporary Anti-Semitism No. 16, New York: American Jewish Committee, 1994.

These two papers, by Russian social scientists, provide the researcher with valuable data derived from attitudinal surveys on attitudes toward Jews in the various countries of the former Soviet Union.

Halpern, Ben. *Policy-Oriented Research on Anti-Semitism: An Inquiry.* Working Papers on Contemporary Anti-Semitism No. 2. New York: American Jewish Committee, 1989.

Halpern, a noted historian, offers a protocol for research in this arena.

Hate Crimes Laws (annual). New York: Anti-Defamation League.

An annual report on the status of hate-crimes legislation in the United States. Covers federal and state jurisdictions.

Highlights from an Anti-Defamation League Survey on Anti-Semitism and Prejudice in America. New York: Anti-Defamation League, 1992.

A summary of data from the first of the Anti-Defamation League polls on antisemitism conducted in the 1990s.

Jodice, David A. *United Germany and Jewish Concerns: Attitudes toward Jews, Israel, and the Holocaust.* Working Papers on Contemporary Anti-Semitism No. 4. New York: American Jewish Committee, 1991.

A report on polling data on attitudes toward Jews in Germany.

Julius, Anthony, Robert S. Rifkind, Jeffrey Weill, and Felice Gaer. *Antisemitism: An Assault on Human Rights.* Submitted to the United Nations World Conference against Racism, Xenophobia, and Related Intolerance, Durban, South Africa, August–September, 2001. New York: The Jacob Blaustein Institute for the Advancement of Human Rights of the American Jewish Committee, 2001.

A superb summary of the international human rights dimension of antisemitism. This report is especially valuable for (1) its summary of international instruments and protocols on human rights and (2) a catalog—the only one of its kind—of legislation throughout history that codified antisemitism into law.

Karmasin, Fritz. *Austrian Attitudes toward Jews, Israel, and Holocaust*. Working Papers on Contemporary Anti-Semitism No. 7. New York: American Jewish Committee, 1992.

Poll conducted by the Gallup Institute of Austria.

Korey, William. *Glasnost and Soviet Anti-Semitism*. Working Papers on Contemporary Anti-Semitism No. 5. New York: American Jewish Committee, 1991.

Korey, one of the leading experts on Jews in the Soviet Union, provides a valuable analysis in this paper.

Raab, Earl. *What Do We Really Know about Anti-Semitism—and What Do We Want to Know?* Working Papers on Contemporary Anti-Semitism No.1. New York: American Jewish Committee, 1989.

This paper, by one of the leading community-relations professionals, is a classic of its genre.

Rosenfeld, Alvin H. *"Feeling Alone, Again": The Growing Unease among Germany's Jews*. New York: American Jewish Committee, 2002.

Intolerance and xenophobia in contemporary Germany are the context for this excellent report on the situation of German Jews.

Setlow, Carolyn E., and Renae Cohen. *1992 New York Intergroup Relations Survey*. Working Papers on Contemporary Anti-Semitism No. 9. New York: American Jewish Committee, 1993.

Poll conducted by the Roper Organization.

Smith, Tom W. *What Do Americans Think about Jews?* Working Papers on Contemporary Anti-Semitism, No. 8. New York: American Jewish Committee, 1991.

Although dated, Smith's analysis of survey data is a useful approach to studying the question of assessing antisemitism.

———. *Anti-Semitism in Contemporary America.* Working Papers on Contemporary Anti-Semitism, No. 18. New York: American Jewish Committee, 1994.

In this work Smith synthesized the data from a number of studies and reviewed the level of anti-Jewish prejudice in a number of arenas.

———. *Holocaust Denial: What the Survey Data Reveal.* Working Papers on Contemporary Anti-Semitism, No. 20. New York: American Jewish Committee, 1995.

A comprehensive analysis of all available survey data on denial of the Holocaust, including 1992 and 1994 polls conducted by the Roper Organization.

———. *A Survey of the Religious Right: Views on Politics, Society, Jews, and Other Minorities.* Conducted for the American Jewish Committee by the Gallup International Institute, 10 May–13 June 1996. New York: American Jewish Committee, 1996.

Smith, who directs the General Social Survey of the University of Chicago's National Opinion Research Center, is one of leading demographers of public opinion and an expert on polling data on antisemitism. This poll of the "religious right"—as do all of Smith's studies—contains data that are important for journalists, scholars, and public officials.

———. *Intergroup Relations in a Diverse America: Data from the 2000 General Social Survey.* New York: American Jewish Committee, 2001.

The General Social Survey of the University of Chicago's National Opinion Research Center is the most comprehensive compilation of demographic data on ethnic groups available and contains much useful information on antisemitism in the United States.

Tuchman, Aryeh. *The Talmud in Anti-Semitic Polemics.* New York: Anti-Defamation League, 2003.

A brief (twelve-page) review of the use of classical rabbinic texts in antisemitic expression, which will be useful to the scholar in getting research in this important area off the ground.

Wistrich, Robert S. *Anti-Semitism in Europe since the Holocaust.* Working Papers in Contemporary Anti-Semitism No. 13. New York: American Jewish Committee, 1993.

A superb review of antisemitism in Europe over the past sixty years.

Periodicals: Journals, Magazines, and Newspapers

The following list is a selection of the most important resources on antisemitism in periodical literature.

American Jewish History (quarterly). New York: American Jewish Historical Society.

An academic journal, *American Jewish History* frequently has articles on the history of antisemitism and related matters. See especially the September 1981 special issue on "Anti-Semitism in the United States," Naomi W. Cohen, guest editor. The issue included the following articles: George Berlin, "Solomon Jackson's *The Jew:* An Early American Jewish Response to the Missionaries"; Jeffrey S. Gurock, "Jacob A. Riis: Christian Friend or Missionary Foe? Two Jewish Views"; Robert Singerman, "The American Career of the *Protocols of the Elders of Zion*"; Dov Fisch, "The Libel Trial of Robert Edward Edmondson: 1936–1938"; John J. Appel, "Jews in American Caricature: 1820–1914"; and Leonard Dinnerstein, "Antisemitism Exposed and Attacked:. 1945–1950."

Commentary (monthly). New York: American Jewish Committee.

Often an important source for articles on antisemitism, particularly with respect to manifestations linked to current events.

Forward (English-language weekly).

The only independent newspaper in the United States reporting on a regular basis on Jewish affairs, including all forms of anti-semitism.

Partisan Review

The summer 1994 issue included a symposium titled "Is There a Cure for Anti-Semitism?" The symposium consisted of brief essays by Saul Bellow, Stanley Crouch, Eugene Genovese, John Gross, Cynthia Ozick, Martin Peretz, Norman Podhoretz, James Sleeper, and Robert Wistrich.

Patterns of Prejudice (quarterly, since 1967). London: Institute for Jewish Policy Research (formerly Institute for Jewish Affairs).

An important journal that covers all aspects of antisemitism and group prejudice.

Articles, Book Chapters, and Lectures

The following is a highly selective listing of some of the more important recent articles exploring antisemitism. Student and other readers are directed to readers' guides and databases—particularly *Sociological Abstracts, Political Science Abstracts,* and *Social Science Abstracts*—for full listings of the many hundreds of articles and reviews that have appeared in recent years. LexisNexis is also a highly useful source for materials.

"Anti-Semitic Political Parties and Organizations." *Encyclopedia Judaica,* 1971: vol. 3, 79–87.

A superb brief review of the political vehicles for antisemitic expression. The material is not up to date, but this is a valuable resource.

"Anti-Semitism." *Encyclopedia Britannica,* 1959: vol. 2, 75–78f.

A standard brief review of the history of antisemitism, useful as a starting point for students but out of date.

"Anti-Semitism." *Encyclopedia Judaica,* 1971: vol. 3, 87–159.

This comprehensive essay is the best brief treatment, from a historical perspective, of antisemitism. The material is not up to date; nonetheless, these articles are valuable resources for scholars, public affairs officials, and journalists.

Berger, David. **"From the Crusades to Blood Libels to Expulsions: Some New Approaches to Medieval Antisemitism."** Second Annual Lecture of the Victor J. Selmanowitz Chair of Jewish History, Touro College, New York, 16 March 1997.

A provocative discussion of the origins of the blood libel by a leading historian of medieval Jewish history. Students will benefit from Berger's review of the historiography of this important issue.

Chanes, Jerome A. **"Antisemitism and Jewish Security in Contemporary America: Why Can't Jews Take 'Yes' for an Answer?"** In *Jews in America: A Contemporary Reader,* ed. Roberta Rosenberg Farber and Chaim I. Waxman, 124–150. Hanover, NH: Brandeis University Press/University Press of New England, 1999.

A comprehensive survey and analysis of antisemitism in the United States.

Cleary, Edward J. **"Silence Coerced by Law: A Look at Recent National and International Efforts to Silence Offensive Expression."** *Washington and Lee Law Review* (Winter 1996): vol. 3, no. 4, 1667–1677.

Putting aside the author's editorial bias, this article is a useful, albeit out-of-date, review of legal developments.

Curtis, Michael. **"Antisemitism: Different Perspectives."** *Sociological Forum* (June 1997): 321–330.

This excellent review essay of six books on a range of historical, psychological, and historical topics—all addressing anti-semitism—will be of use to students and scholars who need to get a "sense" of the field.

Dawidowicz, Lucy. **"Can Anti-Semitism Be Measured?"** *Commentary* (July 1970): vol. 50, 36–43.

An important article for historians and sociologists of anti-semitism and for students. More than thirty years old, yet not dated.

Farrier, Stephanie. **"Molding the Matrix: The Historical and Theoretical Foundation of International Law Concerning Hate Speech."** *Berkeley Journal of International Law,* 1996, 14: 3.

A significant analysis of hate-speech laws; useful to journalists and students and to officials working in the international arena.

Halkin, Hillel. **"The Return of Anti-Semitism."** *Commentary,* vol. 113 (February 2002): 33–36.

An important article, reviewing contemporary manifestations as contextualized by the Arab-Israeli conflict, specifically anti-Israel rhetoric.

Heilbroner, Oded. **"From Antisemitic Peripheries to Antisemitic Centres: The Place of Antisemitism in Modern German History."** *Jewish Social Studies* [New Series] vol. 6 (Winter 2000): 87–106

Historian Heilbroner's essay is an important one in positioning antisemitism—particularly racialist antisemitism—in modern German history. His essay is useful for historians and social scientists.

Iganski, Paul. **"Legislating Morality, and Competing 'Rights': Legal Instruments against Racism and Antisemitism in the European Union."** *Journal of Ethnic and Migration Studies* (July 1999): 509–516.

This essay is particularly timely in light of the spate of antisemitic expressions since 2002. Legal scholars, historians, public-affairs and government officials, and journalists will find it useful.

Katz, Jacob. **"Accounting for Anti-Semitism."** *Commentary* vol. 91 (June 1991): 52–54.

Katz, a magisterial scholar of Jewish history, offers a brief but penetrating analysis.

Keller, Bill. **"Is It Good for the Jews?"** *New York Times,* 8 March 2003, A17.

An op-ed article on conspiracy theories in the context of the 2003 conflict with Iraq.

Little, Lester. **"The Jews in Christian Europe."** Chap. 3 in *Religious Poverty and the Profit Economy in Medieval Europe*. Ithaca, NY: Cornell University, 1978.

A superb essay on the early manifestations of antisemitism under Latin Christendom in the high Middle Ages.

Ofer, Dalia. **"Holocaust Historiography: The Return of Anti-semitism and Ethnic Stereotypes as Major Themes."** *Patterns of Prejudice* vol. 33 (October 1999): 87–106.

The best article that traces the historiography of the Holocaust over the past five decades.

Rosen, Jonathan. **"The Uncomfortable Question of Anti-Semitism."** *The New York Times Magazine*, 4 November 2001, 48–51.

A highly personal, thoughtful reflection from a prominent young novelist on the phenomenon of anti-Israel rhetoric and the anti-semitism of anti-Zionist expression.

Sarna, Jonathan D. **"Anti-Semitism and American History."** *Commentary* vol. 71 (March 1981): 42–47.

Sarna, one of the leading scholars of American Jewish history, has authored an article that is useful to students, scholars, journalists, and public officials.

Shapiro, Edward S. **"The Approach of War: Congressional Isolationism and Anti-Semitism, 1939–1941."** *American Jewish History* vol. 74 (September 1984): 45–65.

Shapiro used the antisemitic statements of members of Congress in the period before the entry of the United States into World War II as a vehicle for exploring the role of national politics in U.S. antisemitism.

Smith, Tom. **"Actual Trends or Measurement Artifacts? A Review of Three Studies of Anti-Semitism."** *Public Opinion Quarterly* vol. 57 (Fall 1993): 380–393.

An important article by a leading demographer—Smith directs the General Social Survey of the University of Chicago's National Opinion Research Center—that offered a critique of surveys of U.S. attitudes toward Jews.

Stacey, Robert C. **"The Conversion of the Jews to Christianity in Thirteenth-Century England."** *Speculum* (1992): 263–283.

An important article, useful for scholars and advanced students, contextualizing antisemitism during the high Middle Ages.

Wieseltier, Leon. **"Hitler Is Dead."** *The New Republic,* 27 May 2002, 19–22.

An important (and highly literate) analysis of contemporary antisemitism, challenging the idea that Jewish security is threatened in any serious way by contemporary manifestations of antisemitism arising out of the Arab-Israel conflict.

Wistrich, Robert S. **"Once Again, Anti-Semitism without Jews."** *Commentary* vol. 94 (August 1992): 45–49.

Wistrich is one of the more thoughtful historians writing about antisemitism in its many manifestations.

Zukier, Henri. **"The Essential 'Other' and the Jew: From Antisemitism to Genocide."** *Social Research* vol. 63 (Winter 1966): 1110–1154.

The role of conflict in shaping national consciousness was explored in this valuable article. The nature of the "other" in the context of the history of Judaism was analyzed; students and scholars will find this article useful.

Nonprint Resources

Films and Videos

Crossfire
Date: 1947
Media: VHS
Length: 86 minutes
Price: $4.79
Source: TCM

Directed by Edward Dmytryk. This classic tells of an investigation of a senseless killing in postwar New York, motivated by antisemitism. *Crossfire*, adapted from the novel *The Brick Foxhole*, is considered to be the first film out of Hollywood—released right before *Gentleman's Agreement*—to deal with antisemitism.

Focus
Date: 2001
Media: VHS
Length: 106 minutes
Price: $14.95
Source: Paramount Classics

Directed by Neil Slavin and written by Kendrew Lascelles. From the path-finding novel by Arthur Miller, this film presents a rich and graphic—and eminently realistic—portrayal of antisemitism in a Brooklyn neighborhood during the waning days of World War II, an era of high levels of antisemitism in the United States. The reaction of most contemporary viewers: "Did these things really happen?"

Gentleman's Agreement
Date: 1947
Media: VHS
Length: 118 minutes
Price: 15.95
Source: Twentieth Century Fox

Directed by Elia Kazan. This groundbreaking film, a classic adapted from the novel by Laura Hobson, was the first to treat social and employment antisemitism (the eponymous "gentleman's agreement") in the United States as the central plot and theme.

Homicide
Date: 1991
Media: VHS
Length: 102 minutes
Price: $14.95
Source: Bison Films

Written and directed by David Mamet. A homicide detective in an American city, shocked by a new case and by antisemitic slurs in his department into an awareness of his own Jewishness, begins to uncover clues to an anti-Jewish conspiracy and to a proudly Jewish resistance. Is he discovering this evidence or hallucinating it? Using the conventions of the police thriller, David Mamet investigated the troubled interplay between self-denial and aggression, real dangers and imagined threats.

Jud Süss
Date: 1940
Media: VHS
Length: 98 minutes
Source: Terra Filmkunst

Directed by Veit Harlan, based on a novel by Lion Feuchtwanger. This notorious Nazi propaganda historical costume melodrama, caricaturing the antisemitic stereotype of the conniving, ambitious Jewish businessman, is a disturbing mix of entertaining camp and deadly propaganda. The film was commissioned by Joseph Goebbels to incite violence against the Jews. It is a notable addition to the cinema of hate.

Longest Hatred: The History of Antisemitism
Date: 1991
Media: VHS
Length: 120 minutes
Price: $29.95
Source: WGBH Boston Video

This documentary (available on video) is from a three-part British series examining the history of antisemitism, antisemitism in the present day, and methods of counteracting antisemitism.

Memories of a River
Date: 1989
Media: VHS
Length: 131 minutes
Price: $15.00
Source: Castle Hill Productions

Directed by Judit Elek and written by Elek and Peter Nadar. In Hungarian. Based on fact, this meticulously realized historical drama is the story of Hungary's last trial of a Jew for ritual murder. Taking place in 1882—a time of modernization in the Austro-Hungarian Empire—but set in a rural logging community, the film concerns a Jewish raftsman, accused of having killed a young Christian girl, and the prosecuting attorney who pressures the man's son to testify against him.

Mr. Skeffington
Date: 1944
Media: VHS
Length: 145 minutes
Price: $15.95
Source: Warner Bros.

Directed by Vincent Sherman and written by Julius J. Epstein and
Philip G. Epstein. One of the first films to address, if not confront,
the issue of social antisemitism. Although antisemitism is not central to the plot of this classic film, it is an important subplot.

Web-Based and Internet Resources

Most organizations and agencies that monitor, study, and counteract antisemitism have Web sites through which up-to-date
data and other resource materials are readily available (see
Chapter 5 for descriptive material on these agencies). Additionally, Web sites will often have links to other sites in allied or an-
cillary areas.

American Jewish Committee
http://www.ajc.org

The American Jewish Committee (AJC) is a community-relations
agency that has long been involved in the monitoring and assessment of antisemitism. Many of the AJC's reports are on-line on its
site.

Anti-Defamation League
http://www.adl.org

The Anti-Defamation League (ADL) is the largest and most visible of community relations agencies that monitor and counteract
antisemitism. This Web site will generate the various reports produced periodically and occasionally by the ADL. These materials
include newsletters on various ADL activities, reports on discrete
areas of antisemitism, methods of counteraction, polls and surveys commissioned by the ADL, and resource catalogs containing
materials produced or distributed by the ADL.

Coordinating Forum for Countering Antisemitism
http://www.antisemitism.org.il

An official Israeli government site that issues periodic reports on antisemitism around the world.

Institute for Jewish Policy Research
"Antisemitism and Xenophobia" Project
http://www.jpr.org.uk

See links to antisemitism for *Antisemitism World Report.*

Jewish Council for Public Affairs
http://www.thejcpa.org

Coordinating body for Jewish public affairs agencies in the United States. The Jewish Council for Public Affairs site contains the many reports periodically generated by the council.

Ministry of Foreign Affairs, Government of Israel
http://wwwmfa.gov.il

Link to manifestations of antisemitism around the world.

The Simon Wiesenthal Center
http://www.wiesenthal.com

Useful site for periodic updates on incidents of antisemitism around the world.

The Stephen Roth Institute for the Study of Contemporary Anti-Semitism and Racism at the University of Tel Aviv
http://www.tau.ac.il/antisemitism

The institute's site includes excerpts from *Antisemitism Worldwide,* the annual report that surveys anti-Jewish activities around the world. Other resources, including libraries, are detailed on this site.

United Nations High Commissioner for Human Rights
http://www.unhchr.ch

This site will generate texts of many of the international treaties and other instruments on human rights, including antisemitism.

United Synagogue of Conservative Judaism
http://www.uscj.org

Link to the Holocaust and antisemitism.

University of Minnesota Human Rights Library
http://www.umn.edu/humanrts

Human rights treaties and other instruments; contains more than 10,000 documents.

The Vidal Sassoon International Center for the Study of Antisemitism
The Hebrew University of Jerusalem
http://sicsa.huji.ac.il

This very rich site generates the many studies, reports, and analyses of antisemitism worldwide that will be indispensable to students, journalists, and public officials. Especially valuable are the many links to other sites on Jewish affairs, anti-Jewish expression, and other forms of bigotry; a good bibliography; and the center's newsletter. From this Web site users can access as well the Felix Posen Bibliographic Project of Antisemitism.

Exhibits and Museums

The Museum of Jewish Heritage
36 Battery Place
New York, NY 10280
(646) 437-4202

Much useful material on antisemitism in the permanent exhibit.

The United States Holocaust Memorial Museum
100 Raoul Wallenberg Place, SW
Washington, DC 20024-2126
(202) 488-0400

A key part of the permanent exhibit is a film on the history of antisemitism.

Glossary

Anti-antisemites   those individuals and groups for whom antisemitism is unacceptable and must be rejected.

Antisemitism   all forms of hostility, which results from no legitimate cause, manifested toward the Jews throughout history. The term was invented by a German anarchist journalist, Wilhelm Marr, as a "scientific" racialist term for anti-Judaism.

Blood libel   the false allegation that Jews murder non-Jews, especially Christians, in order to obtain their blood for the Passover and other rituals; a complex of deliberate lies and popular beliefs about Jews, dating from late antiquity.

Dhimmis   under Muslim law, protected minorities—Jews, Christians, Zoroastrians—in Muslim lands.

Diaspora   the dispersion of an ethnic or religious group from its homeland. The Jewish Diaspora—dating from several centuries before the Common Era—includes Jews of a variety of ethnicities and religious traditions who have settled in virtually every land.

Dreyfus Affair   the court-martial and conviction, on trumped up charges, for treason (1894), and ultimate reversal of the verdict, of Alfred Dreyfus, a French army officer. The affair was a vehicle for French antisemitism and was a turning point in the history of the Third Republic.

Emancipation   the removal of legal disabilities of Jews by the ruler or parliament, thereby enabling Jews to be incorporated into mainstream society.

Galut   the Hebrew word, loosely defined as "exile," is a term-of-art referring to the Diaspora. V. Diaspora.

Hellenistic   the character, thought, or culture of the Greek world after the death of Alexander the Great (323 BCE).

Hellenization   the adoption of the Greek language and customs, particularly by Jews.

Holocaust   The state-sponsored systematic persecution and annihilation of European Jewry by Nazi Germany and its collaborators between 1933 and 1945.

Jews were the primary victims on Nazi Germany—6 million were murdered; Roma and Sinti (Gypsies), people with mental and physical disabilities, and Poles were also targeted for destruction or decimation for racial, ethnic, or national reasons. Millions more, including homosexuals, Jehovah's Witnesses, Soviet prisoners of war, and political dissidents, also suffered grievous oppression and death under Nazi Germany.

Holocaust denial   the claim, motivated or informed by antisemitism, that the Holocaust did not, as a historical reality, take place, or that the numbers of Jews who were murdered in the destruction were grossly inflated. Denial of the Holocaust often accompanies an agenda of promoting fascism.

Holocaust "Revisionism"   the pseudo-scholarly term used by Holocaust deniers for their views. Holocaust "revisionists" cloak their antisemitic agenda of denial of the Holocaust in the garb of pseudo-science and pseudo-scholarship.

Israelophobia   a term-of-art signifying hatred of Israel and anti-Zionism. At this level—that is, beyond legitimate criticism of the policies of Israel—Israelophobia is antisemitism.

Jewish security   the ability of Jews, individually and as a community, to participate in the society without fear that such participation will be compromised by antisemitic animus.

Judeophobia   the fear and hatred of Jews.

Ku Klux Klan (K.K.K.)   a secret society of whites organized in the South after the Civil War to re-establish and maintain white supremacy; a secret society organized in Atlanta in 1915—anti-Black, antisemitic, and anti-Catholic—using violence and terror to achieve its goals.

Libel of the desecration of the Host   the deliberately false allegation that Jews steal the Host and engage in various forms of desecration.

Nazism   the political and social philosophy—nationalism, racism and antisemitism, rearmament, and aggression—advocated by followers of National Socialism (National Socialist German Workers' Party) in Germany from 1919 to the defeat of Germany in 1945.

Neo-Nazism   the racist and antisemitic agenda of those individuals and groups that would advocate the recreation of Nazi power in the post-War era.

Non-antisemites   the overwhelming majority of Americans for whom Jews are not an issue.

Orthopraxis   the day-to-day traditional observance of Judaism.

Philosemitism   the support or admiration for Jews or the Jewish people by non-Jews.

Pogrom   a Russian word for attack or disturbance. The historical connotations of the term include violent attacks by local populations on Jews around the world, often with implicit or explicit government sanction. In modern times, economic and political resentment against Jews, as well as traditional religious antisemitism, have been used as pretexts for pogroms.

Protocols of the Learned Elders of Zion   a late nineteenth-century forgery, perpetrated by the Czarist secret police, that purports to be the secret plans of a group of Jewish leaders to attain world domination. The *Protocols* constitutes one of the most infamous forgeries in history.

Xenophobia   the fear, mistrust, or hatred of the outsider in society. Antisemitism has often been viewed as a form of xenophobia.

Zionism   the movement for re-establishment, and, since the establishment of the State of Israel in 1948, for advancing the Jewish national state in Israel.

Index

About the Author

Jerome A. Chanes has taught at Barnard and Stern Colleges and in Yeshiva University's graduate divisions and is a senior research fellow at the Center for Jewish History at the Graduate Center of the City University of New York. His published works include *Antisemitism in America Today: Exploding the Myths* (1995), *A Portrait of the American Jewish Community* (1998), the award-winning *A Dark Side of History: Antisemitism through the Ages* (2000), the widely-used monograph *A Primer on the American Jewish Community* (forthcoming third edition, 2005), and numerous book chapters, encyclopedia entries, articles, and reviews. His current research is on the organizational structure of the American Jewish community and on the relationship between the American Jewish community and the state of Israel.